Personality Styles
and
Brief Psychotherapy

PERSONALITY STYLES AND BRIEF PSYCHOTHERAPY

Mardi Horowitz . Charles Marmar

Janice Krupnick . Nancy Wilner

Nancy Kaltreider . Robert Wallerstein

Basic Books, Inc., Publishers

NEW YORK

Excerpts from *DSM-III* reprinted by permission from the American Psychiatric Association, *Diagnostic and Statistical Manual of Mental Disorders*, Third Edition, Washington, D.C., APA, 1980.

Excerpts from Peter E. Sifneos, *Short-Term Psychotherapy and Emotional Crisis* (Cambridge, Mass.: Harvard University Press, 1972). Reprinted by Permission.

Excerpts from Habib Davanloo, ed., *Short-Term Dynamic Therapy* (New York: Jason Aronson, 1980). Reprinted by permission.

Library of Congress Cataloging in Publication Data

Main entry under title:

Personality styles and brief psychotherapy.

  Bibliography: p. 331

  Includes index.

  1. Psychotherapy, Brief. 2. Mental illness–Diagnosis.

I. Horowitz, Mardi J.

RC480.55.P47 1984   616.89′14   83–45378

ISBN 0–465–05575–3

To Our Patients

CONTENTS

ACKNOWLEDGMENTS

We acknowledge with gratitude the cooperation of the patients involved in entering a clinical research setting; consenting to the videotaping and scientific study of their psychotherapies; and their continued dedication to this effort to improve treatment by returning for evaluation sessions up to several years after the termination of treatment.

Extensive help was provided by the support of a clinical research center grant from the National Institute of Mental Health. The Center for the Study of Neuroses at the Langley Porter Psychiatric Institute was also supported by the Department of Psychiatry at the University of California, San Francisco. This work would not have been possible without the therapists at this clinical research center who, like their patients, allowed their work together to be recorded on videotape.

We are also grateful to the staff at the Center for the Study of Neuroses who helped greatly to bring the present work to its completion. Daniel Weiss, Kathryn DeWitt, Phyllis Cameron, JoLynne McSweeney, Tony Leong, Matthew Holden, Roy Gesley, Geri Krasner, and John Starkweather especially merit our thanks. The concluding work on this book was facilitated by a fellowship year provided for the first author by the Center for Advanced Studies in the Behavioral Sciences at Stanford University under a grant from the John D. and Catherine T. MacArthur Foundation.

Mardi Horowitz
Charles Marmar
Janice Krupnick
Nancy Wilner
Nancy Kaltreider
Robert Wallerstein

INTRODUCTION

M OST PSYCHOTHERAPIES today begin without any time
limit. The therapies do not necessarily last for a long time:
many patients recover from their symptoms quickly and terminate, while others drop out before termination. Such discontinued
therapies, however, are not specifically construed as time-limited. "Brief
therapy" implies a limitation of time that is set in advance. For many it
also implies a relatively narrow focus—that is, concentration on a particular set of problems or a particular area of functioning.

We began our own type of brief therapy at the Center for the Study of
Neuroses at the Langley Porter Psychiatric Institute of the University of
California, San Francisco. At that center we developed a special research
clinic for stress and anxiety with a focus on stress-response syndromes—
that is, problems brought about by distressing, fairly recent life events.
We developed a time-limited dynamic psychotherapy for the amelioration of such syndromes. Although we concentrated on the effects of the
particular disturbing life event, we found that each patient's personality
characteristics were prominent in our formulations of the patient's problems and in the plans that we developed for the treatment process.

Our patients were not unusual. Anyone who seeks psychotherapy is
under stress, regardless of whether or not a recent serious life event has
brought about this state. And psychotherapy itself imposes a threat because the person anticipates exposure and confrontation with ideas and
feelings that have usually been warded off, but which nonetheless may
have had intrusive consequences. In response to this threat, the patient
will display habitual coping styles, often of a defensive or resistive na-

ture. The more inflexible these styles, the more the therapist will have to recognize and deal with them in order to work on problem areas.

Despite centuries of effort, there has been no generally agreed-upon framework for the classification of personalities. Since dynamic psychotherapy focuses on transferences and resistances to therapy as well as the way in which it progresses, classifying personalities according to various relationship styles and defensive styles appears appropriate. The theory of psychological defense was originated by psychoanalysts, and in that tradition an important dichotomy has grown up between the *hysterical* defenses of repression and denial, and the relatively more *obsessional* defenses of intellectualization, reversal of affects, isolation, and undoing. More recently, *sliding of meanings* and *disavowal* in the narcissistic personality, as well as *splitting* in the borderline personality, have been emphasized. We use these prototypes as a way of organizing the chapters in this book.

While the book does make use of these prototypes, it basically presents a method for approaching personality individually. Each chapter deals with a prototype, but it also indicates individual features that may deviate from that prototype. Each chapter also follows a method, *configurational analysis*, that allows the clinician to examine his or her cases in a highly individualized way. Our aim is to show readers how to identify salient personality patterns in their own patients in the context of a brief therapy approach. Configurational analysis may also, however, be useful in descriptive explanation of long-term therapies or psychoanalyses.

We begin with a review of brief therapy as it has been conducted by others. Imbedded in that review is a controversy about what aims are appropriate when time is to be limited. At one extreme there are clinicians who claim that it is possible to resolve all neurotic character difficulties. At the other extreme are those who feel that only relatively acute symptoms, such as those following a distressing life event, can be worked through in a short time. Our position lies somewhere between these extremes, and is described in chapter 2.

Depending on the aims of brief therapy, different idealized criteria are used for the selection of patients. The more a patient meets these criteria, the more likely it is that the therapy will proceed smoothly with positive consequences. Of course, people who do not meet these criteria may nonetheless seek out brief therapy. Such people may certainly benefit, although perhaps not to the same degree as ideal candidates. In some instances, for example, a brief therapy is the only kind that a patient will accept. Such patients may also resist engaging in an open-ended agreement because they fear that they will become excessively dependent on the therapist without changing for the better. Many patients are less than ideal because of their personality traits. Understanding these personality patterns is important if the therapist is to provide the patient with the best chance for therapeutic success.

In the description of our own approach in chapter 2, we emphasize our aim at symptom reduction, but in a context of work that might allow a patient to learn new coping strategies, to modify enduring attitudes, and to improve habitual strategies for relating to others. We examine each prototype both in terms of symptom reduction and in terms of the patient's progress in a broader sense.

In chapter 3 we present configurational analysis, our method of descriptive explanation. We use this method in chapters 4 through 8 as a way of organizing observations and illustrating different personality styles. The beginning section of each of these chapters considers the presenting picture, and provides a discussion of the reasons behind symptom formation. The next section of the chapter deals at length with the therapy process. Finally, we describe the outcome of each case. These outcomes were assessed through systematic interviews conducted several months after the conclusion of the therapies.

The representative cases described in chapters 4 through 8 are based on our clinical records. In many ways, however, these are composite cases. In order to disguise identity, or to illustrate a given dynamic more sharply, material from a given patient has been changed, deleted, or substituted by material from another patient drawn from the same typology. However, quantitative data, as contained in the Patterns of Individual Change and other rating-scale data reported in the outcome sections of each chapter, is not composited; it is the data obtained from a specific representative case. In changing a patient's individual characteristics, we have paid attention to preserving dynamic implications.

The final chapter considers the change processes in brief therapy, raising for discussion the question of what changes are possible when time is limited.

Personality Styles
and
Brief Psychotherapy

1

THE HISTORY OF BRIEF DYNAMIC PSYCHOTHERAPY

LTHOUGH the history of psychoanalysis has been characterized by a trend toward increasing length of treatment, there have been occasional counter efforts. Those of Ferenczi stand out; for a time he advocated "active therapy" as an effort to shorten the length of therapy. In a paper written in 1920, he presented the theoretical rationale for his approach, citing Freud's observation (1919) that in the treatment of phobic and obsessional anxiety it was often necessary to suggest firmly that the patient confront a phobic situation as a necessary adjunct to the analysis of the unconscious reasons for symptom formation, and to encourage such efforts once they were made. Ferenczi (cited in Marmor 1979) believed that the ideal of a neutral and unobtrusive analyst was unattainable, because each time the analyst interpreted patient material, the flow of the patient's "free" associations was interrupted to some degree, stimulating a new train of thought that otherwise would not have occurred in that exact form or at that exact moment. In this sense, Ferenczi argued that all therapeutic techniques were suggestive to some degree; his explicitly active technique differed only in degree and timing.

Despite this rationale, it was clear that Ferenczi advocated a controversial shift toward directive therapy. He prohibited such tension-reducing activities as masturbation, in an effort to increase the expression of warded-off themes. He advocated restorative care for especially impaired patients who had suffered childhood losses and trauma. This rationale covered such activities as hugging and kissing, and motivated Freud to respond with the now famous "God the Father" letter (Jones 1957) in which he remonstrated with Ferenczi on the dangers of clouding the boundaries between therapeutic and social relationships.

Ferenczi's views on a technique that was brief, more active, and more focused in the present brought him into collaboration with Otto Rank, whose theoretical position was evolving in a similar direction. The result was their publication of *The Development of Psychoanalysis* (1925), a book that criticized some aspects of psychoanalysis and advocated brief dynamic psychotherapy. Some of Ferenczi and Rank's concepts are still used in contemporary therapy; others have been left behind. Rank's work on birth trauma (1924) also led him into confrontation with the prevailing psychoanalytic view of the primacy of oedipal problems. As his thinking evolved, he modified his view that the physical separation of mother and child at the moment of birth was crucial for adaptation, advocating that the later emotional emancipation of the child from the mother was more germane. In so doing, he laid the foundation for the work on attachment, bonding, separation, and individuation by Spitz, Bowlby, Mahler, and others, who were important contributors to recognition of the powerful role of pre-oedipal factors in human development.

Rank's concern with separation led to an emphasis on time-limited treatment and an early focus on the meanings of separation that are currently reiterated in the work of Mann (1973; Mann and Goldman 1982). Finally, Rank's writings on "will therapy" (1947) are seen by Marmor, in his review of historical trends in psychotherapy (1979), as seminal for later selection criteria for brief psychotherapy:

If we substitute the more modern term "motivation" for the word "will," we find that Rank was saying something that has been emphasized by all modern theorists about short-term dynamic psychotherapy, namely, the overwhelming importance of the patient's having a strong motivation to change, if a favorable therapeutic outcome is to be achieved by this technique. In this connection, it is noteworthy that four of the seven criteria for motivation to change that Sifneos (1972) utilizes for selecting [people] for brief dynamic psychotherapy employ the concept of "willingness," i.e., willingness to actively participate in the treatment situation, willingness to understand oneself, willingness to change, and willingness to make reasonable sacrifice in terms of time and fees. What is willingness in this context but the ability to mobilize one's will towards the particular objectives? (Marmor 1979, p. 6)

Alexander and French (1946) followed Ferenczi and Rank as important figures in the historical evolution of brief dynamic psychotherapy. They experimented with methods for accomplishing a time-limited psychoanalysis. Their report on the findings of the research project of the Chicago Institute of Psychoanalysis is best known for the concept of the "corrective emotional experience" as a curative agent in psychotherapy. This is defined in the glossary of the third edition of the *Comprehensive Textbook of Psychiatry* (Kaplan, Freedman, and Sadock 1980) as "reexposure under favorable circumstances to an emotional situation that the patient could not handle in the past." In the approach advocated by Alexander and French, the therapist temporarily assumes a particular role to "generate the experience and facilitate reality testing." If, for example, a person has been traumatized by repeated exposure to a hostile, abusive world, the therapist might adopt a warm, compassionate, empathic role to provide a compensatory or "corrective" experience. At the time it was proposed, this approach aroused major criticism and was rejected by the majority of psychoanalytically oriented theorists.

Use of the "corrective emotional experience" carries therapeutic risks as well. The kindly therapist may play into the patient's unfulfilled wish to establish a relationship patterned on the model of a loving parent caring for an adorable child. This role relationship model may facilitate remission of symptoms, but at the same time it may conceal a neglectful parent, abused child view of the relationship by encouraging an idealized transference. The result may be an increase in the repression, or splitting off from consciousness, of this relationship potential, rendering work on an important interpersonal pattern less accessible in subsequent therapy (Gill 1954). Such negative role representations might easily be reactivated later in the face of the unpredictable and not necessarily "corrective" vicissitudes of everyday life.

An alternative approach, directly counter to Alexander's prescription, is sometimes advocated by brief therapists in the treatment of patients with a history of parental abuse. The therapist adopts a provocatively critical role, in an effort to mobilize negative transference and permit earlier working through. This approach is anxiety-provoking, may intensify symptoms, and may undermine the therapeutic alliance.

Unfortunately, because of the time constraints of brief active therapies, both of these approaches carry risks: either manipulative retraumatization or defensive idealization may occur. In contrast, the meticulously neutral stance of the long-term therapist permits a natural emergence and working through of both idealizing and denigrating transferences. These

5

are more difficult for the patient to disavow precisely because they have not been directly provoked by the therapist.

In presenting their ideas, Alexander and French (1946) challenged the prevailing assumptions that length and depth of therapy were positively correlated, that the stability of the outcome was a function of the duration of treatment, and that the regressions observed in long-term therapy were necessary for the resolution of the patient's psychopathology. They advocated countering regression by shortening the treatment, seeing patients at less frequent and sometimes irregular intervals, and remaining focused on the present rather than fostering a reconstruction of childhood trauma. They believed that the value of formulations concerning the generation of conflicts was not to resurrect the past, but rather to guide the therapist in providing the optimal corrective experience in the present.

The corrective emotional experience approach can be seen as an effort to accelerate the time course of a relatively complete psychoanalysis, rather than an attempt to evolve specific techniques for brief and problem-focused dynamic psychotherapy. By comparison, the contemporary approaches to brief therapy are more restricted in scope, with a single focus (or at most several dynamically related foci) chosen at the exclusion of other possible issues. The theoretical contributions of French (1958, 1970) are relevant in this regard. He introduced the term "focal conflict" to refer to a situation where a wish or impulse, in conflict with a person's enduring values and expectations, leads to a defensive compromise. Since confrontation with all three features—wish, threat, defensive compromise—might help a patient to arrive at more adaptive positions, this model has been referred to as one of several "triangles of insight."

Formulation of the focal conflict in therapy serves to guide interpretive work around an organizing theme, a strategy independently advanced by Balint, Ornstein, and Balint in their influential work *Focal Psychotherapy* (1972). In this intensive, single case study of a brief psychotherapeutic treatment, they explicate the technique of restricting brief psychotherapy to a particular sector of the personality.

Malan (1963) summarized additional departures from techniques that were originally advocated by Ferenczi. These include a time limit set at the outset of treatment, requests for the patient to fantasize about a specific theme (forced fantasies), and the playing of a specific role in relation to the patient in order to facilitate the emergence of transference reactions. The technique of "seeding," or manipulating, the transference has the apparent advantage of accelerating its development and the possible disadvantage of traumatizing the patient, causing him to feel manipulated or to disavow his own contribution (Gill 1954).

The following overview of the proliferation of theoretical and technical reports on brief dynamic psychotherapies over the past twenty years draws on several excellent reviews, particularly those of Malan (1976); Burke, White, and Havens (1979); Marmor (1979); Davanloo (1979, 1980); and Budman (1981).

Intensive Brief Psychotherapy: The Contributions of David Malan and the British School

The British contribution to the theory, practice, and evaluation of brief dynamic psychotherapy is central to contemporary developments. Such work began with the pioneering work of Balint, Ornstein, and Balint on focal psychotherapy (1972) and evolved through the seminal clinical and research contributions of David Malan. A distillation of the British efforts is found in Malan's book (1976a) on research and clinical practice. Malan's book is a noteworthy exception to the statement that psychotherapy research and psychotherapy practice run a parallel but never intersecting course (Wallerstein 1976; Parloff 1982).

The history of the British effort began with Balint's workshop, an alliance of the experienced psychoanalytic psychotherapists working at the Tavistock Clinic and those at the Cassel Hospital, with an initial emphasis on clinical rather than empirical evaluation. As Malan, a participant in the workshop, described this effort, "Judgments, when made, were by consensus of opinion, or in Balint's words, knocking our heads together until something comes out of it, which has its own advantages, like trial by 'jury' " (1963, p. 40). Malan developed and applied methods for assessing process and outcome variables to a sample of cases from the workshop. He later replicated and extended this effort in his own project at the Tavistock Brief Therapy Unit.

ASSESSMENT OF SUITABILITY

Malan considers the initial evaluation and selection process to be critical. The evaluation begins with a psychiatric history, in order to exclude individuals with more serious psychopathology such as mania, depression, schizophreniform psychoses, as well as those who have made serious suicide attempts, had extensive early trauma, or have entangled marital and family problems. Next comes a psychodynamic history, which stresses the quality of interpersonal relations and recurrent conflict patterns. How emotionally open the patient is able to be with the interviewer, and how he responds to early interpretations of derivative aspects of the core neurotic conflict, are indicative of how well the therapy process might proceed.

Like others in the field (Sifneos 1972, 1979; Davanloo 1980), Malan assesses patient's initial motivation for psychotherapy and focality of complaint. He explains the purpose of this:

At the end of the psychiatric interview, therefore, it should be possible to make a full psychodynamic diagnosis, and to see whether there seems to be some circumscribed aspect of pathology that can be made into a focus, and hence, whether there appears to be a possible therapeutic plan. These are all aspects of the therapist's role, and thus represent only half of the information that has been provided. It should also be possible to answer many questions to do with the patient's role: to forecast likely events if he undergoes uncovering psychotherapy, and to assess his capacity for insight, ability to respond to interpretation, strength to face anxiety provoking material, potential for growth, and motivation to carry him through the stresses of therapy (Malan 1976, p. 254).

Malan recommends fixing the time limit from the outset, and prefers a termination date rather than an exact number of sessions. He does report in one of his studies a median length of eighteen sessions for experienced therapists, and a standard limit of thirty sessions for trainees. This is essentially in agreement with Mann (1973, 1980) and differs from the practices of Sifneos (1972) and Davanloo (1980), who set the termination date during mid or late treatment rather than before it begins.

TECHNIQUES OF TREATMENT

Malan (1976) has provided a sequence that might unfold in a prototypical case. He refers to two triangles. One of them has already been mentioned. It consists of the aim, the moral injunction or social threat that makes the aim dangerous, and the defense used to reduce anxiety. Conflict is usually regarded as the play of forces, ideas, feelings, or plans between these impulsive and defensive aims.

The second "triangle of insight," which Menninger (1958) described particularly well, conceptualizes a recurring maladaptive relationship pattern found in three contexts. One of these consists of projections and introjections about the relationship with the therapist (transference). The second is recently terminated or current relationships outside of therapy as described within it. The third context is past real or imagined transactions with parental figures, siblings, and other primary figures.

Malan emphasizes the importance of interpretations that link these relationship patterns in order to establish insight into the patient's constant, recurrent, conflictual, and maladaptive schemata—that is, the internalized relationship pattern. He especially emphasizes interpretations that show the recursiveness of patterns within the transference and those with parental-type figures. He calls the links between patterns of relationship projected into the therapy situation and equivalent patterns with primal past figures the T/P link—that is, the transference-parent link. The skill of a brief therapist is determined in part by the capacity to identify such dynamics quickly but accurately, and to pace the sequence of interpretations about them at the appropriate "depth" or tolerable dosage for a given patient. Malan noted:

1. The impulse-defense triad should be interpreted before the triangle of insight, i.e., the components of the conflict should be clarified in one area before the link is made to another.
2. As far as the individual components of the impulse-defense triad are concerned, the defense should usually be interpreted first, and the anxiety should be interpreted with the impulse. One of the main aims of therapy, however, is to reach the impulse.
3. When this triad has been clarified in one area then the link should be made to another.
4. There is no general rule as to the sequencing with which the triangle of insights should be interpreted. This depends largely on the rapidity with which the transference develops, which is not under the therapist's control. However, as soon as the transference does develop, it should be clarified in terms of the three components of the impulse-defense triad, and the ultimate aim of therapy is to make the link with the past (the T/P link) many times and in as meaningful a way as possible.
5. Finally, all of the above principles converge towards suggesting that of all the different types of interpretations that it is possible to make, it is the impulse component of the T/P link that is the most important (Malan 1976, pp. 261–62).

THE TERMINATION PHASE

The patient's reactions to termination are guided by the nature of the core conflict, and, in a prototypical case, the major therapist-parent linking interpretations are repeated in the course of understanding these reactions. Termination is also seen as having an organizing effect that counteracts the dangers of diffusion of focus.

Short-Term Anxiety-Provoking Psychotherapy:
The Work of Peter Sifneos

At the time that David Malan was articulating the theory and technique of brief psychodynamic psychotherapy at the Tavistock Clinic in London, Peter Sifneos was reaching similar conclusions at the Massachusetts General Hospital in Boston.

Along with Malan, Sifneos departed radically from a tradition of short-term supportive (anxiety-suppressive) psychotherapy by using confrontational interpretations that were usually reserved for psychoanalytic psychotherapy or psychoanalysis. His approach, too, is aimed at effecting enduring characterological changes through resolution of a core neurotic conflict.

Sifneos' procedure emphasizes stringent inclusion and exclusion criteria, determined through screening interviews. Patients need to be able to engage rapidly; to tolerate the anxiety provoked by early and repeated interpretations of defenses, transference, and impulses; and to take an active part in working through in the brief time frame. Patients who display the following characteristics are thought to be most appropriate (Sifneos 1972):

1. Above-average intelligence (reflected in a capacity for new learning).
2. A history of at least one meaningful relationship during the patient's lifetime (implying shared intimacy, trust, and emotional involvement).
3. The ability to interact well with the evaluator (reflected in flexibility in style and access to emotion).
4. A circumscribed chief complaint.
5. Motivation for change. (This is a multifaceted concept involving the ability to recognize that symptoms are psychological in origin; the capacity and willingness to look inward for explanation, and to give an open, honest account of emotions; willingness to participate in the therapeutic interaction; active curiosity about motivational factors; willingness to explore new ways of functioning; realistic rather than magical expectations about the potential for change in psychotherapy; and willingness to make reasonable sacrifices in fee and schedule arrangements.)

FIRST PHASE

Sifneos organizes his technique into five phases (Sifneos 1972). The first, that of the "Patient-Therapist Encounter," involves the establishment of rapport and the building of the therapeutic alliance. This occurs through capitalization on initial positive feelings and early, vigorous interpretations of resistances to working in therapy. During this phase, a crucial task for the therapist is the formulation of a tentative psychodynamic hypothesis that would relate surface symptoms to an underlying conflict. This formulation is constructed from clues about core relationship patterns brought to light in the course of taking a careful developmental history and observing the patient's relationship to the therapist. The next task is the choice of a mutually agreed upon and feasible focus—defined by Sifneos as an emotional problem the patient wished to solve—that is related to the core neurotic conflict.

If there is a misalignment of the therapist's and the patient's goals, a period of negotiation ensues until a realistic compromise is reached. The final task of the first phase is a written statement by the therapist of the minimal acceptable goals, and a prediction of how far a particular patient can advance toward the resolution of the core neurotic problem.

SECOND PHASE

In the second phase, that of "Early Treatment," the therapist continues to differentiate the patient's realistic progress from magical, infantile wishes for gratification without acceptance of adult responsibility for solving emotional problems. The therapist confronts the patient with these positive transference reactions in order to limit the degree of regression in the brief treatment. Sifneos refers to this action as "taking advantage of the long time lag in the appearance of the transference neurosis in fairly healthy patients" as noted in time-unlimited, long-term psychotherapies.

THIRD PHASE

In the third phase, "The Height of the Treatment," the therapist focuses on the patient's past as it pertains to the emotional problem, and shifts to the therapist-patient relationship when transference reactions create resistances to deeper exploration of the focus. As the transference resistances are dealt with successfully, the patient resumes working more boldly on the focus. This cycle of progression, resistance, interpretation of resistance, and further progression is repeated. Anxiety-provoking questions are employed to confront the patient with the reasons for the evasion of painful feelings. Such confrontations frequently activate anger toward the therapist, a reaction that is rendered tolerable by the therapeutic alliance.

As is illustrated in the following quotation, Sifneos is explicit in modeling the therapeutic alliance, which he regards as pedagogical: the therapist-teacher catalyzes emotional problem-solving for the patient-student.

He [the therapist] urges the patient to look at the pattern of his behavior and helps him to learn how his present-day interpersonal relationships are associated with his past neurotic difficulties, and how, for example, his regressive behavior or his tendency to act in a certain way in order to avoid his unpleasant feelings, have created unnecessary complications in his life and caused him much discomfort. By concentrating and focusing on the understanding of the means he has used to avoid anxiety, the therapist helps the patient to examine, and repeatedly re-examine, past problems in the light of the present situations and to experiment with new ways to solve his emotional problem. This role, thus, is clearly one of an unemotionally involved teacher (Sifneos 1972, p. 117).

While Sifneos describes the pleasure of emotional problem-solving as analogous to the mastery of a complicated mathematical puzzle, he cautions against "lecturing" the patient. He differentiates his emotional problem-solving process from a purely intellectual effort, and emphasizes that the former is a process of experimental learning in the context of a charged affective alliance between the therapist and the patient.

Sifneos uses the following transcript to illustrate the working-through process in the "height of the treatment" phase. The transcript is taken from the eleventh hour of the fifteen-hour treatment of a 23-year-old female graduate student whose presenting symptoms were anxiety and difficulties in achieving intimacy with men:

Patient: Well, this being or not being friends business. . . .

Therapist: Yes.

Patient: Well, it is something else. . . . You see, I don't need you as a friend. This is not what bothers me most. I come in here and I have nothing to offer you.

Therapist: There we are again, "offer me something." We went a full circle and got nowhere. Let me recapitulate. There is this feeling of irritation with me for not responding to you for being a "non-structured nothing." You say you offer me nothing; you cannot get excited if there is no response. Then there is the atmosphere in this room that reminds you of something. . . .

Patient: (*Interrupting*) Well, if we had something to do. If, let's say, we could eat a sandwich and talk about baseball or something.

Therapist: You mean like going to your father's office and having lunch together? You "feel so important." You remember?

Patient: I *never* thought of it. I *never* did. Isn't it remarkable!!!

Therapist: How did your father react those times?

Patient: Well, he was friendly. He complimented me on my clothes. He was very nice. It was then that he used to talk to me about his troubles with my mother. I used to get excited, and I would give him advice and stuff like that.

Therapist: And I don't react in the same way.

Patient: Well, no. You don't respond in the same way. You don't make me feel at ease.

Therapist: This frustrates you. I can see that. But you see, my job is not to make you at ease. My job is to help you solve this problem.

Patient: I used to enjoy those visits so much! I felt that I could give something to my father, that he needed me, and this made me feel so good.

Therapist: What intrigues me is your emphasis here on having nothing to offer me. What about that?

Patient: Yes, and this is why the whole thing is confusing, 'cause at these times with my father I felt I had a lot to offer him.

Therapist: But there are other times with your father.

Patient: (*Blushes slightly*)

Therapist: I think I know what you are thinking.

Patient: You mean?

Therapist: Yes—the times you were parading in front of your father with no clothes on, when you were exhibiting yourself to him.

Patient: (*Blushing crimson*) . . . I had nothing to offer him then. Nothing at all . . .

Therapist: So you see how your feelings from two different times in your life are mixed up and expressed here in reference to me. The episodes with your father in his office occurred when you were fifteen?

Patient: Sixteen and later on.

Therapist: Yes, of course. The time you were running around with no clothes on was at the age of five or so, at the time of your brother's birth.

Patient: Yes. And I remember that it happened after my brother was born.

Therapist: So you can see that these feelings really have nothing to do with me personally. Only the situation has revived feelings that have existed a long time ago (Sifneos 1972, pp. 264–66).

This transcript illustrates consistent attention to the transference, even when confrontation with the patient's avoidance causes frustration and anxiety. The transcript also provides an example of how the therapist may make transference/parent linking interpretations.

FOURTH PHASE

This phase is called "Evidence of Change." The therapist ascertains that there have been sufficient shifts in the emotional problem on which therapy has been focused, allowing termination of therapy to be considered. The criteria for improvement include a reduction of tension in the interview situation, amelioration of symptoms, shifts in the specified interpersonal behavior that has been linked to the focus, and evidence that the patient could begin to generalize newly learned problem-solving activities to areas beyond the focus.

FIFTH PHASE

The final phase, "Termination," occurs when the patient and the therapist are in reasonable agreement that the goal defined at the outset has been sufficiently realized. The exact termination date is set at this point. The therapist addresses the ambivalence triggered by the idea of termination and clarifies that such ambivalence is a natural occurrence. The therapist does not, however, attempt to work through all the ramifications of separation. Instead, he or she reminds the patient of the accomplishments attained during the treatment, and encourages the patient to apply successful coping strategies to future adaptive challenges. The therapist as well as the patient work through the resistances to termination, including the temptation to broaden the focus. Often the therapist will feel a growing curiosity and affection for the patient, guilt for providing help that has been limited to a focal conflict area, a sense of frustrated perfectionism, and so forth. The final phase is generally brief and uncomplicated when this progressive (rather than regressive) posture is adopted.

Broadly Focused Short-Term Dynamic Psychotherapy: The Work of Habib Davanloo

Davanloo's approach (1980) is perhaps the most ambitious of those found among the contemporary schools of brief dynamic psychotherapy. He has widened inclusion criteria to encompass individuals who suffer from long-standing, severe obsessional and phobic neuroses, and even to include characterological problems where multiple interactive conflicts prohibit the restriction of therapy to a single focus. Davanloo rejects severity and duration of emotional problems as necessary exclusion criteria. He claims good outcomes in selected cases of long-standing severe character pathology, and points to instances of poor outcomes in certain cases where mild psychopathology of recent onset dominated the clinical picture. Whereas Sifneos recommends short-term anxiety-provoking psychotherapy for a select 5–10 percent of psychiatric outpatients, Davanloo believes that 30–35 percent are suitable for treatment.

Davanloo's selection procedure depends on a specialized pre-therapy evaluation interview designed to elicit the following criteria (Davanloo 1979):

1. The presence of some meaningful relationship in the past.

2. The patient's ability to tolerate anxiety, anger, guilt, and depression.
3. Psychological-mindedness.
4. Motivation to tolerate the uncovering and working through of character problems.
5. Most importantly, positive responses to trial interpretations during the pre-therapy evaluation interviews. The evaluator persistently confronts the patient with the avoidance of real feelings through vagueness, disavowal, or passivity, a process that is often irritating to patients and mobilizes anger.

With regard to the fifth criterion, the therapist adheres tenaciously to the process of confrontation, as illustrated by the following excerpt from an evaluation interview conducted by Davanloo:

Therapist: Going back to yourself, do you see yourself as a passive person?
Patient: Yeah.
Therapist: You do . . .
Patient: In certain situations where I don't feel . . . when I get involved with a man . . . I find I tend to take a passive role, and I don't like that.
Therapist: What specifically do you mean by not liking it?
Patient: I feel upset inside.
Therapist: What is it that you experience? You say "upset" . . .
Patient: Perhaps irritated . . . something like that . . .
Therapist: But you say "perhaps." Is it that you experience irritation and anger or isn't it?
Patient: Ummmm. Yeah. Yeah . . . I do.
Therapist: You say you take a passive role in relation to men. Are you doing that here with me?
Patient: I would say so.
Therapist: You "would" say so, but still you are not committing yourself.
Patient: (*Long, awkward pause*) Well . . . I don't . . . you see, I don't know how to . . . uh . . . I don't know about the situation . . . you know . . . I don't understand this whole situation . . . you know . . . I don't understand this whole situation yet. So I . . . I am here, and I am a passive recipient or a passive participant. I am not passive, really. I am active; I am participating, but I am . . .
Therapist: Are you participating?
Patient: Well, sure.
Therapist: Um-huh. To what extent?
Patient: (*Pause*) I am answering your questions.
Therapist: What comes to my mind is, if I don't question you, what do you think would happen here?
Patient: Well . . . I might . . . I might start to tell . . . I might start something which would indicate . . . would tell you where I am going. It might be very intellectual, though, because I don't really know . . . I don't really understand the source of my depression.
Therapist: Um-hum. In relationship with me, then, you are passive; and it is the same with all men. (*Patient is silent . . . pause.*)

As this point, Davanloo further emphasized the linkages made between the transference and the patient's current relationships. The dialogue then continued as follows:

Therapist: How do you feel when I indicate to you that you are passive?

Patient: I don't like it. (*The patient is laughing, but it is quite evident that she is irritated.*)

Therapist: But you are smiling.

Patient: I know. Well . . . maybe that is my way of expressing my irritation.

Therapist: Then you are irritated?

Patient: A little bit . . . yeah.

Therapist: A little bit?

Patient: Actually, quite a bit. (*The patient is laughing.*)

Therapist: But somehow you smile frequently, don't you?

Patient: It is inappropriate.

Therapist: Hum?

Patient: It is plain inappropriate. It is just nervousness.

Therapist: Let's look at what happened here. I brought to your attention your passivity, your noninvolvement. You got irritated and angry with me and the way you dealt with your irritation was by smiling.

Patient: That is right. That is . . . (Davanloo 1980, pp. 48–50).

In this session, the patient was confronted with her transference resistances and was pushed to own her anger. This process led her to recognize ways in which she was defensively avoiding the experience of anger. The progression of events was regarded as a favorable prognostic sign.

Davanloo recommends that there be between five and fifteen one-hour face-to-face sessions (with a predominantly oedipal focus) for patients with a circumscribed neurotic conflict, fifteen to twenty-five sessions for patients with multiple foci, and approximately twenty to thirty sessions for patients with a severe, long-standing character pathology. The therapist is active and gives priority to the early interpretation of transference (particularly as it is manifested in resistances) and to the determination of the focus. He or she offers linking interpretations with regard to the two triangular configurations described earlier. It is hoped that the initial transference resistances, activated by the confrontational nature of the pretherapy interview, will yield to diminished resistance by the third through fifth sessions. If this occurs, the opportunity for triangular interpretations is ripe and the prognosis favorable. Davanloo advocates this active interpretive stance not only to expedite working through, but also to protect against the dangers of inordinately dependent and symbiotic transferences when he accepts relatively more impaired patients into treatment.

In successful cases, significant working through occurs in eight sessions, evidenced by shifts in the patient's interpersonal relations and alleviation of symptoms. At this point, termination is considered. While there is a prevailing spirit of optimism among the proponents of brief dynamic psychotherapy, Davanloo is in the vanguard of this group. His criterion for initiating the termination phase is nothing less than total cure: "The therapy is not successful unless the patient is free of all symptoms and all of his maladaptive behavior has changed. When this happens, termination is considered. In a successful outcome the patient almost universally refers to himself as a 'free' person, a 'new' person. Termination usually comes about without difficulty" (Davanloo 1979, p. 15). The quality of the empirical evidence that is available to substantiate such a sanguine view of the efficacy of brief dynamic psychotherapy will be reviewed later in this chapter.

The nuances of the technical handling of termination are related to the extent of pathology in the different inclusion groups. Where the oedipal focus predominates, Davanloo agrees with Sifneos that termination does not ordinarily involve a pronounced phase of mourning over the loss of the therapist. However, in instances where the problem of loss is the focus, Davanloo and Malan concur that dealing with such mourning is usually an essential task of the termination phase. Finally, for more vulnerable patients, such as those with passive-dependent characters, or in instances of multiple foci, it is necessary to work through the several levels of meanings of separation. A few additional sessions may be needed for optimal resolution.

Time-Limited Psychotherapy: The Work of James Mann

Mann's work is unique within the brief dynamic psychotherapy movement. He places overriding emphasis on the meaning of time as it relates to termination and to the patient's characterological difficulties in confronting the reality of time, separation, and, ultimately, death. Consequently, the selection of patients, formulation of the focus, techniques of working through, and confrontation with termination are cohesively organized along the conceptual thread of the meanings of time.

Mann distinguishes two kinds of time: categorical or adult time, governed by realistic accommodations to the finite quality of time, and responded to in terms of the watch and the calendar; and existential or child time, governed by infantile omnipotent fantasies of timelessness and immortality. Since the acquisition of a mature awareness of time is a developmental challenge for all persons, especially those with a history of less than optimal early efforts to master separation, the child's perception is never entirely replaced by that of the adult, so that categorical and existential processing occurs in parallel. Specific events in adult life may initiate regression from previously achieved realistic models to incompletely resolved reemergent infantile patterns. In the same individual, adherence to the reality principle may be functional in one conflict-free area (prompt attendance at meetings) and distorted in a conflictual sphere (not planning for retirement as a manifestation of the denial of aging). Mann relates this split in the appraisal of time to symbolic and real parental figures:

> In the way that folklore so often exposes unconscious conflict and meaning, time as a limited commodity is portrayed as Father Time, with a beard and a scythe; limitless time, immortality, is invariably presented in the figure of a woman. Time always represents the reality principle, and the time to wake up is connected with father. By contrast, the attributes of the pleasure principle, the primary process and timelessness, are related to the mother (Mann 1973, p. 4).

SELECTION CRITERIA

According to Mann, ideal candidates are young adults in a developmental crisis, such as college students whose adaptive challenges include mastery of separation from parents and associated conflicts of dependence-independence, as well as the definition of social, sexual, and career identities. Such individuals are seen as having the strength to tolerate the frustration of the time limit. While superior intelligence, emphasized by Sifneos, might constitute an advantage, it is not seen as a necessary criterion for time-limited psychotherapy. Mann suggests that the specificity and fixed parameters of his approach are more consonant with the expectations of those who might be economically or educationally disadvantaged. Research evidence bearing on his point would be of interest, since in a number of previous studies, class has been a predictor of compliance and the outcome of psychotherapy (Garfield and Bergin 1978).

Exclusion criteria for time-limited psychotherapy include severe depression and schizophreniform psychotic disorders, protracted alcoholic and drug abuse, borderline personality disorder, and patients who mask an "ambiguous longing for total passive, narcissistic gratification" by resistance to establishing a specific focus during pre-therapy evaluations.

Mann sees the definition of the focus as a process of gradual interactive clarification between patient and therapist, so that it is not necessary for the patient to initially articulate a specific complaint. In difficult cases, the definition of the specific focus might take from two to four preliminary interviews; Mann did not begin the twelve-session countdown until a mutually agreed upon focus had been defined. If no specific problem is defined during sequential efforts at clarification in preliminary interviews, the patient is referred for some treatment other than time-limited brief therapy.

THE SELECTION OF THE CENTRAL ISSUE

Ideally, the choice of a central issue would serve several aims simultaneously: it would stimulate the development of the therapeutic alliance as well as a positive transference, skirt defenses, alleviate anxiety, link past developmental and current adaptive conflicts, address a privately experienced and chronically endured pain (often a preconsciously known negative self-concept, frequently involving a sense of victimization), and include recognition of the patient's realistic strengths (for example, a way of struggling to overcome a sense of being defective). The chronic pain takes the form of specific, individually colored, troublesome emotions such as constant embitterment.

Here are a few sample "central issues" as stated by the therapist to a patient. These are taken from a course on time-limited psychotherapy given by Mann at the 1980 meeting of the American Psychiatric Association:

1. You have always worked so hard to make things better, but what hurts you is that no matter how hard you try, you end up feeling that you are a loser.
2. You have always devoted yourself to being understanding and helpful, but your inner feeling has always been, and still is, that you are a helpless puppet on a string, controlled by others.
3. You have always given of yourself to so many others, but you always feel that you are both unrewarded and undeserving.

These central problems frequently involve one of four "basic universal conflict situations" that Mann describes: independence versus dependence, activity versus passivity, adequate self-esteem versus diminished self-esteem, and unresolved versus resolved grief. What makes Mann's work unique is the importance accorded to the issue of separation-individuation as it is related to the other conflict areas. Activity-passivity struggles can be formulated in both later and earlier developmental terms: there may be sexually and aggressively tinged wishes to surpass or defer to an oedipal rival; wishes to dominate or submit; and wishes to separate from or merge with one's caretaker. In his writings, Mann weights the latter theme more heavily; Sifneos, Malan, and Davanloo place more weight on the former themes. Undoubtedly, in actual practice, these theorists flexibly combine themes that are geared for the specific individual. Nonetheless, there is a controversy as to whether certain themes, such as conflicts over degree of caretaking needed, feared, or received, are too complex or regressive to be successfully addressed in brief therapy.

THE PHASES OF TREATMENT

Early Phase. The tendency to establish discrete early, middle, and late phases in time-limited psychotherapy is intensified by the initial agreement on a fixed limit (twelve treatment hours). The early phase is marked by the patient's relief in being understood, particularly when the therapist displays empathy in defining the central focus. Initially, the recommendation of brief therapy stimulates hope for a relatively rapid resolution of problems. Anxiety about the time limit and the anticipatory disappointment of "abandonment" are warded off in this early phase. Instead, the magical wish for union and for reparation for all previous disappointments generally triggers some relief of symptoms. Mann refers to this occurrence as a temporary, transference-based amelioration of distress, to be differentiated from the working through of ambivalence toward the therapist in later phases. He writes:

So it is that in this rapid mobilization of a positive transference, one can observe the dynamics of the transference cure within the first three or four of the twelve meetings. In essence, the ambivalence experienced and endured in relation to early significant persons is temporarily resolved in the expectation of enormous fulfillment and relief (Mann 1973, p. 33).

Middle Phase. The patient, narcissistically fortified by the hope for gratification, is generally bold in presenting problems and optimistic about rapid resolution of these problems. However, the failure of the therapist to meet these expectations initiates a process of disillusionment, ushering in the middle phase. This transition frequently occurs at about the sixth session, perhaps with exacerbation of symptoms as the ambivalence emerges. As Mann describes this phase:

The characteristic feature of any middle point of treatment is that one more step, however small, signifies the point of no return. In the instance of time-limited psychotherapy, the patient must go on to a conclusion that he does not wish to confront. The confrontation that he needs to avoid and that he will actively seek to avoid is the same one that he suffered earlier in his life, namely, separation without resolution from the meaningful, ambivalently experienced person. Time sense and reality are co-conspirators in repeating an existential trauma in the patient (Mann 1973, p. 34).

Ending Phase. With the pressure of termination, a deepening of the negative transference is characteristic of the end phase, occurring usually, but not invariably, during hours eight through ten. There is a preconscious and unconscious processing of the threat of termination, combined with a conscious struggle to defend against awareness of the prospective termination. The patient might be vague about the date of termination and exaggerate the number of sessions remaining. The therapist then deals repeatedly with the meanings of termination as related to the patient's central problem. The negative transference made manifest a here-and-now replica of a conflicted fundamental relationship, intensifying the "bad self-concept" as defined in the original focus. Transference interpretations link current patterns with past ones, and afford an opportunity for correcting distortions. In his key emphasis on transference interpretations, Mann's approach is consonant with those of other theorists already discussed. During termination work, the problem issues described earlier might result in linking interpretations of the following kind (these are extrapolated from Mann's theory):

Therapist: Just as you always tried too hard in the past, but ended up feeling like a loser, you feel that our ending now is a rejection of you, a further confirmation of you as a person who is destined to lose out. Yet in reality our ending is not a personal comment on you; it only feels that way.

Therapist: Just as in previous experiences, you devoted yourself here in therapy to being understanding and helpful, and you find that with our ending you once again feel like a helpless puppet, this time on a string controlled by me.

Such interpretive work would in reality be more complex, involving linkages to themes of defensive avoidance of anger, denial of loss, guilt for anger over separation, and wished-for but feared reunion. With the following transcript, Mann illustrates some of the recurrent themes in the termination phase. The dialogue is taken from the last moments of the twelfth hour of the "Case of the Conquered Woman," a thirty-nine-year-old white Catholic woman, married and the mother of six children. In this instance, the central problem was defined as "a constant sense of nagging discomfort, irritation, and irritability," later clarified to include the use of sickness in the service of passive-avoidance of conflictual feelings and adaptive challenges.

Patient: I have feelings, but sometimes they work in the wrong way.
Therapist: You are right.
Patient: And that's what a lot of my problem is.
Therapist: When you say they work in the wrong way, what do you mean?
Patient: I don't know. I think that I fight it a lot.
Therapist: In which way?
Patient: Offhand, I don't know.
Therapist: Well, I will give you an example. How did you feel before you came in here today?
Patient: I felt sick.
Therapist: That's one way you fight your feelings.
Patient: But, like I said, I don't know—I knew it wasn't bothering me coming here today.
Therapist: I *know* that it was bothering you.
Patient: All week all I have been thinking of was the dentist, and I don't want to go there.
Therapist: I know that you were thinking of the dentist so that you wouldn't have to think about coming here for the last time.
Patient: I could be, but I know all I had in mind was the dentist.
Therapist: This is your way of fighting off certain feelings. All you could think of was the dentist, feeling sick to your stomach, nauseated, and vomiting. But no thought about the fact that this was your last visit here with someone where you feel that you have gotten some help and with someone you like—no thought about that.
Patient: So I used the dentist.
Therapist: This is one of the ways you avoid your own honest feelings. Next time when you feel nauseated or have a headache—not every time—but especially if you come down with some other symptoms, ask yourself—
Patient: Why?
Therapist: What it is that you are feeling about somebody else or something else that you are not allowing yourself to feel—instead you are feeling like this.
Patient: Getting sick.
Therapist: Yes, getting sick. Ask yourself what it is that you don't like.
Patient: So instead of fainting I sometimes invent a sickness.
Therapist: Don't be hard on yourself. You know, it's not that you are a bad person to invent sicknesses, you simply find it hard to face what you feel about people (Mann 1973, p. 192).

The above dialogue clearly illustrates the value of linking the reaction to termination with the centrally defined focus, with the manifestation of the central problem in the transference, and with the clarification of core characterological defensive configurations.

Short-Term Interpersonal Psychotherapy: The Contributions of Klerman and Weissman

Researchers at the Boston–New Haven Collaborative Depression Research Unit have developed a brief psychotherapy tailored to the treatment of depressive disorders. The focus of the treatment is on interpersonal behavior rather than intrapsychic phenomena, with relatively little attention directed toward the uncovering and exploration of unconscious core conflicts or the relating of childhood antecedents to current adaptive struggles (Neu, Prusoff, and Klerman 1978; Weissman et al. 1981). Treatment is time-limited, and in one study averaged fourteen sessions. Treatment is provided on a once-weekly basis for about fifty minutes, and is seen as particularly appropriate for treating depressions triggered by interpersonal problems.

The authors describe seven classes of technical interventions, organized hierarchically from simple to more complex approaches (Neu, Prusoff, and Klerman 1978). The first three are classified as descriptive, beginning with "nonjudgmental exploration." This approach, which is particularly relevant in the early phases of treatment, involves supportive acknowledgment, encouragement for the patient to continue presenting material, and receptive silence. The therapist's continuously available and empathic neutrality is essential.

"Elicitation of material" is a more active technique, involving "nonjudgmental neutrality" but extending this to include active probing for new information. Such probing is advocated at any phase in treatment when a more complete picture of past or current functioning is required. Next is "clarification," or "making understood." This involves rephrasing material, pointing out inconsistencies or verbal-nonverbal incongruencies, and making partially developed thematic material more explicit.

Several additional techniques are directed toward the effecting of change in interpersonal behavior. "Direct advice" is provided to guide more adaptive interpersonal behavior, particularly in the short-term management of people with impulsive characters. "Decision analysis" involves an examination of alternative courses of action in order to expand the patient's understanding of short- and long-range consequences of behaviors. "Development of awareness" involves stimulation of insight into interpersonal behavioral patterns and clarification of defensive efforts to ward off awareness of these patterns. Finally, a class of "other" techniques is employed, including supportive therapist "affective responses" to encourage patient productivity.

In a study of thirty-three patients (Neu, Prushoff, and Klerman 1978), the most prevalent therapeutic techniques were nonjudgmental exploration, elicitation, and clarification. This replicates an earlier finding in a study of maintenance psychotherapy for depressed women, in which patients' descriptions of daily events such as family conflicts predominated (Weissman and Klerman 1973).

Brief Behavior Therapy

Behavior therapy is often thought of as a brief treatment of between one and twenty-five sessions. However, in a recent review, Wilson (1981) points out the considerable variability in treatment duration within the behavioral approach. He cites an unpublished report by Fishman and Lubetkin indicating that over a four-year period the behavioral treatments provided at the Institute of Behavior Therapy in New York City averaged about fifty weekly one-hour sessions. The extension of the inclusion criteria beyond symptomatic neuroses to complex disorders such as drug addiction, obesity, and gender identity confusion may have necessitated the development of such longer-term strategies, in an effort to maintain behavioral change rather than achieve only transient improvement.

Wilson believes that the range of disorders amenable to brief behavior therapy includes specific phobias (including some agoraphobias), obsessive thoughts and compulsive rituals, and sexual disorders. Treatment frequently consists of graduated *in vivo* exposure, with or without participant modeling, so that the patient can confront the behavior at tolerable levels of anxiety. *In vivo* exposure involves real confrontation with phobic situations, places, or things, and contrasts with the use of visual imagery or other exposure-in-fantasy procedures. Participant modeling involves another person, present with the patient, who demonstrates more adaptive patterns of coping. Practitioners vary in setting the parameters of treatment; a therapist will establish an individualized treatment contract with each person. The time limit could be established at the outset or determined during the process, allowing for eight to twelve sessions over a two- to three-month period. The rate of incremental achievements toward target goals guides the therapist in determining the final termination point.

During the termination phase the frequency of sessions is gradually decreased from weekly to every other week and then finally to monthly intervals. The later sessions might be shorter than earlier ones, with emphasis on maintaining and generalizing positive changes. Periodic posttreatment booster sessions are used to sustain gains. In psychoanalytic therapies, such booster sessions have sometimes been regarded as too evocative of dependency. However, behavioral therapists have not reported such negative effects. In actual practice, psychodynamic therapists also see patients for single subsequent sessions, but usually in an unplanned manner timed by a patient's requests for visits after termination.

While there are roughly accepted standards guiding the decisions made about length, frequency, and duration of sessions in behavorial therapies, Wilson notes the inadequate number of empirical studies dealing with the results of different ways of organizing the therapy situation. Surprisingly few behavioral studies have compared the efficacy of massed versus distributed sessions, long versus short sessions, and fixed versus variable treatment intervals. The difficult problem of empirically validating the optimal contexts for clinical practice has been discussed elsewhere (Garfield and Bergin 1978; Parloff 1982; Horowitz 1982).

Despite these problems in research, theoretical models of the change process in behavioral treatments have undergone revision in response to research findings. There has been a shift in emphasis from the early optimism concerning the power of discrete techniques to effect change universally to a consideration of dispositional factors—including motivation, coping style, and social supports—that necessitate individualized approaches. The quality of the patient-therapist relationship, seen as largely irrelevant in earlier years, is receiving greater attention (Wilson 1981; Wilson and Evans 1976). The self-characterization of behaviorists has shifted from that of "behavioral engineers" (Ayllon and Michael 1959) to that of "behavioral psychotherapists" (Marks 1978).

Wilson and Evans (1976) provide an excellent detailed discussion of the ways in which behaviorists address the issue of resistance, as well as the biases that the client and therapist bring into the treatment situation. These writers also point out the importance of the therapist's style in modeling problem-solving strategies and in identifying and altering patient expectancies. Avoiding use of the dynamic concepts of transference and countertransference, Mahoney (1974) defines such expectancies as a "complex of mediational processes which influence selective attention, response utilization, and unanticipated consequences" (p. 275). The behaviorists Ullman and Krasner (1969) define such expectancy as "a verbal description of a role enactment likely to be reinforced in a given situation" (p. 72).

While these concepts relate to the psychodynamic view of transference and countertransference, exploration of relationship issues in behavioral therapies is usually more restricted than in psychodynamic therapies. The goal is to increase patient compliance by stimulating hope and increasing the power and credibility of the therapist. This is technically referred to as augmentation of the reinforcing and discriminative stimulus value of the therapist.

Behavioral therapists have paid increasing attention to internal variables such as conscious cognitions and what we would call enduring attitudes, especially in regard to irrational but persisting self-concepts and views of others. The usefulness of some of the behavioral techniques has also caught the attention of persons trained in the conduct of psychodynamic psychotherapy (Marmor and Woods 1980; Meichenbaum 1980). Such techniques are sometimes useful as supportive or teaching approaches that complement gains due to insight, altered decisions, and new assumptions or schematizations.

Brief Cognitive Therapy: The Contribution of Aaron Beck

The convergence of psychodynamic and behavioral approaches is best exemplified by the contribution of Aaron Beck. He originally was trained as a psychoanalyst, then learned behavioral therapy techniques, and is a founder of important forms of cognitive-behavioral therapy for depressive and anxiety disorders.

The importance of Beck's approach (1976; Beck et al. 1979) is attested to by the inclusion of cognitive therapy as one of the two contrasting psychotherapeutic treatments in the Multi-Center Collaborative Study of the Outpatient Psychotherapy of Depression conducted by the National Institute of Mental Health (Waskow 1981). Cognitive therapy has taken its place alongside psychodynamic and behavioral therapies in comprising the three dominant forces in the contemporary psychotherapeutic scene. Indeed, it is our impression that "pure" behavioral therapy is on the wane as an unaccompanied set of techniques [for example, Lazarus (1980) has described a multi-modal behavioral effect; see also Marmor and Woods 1980].

Beck and his colleagues (1979) define cognitive therapy as follows:

... "an active, directive, time limited, structured approach used to treat a variety of psychiatric disorders (for example, depression, anxiety, phobias, pain problems, etc.). It is based on the theory that an individual's affect and behavior are largely determined by the way in which he structures the world. . . . His cognitions (verbal or pictorial "events" in his stream of consciousness) are based on attitudes or assumptions (schemas), developed from previous experience (Beck et al. 1979, p. 3).

Beck traces the history of cognitive therapy from its earliest origins in Stoic philosophy, through to the twentieth-century contributions of Freud [1953 (1900)], Adler [1958 (1931)], Piaget [1937, 1950 (1947) 1970], Kelly (1955), and more recently Ellis (1973), all of whom have advocated the substitution of rational thinking to counter irrational beliefs that generate maladaptive emotional responses. Beck also credits Meichenbaum (1977) and Kazdin and Wilson (1978), who stress the importance of cognitions as behaviors subject to modification.

THEORETICAL ASSUMPTIONS OF COGNITIVE THERAPY

Beck outlines seven broad assumptions as the basis for the technique of cognitive therapy:

1. Perception and experiencing in general are active processes which involve both inspective and introspective data.
2. The patient's cognitions represent a synthesis of internal and external stimuli.
3. How a person appraises a situation is generally evident in his cognitions (thoughts and visual images).
4. These cognitions constitute the person's "stream of consciousness," or phenomenal field, which reflects the person's configuration of himself, his world, his past and future.
5. Alterations in the content of the person's underlying cognitive structures affect his or her affective state and behavioral pattern.
6. Through psychological therapy a patient can become aware of his distortions.
7. Correction of these faulty dysfunctional constructs can lead to clinical improvement (1979, p. 8).

Beck differentiates cognitive therapy from dynamic therapy by noting that the former stresses the here and now, without reconstruction of childhood experiences, and holds that the interpretation of unconscious aims should be avoided. Additionally, cognitive therapy involves the prescription of homework assignments that are reviewed later, and the addition of booster sessions after planned termination. Beck also contrasts cognitive therapy with behavior therapy, noting that the former gives greater attention to internal processes such as automatic thoughts.

The parameters of cognitive treatments are worked out in the most systematic form for the depressive disorders. For these conditions, treatment typically involves an initial four-week period of twice-a-week therapy followed by approximately seven to fourteen once-a-week sessions. The timing varies with the severity of the presenting illness. An initial phase of twice-weekly therapy is advocated to counter the despair of the depressed person, facilitate a therapeutic alliance, and reduce the risk of an early dropout. During the termination phase, Beck recommends tapering off to biweekly and monthly sessions in order to consolidate gains and permit mastery of the separation.

In 1976, Beck advocated a sequential approach using the following steps:

1. *Establishing the Therapeutic Alliance and Identifying a Mutually Agreed upon Focus.* The focus is generally elucidation and alteration of pathogenic beliefs. The patient is encouraged to view therapy as a valuable opportunity to solve emotional problems rather than as a dreaded confrontation with defective self-images. This approach is designed to counter excessive feelings of guilt and shame, a suggestion in the spirit of the recommendations of Sifneos and Mann for establishing a focus.

2. *Filling in the Blank.* The technique of filling in the blank involves the clarification of the sequence of external events that trigger automatic thoughts and lead to characteristic reactions. By consciously turning his attention to the thought process itself, the patient is helped to observe the intervening thoughts as they occur—in slow motion, so to speak. Beck provides the example of a patient who had seen an old friend (external event) and then experienced sadness (reaction). The patient was asked to recall the thoughts triggered by the reunion and reported: "If I greet Bob, he may not remember me. . . . He may snub me. . . . It's been so long, we won't have anything in common. It won't be like old times." This technique is a circumscribed application of the psychoanalytic technique of free association.

3. *Distancing.* Greater objectivity is gained after the patient repeatedly becomes aware of automatic thoughts, and there is a gradual increase in understanding of the subjective distortions involved in beliefs that were previously assumed to be accurate. Beck defines distancing as "being able to make the distinction between 'I believe' (an opinion that is subject to validation) and 'I know' (an irrefutable fact). The ability to make this distinction is of critical importance in modifying those sectors of the patient's reactions that are subject to distortion" (1976, p. 243).

4. *Decentering.* The aim of this technique is to counter the tendency of individuals to inappropriately *personalize* events that are not, in reality, linked to them. This tendency is countered by directing the patient to make a rational reappraisal of the egocentric nature of these automatic beliefs.

5. *Changing the Rules.* Personalization, illustrated above, is one instance of a systematic error in appraisal. In a later work, Beck et al. (1979) outline a more comprehensive list of patterns of distorted thinking. These include arbitrary inference (drawing specific conclusions in the absence of sufficient information and/or ignoring contradictory information), selective abstraction (taking a detail out of context), overgeneralization (drawing generalizations from unrepresentative incidents), magnification and minimization (making errors when estimating the magnitude of events), and absolutist, dichotomous thinking (placing all experience in one of two mutually exclusive categories). Specific therapeutic counters are employed to correct for each of these distortions in information processing. Beck refers to this process as "changing the rules."

The working-through process consists of a modification of false beliefs through reality confrontation, leading to freedom from previously automatic neurotic reactions. Success in one sector of difficulty increases the likelihood of correcting distortions in other spheres, either in therapy or through the patient's extratherapeutic efforts at successful generalization.

Beck's concept of "changing the rules" is somewhat analogous to our own attention to the individual information-processing style. It is not, however, Beck's primary intention to relate patterns of information distortion to structural aspects of character, or to personality development. He believes that such dimensions of personality play a secondary role, as far as change is concerned, to the identification and intense effort at correction of inaccurate cognitions. Yet each of his suggested procedures can be related to prototypes of cognitive distortion noted in certain character styles that are elaborated in later chapters. Arbitrary inference and overgeneralization are frequently seen in the hysterical personality style, selective abstraction is a predominant feature in obsessional characters, magnification and minimization are features of the narcissistic personality, and absolutist, dichotomous thinking is an important component in the splitting processes characteristic of borderline personalities.

Beck illustrates some steps of the technique of cognitive therapy in a condensed fashion in the following transcript:

Patient: I have to give a talk before my class tomorrow and I'm scared stiff.
Therapist: What are you afraid of?
Patient: I think I'll make a fool of myself.
Therapist: Suppose you do . . . make a fool of yourself. . . . Why is that so bad?
Patient: I'll never live it down.
Therapist: "Never" is a long time. . . . Now look here, suppose they ridicule you. Can you die from it?
Patient: Of course not.
Therapist: Suppose they decide you're the worst public speaker that ever lived. . . . Will this ruin your future career?
Patient: No. . . . But it would be nice if I could be a good speaker.
Therapist: Sure it would be nice. But if you flubbed it, would your parents or your wife disown you?
Patient: No. . . . They're very sympathetic.
Therapist: Well, what would be so awful about it?
Patient: I would feel pretty bad.
Therapist: For how long?
Patient: For about a day or two.
Therapist: And then what?
Patient: Then I'd be okay.
Therapist: So you're scaring yourself just as though your fate hangs in the balance.
Patient: That's right (Beck 1976, pp. 250–51).

This overview has touched on some important points in descriptions of brief therapy techniques. Work on short-term psychotherapy and its techniques has led to over 1,500 references in 125 professional journals and books. Review of this literature is beyond the scope of our present purposes, but it has been summarized by Mandel (1981). The major themes that are consonant with the work to be described in this book are the attention to individually described problematic states of mind, and conflicts involving diverse relationship patterns and incompatible aims, purposes, and values.

The Efficacy of Brief Psychotherapy

How effective different kinds of psychotherapy are is a vital research question, but it is one that is difficult to answer easily because of such methodological impediments as the difficulty in assembling sufficient numbers of homogeneous cases treated under controlled circumstances. The majority of research studies have focused on brief therapies. The most comprehensive recent review of research on psychotherapy has been provided by Smith, Glass, and Miller (1980), who conducted a meta-analysis of hundreds of published studies on psychotherapy. What is of interest to us here is that the average length of treatment in the 375 studies included in the major data analyses was seventeen sessions. Hence, the report by these researchers focuses predominantly on the outcome of brief therapies. In general, the average patient who received therapy was more improved than 75 percent of those who received no treatment or who were waiting-list controls, although the relative efficacies of various types of brief therapy were not well differentiated.

Brief therapy is generally conducted both by those who see it as an effort to accomplish the same ends as long-term psychoanalytic psychotherapy or even psychoanalysis, and by those whose goals are to work through a focal issue to the best possible resolution, with a concurrent reduction of acute symptoms. Before going further, the reader should be advised of our own position. We believe that characterological change is best accomplished by long-term psychoanalytic psychotherapy or psychoanalysis. This does not mean that characterological changes never occur in brief therapy, but rather that, for the average patient, brief therapy can be expected to ameliorate focal symptoms, to change delimited irrational beliefs, and, perhaps, to put the person back on the track of adaptive life development. We believe that the patient has to learn new patterns of behavior, to live the changes, after the termination of therapy in order to gain maximum benefit.

The relative efficacy of brief versus long-term treatment has been discussed by Butcher and Kolotkin (1979), in a review of their own study and that of Luborsky, Singer, and Luborsky (1975). Butcher and Kolotkin have found no strong evidence that the differential efficacy of psychotherapies is a function of duration. This may be due, however, to a limitation in the ability to make reliable outcome assessments of characterological changes that occur more often in long-term treatments. The difficulty in assembling appropriate psychodynamic formulations has been discussed elsewhere by our group (Kaltreider et al. 1981a). Research problems include defining patients who terminate early from a long-term therapy as if they were brief therapy cases, and the tendency to evaluate long-term treatments by the more limited goals of many brief therapies (symptomatic remission and restoration of premorbid social functioning).

The question of which kind of therapy is best for a particular person is unanswered by available research data. This is especially the case with reference to character style or the nature of Axis 2 diagnosis (presence of personality disorders) in the American Psychiatric Association's *Diagnos-*

tic and Statistical Manual (DSM-III) (1980). What we present in this book, then, is a consensus of clinical opinions derived from case reviews. The assertions are consistent with what quantitative data has been reported. For example, various psychotherapy research studies have indicated the importance of the therapeutic alliance as one of the predictors of outcome (Moras and Strupp 1982; Bordin 1974; Luborsky 1976; Marziali, Marmar, and Krupnick 1981; Gomes-Schwartz 1978). Our own studies have indicated that the therapeutic relationships may interact with pre-therapy patient qualities to effect the eventual results (Marmar et al., forthcoming; Horowitz et al., in press).

It is of interest that brief therapy for outpatients with fairly severe psychiatric conditions has been demonstrated to be effective in reducing symptoms and maintaining symptom improvement. In our studies, brief therapy has been effective in treating the post-traumatic stress disorders (Horowitz et al., in press; Marmar et al., forthcoming). Our approach will be described in the next chapter. Rush et al. (1977) have found cognitive therapy to be more effective than antidepressive agents alone in reducing the symptoms of major depressive disorders. Weissman et al. (1981) have found that interpersonal psychotherapies averaging fourteen sessions in length are effective in dealing with major depressive disorders.

We should note here as well that few studies of psychotherapy have reported negative effects. Patients are usually reported as "not improved" rather than "worse." One result that may be viewed as a negative effect is a reduction in a patient's motivation for more fundamental change. A brief therapy may cause the person to be satisfied with circumscribed improvement, attenuating the possibility of a major effort toward personality change (Strupp, Hadley, and Gomes-Schwartz 1977; Malan 1976). This is an area of controversy that will be addressed later in this book, through specific case examples.

Summary

Brief dynamic psychotherapy has gradually evolved over several decades. There is general consensus about its utility in helping people work through focal current conflicts and acute symptoms. The controversy regarding the value of brief dynamic therapy for revising core neurotic characterological structures, or habitual information-processing styles, has not yet been resolved. From case reports, such as those of Malan (1976), Sifneos (1979), and Davanloo (1980), there is evidence that in some instances major characterological changes can be accomplished. However, these may occur in the minority of patients treated in brief therapy. With an individual patient, the issue is always whether to aim for such major characterological revisions or for the partial changes that are more likely to be achieved.

2

OUR APPROACH TO BRIEF THERAPY: FOCUSED ON CURRENT STRESSORS

WE HAVE CHOSEN to study time-limited psychodynamic psychotherapy for individuals who exhibit a stress response syndrome. This decision was made because a recent important life event can provide an appropriate focus for brief treatment. The objective is to help patients to master their responses to the threat, injury, or loss involved in the event. A stress response syndrome involves not only reactions to the event itself but some degree of predisposing personality characteristics or underlying conflicts. Thus, the therapeutic process associated with the established focus necessarily relates to long-standing as well as recent issues.

We began our work by detailing the phases of response to serious life events, typical symptoms of stress response syndromes, and methods for systematically evaluating a patient's condition both before and after therapy. We developed further existing dynamic techniques for treating stress response syndromes (Horowitz 1973, 1976). We were able to examine the effect on the therapeutic process of various preexisting personality styles.

In 1973 we established a stress and anxiety research clinic at the Langley Porter Psychiatric Institute of the University of California, San Francisco, for this purpose. Patients signed informed consent statements, allowing us to make audio and video recordings of therapy and evaluation sessions for research and teaching purposes. The recordings gave us an opportunity to systematically review the content and form of communication that was used during therapy sessions. Before and after therapy, separate rating scales that related to the patient's condition were completed by the patient himself, the therapist, and the evaluating clinician. Thus, both the outcome and the nature of the therapeutic process were assessed.

We initially studied responses to a wide range of traumatic events. Then, in order to keep as many variables as possible constant, we narrowed our focus to the study of specific inciting events. The cases in this book involve individuals who entered treatment after the death of a parent. This particular event heightens issues that concern self-concept and the evolution of developmentally important relationships with others. Time-limited dynamic psychotherapy for a neurotic-level response to the death of a parent would be likely to focus, in a concentrated way, on issues found in general analytically-oriented therapy, especially issues of transference as they relate to difficulties in current relationships.

Stress Response Syndrome

Stress response syndromes are reactions to serious life events or very threatening life circumstances. Depending on events, symptoms, and their duration, the official nomenclature classifies these reactions as post-traumatic stress disorders, adjustment disorders, flare-ups of other varieties of anxiety and depressive disorders, or as exacerbation of personality disorders. A characteristic state of mind in stress response syndromes contains intrusive ideas, feelings, or compulsive enactments, as well as contrasting states of mind characterized by denial of important ideas, ignoring implications, with emotional numbing, avoidances of situations, and general behavioral constriction (Horowitz 1976; Horowitz et al. 1980a).

When a serious life event occurs, an individual will generally go through the phases of outcry, intrusion, and denial. Each person, however, brings his own individualized response to the situation (Horowitz 1976).

Phases of Response

The immediate response to a serious life event may be an outcry such as "Oh, no! It can't be true!" or a stunned inability to take in the meanings of the loss. The shattering of the illusion of invulnerability can be particularly threatening. For a person who ceases to think of himself as an idealized, omnipotent self, there may be an initial phase of effective, well-modulated behavior that involves the use of familiar defenses such as intellectualization, a shift from passive to active behavior, and isolation of affect. Over time, however, the multiple painful meanings of the event and its disruption of the patient's homeostasis lead to other, less well-controlled states of mind (Horowitz 1973). The common sequence of phases, with normal and pathological variations, is summarized in figure 2.1.

Figure 2.1
Stress Response States and Pathological Intensification

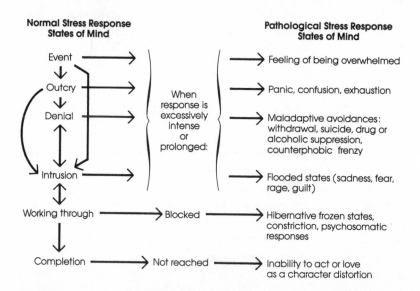

Particularly prominent is a state of mind characterized by intrusive symptomatology such as unbidden thoughts and images, nightmares, pangs of emotion, and compulsive behavior. The range of affects that might become overwhelming, despite attempts to defend against them, includes emotional states found in many of the psychoneuroses: distraught sadness, rage, guilt, shame, and fear. The attempt to deflect such experiences may lead to avoidant symptoms such as warding off of thoughts about the event, isolation of affect, and denial of consequences of the loss. In most individuals, the implications of the event are eventually worked through, leading to relative completion of the stress response. The typical symptoms of the denial and intrusion phases are found in tables 2.1 and 2.2.

TABLE 2.1
Symptoms of the Denial Phase

Perception and Attention	Daze
	Selective inattention
	Inability to appreciate significance of stimuli
Consciousness	Amnesia (complete or partial)
	Nonexperience of themes implied as consequences of the event
Ideational Processing	Disavowal of meanings of stimuli associated with the event
	Loss of a realistic sense of being connected with the world
	Constriction of associational width
	Inflexibility of organization of thought
	Presence of many fantasies to counteract reality
Emotional	Numbness
Somatic	Tension-inhibition type symptoms
Actions	Frantic overactivity
	Failure to respond to consequences of the event
	Withdrawal

Evolution of the Therapy Model

Patients in our Stress and Anxiety Clinic were originally seen on a weekly basis for up to twenty sessions, with the length decided on during treatment. While there were individual variations, the systematic study of data from these treatments suggested a common pattern. Substantial remission occurred in the early sessions, followed by a mid-therapy phase during which the focus was diffused or the patient dropped out of therapy before termination work was begun. After reviewing the work of Mann and others, we established a set time limit of twelve sessions.

TABLE 2.2
Symptoms of the Intrusion Phase

Perception and Attention	Hypervigilance, startle reactions
	Sleep and dream disturbance
Consciousness	Intrusive-repetitive thoughts (illusions, pseudohallucinations, nightmares, unbidden images, ruminations and preoccupations with various emotionally charged themes)
Ideational Processing	Overgeneralization of stimuli so that they seem as if associated with the event
	Inability to concentrate on other topics, preoccupation with event-related themes
	Confusion and disorganization
Emotional	Emotional attacks or "pangs" of anxiety, depression, rage, shame, guilt, or other mixed affects related to the event
Somatic	Symptomatic sequelae of chronic fight or flight readiness, tension, and exhaustion
Actions	Search for lost persons and situations, compulsive repetitions of actions associated with the event, displaced reparations, self-punishments

Experience over several more years indicated that the shortened time period was successful, and the time limit encouraged determined, active, goal-oriented work on the part of the therapist. As emphasized by Mann (1973), establishing a time limit allows one to deal with termination throughout therapy, especially at the mid-therapy point when the emotional valences can be gradually expressed over several hours.

As emphasized by Sifneos (1972, 1979), Malan (1963, 1976), Mann (1973), and other modern pioneers of brief therapy, early case formulation is essential to development of a focused intervention strategy, one geared to individual personality styles and issues (see also Basch 1980; Davanloo 1980). In our approach, this formulation would have to do with the personal meanings of the stressful life event and with any important ways in which the patient is stymied in his attempts to process the event. The therapist would also seek to relate the event to current developmental issues that are facing the patient.

Our goal for the treatment process was to facilitate a working through of reactions to the current stressors. We aimed to help people improve their functioning while ameliorating or eliminating symptoms. This was to be achieved by working through focal conflicts, especially conflicts that had flared up significantly because of association to a serious recent life event. The desired outcome would be that patients had returned at least to their previous level of functioning, possibly working through some impediments to further developmental progression.

Rationale for Brief Therapy with Persons Who Display Stress Response Syndromes

The particular content that intrudes in an unwelcome way may directly or indirectly indicate the thematic area that troubles the individual. The other cardinal symptoms of stress—that is, denial and numbing experiences and behaviors—are part of an effort to stifle these themes and to prevent the flooding with emotion that may occur with intrusive experiences. A rational approach to helping the person work through a currently stressful theme or conflict should be based on a theory that would explain such intrusive ideas and feelings, and the seemingly opposite experience of warding off ideas and feelings. A detailed exposition of this theory has been presented elsewhere (Horowitz 1976; Horowitz and Kaltreider 1980). It has led to some revision of the classical theory that differentiates between normal and pathological grief, as well as between normal stress response and post-traumatic stress disorders (Horowitz et al. 1980b; Horowitz et al. 1981). A synopsis of an aspect of this theory provides some of the rationale for our treatment approach.

A serious life event such as the loss of a parent presents the individual with news that must be assimilated. Recognition of all implications of this news will eventually lead to some change in inner psychological structures of meaning, which might be called inner models. It takes time to change these inner models, time in which the person reviews the implications of the news and determines what responses are available to him. Until such a review is completed, and inner models are brought into accord with the new realities, the mind will tend to store the news in a form of active memory. The news in this form, as supplemented with personal associations, will then be repeatedly represented in the conscious mind, and as information processing occurs, inner models will be brought up to date with the actual world. This important tendency to integrate reality and inner schemata can be called a *completion tendency*.

Until completion occurs, the news, with associations to it, is stored in active memory. According to this theory, active memory contents will be transformed into mental representations that can be consciously experienced whenever that process is not actively inhibited, or set aside because channels are occupied with matters of currently higher priority (Horowitz and Becker 1972). This tendency for repeated representation will end only when these contents are no longer stored in active memory. When the contents are very important, termination in active memory will not occur in a decaying fashion, as may take place with less important contents, but only when information processing is complete. At that time, the news will become a part of long-term models and revised inner schemata.

A stress event is by definition a very significant change in the quality of a person's life and his relationship to the environment. There will always be a discrepancy between the news of a stress event, while it remains stressful, and inner models. The person who is aware of this discrepancy will often have strong emotional reactions. These reactions can take the form of various states of mind, such as those that are commonly associated with stress response syndromes and those that are the essential features of anxiety and depressive disorders in general.

The loss of a loved one, for example, is so different from the inner model of attachment that a person may experience very painful emotional responses whenever he attempts to process information about the deceased. The unpleasantness of these states of mind, and the anticipation of possibly being flooded with out-of-control responses, triggers certain regulatory processes. That is, unconscious decisions are made that aim at avoiding entry into dreaded states of mind through selective inhibition of painful themes.

The treatment of a person with a stress response syndrome is intended to facilitate his review of stored information about the serious life event as well as his association to that event. The treatment follows the person's natural healing tendency—that is, it supports the patient's tendency to move toward completion. The therapist aims to facilitate the patient's mastery of experience by bringing about a gradual, in-depth contemplation of the personal implications of the event. An important part of this process will involve helping the person to contemplate new ideas and to differentiate realistic appraisals from fantasy-based conceptions.

In the type of therapy we use, the focus is not only on the meanings of the stress event but on the constellation of associated ideas relating the event to issues of self-conceptualization These ideas are themselves composed of memories and fantasies. For example, after the death of a parent, various preexisting fantasies about the relationship with that parent, as well as actual memories of interactions, will be activated for review. This provides an occasion to do a kind of differentiation between reality and fantasy, now with an adult mind, that the individual may not have accomplished since the original fantasies were established during childhood. In this manner, review of themes activated by a stressful life event, such as the death of a parent, may be analogous to issues that are present in all brief therapies of neurotic conditions, even those not precipitated by a recent serious life event (Krupnick and Horowitz 1981). As it happens, many patients do come to psychotherapy because of a recent life event, although not necessarily one of traumatic proportions. Separations, failed love affairs, the experience of being fired, or disruption in competency as a parent or worker often provides the impetus for a person to seek help. Many people with chronic difficulties are not seen by a therapist until a relatively dramatic event occurs.

The effectiveness of psychotherapy depends partially on whether a safe relationship can be established; once this is done, work within the therapy alters the status of the patient's controls. With a safe relationship and gradual modification of controls, the patient can proceed to reappraise the serious life event as well as the meanings associated with it, and can make the necessary revisions of his inner models of himself and the world. As reappraisal and revision take place, the person is in a position to make new decisions and to engage in adaptive actions. He can practice with the altered models until they gradually become automatic. Overlapping with the processing of the stress event is the necessity to work through reactions to the approaching loss of the therapist, which often becomes a replay of the earlier loss.

Within the time limits of a brief psychotherapy, the therapist works to establish conditions that will help the patient to examine the personal sets of meanings that are evoked by thoughts of the painful event. Early in the treatment, the patient tests the safety of the relationship and the therapist's ability to help him cope with symptoms.

The pattern of treatment onset depends in part on the phase of stress response exhibited by the patient. Most commonly, patients seek help for intrusive symptoms that seem overwhelming. Operating within specific guidelines, the therapist provides support, suggests some immediate ways in which the patient can structure his time and plan for events, prescribes medication for episodic use if anxiety or insomnia is too disruptive, and gives "permission" for the patient to work through his feelings one step at a time rather than as quickly as possible.

Patients in whom the mourning process has been stymied by avoidance symptoms are encouraged by the therapist to recollect the stress event with associations and abreaction. At the same time, the therapist tries to help the patient to modify his exaggerated levels of control.

Frequently, stress-related symptoms subside rapidly once a firm therapeutic alliance is established. Therapy can then focus on the relationship of the stress event to the patient's various self-concepts and inner assumptions.

Plans for termination are introduced several sessions before the final one, and this sometimes leads to a reexperiencing of the sense of loss. Occasionally, there is a return of symptoms. In contrast to the original stressor, the loss can now be faced gradually, actively rather than passively, and within a communicative, helping relationship. Specific interpretations are made that link the termination experience to the stress event, and the final sessions center on this theme. At termination, the patient may still have some symptoms, partly because of the time needed to process a major loss and partly because anxiety about termination is reactivated. Follow-up evaluations have suggested to us that stress-focused therapy serves as a catalyst for positive changes in work functioning and interpersonal patterns over the ensuing year or more. This general overview for a model twelve-hour therapy is presented in table 2.3.

Establishing a Therapeutic Relationship

The therapist, in the role of expert and healer, should remain compassionate, understanding, nonjudgmental, and natural. He or she may be sympathetic, but should avoid gratifying his or her own wishes and those of the patient that extend beyond the purposes of the therapy. The therapist should remain respectful of the patient's autonomy, leaving it to the patient to make any final decisions, including choice of the essential themes in therapy.

The therapist pays close attention to the patient's tendency to repeat role relationship models that have been internalized following earlier interactions with important figures. These are called transference potentials, and they powerfully influence the way in which the patient experi-

TABLE 2.3

An Example of Timing in Brief Psychotherapy Focused on a Recent Stress Event

Session	Relationship Issues	Patient Activity	Therapist Activity
1	Initial positive feeling for helper	Patient tells story of event	Preliminary focus discussed
2	Decreased pressure as sense of trust is established	Event related to life of patient	Takes psychiatric history
3	Patient tests therapist	Patient adds associations	Realignment of focus. Interpretation of resistances with empathic recognitions of why they are currently reasonable, based on past relationships
4	Therapeutic alliance deepened		Further interpretation of defenses and warded-off contents,
5		Work on what has been avoided	with linking of the latter to stress event and responses
6			Time of termination discussed
7–11	Transference reactions interpreted as they occur and linked to other configurations	Continued working through of central conflicts and issues of termination as related to the life event and reactions to it	Clarification and interpretations related to central conflicts and termination; clarification of unfinished issues and recommendations
12	Saying goodbye	Realization of work to be continued on own	Acknowledgment of real gains and real *future* work involving continuation of mourning and experimentation with new relationship patterns

ences interventions made by the therapist. Any intervention may be simultaneously interpreted by the patient in multiple ways, according to how he or she views the patient-therapist relationship. As a therapeutic alliance is developed, it can be contrasted with the patient's transference reactions or expectations. It is possible to develop a triangle of insight, described on page 8, that shows the maladaptive and repetitive application of an inappropriate role relationship model from past situations to current ones and to the therapy situation itself.

The interpretation of transference in and of itself may not lead to change. It is necessary for the patient to engage in some kind of parallel processing—a comparison of the transferred relationship pattern with a more realistic alternative for relating to the therapist. We will describe this process in each chapter in detail, and will refer to this relatively realistic and desirable relationship as the therapeutic alliance. In such an alliance, the patient's role is to express ideas and feelings freely and much more openly than would be customary in social circumstances. The therapist's role is to be receptive, understanding, and helpful, and to refrain from moral judgments.

In practice, the therapeutic alliance, as experienced by the patient, always has some elements of transference, in that it is based on the patient's existing repertoire of reactions. But the alliance is closer to the actual potentialities of the relationship with the therapist than the more extreme transference potentials. The interpretation of the transference potentials may be a route to developing a better therapeutic alliance. Interpretation of transference reactions is also needed when these reactions impede the therapy, and may be necessary in order for the patient to engage in appropriate processing of recurrent conflicts and issues.

Work with Defensive Styles

In brief therapies, the therapist must counter the patient's defensive maneuvers effectively in order to maintain a progressive line of work on the focal problems. Some patients may react to this countering of defenses and to the resultant emotional pain as if the therapist aimed to hurt them, to force them to submit to his aims, or to magically restore them to happiness. When such unrealistic expectations are recognized during the therapy, they can be set aside by comparing the fantasy with the realities of the therapeutic relationship.

Specific nuances of character style will play a part in the formation of a therapeutic relationship. First, with patients who fit the stereotype of a hysterical personality style, we are alert for signs that the patient expects of therapy not only expert therapeutic treatment but also personal repair of all injuries and satisfaction of all needs. Such patients who also have characteristics of the narcissistic personality tend to present such expectations as imperatives, feeling that they are entitled to the relationship they desire because they are in need. When it becomes evident that the therapist will not play this expected role, the patient will be more likely to become enraged or to withdraw.

Faced with such expectations, the therapist must walk a moderate path, giving no signals that such gratification may be expected. At the same time, the therapist should not appear so cool and detached that the patient feels abandoned at just the time when symptoms are at the most distressing levels. At this time, the realistic expectations for the therapy are being clarified, and potential impasses and frustrations are predicted. During this stage, the therapist should be empathic, understanding, and hopeful, in an effort to restore morale, as described by Frank (1978). Later, when the patient feels less overwhelmed and begins to strive for attention, the therapist may have to be alert to positive transferences. The earlier clarification of patterns is now repeated, so that the patient gradually comes to understand and accept deeper meanings.

The patient with a hysterical personality style tends to prefer to keep the therapy at a level of ordinary social discourse rather than one of therapeutic communication. Because of his labile mood, he may also turn the therapy into a wildly emotional scene. Superficially, the patient will often appear incapable of communicating clearly or understanding the therapist's observations. In reality, however, the patient usually pays close attention to certain therapist responses (although other therapist messages may be missed). If the treatment occurs after the patient has experienced a recent personal injury or loss, this trauma may be worn as a badge that is expected to elicit sympathy and call forth advice on how to manage everyday affairs. To some extent these requests are realistic, in that the patient finds it difficult to plan adaptive actions. However, these requests are also tests to see whether the therapist will turn aside from the particular focus of the brief therapy and take on larger responsibilities for the patient. As work on the focus continues, it will often be necessary to explore concomitant interpretations of the meaning of the patient's attempts to place inordinate responsibility on the therapist. The latter's responses need to be explained in a sympathetic rather than a cold or intellectual way, so that the alliance can be maintained.

With a patient who has a compulsive style, the major question concerning the therapeutic relationship may at first be whether or not the therapy can move to an emotional type of communication. Underneath the patient's effort to set up a social or intellectualized storytelling type of relationship, there may be a covert struggle for control over the topics that will be discussed and over the degree of direct emotional communication that will be permitted. In a way, the patient is presenting the therapist with a test—namely, will the therapist demand that the patient display the emotions that are being withheld, both from the therapist and from his own conscious experience? In response to this implicit question, the therapist strives to answer that the situation is basically a safe one, but one in which there is some pressure toward dealing with central and emotionally loaded ideas. The therapist does this by displaying both compassion and objectivity in a steady manner that conveys firmness.

The compulsive patient may be relieved if he finds, in the midst of this process, that the therapist remains calm and consistently treats him like an adult equal. The persistent focus of the therapist on emotionally charged ideas, rather than on peripheral ideas that only seem important, may allow the patient to proceed through a normal mourning pattern instead of experiencing a pathologically frozen grief.

The patient with a narcissistic style may bring to therapy the expectation of being admired or special, or of being shamed or criticized. Any injury to the self, such as the loss of an idealized parent figure, can elicit a strong pull on the therapist to replace that which was lost, thereby restoring the patient's sense of competence and worth. The patient will use the kind of minimizations and magnifications mentioned in an earlier chapter to avoid disclosing aspects of previous relationships or of the stressful event that might otherwise reflect poorly upon the self. Here, the therapist must be extremely tactful while continuing to help with confrontation and reality testing. Strongly phrased interpretations of an idealizing transference (if one seems to occur) may serve no useful purpose if, by such interpretation, there is disruption of a patient's increasing sense of calm and personal coherence (Goldberg 1973).

Time-limited therapy is usually not the best choice for a borderline patient. Nonetheless, in some instances it is the therapy that the patient selects as least threatening. Alternatively, the diagnosis may only become clear after the patient embarks on brief therapy. In other situations, institutional requirements restrict professionals from providing long-term therapy. In such cases, the therapist should be attuned to the person's tendency to dissociate meanings into all-good or all-bad composites. The therapist should take care to repeatedly point out what has taken place in the therapeutic relationship and what will not occur. Intense expressions of anger by the patient are not encouraged because these precipitate out-of-control states. Instead, small, early signs of irritation are dealt with promptly in an attempt to avoid explosive outbursts and to allow conscious suppression. In doing this, the therapist aims to clarify that his or her own real role with the patient is neither that of protector or persecutor; rather, the therapist serves as the facilitator of a working-through process.

Working Through Ideas and Feelings
Related to the Focus

The patient who seeks treatment may have personal themes that are too problematic to resolve through independent contemplation.

When the person experiences relative failures of control, the activities of the therapist are geared toward helping him to regain a sense of his ability to be self-regulating. This is done through the usual methods of psychotherapy: by helping the patient to focus attention, by asking questions or repeating comments, and by seeking clarification of statements. Most importantly the therapist helps the patient to feel more in control by arriving at ways of organizing information through reconstructive interpretations. Such efforts help the patient to place memories and responses into an orderly sequence, to make appropriate linkages, and to differentiate reality from fantasy.

One aspect of working through a problematic theme is review of the various concepts of self and others, and of the fantasy elaborations that are associated with the theme. Because of the emotional pain aroused by this review, most patients will interrupt some aspects of their contemplation of it. In therapy, the controls used in that interruption are gradually set aside. Most of this is done by the patient, once he has established a safe relationship with the therapist. When there is reluctance to do so, the therapist may counter the barriers to communication by interpreting defenses and the reasons for them, by increasing attention to warded-off material through interpretation and labeling, or by simply directing attention to emotionally evocative situations.

Certain themes are relatively universal. Emotions that are commonly experienced after a stressful life event include:

Sadness over the loss
Fear of repetition
Fear of merger with the victims
Shame and rage over vulnerability
Rage at the source of the event
Rage at those exempted
Fear of loss of control of aggressive impulses
Guilt or shame over aggressive impulses
Guilt or shame over surviving
Guilt stemming from an exaggerated sense of responsibility

47

The person will examine many of the above themes independently and without difficulty. One or another theme, however, will be accompanied by flooding of emotions, be warded off by pathological defensive maneuvers, or comprise a combination of both. These themes will be a primary focus in therapy.

Working with Control Operations

In the process of working on a conflictual theme, each patient will use his own habitual defensive styles of inhibiting or distorting the flow of ideas and feelings. The techniques of the therapist must be sensitively geared to these habitual modes.

Patients with a hysterical personality style have a defensive pattern geared to preventing conflictual themes from reaching consciousness or from triggering threatening associations. The vague style of such patients can be countered by simple repetition, often with use of their own phrases (Horowitz 1974). Within the security of the therapeutic alliance, the patient hears meanings more clearly and can move forward to new associational connections. The therapist, by encouraging the translation of imagery into words and by labeling the emotions that the patient experiences, can promote a new clarity. Calm and supportive questioning helps to hold the patient in thematic areas that were previously short-circuited because of the dread of entering mental states with unbearable emotions. The emphasis on detail and structure counteracts global perceptions and encourages working through of the conflictual material.

In contrast, patients with a compulsive style tend toward a more acute awareness of ideas, so that staying with and delving deeply into one theme may be experienced as dangerous. Frequently, the patient alternates between opposing viewpoints to avoid unpleasant emotional aspects of the theme. A major goal for the therapist is to help the patient deepen emotional thought about a given topic by staying with the theme long enough to allow conceptual mastery. This can be carried too far: attempts to lock the patient into a theme selected by the therapist will increase the dominance-submission struggle that frequently preoccupies such patients. Instead, the therapist should act to slow the patient's defensive deflection from the heart of a theme by often returning to the content that was under discussion just before a shift occurred. Detailed, intellectualized perceptions are countered by questions about emotions and the specific personal implications of the recent experience. The aim is to move from an abstract to a subjective level so that the patient can contemplate warded off themes. By phrasing interpretations as questions, the therapist can avoid struggles over control or loss of self-esteem.

For a patient with a narcissistic personality style, work on thematic processing is further complicated because of the patient's tendency to exaggerate or minimize personal actions in memory in order to place himself in a better light (Horowitz 1975). Undesirable actions, emotions, or ideas are disavowed or attributed to others. Here the therapist works within a narrow zone of safety to counter reality distortion in a tactful manner, avoiding praise or blame (Kohut 1971). Recurrent clarifications and definitions help the narcissistic patient to reappraise problematic themes. With emphasis on maintenance of realistic self-esteem, a gradual reduction in grandiose expectations is carried out. Empathic support of the patient's defenses in the early therapy sessions may allow the patient to use the therapist as an external support to stabilize his fragile ego state (Goldberg 1975).

Thematic processing in the borderline patient may sometimes be derailed by the patient's biased interpretive scheme in which all good and all bad attributes of persons and things are segregated (Kernberg 1975). The initial train of ideas may proceed rationally, but when shame, rage, fear, or sadness is anticipated, a distorted set of associations may ensue. This tends to shift the direction of the ideas away from themes that are associated with threatening emotional states. In a reappraisal of familiar sequences of behavior, the patient may use the same chain of questionable logic rather than correcting his errors in linking one idea with another.

In such sequences, in order to help the borderline patient overcome such derailments, the therapist makes clarifications that differentiate reality from fantasy attributions. In such instances, he or she deals not only with the manifest reality and fantasy contents, but with attempts to comprehend and acknowledge aloud, in an accepting way, the danger of expression of warded-off ideas and feelings. Intellectual discussion of anger themes is not discouraged but accepted. The issues of safety of self-esteem, and the continued coherence of self-feeling, are considered as aspects of each thematic topic.

Termination

The approach of a previously agreed upon end-point of therapy may be misinterpreted by the patient as a rejection because he is unworthy, as a separation that he is too weak to tolerate, or as a retaliation for his hostile ideas and feelings. When interpreting the transference reactions stemming from such views, the therapist can indicate that they relate the person's reactions to the life event and to configurations of his developmental past.

In this linking work, the focus on the stressful event is not lost. Rather, it is intensified by useful linkages to recurrent patterns of self and object conceptualization that make separation difficult. Failed expectations concerning the therapy can be openly discussed, and the anger at abandonment worked through. Equally important, the therapist encourages the patient to discuss the meaning of the therapy experience, to be able to say "thank you," and to share positive feelings. Together they anticipate a period of appropriate sadness after termination.

In a twelve-session therapy, the topic of approaching termination generally should be raised by the eighth hour. Review of the cases in our clinic suggests that patients frequently pace topics and relate themes to termination well before the issue is "officially" brought up by the therapist. Recurrent linking of the termination to both past and current losses allows the patient to develop a sense of new mastery. Open exploration of termination themes generally peaks in the eleventh session. In the final, twelfth session, when the patient feels less inclined to open the door to strong and still incompletely resolved feelings, the patient and therapist usually discuss future work that the patient will conduct on his own, in social and work relationships, or perhaps, if needed, in subsequent psychotherapy.

3

CONFIGURATIONAL ANALYSIS: AN APPROACH TO CASE FORMULATION AND REVIEW

MANY PATIENTS have personality characteristics that stand in the way of their rapidly working through a conflict. With these patients, a procedure such as configurational analysis can provide useful descriptive explanations that help us to understand and so to modify resistances. It is also a method to review what has happened after the completion of treatment.

The word "configurational" is used to indicate a patterned and understandable complexity composed of multiple variables. In dealing with the explanation of mental phenomena it is essential to consider how many variables interact since thoughts, emotions, and actions are overdetermined. Elements in thought recur but they also change according to any new factors in the present environment. Mental life is considerably affected by who is listening to or studying it (Wallerstein and Sampson 1981). A system for describing and explaining thought products, especially when inferences about unconscious thought processes are necessary, needs to be open to discussion of diverse variables. Yet it must confront these variables in some kind of orderly way if the path followed is to be reproduced.

The case study has provided the major discoveries about unconscious factors. Yet case conferences, based on case studies, are often confusing when there are multiple authorities discussing the case (Meehl 1973). Each clinical expert tends to focus on a different dimension. The configurational analysis method was developed by reviewing and organizing these dimensions of a case. These organizing dimensions are assembled into an order that proceeds from judgments based mostly on observation to the most inferential ones. By having a systematic order of description and explanatory inference, the pathway taken by one clinician or team of a clinicians can be repeated by another team. Arranging descriptions according to a similar order and format enables the formulations of varied clinicians to be compared.

The background to the configurational analysis method is described in detail in an earlier book (Horowitz 1979). In brief, this method utilizes points of view from both psychoanalytic theory and cognitive science, attempting to meet earlier criticisms about psychoanalytic language (Holt 1968; Peterfreund 1971; Klein 1976; Schafer 1976; Meichenbaum 1977; Beck 1976). It condenses issues to avoid the cumbersome nature of procedures such as the Hampstead index, and utilizes component methods developed by other clinical investigators (Murray 1938; A. Freud, Nagera, and W. Freud 1965; Jacobson 1966; Sandler and Joffee 1969; Gaarder 1971; Kohut 1971; Greenspan and Cullander 1973; Gedo and Goldberg 1973; Knapp 1974; Kernberg 1976 and Luborsky 1977).

Methods

Two teams, each composed of two to three clinicians, independently reviewed all materials relating to a given case, following the ten steps of configurational analysis that will be discussed shortly. The teams then met together to review their reports, again following the same procedure. Disagreements or gaps in the reports were located and resolved by review of case materials, and a consensus document about change and change processes was written according to the steps of configurational analysis. The ten steps are completed in the following order.

First, the phenomenology, such as signs and symptoms, is clearly described and the major problems of the patient are formulated. The second step involves analysis of states of mind. In the third step, self-concepts and relationships with others are discussed in terms of recurrent, maladaptive interpersonal relationships, problems of self-esteem, and internalized schemata with regard to roles, aims, and assumptions. In the fourth step, the currently conflictual themes or important current life issues and decisions of the patient are examined in relation to his or her information-processing and self-control strategies. The fifth, sixth, and seventh steps involve examination of the states, relationships, and information-processing themes as they occur during therapy. The final three steps consider the outcome of a treatment. States are discussed in terms of changes that have taken place and the influence of extratherapeutic factors such as an altered life situation. Current relationships are reviewed with attention given to modifications that have occurred. Information is described from the point of view of changes in the patient's habitual strategies and attitudes, as well as the degree of working through that has occurred concerning important themes or decisions that were previously conflictual.

Below, the ten steps are described in a more systematic way, as they would be followed by two teams of clinicians reviewing recorded case material.

STEP 1: PROBLEMS

Define the patient's condition through a statement of the problems of current concern. Describe major phenomena and list the problems of the patient, starting with the chief complaint. Separate the initial complaints from those reported subsequently. Include a statement of difficulties that the observer recognizes but the patient does not. Make *DSM-III* diagnostic judgments on each of the five axes, listing all criteria.

The next three steps involve formulating the condition as it stands before therapy. All information derived during and even after the therapy is used for this purpose.

STEP 2: STATES

The goal is a language for describing briefly the most important recurrent states of mind of the patient. Extended descriptions for each state are summarized by labels which can then be used for brevity in describing later steps. Include descriptions of observed behavioral patterns with summaries of reports of subjective experiences.

1. List first those states that contain the major symptomatic phenomena described in Step 1. Then list and describe states colored by intense and negative emotion, ones that seem overtly to be most undercontrolled. Continue to list other undercontrolled states of mind.
2. Next list states in which the subject seems overtly more controlled.
3. Complete the list of states by describing the qualities of overcontrolled states of mind, those that overtly appear to be used for purposes of concealment or conformity. This will result in a list of states ranging from undermodulated, to those that are relatively well-modulated, to those that are overmodulated.
4. Discuss these states according to their defensive arrangements, in terms of problematic, dreaded, desired, and compromise states of mind. Include and designate warded-off states that rarely occur but have a motivational function—for instance, when the patient seeks to remain in certain compromise states to avoid entry into the dreaded states. Include and designate any ideal states that are desired, even if they are rarely or never achieved.
5. Review the occurrence of each state in the context of the triggers or events that influence the subject to enter it or exit from it. Include social, subjective, and biological factors such as events, situations, dreams, drugs, fatigue. Where patterns are noted, derive a model of state transitions and cycles. Describe the nature of state transitions, noting abrupt disjunctions or smooth blendings from one state to another.

STEP 3: RELATIONSHIPS.

Describe each state in terms of the most prevalent *self-concept* during the time of its manifestation. State transition patterns noted earlier in Step 2 may now lead to inferences about the degree to which elements in the individual's self-concepts repertoire are organized into a supraordinate self-concept. Describe concepts of others as another important repertoire of inner forms. Describe *role relationship models* characteristic of each state. A role relationship model includes at least three elements: a self-concept or role; the role of another person; and intended or expected aims for interaction of self with other. As with states, describe defensive layering of *problematic, dreaded, desired,* and *compromise* role relationship models. Describe sequential patterns in which roles or aims change in a *story line*. Derive a model of the conflicts or deficiencies embedded in maladaptive story lines, using the *conflictual relationship schematization* form. This form requires specification of a personal aim, usually one embedded in a key relationship that is conflicted because of anticipated consequences. Many conflictual relationship themes involve progressive and regressive aims in conflict; in such instances, use the progressive aim as the initial statement and failure to gratify the regressive aim as an anticipated negative consequence. (Forms are found in chapters 4–8.)

If information is available, describe the developmental basis for these role relationship models. Relate shifts in self-concept to recent life events, changes in social context, or physical occurrences. A formulation of the organizational level of self and object schemata may be made here, with comments on stability or instability.

STEP 4: INFORMATION PROCESSING

Themes. Indicate major constellations of ideas, feelings, and actions that influence current states of mind, especially those related to the symptomatic phenomena described in Step 1 and the problem states described in Step 2. Describe trains of thought that activate the problematic self and object concepts described in Step 3. Relate these constellations to recent life events, environmental or physiological deficiencies, and support systems. Derive a model of the degree to which outer reality accords with the subject's views, assumptions, and schematizations, including self-concepts and role relationship models. Indicate how discrepancies between outer world and inner assumptions evoke emotional responses and lead the subject to self-regulations and entry into various states of mind. Also derive a model of how control operations influence the processing of themes consciously and unconsciously. If information is available, indicate why progression toward completion is blocked for each theme, noting the developmental basis for the blockage and the potential course to take toward resolution.

Habitual Styles. Indicate the subject's typical use of specific information processing strategies. Include the particular use of any specific mode of expression, defensive operation, and coping strategy. Relate different modes for processing or representing information to different states of mind noted in Step 2. Include statements of any enduring attitudes that lead to maladaptive repetitions of a thought cycle, or inappropriate responses to external situations.

The next three steps utilize the concepts evolved in the first four steps in order to examine key issues in the therapeutic process.

STEP 5: STATES

Divide the therapy into phases corresponding to distinct changes in observed state patterns. Describe newly emergent states and changes in the frequency or intensity of pre-existing states. Add descriptions of the states of the therapist, and of the therapist and patient as a pair. Describe the effect of interventions on the transitions between states.

STEP 6: RELATIONSHIPS

For each phase of the therapy as described in Step 5, describe change processes in terms of the self-concepts and relationship models of the patient. Use the self and other concepts as defined in Step 3. Discuss interpersonal patterns outside the therapy as well, including separations and new attachments. Then discuss the various relationships of the patient with the therapist, using or modifying concepts in Step 3. Consider actual and potential relationships, and then relate them to forms of social alliance, therapeutic alliance, transference and countertransference.

Focus on key dilemmas. Discuss actual and potential errors of technique provoked by the patient and the therapist. Describe useful techniques. Include analysis of tests by either party to determine what kind of relationship pattern might be more fully developed.

STEP 7: INFORMATION PROCESSING

Classify interventions by the therapist in relation to key dilemmas described in Step 6. The effect of interventions and interactions should be related to the change in states, self and object concepts, and relationship models. Focus on: (1) work (or failure to work) on the main themes and habitual styles described in Step 4; (2) explanations of the shifting state patterns in different phases of therapy described in Step 5; (3) explanation of the processes of changing relationship patterns described in Step 6; and (4) descriptions of how therapist interventions affected the patient's control processes and core attitudes.

The final three steps examine outcome.

STEP 8: STATES

Describe outcome in terms of changes in signs, symptoms, and states. Use the labels developed in Steps 2 and 5.

STEP 9: RELATIONSHIPS

Describe outcome in terms of modifications in self and object organizations.

STEP 10: INFORMATION PROCESSING

Themes. Describe outcome in terms of the changes in major themes and defensive styles described in Step 4. Relate these modifications to changes in emotional responsiveness and action patterns. Describe changes in how the person is experiencing the world and communicating with others. Include any comments about increased or decreased aims and scope of life purposes or plans.

Habitual styles. Describe any changes in styles and enduring attitudes that were noted in Steps 4 and 7.

We applied the configurational analysis method to a series of brief therapies. The patients in this series came for treatment after the common experiences of the death of one of their parents. By having this common feature as part of the complex precipitation of a neurotic syndrome, we were able to understand some individualized variations in response, resting in part on personality styles.

The death of a parent is, we think, an apt choice for this purpose. It calls into question the past, present, and future implications of a developmentally important relationship. The event instigates what might be a normal grief process, but in the patients we saw, there was a pathological grief reaction based on pre-existing neurotic conflicts. Each person brought to the mourning process both pre-existing neurotic conflicts and a particular repertoire of habitual coping and defensive styles. This similarity of life events allowed us to focus on the typological differences in personal styles and conflicts.

Among the important conflictual themes for this group is rage at the parent for dying, accompanied by guilt for these feelings of rage (Horowitz et al. 1980b, 1981, 1982; Krupnick and Horowitz 1981). In order to provide a simplified model of how a case is formulated through configurational analysis, this rage theme will be modeled as if it were isolated. (More complex cases will be presented in ensuing chapters.) While such isolation never occurs in clinical contexts, this modeling effort demonstrates how case formulation may help a therapist to understand relationship problems based on individual personality styles.

In this simplified model of a conflictual theme, we focus only on those intrusive emotions and ideas that contain hostility toward the deceased parent and, as intrusive symptoms, served as a motive for seeking help. We want to understand the nature of that motivation, the kind of help that is required, and the reason for the patient's inability to resolve conflict on this theme without help. In addition, we want to know if help will be easy or difficult to provide, and if difficult, to understand why that is so.

Let us consider a patient who experiences intrusive and intensely felt hostile states after the death of a parent. Before the death, the patient believed that her mother or father would live on and eventually provide something she desired. In the cases we have studied, these desires may involve the parent accepting the patient's chosen career, forgiving a wrong the patient had committed, apologizing to the patient for a wrong committed by the parent, bestowing a blessing on the patient's life accomplishments, or providing a special skill or endowment. At this somewhat irrational level of information processing, the act of dying is considered to have been a deliberate and surprising act.

The idea that the death was deliberate stems from a phase of the childhood development of the individual when it was believed that a parent could do anything and everything. Whatever happened then seemed to be the result of the parent's deliberate actions. Since the parent died "on purpose," before delivering "it," anger is appropriate. In this belief system, expression of anger is felt to be a potentially effective action, since past expressions of hurt and resentment by the child did affect the behavior of the parent.

Once activated, a motive for aggressive retaliation will persist until some point of completion is achieved. Such a motivation may erode with time, when completion is untenable. However, the implications of the parent as now dead are so important that the actuality of the death must be repeated until it is assimilated, and each repetition may rekindle the anger theme. In order to understand the complete working through of this theme, we will first consider a simplified "model" case:

Patient: I am angry with my father for dying before he apologized for declaring me a bad person, and before he declared me to be a good person.

Therapist: Why does that trouble you?

Patient: Because now I will go on feeling like a bad person forever.

Therapist: Are you a bad person?

Patient: No.

Therapist: Do you think your father died on purpose, in order to deprive you of his blessings?

Patient: Yes.

Therapist: Is that rational?

Patient: No. He just died, not on purpose. So I will change my mind about the idea that he died on purpose.

Therapist: Can you call yourself a good person on your father's behalf?

Patient: Yes. He actually would like me as I am. There are some bad things, but I'm pretty much okay.

Therapist: Can you forgive your father?

Patient: Yes. He had problems of his own.

Therapist: Can you accept yourself for being angry with him?

Patient: Yes. My anger was based on an irrational belief that he died on purpose, in order to deprive me of his blessing. But that is the way the mind works, and I know that it is not true. That cuts down the anger now. But my feeling angry did not hurt him. So I have changed my mind and do not feel that I am to blame for his death.

Therapist: Then I think we can terminate therapy.

Patient: Yes. Thank you.

Nothing in real life is this simple, of course. However, let us carry forward this oversimplification to the situation in most therapies where the working-through process is countered by defensive resistances.

Steps in Configurational Analysis: A Simplified Model

In Step 1 of configurational analysis, we would outline the problem. One problem that the patient might present as a chief complaint is the experience of excessive rage. She might also complain of overwhelming sadness. In Step 2, these complaints would be considered as states of mind that are found in patterns related to other, less problematic states of mind. The rage and sadness states would be regarded as undermodulated, or out of control. This model also might include any relevant states that the patient feared, did not experience, and wished to avoid.

In this simplified case, one such warded-off state is listed in figure 3.1 as *panicky guilt*. This state would be out of control and stands in sharp contrast to the well-modulated state that this patient wants. We will call that desired state *intimate give-and-take*. Perhaps the patient experienced this state during some good moments achieved with the parent; alternatively, the state may only be the patient's ideal for a relationship with the parent and other companions.

When she is distressed, our patient seldom enters the desired state. Instead, she enters a state that is a defensive compromise between what is feared and what is desired. It is not quite *intimate give-and-take*, but at least it is not *panicky guilt, distraught sadness,* or *explosive fury*. It is a state of *social chitchat* in which only superficial matters are touched on as a

59

Figure 3.1
Defensive Organization of States of Mind

Problem States	Distraught sadness
	Explosive fury
Warded-Off State	Panicky guilt
Compromise State	Social chitchat
Desired State	Intimate give-and-take

way of avoiding intrusive and potentially out-of-control ideas and feelings. This is an overcontrolled, excessively modulated state. The cycle of different states, and some reasons for state transitions, are presented in figure 3.2.

Figure 3.2
An Oversimplified Cycle of States of Mind

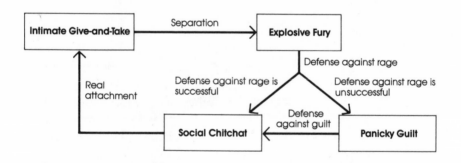

In Step 3 of configurational analysis, an attempt is made to model themes of a relationship both in the external world and, importantly, as conceptualized within the mind of the patient. In our example, one aim is to express anger at the parent for dying before providing "it." This aim, were it not for psychological conflict, would resemble an aroused appetite that could be satisfied by certain actions (Dahl 1980). For example, anger at a suitable target could be expressed as in the following dialogue.

Patient to deceased parent: "I am angry that you hurt me by dying on me." Deceased parent: "Oh, I am sorry I did that. I realize now that it hurt you, so I will stop neglecting you and attend to you more closely."

Were this possible, the patient would complete the cycle of yearning and of being angry, and enter the state of *intimate give-and-take* with the parent. But the parent is dead, the dialogue cannot take place in real life, and the urge to express anger is in conflict with the common attitude that expressing anger at a dead parent is unjustified. (Indeed, expressing anger at the live parent is also usually associated with guilt.) The patient expects recognition of that lack of justification in the form of either self-criticism or punishment from another person. In addition, there may be an irrational belief that the anger, present before the death, contributed to the death.

This activated set of ideas may find a new target, by transference onto the therapist. The patient will tend to express anger toward the therapist for terminating therapy before providing "it" as a replacement for the lost relationship. This transference parallel is shown in figure 3.3, and may provide an opportunity for working through this theme.

Figure 3.3
A Transference Parallel to an Important Theme in the Parental Relationship

Target	Activated Theme	Conflicts over Expression of Theme
Potential response to parent:	Expresses anger at parent for dying before providing "it" $\longrightarrow$	Expects punishment for being unjustly angry at parent
Potential transference:	Expresses anger at therapist for termination before providing "it" $\longrightarrow$	Expects punishment for being unjustly angry $\begin{cases} \text{at parent} \\ \text{at therapist} \end{cases}$

This theme of conflicted anger can be patterned as a story. A *story line* is an organized sequence of changes in role relationship models. A positive story line would involve roles for self and others that remain complementary even though they change. Story lines are also called nuclear scripts because they contain expectations of how different roles for self and others will be reenacted. As the story moves along a progressively unfolding line, the roles assigned to self or others may change. In Step 3 of configurational analysis, these roles and the expectations of a story line are described. In our simplified case, the roles might be those shown in figure 3.4.

Figure 3.4
Common Roles and Aims Used by this Patient in Organizing Self-Concepts and Interpersonal Expectations

Roles	Aims
Caretaker ————————	Provides
Waif/Victim ————————	Receives
Aggressor ————————	Hurts
Independent adult ————	Freely moves ahead
Critic ————————————	Assesses blame for any harm done

The roles of caretaker, waif/victim, aggressor, independent adult, and critic may each predominate in different states of mind. For example, the *social chitchat* state of mind may be the result of a pseudo-adult role presentation, in which the patient wants to present herself as an independent adult in terms of exterior communications, although her interior communications (such as reflective thoughts) are closer to the waif role. This is illustrated in figure 3.5.

Figure 3.5
A Story Line Maintaining Positive States of Mind

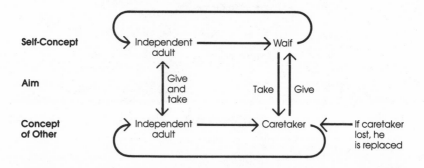

As psychotherapists, we are interested in the failure to achieve such positive story lines, and in the story lines that produce negative states of mind. For this patient, the negative states of mind may include the *rage* state already mentioned, states of *distraught sadness*, and *mixed states* that combine emotions of guilt, anxiety, depression, and rage. As illustrated by these numbers in figure 3.6, this negative story-line sequence begins with (1) the search for a caretaker to replace the lost relationships with the parent; and (2) the death of the parent, experienced as if it were a deliberate abandonment of the self in a waiflike role. The result is (3) a shift in the self-concept toward being an aggressor who obtains justifiable revenge on a neglectful caretaker, or at least prods the reluctant caretaker with enough hostile stimuli to make him alter the situation of neglect. (4) However, the hostility is appraised as unjust. The other person is not a remorselessly neglectful caretaker but is (5) viewed as a critic who seeks to (6) punish the aggressor. Alternatively, the patient may take on a self-critical role, punishing himself for the unjust aggression (6'). The injured, depleted person may (7) return to a self-concept as a waif, seek a caretaker, and so repeat the cycle.

Figure 3.6
A Story Line Producing Negative States of Mind

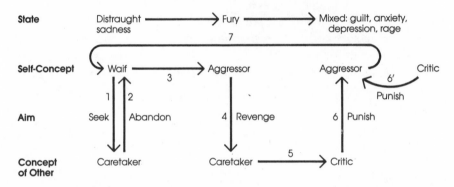

Just as the states were divided in figure 3.2, we can model the desired, dreaded, and compromise relationships of this patient as she approaches a closer attachment to the therapist. The desired relationship is shown in figure 3.7. Within the given theme of our simplified focus, she is an angry child, an aggressor telling a caretaker she has been hurt because the caretaker died before giving her something she felt she had been prom-

Figure 3.7
Desired Role Relationship

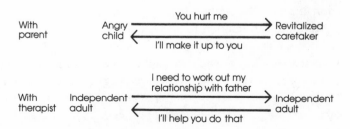

ised, something that was essential to her well-being. This aggressiveness has its purpose: the caretaker is revitalized and promises redress for the hurt. While this is the desired relationship with the father, the desired relationship with the therapist is for the patient to be an independent adult who asks for and receives expert help in working out the past relationship with her father.

Unfortunately, the patient also has a latent but dreaded role relationship model or schemata activated by news of the parent's death. This model also may lead to a story line while thinking about the implications of the death. Within this role relationship model she would experience herself as a bad, destructive child who has unjustly unleashed destructive anger upon her father. The role of her father switches from that of a caretaker to that of a punitive critic, one who tells her how bad she is for experiencing such anger. In response, as this story line unfolds, she enters a state of despondency because she believes that she can never undo her expression of hostility. This dreaded relationship pattern, which is in conflict with the desired relationship pattern, is shown in figure 3.8.

Figure 3.8
Dreaded Role Relationship

Just as the desired and dreaded role relationship patterns or models incorporate self-concepts that have been activated from an already existing repertoire, so does the actual role relationship model. The patient, in this compromise relationship pattern, presents herself to the therapist as a combination of adult and waif. She gives mixed messages which, if not unraveled by her and by the therapist, may impede work on the theme of her relationship with her father. Half of the message, spoken as a pseudo-competent adult in relation to a caretaker from whom she fears criticism, is that she has already accepted the death of her father and has no hostility, or that she has already worked out her hostility and need confront it no longer. The other half of the message, spoken as a waif, says that she needs help but, because of guilt, cannot be permitted to accept it. These mixed messages can also be diagrammed, as in figure 3.9.

Figure 3.9
Defensive Compromise Role Relationship

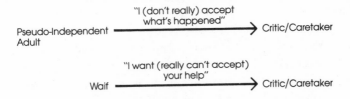

When she came to a psychotherapy session, this imaginary patient might present herself in the social chitchat state of mind, which is a defensive one, as indicated in figure 3.2. When on the topic of her father, she would present her ideas and feelings in the contrived manner of this state. Yet there might be signs of her anger leaking through this facade. The therapist might wish to address these signs of anger in order to help her. In a patient with whom such work is easy, as in the earlier dialogue, once the therapist addresses the anger, the patient might shift into the intimate give-and-take state of mind, as also shown in figure 3.2.

In this more expressive, less defensive state, she might describe how she has felt and how she is now feeling during the session, and might transfer her feelings of anger toward the deceased parent onto the therapist. If she were to transfer this feeling toward the therapist, perhaps in relation to the issue of terminating the time-limited treatment, she could confront her guilty, anxious, and sad feelings that occur in a parallel way in both relationships. The therapist would be able to help her reexamine the irrational idea that her thoughts of anger had harmed her father, as well as the idea that his death was a deliberate abandonment. Such communication would be likely to lead to a shift toward more rational appraisal of these ideas. The patient would then think through implications of her father's death that she previously warded off. She might develop plans for achieving "it" in some realistic way, which may involve modification of her goals and expectations. She may also belatedly progress through her own mourning process.

However, if our imaginary patient has a very neurotic character style, this working-through process may be impeded. The overcontrolled states, such as social chitchat, may be habitually used to avoid unmodulated outbursts. There may be a character attitude against intimate give-and-take.

For a patient with such personality patterns, when the therapist addresses the anger by inferring its presence from various signs, the patient will be very frightened that she will experience the anger too intensely. At some level, conscious or unconscious, she harbors the fantasy that she might conceivably harm the therapist by expressing her hostility.

In such a patient the therapist would face a dilemma—the kind of dilemma that keeps psychotherapy from being anywhere near as simple as the dialogue and simplified model presented earlier. The therapist is motivated to help the patient move from the social chitchat state of mind to one in which feelings and ideas would be expressed more openly. But the therapist does not want to precipitate the patient's entry into a state of explosive fury, overwhelming guilt, or searing shame. Nor does the therapist want to see the patient thrown into confusion because of the threat of explosive fury.

Faced with this dilemma, the therapist might address the anger in a tactful way. Using a dose-by-dose manner, he or she may hope that the patient can lower her defenses without entering the state of explosive fury, or hope that if she does enter that undermodulated state, she can master the anger. Through nonverbal communications, the therapist may indicate uncritical and sympathetic acceptance of the patient.

Let us suppose that this therapist, in an effort to be very tactful, speaks in an especially gentle tone of voice. With a patient who has certain other personality characteristics, this soothing approach might be interpreted as a seductive gambit. Instead of letting down her defenses, the patient may become anxious about the threat of sexuality (a different type of transference reaction).

In such a patient, the personality characteristics present the therapist with two dilemmas. One dilemma is that if he tries to address the patient's anger, she will feel that he is inviting her into too dangerous a territory; if he does not address the anger, she will not confront and work through that theme during therapy. The other dilemma involves the manner of addressing the patient's anger. If he does this in too firm a tone of voice, the patient will feel that he is critical of her for being hostile or for not telling him about her anger; if he uses a gentle tone of voice, then the patient may feel that he is trying to seduce her.

The configurational analysis approach may help in identifying such complex issues in the psychotherapeutic process. Even when compounded dilemmas occur, clear formulation will allow the therapist to discuss the dilemmas openly with the patient. The therapist and the patient may then work together to find ways of approaching a solution, a maneuver that may strengthen the therapeutic alliance.

In the following chapters, we will emphasize the difficulties in establishing a therapeutic alliance with persons who have different personality styles and will describe the processes in therapy by which this came about. In doing so, we will not be presenting perfect treatments but will show the advantages and disadvantages of various techniques that were actually used.

4

THE HYSTERICAL
PERSONALITY

W ITH THIS CHAPTER, we begin a series of descriptions of
people with different personality styles who were seen in brief
psychotherapy. We will describe personality style as a repertoire of states of mind, self-concepts and patterns of relationships, and
ways of coping with stress and defending against threat. This includes
characteristic patterns of regulating perceptions, thought, feelings, decisions, plans, and actions.

This approach seeks to advance the contemporary psychiatric nomenclature, as exemplified by *DSM-III*. That manual does contain the concept
of multiaxial diagnosis, which is in keeping with the types of formulations we present. However, it does not include the types of diagnostic
observations of information-processing style that we will describe. We
hope that *DSM-IV* may contain such aspects of typology, as the multiaxial system evolves to meet its present promise.

Our clinical examples relate to patients who would meet the criteria of
either Post-Traumatic Stress Disorders or Adjustment Reactions of Adult
Life on the first axis of *DSM-III*. The patients had intrusive and denial
symptoms of stress response syndromes after the death of a parent. However, it is the second axis of *DSM-III* that contains descriptions of person-

ality disorders and that is the most pertinent to the distinctions found in the ensuing chapters. In an attempt to place our examples in typological context, we first describe *DSM-III* descriptions. Following this description, we briefly summarize other literature relating to a given style, and then give our own observations.

We believe that a descriptive diagnostic nosology should also include the organizational level of the self-concept and object conceptualization (Horowitz and Zilberg 1983). This dimension would range from normal, to neurotic, to narcissistic, to borderline, to schizoid as suggested by Gedo and Goldberg (1973).

We will separate what is now Axis 2 of *DSM-III* into two separate dimensions. We would distinguish between pathological styles and the capacity for maintaining cohesive and realistic self-concepts. For example, a person may have a hysterical style in which impressions tend to be global and inhibition is used to reduce stress that is experienced. That person may have an advanced capacity for maintaining a coherent self-concept even under stress. In contrast, a person may have essentially the same style but may be vulnerable to loss of coherence in the self-concept under stress. Similarly, a person with an obsessional personality style is one who utilizes defenses such as isolation of emotion, undoing, and intellectualization. Such a patient could range from a neurotic through a narcissistic or even a borderline level of self-organization.

Before the nomenclature can be advanced in these ways, however, more systematic observations are needed. We will provide what we can in this direction. The first two cases that are presented both relate to the prototype of the hysterical style, although the first person has less vulnerability to disorganization of self-concept than the second. That is, the person described in the first case, the one to be presented in this chapter, is relatively less vulnerable to sudden regressions to very primitive or immature views of self and others, and less likely to confuse traits of the self with traits of others. The second case of the hysterical typology, which is given in the next chapter, will deal with a person who is more vulnerable to feeling chaotically deflated in self-esteem and who more often acts on impulse in a desperate search for self-stabilization.

In the ensuing chapters we will present an additional three cases. Each of these patients uses obsessional-style defenses to some degree (especially intellectualization and isolation of emotion), and each case varies in degree of vulnerability to self-disorganization. These issues will be clarified in the course of each case presentation.

Diagnosis

In contrast to *DSM-III*, which uses the term "histrionic," we have chosen the label "hysterical" to describe the first personality disorder in our series. Our reasons for making this selection will become clearer as we examine both terms.

In terms of the characteristic disturbances of interpersonal relationships, *DSM-III* defines individuals with a histrionic personality disorder as overly dramatic, reactive, and intensely expressive. According to *DSM-III*, such persons

> . . . [are] always drawing attention to themselves. They are prone to exaggeration and often act out a role, such as the "victim" or the "princess," without being aware of it. Behavior is overly reactive and intensely expressed. . . . Such individuals are typically attractive and seductive. They attempt to control the opposite sex or enter into a dependent relationship. Flights into romantic fantasy are common; in both sexes overt behavior often is a caricature of femininity. . . . Individuals with this disorder tend to be impressionable and easily influenced by others or by fads. They are apt to be overly trusting of others, suggestible, and show an initially positive response to any strong authority figure, who they think can provide a magical solution for their problems. Though they adopt convictions strongly and readily, their judgment is not firmly rooted, and they often play hunches. (*DSM-III*, 1980, pp. 313–14).

We have retained the term "hysterical personality" because the repetitive, expressive, and defensive style described above is found in both dramatic (histrionic) and subdued self-presentational patterns. Some people with hysterical personalities present in terms of timidity and shyness. They may seek attention in an imperative way, but they do so through passivity, shyness, and displayed vulnerability rather than through flamboyant dramatics. Our diagnostic description of this typology will emphasize the defensive inhibition style, which is omitted by *DSM-III*. A more detailed review of the history, understanding, and treatment of persons with hysterical personalities is available elsewhere (Horowitz 1977*b,c*).

Observation of Style

The attributes of the hysterical personality can be elaborated and grouped by what the clinician may observe in three time periods. The first of these are short-order patterns that can be noted during a clinical interview. These are patterns of thinking and communication observed as the patient describes a theme of importance. Medium-order patterns may also be observed during interviews. These patterns include the patient's manner as he or she interacts with the therapist while describing several themes. Long-order patterns are those observed in the patient's history of interpersonal behavior, work productivity, and self-development.

SHORT-ORDER PATTERNS

As already mentioned, the official nosology (DSM-III) overemphasizes dramatic acts that are carried out by a person typed as hysterical-histrionic. DSM-III pays less attention to the disordered perceptual, cognitive, and verbal communication patterns one may commonly observe in such patients. Shapiro, for example (1965), has described the hysterical patient's global perceptual manner, impressionistic grouping of constructs, and shallow repertoire of memories of self and others. In addition, inhibition of associative lines of thought, as well as a shifting of self-concept from active to passive, have been noted during communication about an important theme in the context of an evaluative or psychotherapeutic interview (Horowitz 1977a).

Another operation that reduces the intensity of unpleasant emotions is the loss of reflective self-awareness in a dissociative manner. This might mean entry into a slightly dazed or slightly depersonalized state. The "I" of this particular moment may be regarded as the total self, with the patient forgetting the somewhat different "I" experiences of other moments. The meaning of associative linkages, even if fully understood for a moment, may not be retained. What is learned is transient rather than consistently remembered, and is not available in other experiential moments. Through such alterations in the state of consciousness, a person with a hysterical personality reveals that he or she has unconsciously decided to avoid conscious recognition of conflict.

Such short-order patterns involve defenses such as repression, denial, avoidance, and constriction, the operations most prominent when these persons are under strain. These habitual cognitive maneuvers can be placed in a hierarchical list, which indicates the order of the patient's options as he or she tries to end or prevent a dreaded state of mind:

1. Inhibit representation of conflicted aims.
2. If this fails, inhibit translation of ideas into other forms of representation (for example, do not translate visual images or bodily sensations into words).
3. If this fails, avoid associational connections that might amplify on the implications of represented ideas. Three ways of avoiding associations are (1) to inhibit all surrounding concepts linked with the representation that is present and threatening; (2) to conclude a train of thought as quickly as possible by short-circuiting to a premature conclusion; or to (3) conclude a train of thought by declaring it an insoluble problem or unknowable recollection.
4. Alter state of mind by shifting self-concepts, usually from active to passive in relation to others. This includes regressive shifts to cognitive organization from more secondary-process to more primary-process thought. It also includes the clouding of consciousness that may occur as the patient adds more aspects of his interior landscape to impressions of the external environment.

MEDIUM-ORDER PATTERNS

The patient will often display a variety of attention-seeking behaviors. While these characterize any patient, the hysterical personality is especially alert to what is likely to evoke maximum interest on the part of the therapist. A variety of pleasing gambits may occur while the patient seems naively unaware of initiating these maneuvers. Charm, vivacity, helplessness, sex appeal, ideological appeal, naiveté, passivity, or spirituality may all be displayed to elicit the therapist's interest and to secure attachment. Similarly, a patient may convey interest in therapy and in the apparent theories and personal preferences of the therapist. Such behaviors may all be motivated by a desire to obtain attention.

When there are successes or failures in obtaining attention, there may be fluid changes in mood. The expression of positive or negative emotions may escalate rapidly to intense, seemingly uncontrolled levels. This lability of mood makes the person appear inconsistent in his values or attachments, or quite suggestible. The flexibility of emotional response, however, may also give the therapist a "gut level" feeling of enthusiasm for this particular patient and may generate optimism about the likely treatment outcome.

LONG-ORDER PATTERNS

As one scans a patient's life history and listens to the week-by-week unfolding of current interpersonal relationships, one often notes that there is a "cardboard" repetition of characters. Both self and others are portrayed as living out role relationship models that may have the exaggerated quality of a caricature. Certain story lines are frequently repeated, although they usually end badly. These story lines may involve romantic and sexualized connections between heroes and heroines, or between good children and kind parents, only to become struggles between victims and aggressors, with the patient experiencing anxiety and guilt following sexual misconduct or excessive demands for caretaking (Reich 1949; Marmor 1953). The repetition without learning that is implied by these story lines may have led to drifting but possibly dramatic lives. Someone living a dramatic and turbulent life may do so with an existential sense that reality is not quite real, and that the self is not in control or responsible for the events that occur.

Typical Problems for the Therapist

A patient who markedly exhibits the common traits of this typology will place special demands on the therapist to be active, to rescue him from distress, and to replace deficits. While such a patient displays or seems to "leak" many nonverbal cues, he tends to inhibit verbal expression of key ideas and feelings. As the therapist tries to focus on a specific problem, the patient will avoid clarity, limit associational connections, and abruptly change mood. If the therapist persists with a specific focus, the patient is prone to feel neglected or misunderstood, forget what just happened, or simply comply without real efforts at understanding or changing. Such a patient expects more than he is likely to receive.

The therapist is then placed in this dilemma: if the therapist provides clarification and insight rather than solace, the patient will feel neglected and believe that the therapist is insensitive to his or her needs. If the therapist tries to give "more," the patient will feel that a special "beyond therapy" relationship has been established. When it turns out that this is not so, the patient may respond with shock, disbelief, sadness, or rage.

Tactics in Therapy

The therapist may help by countering the hysterical patient's habitual style of dealing with conflictual themes, which tends to be diffuse, global, inhibitory, and short-circuiting. In a brief therapy, it is illuminating to focus on repetitive clarification of a focal theme and the reasons for seeking help. Simple repetition of what the patient has said may bring about a noticeable effect, because the patient hears meanings quite differently when they are echoed by the therapist. The warded-off ideas and feelings may seem less threatening when the therapist repeats them. Such repetitions often label an idea or emotion more clearly; where the patient has said "it" or "something," the therapist speaks concretely and specifically. This approach indicates the relative safety of saying what the patient has feared as too dangerous to fully express.

In a similar manner, the therapist restates what the patient has said, referring to events in the context of temporal and causal sequences. Such a tactic helps the patient to understand the reasons for actions, to realize what has happened, and to learn why maladaptive patterns are repeated. Restatement of what the patient has said clarifies alternatives and counters the usual disavowal of having a choice in deciding between courses of action.

In order to counteract the habitual "I don't know" attitude of the hysterical personality, the therapist asks for details and reconstructs the way in which events have led to problematic states of mind. He encourages ideas about feelings and keeps the topic open when the patient attempts to avoid anxiety by premature closure. The therapist also provides support so that the patient can tolerate thoughts that otherwise would be repressed or experienced as intrusive. When the patient is vague, the therapist clarifies, providing word labels for otherwise unclear referents like "it" and "you know."

Added to these general tactics are interpretations of warded-off ideas and feelings. These interpretations also reveal the continued calm attention of the therapist, at precisely the time of maximum danger (when warded-off themes emerge). This tactic may help to stabilize the otherwise labile shifts in state of mind that occur when threatening topics are broached.

The strong need for care and attention to help control emotions that would otherwise flood and overwhelm the patient creates a special tension. If care and attention are provided, anxiety may increase because with closeness there may be activation of conflictual sexual or aggressive themes. The therapist then feels a demand for caretaking. Without the support of another person, the patient may feel too frightened or devastated by events to confront issues with courage and realism. At such times, the therapist moves just close enough to the patient to provide hope. The degree of communicative intimacy may then appear threatening, and the patient may fear being intruded upon, taken over, or seduced, as described at the end of chapter 3. The kindly attentiveness that helped in an earlier distraught state may now be "too close," and the therapist may take a stance that is somewhat "cooler" but still interested and concerned. In this way, the therapist, while behaving in a neutral manner, oscillates the intensity of empathy in order to help the patient feel the presence of a safe zone for therapeutic communication.

Connie, a Representative Case

PRESENTING COMPLAINTS

Connie was a twenty-four-year-old single graduate student who sought therapy three months after her father's death. She came for treatment complaining of uncontrolled sobbing, preoccupation with death, and confusion. She had no history of previous psychiatric disorder or therapy. She presented herself as shy, timid, and vulnerable, but also as sensitive, attractive, and intelligent.

Her father's death had been sudden and unexpected. Connie attended the funeral and felt extremely sad but was not overwhelmed by these feelings. She then began to have fearful thoughts about dying herself. She broke off a relationship and began to sleep excessively as a form of withdrawal. She became progressively more distracted and unable to concentrate on her work.

When Connie tried to socialize with others, she experienced episodic outbursts of sobbing about which she felt intensely embarrassed. She could not follow the thread of meaning in many conversations. She sensed that she was seriously upset about the death in a way that she did not understand.

During an evaluation interview for our research project on brief therapy, Connie described her response to the death of her father as "too intense and confused." She hoped that if she could understand what was happening, then something might emerge that would be valuable to her.

She had not understood her relationship with her father for some years, and felt that it would help now if she could come to accept what she and he had meant to each other. She was uncertain about the wisdom of her recent choice of a new career direction, a problem that was intensified by her father's death.

Connie seemed less distressed about the loss of the relationship with a male companion, noting that this separation had seemed likely even before her father died. She did have a pattern of unsatisfying relationships with men. An aspect of her pattern was to become attached to men at least ten years older than herself, to soon feel emotionally deprived, and to then lose the person. This pattern seemed to repeat the role relationship model she had experienced with her father.

BACKGROUND

Connie's family had emigrated from a Latin-American country. Her family had been members of an upper-class circle of friends who, fearing a Communist take-over, had moved to the United States even though that had meant leaving their property and savings behind. This abrupt change in culture occurred when Connie was ten years old; and she was part of a generation expected to establish the family name in this new country.

Sacrifices for her education were made so that she could obtain the best possible start in life; this was, however, the best possible start as determined by her father. She completed college in business administration, and then decided that she wished to obtain graduate education in cultural anthropology. As her father saw it, her change of field could lead only and at best to a low-paid career as an educator, and he disapproved of her choice. This attitude caused Connie's sense of estrangement from her father to increase, a situation she hoped to correct in the future.

The relationship with her father had seemed to Connie to take a downward course. She was a child the father seemed to prize highly until shortly after the move to this country, at a time when she was in her puberty. Early in her adolescence, Connie's father enjoyed having long philosophical talks with her. Then he seemed to disapprove of her interest in normal dating. He was pleased again with her when she was accepted to an excellent university, and close to her throughout the next few years, during which he divorced her mother.

After the turbulent divorce, during which she felt more "on her father's side," Connie felt rejected when he married a woman younger than himself, and not too much older than she was. Her father's disparagement of her change in personal goals heightened the sense of uncomfortable separation that she already experienced. During this period Connie drew closer to her mother, but remained distressed, although hopeful, about her father. These factors made his sudden death seem like an unfair, unexpected, and heavy blow to her.

The evaluation interview indicated a person who seemed urgent to begin treatment, and whose features suggested a good prognosis for the outcome in a brief psychotherapy. She was referred to a therapist, a man older than herself, and began sessions within a week.

IMPORTANT STATES OF MIND

Connie's states of mind could be grouped into three categories. These categories included undermodulated states, in which she felt emotionally flooded and out of control, well-modulated states in which she would experience emotions such as sadness but without a sense of loss of control, and overmodulated states, in which defensive avoidances were so pronounced as to preclude authentic experiencing or expressing. In this case example and in the ones that follow, the first states to be described are those that are presented as problematic.

Most Problematic States. Connie's chief complaint was out-of-control crying. In order to label states briefly, we will refer to this state as that of *despair.* Throughout this book, labels of states will be italicized in order to indicate that they refer to a more extended and individualized description.

For Connie, the state of *despair* was characterized by sudden sobbing in the company of others, which was intensely embarrassing to her. She also experienced pangs of anguished despair when alone. The *despair* state was associated with unwelcome ideas about her own mortality as well as that of her father. It included anxiety about her future, a sense of foreboding about the present, and rage and grief over her loss. When she was in this state, Connie's self-concept was that of a bereft child, abandoned and crying in vain. She tried desperately to avoid *despair* because she did not view it as an aspect of normal mourning. She also felt that it would interfere with her work. To avoid this state, she attempted to hold back tears. This led to a state that was not so much *despair* as a *struggle against crying.*

During the *struggle against crying* state, Connie felt as if she were a deserted "messy emoter" in relation to a scornful critic. She attempted to portray herself as a person who was in control, and braced herself to hold back tears or the sounds of sobbing. She wanted to be seen as competent, in order to receive recognition and attention from others, and anticipated that other people would be repelled by her constant crying.

There was a third problematic state in which Connie felt *highly pres-*

sured, as if she had too much energy. During it, she sometimes felt "as if she were crazy." Her thoughts raced, she was unable to concentrate on her work, and she experienced great muscular tension. Even her bodily organs felt as if they had been speeded up. She also felt frustrated, saw herself as worthless and incompetent in relation to others, and had intrusive, jumbled, unclear thoughts. During this state she did not know what to do, but had a desperate feeling that she ought to be doing something.

Series of States. The above problematic and dreaded states of mind were a contrast to those Connie desired, in which she would feel attractive because she was especially moral, knowledgeable, or loving. She would relate well to another person with equivalent characteristics, in an intimate, mutual give-and-take. This was her *shining state.* When she was in it, her face glowed, she smiled, and her eyes glittered with joy. This is one example of her well-modulated states, which also included ones that were colored predominantly by sadness and anger, as described in table 4.1.

Since Connie was unable to stabilize herself in a well-modulated state of mind, and since she dreaded her out-of-control *despair,* she presented overmodulated states to the world. These states were not desirable but were less painful than the severe problematic states. In her most important overmodulated state, she felt and appeared *meandering* (or *distracted*). When in this state, she felt out of touch with anyone who might turn out to be unavailable or scornful. During this state Connie inhibited ideas, presenting herself as a compliant "good girl." She meandered from topic to topic in an effort to please. As in many overmodulated states, there was an incongruity between her verbal behavior, which implied compliant communication, and her inner sense of being out of touch and the way she conveyed this nonverbally.

Defensive Organization of States. As described earlier, states may be related in terms of those that are problematic, warded off, desired, or used as compromises between wishes and fears.

Table 4.1 summarizes nine of Connie's important states of mind. Four of these may be placed into a motivational and defensive matrix as in table 4.2. The problem state is *struggle against crying,* the warded-off state is *despair,* the desired state is *shining,* and the compromise state is *meandering.* The table also provides additional delineation by adding key self and object concepts. In addition, Connie's typical aims as she interacts with another person were added, to indicate the story-line expectations. As mentioned in the description of Connie's *meandering* state, there was an incongruity between her inner experience, her nonverbal communication, and her verbal expressions. This incongruity is based on discrepant

TABLE 4.1
List of Connie's States

Label	Description
Undermodulated States	
Despair	Embarrassingly uncontrolled sobbing when with peers and pangs of despair when alone, associated with ideas about death.
Struggle against crying	Verbally minimizing sadness while lips are trembling and eyes are brimming. Looking toward others and away. Ranges from blinking off tears to crying and quickly wiping away tears. Looking ashamed or pained.
Highly pressured	Subjective experience of too much energy. Unable to concentrate on ordinary work, tension. Speeded up sense of time. Feels frustrated, has intrusive thoughts, doesn't know what to do. Feels "crazy."
Well-Modulated States	
Sad crying (ranging to sadness)	Open, forlorn, pining. Full-bodied movements may show discomfort that is congruent with content.
Bitter crying (ranging to resentment)	Crying while speaking in a resentful, whiny voice. Subdued, head down, twisting hands in lap; tension, pouty facial expression; angry, frustrated tone.
Annoyed, skeptical, challenging	Hesitant to be "sucked in"; remote, slight, covert hostility undone by small laughs, ranging to mild hostility in terms of complaints. Hits chair, has edge to voice. May blame others.
Reflective, active, earnest	Open, cooperative, makes intermittent eye contact, self-observing, congruently expressive, often with soft tone of voice.
Shining	Has new idea or develops positive views of events or present situations. Has beaming eyes, smiles, expresses openness, and makes appealing looks to the other person for mirroring.
Overmodulated State	
Meandering (or distracted)	Shifts topics in vague, disengaged way; uses flat voice; is "reasonable" to the point of intellectualizing. Looking off into space, slowed down, stroking hair, poor eye contact, silent or role-playing compliance. Feeling and seeming remote.

roles for self and other, as shown in table 4.2 by the concepts listed in parentheses. For example, she verbally presented herself as a good, compliant "girl" while feeling inwardly that she might at any moment be

TABLE 4.2
Defensive Organization of Connie's States

State	Self	Aims	Concept of Other
Problematic Role Relationships			
Struggle against crying	Messy emoter	Get recognition and attention ⟶ Reduces interest ⟵	Scornful critic
Dreaded or Warded-Off Role Relationships			
Despair	Bereft child	Cries for rescue ⟶ Deserts ⟵ ⟶ Rage	Willful abandoner
Desired Role Relationships			
Shining	Moral, knowledgeable, attractive woman	Mutual ⟵⟶ give and take	Admiring and worthwhile man
Compromise Relationships			
Meandering (or distracted) ↓ or Compliant (or disinterested)	"Good girl"	Pseudo-compliance ⟶ ⟵ Pseudo-interest	Remote ↓
(Potentially a worthless incompetent)		(Withdraws) ⟶ (Abandons) ⟵	(Potentially scornful)

seen by the other as a "bad girl," a "potentially worthless incompetent," or a vengeful wrongdoer.

Formal discussions in psychiatry and psychology tend to separate descriptions of emotional phenomenology from those of conceptual, or "cognitive," expressive phenomenology. The states-of-mind approach does not segregate these expressive forms. One example in the state list for Connie is found in her several states of mind related to sadness and crying.

There are, in the nine states listed and described in table 4.1, four entries for crying since expressive sadness was so prominent. These were *despair*, a state in which there was explosive sobbing; *struggle against crying*, a state in which there was both intrusive expressions of partial crying, and tense avoidance of other aspects of weeping; and then two less out-of-control crying states. These were *sad crying*, which had an open quality, and *bitter crying*, which had angry and whining components of emotion and form. There was also a fifth state, which was an overcontrolled avoidance of crying and other affects, her *meandering* (or distracted) state.

Connie's communication in treatment was heavily oriented toward the theme of sadness about her father's death, with additive complexities of other emotions and ideas involved in their relationship. Gradients in control over crying were important in observing the therapy process. The major therapeutic interventions related to state shifts, from out-of-control crying states (*despair*, *struggle against crying*) and overcontrolled avoidant states (*meandering*) toward well-modulated expressive states (*sad crying*, *bitter crying*).

Implications of Defensive Layering of States of Mind for Therapy. The prototypical hysterical personality style is one in which lability of mood is common and a potential source of difficulty in therapy. Connie was motivated to develop more self-control and to have less frequent undermodulated states such as *despair* or *struggle against crying*. Yet any effort by the therapist to deepen her awareness of the focus, such as her relationship with her father and what his death meant to her, would precipitate entry into the undermodulated states. Connie often resisted the efforts to focus in order to avoid that consequence. Recognizing this, the therapist tried to help her stabilize in a better-modulated state of mind, one in which her ideas and negative emotions could be gradually processed. *Sad crying* and *bitter crying* were such states for her. Success in helping her gain a sense of control, however, sometimes led Connie to enter the *shining* state, with its component of idealizing transference. For Connie, that would be a fantasy restoration of what she had wanted from her father.

Connie's own efforts to avoid the *despair* state sometimes led to a compromise, manifested in overcontrolled states such as *meandering*, rather than a modulated, expressive state such as *sad* or *bitter crying*. Her therapist, recognizing the incongruities in the *meandering* state, tried to help her to experience the therapy in a deeper, more authentic way. At times, Connie reacted to that effort by entering an undermodulated state, such as *struggle against crying*, in which she experienced the therapist as scornful of the way she had expressed herself during the *meandering* state.

MODELS OF ROLE RELATIONSHIPS AND SELF-CONCEPTS

Connie's thoughts during her problematic states of mind were focused upon her father or were clouded because of inhibitions of thinking about him. When she spoke of her father she described memories and fantasies in which certain role patterns recurred. In some memories or fantasies about him, he was an ideal, worthwhile man who admired her, especially during her prepubescent period. In other reminiscences, ones later in adolescence and more recently in young adulthood, he was a scornful and remote critic. In a reflective way, her positive self-concepts involved qualities that her father had regarded as admirable: she viewed herself as upright, idealistic, intelligent, and knowledgeable. In contrast, her negative self-concepts were related to her father's perceived scorn of her as too emotionally excitable, and hence as somewhat disgusting or worthless. These two role relationship models were already indicated in table 4.2, for the *struggle against crying* state and for her desired *shining* state.

This polarity of self-concepts and role relationship models was predominant in a compulsively repeated rumination about her career choice. She had pursued the financial career that met his favor. However, she did not find it rewarding, and, after several years of trial effort in which she was unsatisfied though successful, she decided to retrain herself for a career she might enjoy. She made this change boldly, hoping to gain her father's approval and to achieve her own ambitions as well. He died before this hope could be realized.

Connie was mystified by his rejection of her before and during an unsatisfactory holiday visit just prior to his death. She saw him as having been a cold, selfish man. When he was struggling to separate from her mother, he needed Connie's support. When he remarried and no longer needed her, he became remote. To Connie his death was a further abandonment; it preempted the future plan of gaining his approval.

Her experience of herself as a "messy emoter," while in the *despair* or *struggle against crying* state, was an identification with her mother's episodic lapses in control in expressing rage and despair in relation to Connie's father. According to her father, the mother's labile moods, rages, and uncontrolled sobbing were among the reasons for the divorce. Connie feared that she too would be rejected if she displayed emotions. That was one reason for her efforts to avoid ideas that led toward emotional expression; her fear of rejection was the motivation for her defensive inhibition.

These were some of her thoughts, examined during therapy, about why the good relationship with her father had been lost in adolescence:

1. Her father seemed caring, but he was actually selfish. He had only used her while *he* needed support, and was not available when she needed support.
2. He was caring, but stopped short. He rejected her because of her increased sexuality and emotionality: that is, she became excitable, intellectually worthless, and defective like her mother. He found another woman to love and admire, and she resented this rival, her stepmother.
3. He was caring, but stopped short because her assertiveness made him too nervous.
4. He was caring, but his own life disappointments depleted him so that he could not care anymore. He may have given up and died a psychosomatic death because Connie did not care enough for him. His death was on her head, and she had to feel guilty.

Connie repeatedly cast her life in terms of story lines that involved a triangular relationship between herself, a man, and another woman. In the most common form of the story, the man (her father) was ideal and desired by both women. One woman (her mother or herself) was rejected because she was too defective or demanding. The other woman (the stepmother, the mother in earlier years, herself in prepubescence) was desired. The man and the desirable woman established a bond. There was then hostility, contempt, identification, and ambivalence between the two women. The rejected woman ambivalently desired and hated the man, was envious of the bond between the ideal man and the desired woman, and was ashamed of her rejected and worthless position (see figure 4.1). The triumphant woman might also feel guilty about winning at the expense of the other woman, causing the latter suffering. In the version of these dynamics most prominent in Connie's brief therapy, which took place after the recent death of her father, the theme of herself as the rejected woman was more prominent. The theme of herself as the triumphant woman was less salient.

Connie's self-image shifted, so that at times she occupied different positions in this triangle. Sometimes she was the desired woman, her mother the rejected one, and her father the admiring man. Sometimes she was the rejected woman, her stepmother the desired woman, and her father a betrayer of their previous bond.

The above condensed summaries of Connie's memories, stories, fantasies, and associations indicate various roles for self and others. These self and object concepts can be related to her important and recurrent states of mind, as in table 4.3. In this table, each labeled state (described in

Figure 4.1
Conflicted Triangular Relationship Model for Connie

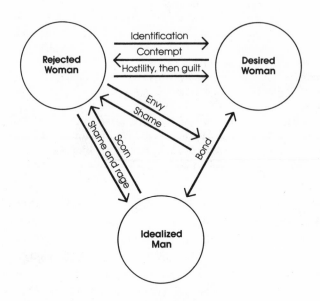

TABLE 4.3
The Example of Connie: Relating Role Relationship Models to States

States	Self	Other
Undermodulated States		
Despair	Bereft child (en-raged, envious, and guilty child)	Willful abandoner (triumphant rival)
Struggle against crying	Messy emoter	Scornful critic
Highly pressured	Worthless	Unavailable
Well-Modulated States		
Sad crying	Bereaved woman	Empathic listener
Bitter crying	Rejected woman	Scornful critic/rival
Annoyed, skeptical, challenging	Scornful critic	Manipulator
Reflective, active, earnest	Companion	Companion
Shining	Desired or admired	Idealized man
Overmodulated State		
Meandering (or distracted)	"Good girl"	Remote

more detail in table 4.1) is related to the predominant relationship model that is inferred to organize ideas and feelings during that state.

DEFENSIVE ORGANIZATION OF ROLE RELATIONSHIP MODELS

Earlier, in table 4.2, states and role relationship models were shown as a defensive arrangement which included wishes, fears, and compromises. Such considerations of impulse, threat, and defense can be formulated for a specific relationship aim by following a format that includes expectations of the consequences of that aim. Such a format, part of Step 3 of the configurational analysis method, is called a "conflictual relationship schematization." It is an elaboration of the "core conflictual relationship theme" format developed and tested by Luborsky (1977).

A major relationship theme for Connie involved the aim of getting support and attention from her father as she pursued her own values. The conflicts, coping or defensive strategies, and consequences of this constellation, are schematized in table 4.4.

In addition, there was an inferred dissociation in Connie's views of the role relationship between herself and a sought-after father figure. The father figure was idealized insofar as conscious fantasies were concerned. Unconscious sexual themes were also inferred. They would be dissociated and repressed to avoid guilt and to protect the idealization of the father.

IMPLICATIONS OF ROLE RELATIONSHIP MODELS FOR THERAPY

This method of summarizing self-concepts and identifying models that are used in organizing any potential new relationship allows us to formulate how Connie is likely to relate to her therapist. She will want to test the therapist to see if he will be attentively admiring or coolly rejecting of her, as she felt her father had been at various times. She will want to test the therapist to see if he is emotionally labile or encourages her to be a "messy emoter," as she sometimes viewed her mother or (in instances where Connie identified with her mother) herself. She will be more likely to test a male therapist for the former qualities, a female therapist for the latter ones. She would be more likely to test a therapist older than herself for the former, a peer-aged therapist for the latter.

The relationship between patient and therapist can be examined in terms of the potential *social alliance*, the potential *therapeutic alliance*, and the potential positive and negative *transference reactions*. All of these relationships are transferences in the sense that they are based on the patient's initial repertoire of self and object concepts. Only gradually can a

TABLE 4.4
A Conflictual Relationship Schematization for Connie

Aim:	I want support and attention from my father.
But I have these impediments:	
Personal deficiencies	I am too emotionally excitable and uncontrolled, not worthwhile enough intellectually.
If I get what I want, then:	
Internal positive responses	My sense of being a worthwhile person will be restored.
External positive responses	Others will like me.
But if I get what I want, then:	
Internal negative responses	I will feel too anxious and guilty about the close relationship with my father, and will feel that I hurt my rivals.
External negative responses	My rivals will be very envious and angry with me.
So I will use these coping strategies:	
Interpersonal attitudes or behaviors	I will withdraw to avoid social excitations or embarrassment.
Intrapsychic attitudes	I will believe that I no longer care about what my father, or men like him, think of me.
Intrapsychic styles	I will inhibit ideas that remind me of my sadness and anger about my father.
And the results will be:	
Recurrent states of mind	High-pressured, confused state due to lack of relationships or work accomplishments.
Patterns of state transition	Explosively sudden entry into despair state, with any reminder of the father as a triggering event.
Likely life course (accomplishments in working, relating, experiencing):	
Short-range	Inability to concentrate or boldly pursue aims.
Long-range	Poor career development; recurrent brief and unsatisfactory liaisons with men.

new role relationship model be developed, on the basis of newly perceived and actualized possibilities for transactions.

A brief, problem-focused psychotherapy requires development of a therapeutic alliance. Connie may be expected to develop such an alliance because of her capacity for an adult give-and-take relationship between companions, as listed in table 4.3 for her *reflective, active, earnest* state, and between a bereaved woman and an empathic expert as listed for her *sad crying* state. But there will be fluctuations in this therapeutic alliance. Connie may, early in therapy, react to the therapist's sympathetic listening to her sad story by developing a positive transference reaction in which she organized her experience of the immediate relationship by the roles of herself as an admired, perhaps desired woman, and the therapist as an idealized man (Connie was assigned to an older male therapist). Her positive reaction would be manifested as the *shining state.*

This positive transference potential might frighten Connie, because of her high potential for anxiety and guilt, as indicated in table 4.4. She might then defensively seek a social alliance, or exhibit an avoidant relationship pattern. She might enter the *meandering* state, acting like a pseudocompliant but also uninterested "good girl." In this state she would avoid expression of authentic feelings.

Of course she might wish to restore her hopeful fantasy by replacing her father through a positive transference to the older male therapist, especially if the ordinary compassion and empathy expected in dynamic psychotherapy resembled his earlier love and attention. She might find that the therapy is seductively in accord with this fantasy, and yet quite frustratingly falls short of fulfilling it. She might then develop a negative transference reaction in which she feels that the therapist scorns her and finds her worthless. She might react angrily and feel anxious and guilty about her anger. These negative transference potentials might also be warded off by avoiding a therapeutic encounter and attempting to maintain the social alliance of being a "good girl" (getting some attention by compliance) while remaining remote. Connie's relationship potentials are summarized in table 4.5.

TABLE 4.5
Summary of Key Relationship Potentials for Connie's Therapy

	Patient Role	Therapist Role
Potential negative transference	Rejected woman	Scornful critic or abandoner
Potential positive transference	Beloved daughter	Idealized father
Potential therapeutic alliance	Bereaved woman	Empathic expert
Potential social alliance	Pseudo-compliant "good girl"	Attentive expert

INFORMATION PROCESSING: THEMES AND STYLES

Connie's important constellation of ideas and feelings, and her habitual defensive styles—which were activated during this time of stress—have already been partially described. They will be recapitulated and elucidated at this point.

THEMES PREDISPOSING CONNIE TO PATHOLOGICAL GRIEF

Connie's father favored her during her prepubescent and early adolescent period. She hoped that this positive relationship would continue as she developed from girl to woman, with an adult career and sexuality. But she experienced her father as rejecting her, as he had rejected her mother during Connie's early adolescence. He centered his attention on another woman, and seemed remote or scornful when Connie attempted to change her work. She hoped that he would once again recognize and support her when she became successful in her new career. This plan was interrupted by his death. That event heightened her feelings of loss of support and activated themes of sadness, inferiority, and anger. These themes had been present, though dormant, before her father died.

Sadness Theme. Connie was sad and bereft over the loss. When she cried, she felt too much like her mother, a defective "messy emoter" in her father's eyes. She tried to stifle her emotional expressiveness through rigid inhibition, but at times the realization of her father's death would sweep over her. This led to a vicious cycle of feeling out of control.

Inferiority Theme. Connie feared she could not maintain her self-esteem without the approval of her father. The idea of regaining the idealized relationship had been a sustaining fantasy for many years. With the death of her father, Connie lost her fantasy of reparation. Her work, which had the capacity to provide self-approval and increased self-esteem, was impeded by guilt, grief, and loss of confidence.

Anger Theme. At an irrational level of thinking, Connie tended to interpret her father's death as a punishment he rightly deserved. In this sense, she actively rejected her father, a reversal of the relationship in which he rejected her. This conversion from passive to active permitted her to feel a sense of control over the loss. However, when she saw herself as active, she feared that her anger had punished her father (as a magical wish for his death) or, at least, that she was being punished for feeling that her father's death had served him right. Her emotional reaction to these ideas was guilt.

On the other hand, when she saw herself as passive, she had problems because she then identified with her father as a victim of death and feared her own death. On an irrational level, she believed that he had died because his guilt and despair had been converted to bodily problems. She feared that the same thing might happen to her, because of her guilt and despair at failing to have saved him.

STYLE OF COPING AND DEFENDING

The themes just described aroused strong feelings of anger, shame, remorse, fear, and sadness. She used various controls to ward off these affects and to prevent the problematic mental states they would evoke. The controls included the following habitual maneuvers to avoid emotional flooding (an out-of-control state) in times of strain.

1. She inhibited thought about these themes. In communicative situations, she avoided explicit meanings and instead filled gaps by saying "you know," "maybe," "I don't know," "whatever," and "nothing specific." Sometimes she lost her memory when pursuing an immediate train of thought, or entered a distracted state. Connie also provoked the evaluator to pursue a nonthreatening line of thought by saying "really" or "that's right" when she did not want to fully explore a different set of ideas and feelings. On emotionally evocative themes she interrupted him in order to agree quickly and avoid deeper discussion. Sometimes she did not listen to threatening information, a form of selective inattention.

2. She used positive memories of her father to disavow and substitute for negative ones. When negative memories were evoked, she trailed off and fell silent.

3. Emotions occurred and were reflected in facial expressions, but they were not verbalized, as noted in the description of her *struggle against crying state. She disavowed emotions as not self-induced:* "I cried for no reason at all," and "I don't know why I'm crying." Sometimes Connie made statements that contradicted her nonverbal behavior.

4. She often shifted to passivity to avoid active thinking, feeling, and planning. She externalized her own anger by attributing it to her siblings, citing their angry responses after the father's death, but disavowing or not indicating her own reactions.

IMPLICATIONS OF THEMES AND INFORMATION-PROCESSING STYLE FOR THERAPY

A path out of the morass of these conflicted ideas was to differentiate rational from irrational associations, to help Connie accept the fact that she was not responsible for her father's death, to help her understand that her grief response was not a capitulation to complete identification with her mother, and to enable her to grieve openly and continue with her plan of developing independent values, goals, and skills. Connie's inability to think through each conflictual theme became a barrier in her path. She could not accept the pain of knowing that her father was dead and that she could never undo his rejection of her. (In the first evaluation interview, she had stated this as the problem she wanted to resolve.)

If she continued to believe that her father had scorned and rejected her because of her worthlessness, it would be difficult to restabilize her own competent, independent self-concept. If she conceptualized him as selfish and manipulative, she experienced anger and felt anxiously guilty. Contemplation of any of these themes made her feel so fearfully alone that she aborted the train of thought.

There was another alternative. She could appraise her father as a conflicted man who coolly avoided showing his suffering because of his own pride and shame (or anxiety) about needing to be close to her. (The anxiety might have been due in part to his fear of relating to her as a grown woman because for him, and for her, mutual affection was tinged with the threat of incestuous thoughts.) If she thought it out this way, she would then have felt too anxiously guilty for "letting" him die without some magical effort on her part to restore the positive relationship.

Whenever threatening ideas occurred, Connie experienced them as insoluble and hopeless, and viewed the associated emotions as inexorably out of control. As a protective measure, she inhibited her train of thought. This led to vagueness and a "Pollyanna" quality of focusing on positive views.

The threatening ideas that arose kept Connie from reaching this potential solution: viewing her father as remote because of his own weaknesses and conflicts, nonetheless being angry at him for rejecting her, and ceasing to feel unduly responsible for his fate. She could plan to develop her own strengths without guilt, cherish the positive memories she did have, and, during the mourning process, give up the fantasy of future reparations. She would select an appropriate man for a mutually rewarding relationship, and could stabilize her identity as competent by accepting real tasks and carrying them out capably.

After the death of her father, Connie entered therapy with these complaints: intrusive episodes of crying, inability to control her thoughts when they turned toward frightening themes of death, excessive sleeping, no sense of purpose, and feelings of being defective. She also seemed to have an excessive tendency to idealize others, to be unduly suggestible in entering relationships, and to find her relationships with men too unsatisfying and brief.

She saw her father as a cold and selfish man who had tricked and used her. She also saw him as a loving man who yearned for her. These ambivalent feelings led to unacceptable rage about the former, and anxiety and guilt about the latter. Because Connie inhibited so many themes, she was confused about the meaning of the relationship she had had with her father. She tended to reenact her relationship with him when interacting with other men, because of her yearning to restore the ideal aspects of that relationship. Before her father's death, her self-concept in terms of competence had been stabilized by the fantasy of having a future ideal relationship with a father surrogate. When he died, this stabilization was lost. The result was more frequent states in which she experienced a sense of personal defectiveness.

This constellation of dynamics made Connie feel sad and potentially angry. She could not express these feelings because then she would be a "messy emoter," overwhelmed by feelings—the role scornfully attributed to her mother by her father. She inhibited the expression of emotions, but at times her suppressive and repressive efforts failed. This resulted in a vicious cycle of feeling out of control and trying harder to be in control.

We will now look at how these features affected the relationship with the therapist in the context of a brief psychotherapy focused on the amelioration of Connie's pathological grief reaction.

ESTABLISHING A THERAPEUTIC ALLIANCE AND A FOCUS

As mentioned earlier, the therapist was an older male. It was possible that Connie would relate to such a therapist as a replacement for her idealized relationship with her father. More dangerous than this positive transference was the possibility of a compulsive repetition of the rejection story. In that scenario, Connie might realize that the therapist expected her to frankly disclose her sadness, anger, and thwarted desires. If she were to do so, however, he might respond as a scornful critic who saw her as emotionally labile and demanding. She might even see the termination of therapy as a sign of his disgust with her because of her resemblance to her mother.

These issues of potential positive and negative transferences were well illustrated in Connie's dilemma over crying. Her chief complaint to the evaluator concerned the intrusiveness and social embarrassment of sudden sobbing. She did cry in that manner, exhibiting her *despair* state, during the evaluation session. She did not cry in her early sessions with the therapist, but entered the *struggle against crying* state instead. The therapist interpreted her inhibitory efforts and related them to her fear of being a "messy emoter" like her mother. This had the effect of clarifying the therapist's acceptance of her. She then entered both a *despair* state of sobbing and, momentarily, a new *open crying* state in the third therapy session. After that session she spent a whole day sleeping.

During the fourth session she reported the "big effect" of the third session. In doing so, she beamed at the therapist in her *shining* state. This vignette, so far, indicates the negative transference potential (expectation of criticism for being a "messy emoter"), the therapeutic alliance (direct communication, with the therapist accepting Connie), and the positive transference potential (mutual excitement that the therapy was having a good effect).

Connie's moods were labile due to the fluctuations in her self-concept and role relationship models. The potential story line of shifting self and other concepts that could disrupt the alliance might be modeled as in the following imaginary condensed interchange.

Connie: Here I am. What should I do?

Therapist: Tell me what is bothering you.

Connie: I feel sad and angry about my father *(cries bitterly)*.

Therapist: I can see how upsetting that is for you.

Connie: I feel good with you. Please be my good father.

Therapist: You seem like a nice girl.

Connie: You scare me *(because you are sexually interested in me and I scare you because you cannot tolerate me as a woman)*.

Therapist: You don't appreciate my help *(resentful tone)*.

Connie: *(Cries bitterly)*

Therapist: Try to get hold of yourself *(disgusted tone)*.

Connie: *(Leaves)*

The therapeutic alliance (T: "Tell me what is bothering you"; P: "I feel sad and angry") is short-lived in this fictional version in that the alliance is unstably attached to the role relationship models of mutual idealization. The patient might easily shift to a view of herself as defective in relation to a scornful other. Connie struggled to stabilize her self-concept as that of a woman realistically worthy of help in relationship to a competent, sympathetic expert interested in providing her with help. If she could stabilize that concept, she would see herself as an ambitious person struggling to find new goals in work and intimate relationships. As she moved into that position, however, she also activated a view of herself as moral, good, lovable, and longingly attached to an idealized father surrogate. In therapy this "sharing of ideal values" would permit openness and emotional frankness. Since the therapist valued emotional frankness, he could be seen as even better than her real father, who criticized messy emoters.

If she moved too far in this direction, the therapeutic alliance would be replaced by a positive transference that could then frighten Connie. She could be too captivated, seduced into a relationship that she might want, but one associated with anxiety-provoking incestuous rather than therapeutic meanings. At the same time, the potential for a relationship pattern leading to a negative transference reaction was also present. If the focus was on understanding the meanings of the relationship with her father—her initial suggestion—then Connie would express the kind of feelings that had led her father to reject her mother. If the therapist seemed to "force" her to be open about her feelings, he would be trapping her into being messily emotional so he could then criticize and reject her. Despite these potential story lines, acting as expectations, it was not difficult to establish a therapeutic alliance in the initial sessions. That was because Connie had a strong need for help, believed that it would be forthcoming, and had a relatively stable and positive world view. After several therapy sessions, she felt markedly improved and much more in control of her states of mind between sessions. Her intrusive crying episodes stopped, and, with this reduction in symptoms, she began to test the therapist to see if either positive or negative transference dangers were likely.

During the first four sessions, the therapist interpreted the differences between the role relationship models of the therapeutic alliance and those of the potential negative transference. He clarified the difference between Connie's view of herself as bereft (crying to an accepting listener) and her tendency to be a "messy emoter" (demanding succor, but in an unpleasant way, from a scornful and critical companion). Similarly, there were active interpretations of the differences between the therapeutic alliance and potential positive transference. The therapist clarified the difference between being openly emotional with an accepting therapist and being a romantic idealist with an approving father. This interpretive work stabilized the therapeutic alliance, clarified Connie's understanding of her relationships, and allowed her to contemplate the continuity that existed among her various self-concepts.

Initially, the focus was fairly clear. Connie wanted to overcome her despair by achieving a clear understanding of the relationship she had had with her father. This would clarify her sense of self and her career directions. She also thought that therapy might help her to better understand her relationships with others. However, she quickly indicated a readiness for passive compliance to whatever the therapist might want her to do; this meant a readiness to permit diffusion of the focus in any direction he chose. In response, the therapist listened reflectively but did not shift away from the focus on Connie's relationship to her father.

Since the focus was on a conflictual theme, Connie's discussion of it halted periodically, and she either would lapse into the overcontrolled *meandering* state (to avoid intrusive crying) or would talk about her mother in a clearly ambivalent way that was not defensive. The difference in her manner of confronting the two themes, in terms of the level of observable defensive maneuvers she used, substantiated the therapist's supposition concerning the salience of the initial focus.

Early in therapy, the therapist focused on the question of what Connie thought her father's opinion of her had been. This topic evoked maximum defensiveness in the form of vagueness and inhibition of thought. The therapist made clear interpretive statements of what Connie wanted her father (the idealized father) to say as well as what she feared he (the contemptuous and scornful father) would say. The therapist related these ideas to the transference and the current repetitions of behaviors in Connie's various relationships with men. The technique of clear statement helped to counteract her defensive style.

ILLUSTRATION OF HOW RESISTANCES ARE DEALT WITH
AND THE FOCUS IS SET

In order to avoid dreaded states, Connie spoke of her mother rather than her father. While this was of interest for the formulation of dynamics, it was not an optimal focus. Here is an illustration.

The third session began with Connie saying, "Good morning." She said she felt awkward, and appeared to be in the *meandering* state. After several gambits, with an air of ready willingness to comply, she asked the therapist how to proceed. The therapist answered by saying that she seemed to feel awkward. She asked, "Is there a way to get past that easily?" This was simultaneously both a request (in the therapeutic alliance) for useful instruction and an aim (in the social alliance) toward a passive role. By complying, she hoped to get the therapist's approval and to restore her lost relationship with her father, but without getting excited. The therapist was alert to the danger of providing excessive warmth and structure (encouraging passivity and dependency) or excessive coolness (making her feel rejected). In response to Connie's question, he said, "I think if we just went ahead, we'd get past it . . . unless you'd like to tell me what you feel awkward about."

This response did not alter her state. Noting this, the therapist asked her about her overall impression of the therapy so far. She trailed off, saying, "I don't know." She shifted to an *earnest* state and then talked about her mother. In describing her relationship with her mother, she used the kind of intelligent and interesting articulateness that her father had probably found appealing.

The therapist then attempted a link to the father theme by saying, "I guess in a way, with your father being dead, it leads to a reexamination of your relationship with your mother." Connie agreed and continued to talk about her mother. Then the therapist said, "You kind of know where you stand with your mother. With your father, you hadn't reached that point." Her response to this was to say, "Well, I hadn't rejected, um, he probably wanted me to be the same." In context, the latter part of this cloudy sentence meant that her father was the same as her mother in wanting her to stay in the career that she found unsatisfyingly constricting. The therapist then made a more precise interpretation. He said, "You felt vulnerable to his opinion of you when you launched a new path for yourself." Connie interrupted him twice as he began this sentence, by saying "right." As she did so her eyes grew moist, but her facial muscles resisted any display of sadness. She entered the *struggle against crying* state.

The therapist said, "Tell me how you are feeling right now. Something just happened." She then sobbed, briefly entering the *despair* state, and said, "I don't know." She struggled to go on talking about her mother rather than her father. Her verbal manner of partial poise was incongruent with her nonverbal communication of tension and warded-off sadness. She entered into the *struggle against crying* state again. The therapist continued, "You know, I would like you to tell me that you are crying. I know I can see it, but if you tell me, then I know we are talking about the same thing. Something I said, or you thought, brought tears to your eyes."

Connie's state did not change abruptly, but it did change slowly. She went on talking about her mother for a minute. During this transition between topics, the attributes that Connie described in a story about her mother seemed to apply to her father. For example, she said that her mother wouldn't understand what she was doing in her new career. The underlying meaning was that her father wouldn't understand what she was doing. The therapist then repeated what he had already said, that she seemed to be on a firm footing with her mother, while she still had quite unsettled ideas about her father. Then he added, "You may have had a plan before your father died. He disapproved of you for changing your field of study, but you thought you would do so well in your new career that he'd have to eventually see its high quality."

The therapist was thinking out loud in the foregoing remarks. He had not yet found the most accurate wording. What he meant was, "You changed your field hoping that your father would come to approve of you in your own chosen work. But he died before you could get his approval, while he was still scornful of you for quitting the work he had chosen for you." The meaning of the therapist's actual statement was, nonetheless, clear enough to Connie. She elaborated further on this theme, in an *open crying* state.

As she began to cry, she laughed anxiously. This laughter probably reflected both her anxiety at displaying emotion and a sense of relief in expressing the theme without seeming like a "messy emoter."

WORKING THROUGH

We begin this discussion of working through a theme by modeling how Connie might have worked through her problems on her own had she not been impeded by her conflicts and defensive style.

Until his death, Connie's relationship with her father had been ambivalent. She fantasied a reparative relationship with him that would be realized in the future. When he died, she had to mourn the loss both of the real current relationship and of her hopeful fantasy. Hypothetically, these near-conscious ideas could be summarized as follows:

"My father prized me once, and I loved and respected him. Then he rejected me, perhaps seeing me as defective. Now I am angry and disappointed (punished). Despite this, I hope he will come once again to prize and respect me as an adult worthy of his love and esteem. I hope that I can once again esteem my father as honorable and moral, even though in my own partially biased view, and also in the real examination of his acts, I came to feel he might be otherwise. These hopes sustain me."

When Connie reacted to the death of her father, this constellation of ideas changed. To continue with our hypothetical example: "Because my father is dead he can never again prize me, or I him. If I cannot have this in the future, I will feel too abandoned and defective to stabilize my own life. That is why I feel frighteningly sad." She would continue progressively along this train of thought during mourning: "No, this is not so. I had that hope, and that anger. I am sorry we never got past that ambivalence together. But I can continue, on my own, because I am a competent and worthwhile person. I will review this story and decide for myself what it all means. I will know what was real and what was fantasy. He was neither so bad nor so good as I believed. He was a human being with self-preoccupations, with both love and resentments. I can see myself as reasonably good and human also, with both good and bad feelings. I can get approval from others, because of my real traits, but I don't have to continually diminish or justify myself.

"As I think this over I realize that my father did not reject me because I was worthless but because he was anxious about relating to me, as I was with him. I was jealous of his new life, and a bit confused over what I did want from him. I needed to grow up and be away from him, and I do not have to feel guilty about his death or even his suffering before his death. He had his limitations, but I will cherish my memories of him as my father. I will not feel compelled to repeat my difficulties with my father in relationships with other men. Instead, in my relationships with new lovers, I will explore our real potentials for intimacy."

Connie's defenses blocked these types of thoughts. When she faced the loss of her idealized father, she felt too sad to think along these lines. When she thought of him as the rejecting father, she felt too outraged and ashamed of herself (for resenting him or not saving him). She warded off clear expression of these ideas to prevent entry into an excessive, uncontrolled emotional state. When, with the development of a therapeutic alliance, Connie became able to stay on a topic, and when the therapist clarified and interpreted her inhibitions over recognizing these particular ideas, strong emotional responses occurred without Connie feeling as out of control as she had before. She could process the previously warded-off trains of thought in reassessing her self-concept in relation to her father. With that overview in mind, we will briefly describe the twelve sessions, with key features highlighted.

Session 1.   Connie began the first therapy hour in a passive manner, which is a frequent stance of patients who want to first see what the therapist will accept as appropriate. She was dressed in black and had a somber expression on her face, indicating that she was in mourning. She sat silently, looking vulnerable and compliant. Her nonverbal communications to the therapist indicated that she was confused and wanted him to begin. The therapist said that he had talked with the evaluating clinician, but that it would be good for her to start by telling him why she had come to seek help at the clinic. She immediately agreed and launched into her story, indicating embarrassment by nervous laughter. Her voice broke when she said that she had come because her father had died, but she shed no tears.

She then gave her history. Unlike some persons in the hysterical typology, she was capable of organizing this history into a coherent, linear story. However, she left out her own reactions, instead focusing on the interplay of other people at her father's funeral. She did say that her main problem was feeling out of control. She experienced intrusive ideas about her father's death in particular, and about death and depression in general. She had difficulty sleeping and was feeling overwhelmed. She was unable to get herself to move in any direction, and was frightened about her labile changes in mood.

As much as he could, the therapist urged Connie to take responsibility for what was to happen in therapy. At the end of the session, the two agreed to focus the therapy on what the father's death meant to her. One interpretation was made: the therapist commented that possibly her father had felt uncomfortable with her as she grew to be a young woman. She said, "I don't know."

Session 2.   Connie began the second session by referring to the foregoing interpretation. She said that she had not arrived at any conclusion, but had found herself thinking about her relationship with her father. She wondered whether he had been able to accept her as a grown woman. She quickly moved away from this idea when the therapist said nothing. Instead, she raised the issue of whether or not she currently had any responsibility to develop a good relationship with her young stepmother.

This topic led to a description of the relationship that had existed between her mother and father. Connie focused on how her mother had become "distraught and crazy" when the father lost interest in her. Connie indicated that at points earlier in her life, she herself had found her mother's labile moods, especially those of sadness and anger, to be contemptible. She favored the tighter control of her father. That attitude led the therapist to realize how important the "messy emoter" role concept was to Connie, particularly as this role related to her fear of identification with the mother. More recently, Connie felt that her mother had added things to her life, especially in the area of aesthetics.

The therapist pointed out the similarity between her own position and her mother's position in relation to the father. Now Connie had lost her father, and was like her mother at the time of the divorce, enraged at him and saddened by the event. Like her mother, she felt that these emotions were shameful and inappropriate. She attempted tight control, but had intrusive episodes of these feelings.

Connie acknowledged this interpretation, and said that she was embarrassed to cry where others could see her. The therapist said that she need not be embarrassed to show her feelings during the therapy sessions. This remark encouraged Connie; it also seemed to enhance the positive transference. She reacted with cheerfulness, entering the *shining* state, because she saw in his comments the possibility of a new, shared ideology (the idea that expressing feelings is worthwhile).

Session 3.   Connie came to the third therapy session appearing much more composed than in previous sessions. She said she had been feeling much better. She was having fewer intrusive experiences of any kind, and she stated that the work of talking about the death of her father in the therapy seemed very important to her and might accomplish a great deal. Again, she seemed to be responding to more than a therapeutic alliance. The therapist inferred that Connie hoped for a reparative replacement of the idealized future fantasy with her father, to take place here with the therapist. This was one reason she felt so much better, and was again working and socializing. These improvements in functioning had positive effects, such as increasing her senses of self-esteem and confidence.

Connie talked about her mother in a *reflective, active, earnest* state. She noted her own ambivalent feelings and described her mother's love as too conditional and selfish at times. She also stated that she would not accept her mother's invitation to live with her and to go into business together. Without seeming to feel anxious, guilty, or resentful, Connie was able to discuss ways in which her mother criticized her present life and preferred that she be married and have children. The therapist recognized that the discussion about the mother, while providing useful information, allowed Connie to maintain a well-modulated kind of self-control while she avoided the more emotional topic of her father.

The therapist gently communicated this observation, and Connie—partially in real agreement with him, and partially because of her style of compliance—switched to talking about her father. She was more defensive but stayed on this topic. Her state changed to *sad crying*, and she looked at the therapist as if to see whether he would criticize her as a "messy emoter."

The therapist took a neutral and sympathetic stance, repeating what she had said and making a few clarifications, in order to occupy a neutral zone between the positive and the negative transference dangers. He did not appear pleased that she was crying, which would have promoted the positive transference potential (the therapy as a new, idealized relationship in which Connie could win approval and attention by being emotional). At the same time, he did not want to appear critical, because of her fear that the therapist, like her father, would see this outpouring of tears as messy and inappropriate.

Connie cried several times as she talked about how her father had neglected her and described the conflicts she had had with him. The therapist's main efforts were to help her clarify her wish that her father had accepted her decisions about the direction her life would take, and to confront the loss of her fantasy that this would happen in the future.

There were also linking interpretations about how she was now in the position that she felt her mother had occupied with respect to her father, in that her father (boyfriend, or therapist) would be dissatisfied with her for being a "messy emoter," having too much sadness or rage.

Session 4. Connie reported that she had slept through the day and night following the preceding therapy session, waking periodically to think about it. She thought especially about how she had cried about her father so unexpectedly during that session. She thought about the remarks made by the therapist, which clarified what she had already been thinking herself. She felt better during the week, and did not enter the *despair* state at all. She reported improved concentration at her training program. It was also easier for her to socialize.

During this fourth session, Connie sobbed when she returned to the themes of rejection by her father and her wish for him to approve her new career. She then told the story of her father's life, trying in that way to trace her relationship to him at different ages. Her main concern was how to interpret his divorce from her mother, his apparent selfishness and disinterest in Connie afterward, and the degree to which this might have been caused by her failure to live up to his ideas and expectations for her career. There were associations related to money, and the therapist asked Connie about her inheritance. She described the will, in which her father had made no provisions for her. She felt bad that there was no money which might have sustained her during her studies. The therapist attempted to identify Connie's feelings, apparently angry ones, about this. She warded off the therapist's attempt by becoming increasingly vague. She shifted to the *meandering* state and then short-circuited to the *compliant* state ("yes, I am angry"), but did not seem to be feeling the anger.

Session 5. Connie said she had been crying more during the last week, but in the *sad crying* rather than *despair* state of mind. She continued with the history of her father. She said he had been dissatisfied with her stepmother after his remarriage. That marriage had come to resemble the earlier marriage to her mother. Connie said that in the past she had been resentful toward her father for rejecting her offers of help in resolving his dissatisfaction with his new, young wife.

At one point Connie had been using positive special memories about her father as a way of avoiding the anger theme that had already been communicated. She feared experiencing and expressing this anger. She was afraid that the direct experience of anger would mean that she could not preserve good memories of her father in the future. The therapist said, "I think you can be angry with your father about that, without losing sight of his positive aspects." In response, Connie momentarily entered the *struggle against crying* state. She then switched to the intrusive crying of the *despair* state. From this out-of-control state, she made a quick transition into the overcontrolled *meandering* state, saying "I guess so" in a vague manner.

Recognizing this transition, the therapist then said, "You don't really agree with me, though. You are fighting something back right now." She entered a state of *bitter crying* in which she wept and spoke in a whiny tone of voice. She said, "Well, I can't be angry with him for not leaving me money, you know. Or maybe I feel funny [guilty] about thinking that I should have gotten money. I don't know what I would have, I mean . . . (trails off). I know (more angrily) that all the people I know who are doing something worthwhile or meaningful have all started from money they were given by their parents."

Session 6. Connie reported that she had been a little depressed during the past week, but was not sure why. For the first time she challenged the therapist after he interpreted her grief and anger. Basically, this challenge took the form of: "So, what am I supposed to do about that!"

During this sixth session, the therapist interpreted the sadness that Connie had expressed about a roommate leaving. He linked this sadness to her potential sadness about losing the relationship with the therapist when the time-limited therapy came to an end in six weeks. Fear of losing the relationship with the therapist was then linked to despair over losing hope for an eventual ideal relationship with her father. Warded-off anger at the infliction of the loss upon her was interpreted. The idea that the therapy would end while she was still mourning her father, rather than continuing until she had completed mourning, emerged and clarified a reason for resentment toward the therapist. This anger toward the therapist was linked to anger with her father for not being there to support her in the future, and for not supporting her in the recent past. Working with the anger theme, Connie reported a memory of a specific behavior by her father that she found underhanded and contemptible. Her present longing for a reparative relationship with a man was interpreted in terms of her repetitive search for a surrogate father in older, idealized men.

An important new theme emerged: her fantasy that her father's stroke had been psychosomatic. She thought it had been partly caused by his feelings of self-disgust and failure, in that he was repeating the pattern of an unsatisfactory marital relationship with his second wife. Connie felt badly that she had not been able to rescue him. This was linked to her guilt over being angry with him.

Session 7. Connie reported that she had cried profusely, yet comfortably, while watching a film on television about the death of a parent. The movie was about an ambivalent relationship between a son and his aged, angry, widower father whom he eventually had to leave.

Connie then began to talk about her own future career activities. This was done in a way that tested the therapist to see how he might respond to her. She said she was now trying to decide whether to go to the country and live a quiet life, or to continue with her new career goals. The move would be immediate, interrupting the therapy before the planned end. In this way she provoked the therapist to choose for her, with his decision meaning that he either agreed to her departure (rejection) or wanted her to stay in therapy. The therapist did neither. Instead, he brought up the theme of planned termination and her reactions to it. She then entered a *sad crying* state while expressing her feelings and ideas about eventual separation from the therapist. There was further work linking the meaning of termination to her feelings of abandonment by her father, repeating and working on themes emergent during the preceding session.

Session 8. Connie reported that she felt much better since the last session. She said that she was crying less often than she had previously, and when she did, it was *sad crying*, not *despair*. She talked again about how her father had been cold to her, and noted that now she could be angry with him in order to motivate herself to pursue her quest for independence through a new career. She saw her independence as moving along a path that her father had never been able to follow. He had not fully left his own parents when he married his first wife. Upon divorce, he immediately married his second wife, and then he died.

She told more stories about herself and her father. She emphasized how some of his plans had been unfulfilled, although he was regarded as successful. She also saw him as cold and remote in many of his relationships. She began to feel he had tried to love her but had had his own conflicts about intimacy. She began to discuss her anger toward men, although this theme tended to be one that caused her to ward off all possible interpretations and convert them instead into self-criticism. At other times she inhibited such ideas, replacing them with positive ones.

Session 9. In the ninth session, Connie described her sense that her father had tried to be superior in their relationship. She felt that he had not valued her sufficiently as an autonomous person. Instead, he had shown off in front of her, indicating only cursory interest in supporting her emotionally. She began to think of "telling off" her father. She wanted to say how he had disappointed her by talking about high ideals but not living up to them in their relationship. She said that she had never shown any anger toward her father, with the exception of one episode. During this occurrence, she had screamed uncontrollably at him because he would not give her money for advanced education. This event was like a "mini-trauma," now integrated in the course of working through her grief. The therapist helped Connie to reexamine issues of anger and guilt by differentiating reality from fantasy concerning the magical effects of hostile wishes.

The therapist also clarified her pattern of finding and then giving up on selfish men. She chose men who were like her father, hoping that each relationship would work. These men turned out to be self-preoccupied and often rejected her for another woman, recapitulating the triangular relationship theme of her father, her mother, and herself (and, subsequently, of her father, her stepmother, and herself).

In response to this line of clarification and interpretation, Connie brought up the news that she had recently been attracted to a current teacher. She did not know if he was married or whether she really wanted a relationship with him. She discovered, however, that she was trying to attract his interest. The therapist commented on the similarity between the teacher and her father. He wondered if this new interest could be related to the therapist's impending and announced two-week absence.

Session 10. There was then a two-week break because of the therapist's vacation. During that time Connie began a relationship with a teacher, which she described in the tenth session. She reported that she had once again been in a *highly pressured* state before the session and had found it quite distressing. She began the hour, however, in the *meandering* state. She asked about the therapist's vacation, saying that he looked tanned and rested. Then, as in the early sessions, she was passive, asking where she ought to begin.

The therapist, noting her *meandering* state, inquired more about the *highly pressured* state she had reported occurring just before the session. This inquiry led Connie to describe her physical sensations and how she had been hyper-alert, as if speeded up. She said she had felt as if she was going crazy because of her enormous energy, for which there seemed to be no outlet. She attributed her entry into this state to recent events.

At this point Connie changed to her *reflective, active, earnest* state and in a more open manner told the therapist about the new relationship. She linked this to material discussed in the previous therapy sessions, saying, "I should think more about these things. I should think about what I'm getting into (*before getting into it,* implied). We talked about relationships and . . . but I don't know . . . I mean. . . . " With a great deal of trailing off and saying "I don't know," but with efforts to counteract these aspects of inhibition, she began to describe the positive and negative aspects of the relationship.

She started to cry, possibly because she expected the therapist to be critical of her for once again starting a relationship with a man similar to her father. She warded off the tears and attempted to change the subject to her work, commenting on how her retraining was proceeding, but did not give her full attention to this important topic.

At this point the therapist reviewed the preceding session. He reiterated the similarity of the man to her father, and linked impulsive entry into the relationship to her feelings of loss of support when the therapist had left her to go on his vacation. He related the *highly pressured* state to her fear that he would criticize her for starting a relationship with the teacher (for being disloyal to the therapist) and would become a "scornful critic" in the manner she had experienced with her father. Connie admitted that she felt uncomfortable. She said that she didn't want to be weak and repeat a pattern because she wasn't strong enough to act differently. The therapist said, "You're especially embarrassed about wanting to be held, comforted, or listened to, as if those were bad wishes."

Work continued on this pattern of seeking an idealized older man who was also somewhat remote. As Connie talked about this theme, she brought up her anger at the lack of response she got from men. The therapist had gone on vacation, the teacher had used her without interest in her personality, and her father had rejected her before and with his death.

Session 11. Connie reported that it had been a good week. She seemed composed, and said that she did not expect to cry during the hour because she was feeling so well. Most of the time was spent discussing her relationship with the teacher. The focus was on her tendency to develop an inferior and defective self-image in relation to a disinterested man. Once again she had formed a relationship in which she was looking for signs of approval or disapproval from an older man. Once more she seemed doomed to a repetition. She had again selected a man who was older and was superior to her in status, and she felt unable to insist that she be treated as an authentically valuable woman and equal companion.

She indicated that the discussions with the therapist had clarified these issues and had led to some new behavior patterns. That was what she wanted. However, she feared that after the therapy was over, she would be unable to maintain this perspective. She said, "I fear, in any future relationship, that I won't be able, be strong in myself enough to . . . I think, I would really like to have, you know, a relationship that was. . . . I'd like to have some stability in my life (*laughs anxiously*)."

The therapist responded by asking how she felt about the next session being the last. He reviewed some of the material they had discussed during the eleventh session, particularly the repetitive quality of her relationships with men. He labeled such material as "unfinished business" that she might contemplate after the therapy. She was reminded that she would be coming in a few months later for reevaluation, and at that time could discuss additional therapy if she felt it was desirable.

Session 12. Connie began the hour in the *reflective, active, earnest* state, reviewing her career plans. She entered the *sad crying* state during the session, when talking about separation from the therapist, whom she felt had been very helpful. She said that she feared not being able to maintain what she had learned in therapy, but was hopeful that she would. She commented that having a fixed end to the period of therapy was better than not knowing when the end would come, because she had been able to pace herself to accept this moment. The ending was still painful for her, however.

Outcome

Our research group has developed an outcome assessment device that is called the Patterns of Individual Change Scale (Kaltreider et al. 1981). This device provides a quantitative assessment that is arrived at by independent reviewers who look at evaluation and follow-up videotapes on symptomatology, personal capacities, and current interpersonal relationships. As figure 4.2 indicates, each clinician rates the outcome of a case, by comparing pre-therapy and post-therapy statuses. Placement of the mean scores for each patient on a concentric-wheel graphic display allows quick recognition of patterns.

The Patterns of Individual Change Scale battery was designed to measure complex changes in personal functioning that are seen in bereaved persons. Each of the thirteen scales has seven scale ponts, anchored by descriptive phrases. The domains covered are symptoms, relationships with others, and self-concept. These scales were used by six experienced clinical judges who reviewed videotapes as the basis for rating a patient's status at each evaluation session. The ratings were found to be reliable and to discriminate among subjects in clinically meaningful ways.

Figure 4.2
The Pattern of Change: The Case of Connie

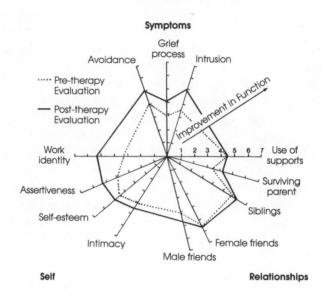

The hub of the circle in figure 4.2 contains the most pathological ratings on each of the scales, and the other rim the more adaptive functional levels. The figure shows symptomatology at the top. There are three separate scales for grief process, intrusive symptoms, and avoidant symptoms. Note that there was improvement on all three symptom scales from the time before therapy to a follow-up evaluation four months after termination.

In the lower left quadrant of the web of the scales are four scales having to do with personal functioning: work identity, assertiveness, self-esteem, and intimacy. Again, clinicians rated all four of these factors as improved by the time of follow-up.

The other six scales illustrated on figure 4.2 covered these aspects of interpersonal functioning: same-sexed friendships; opposite-sexed friendships; relationship to stepmother, to mother, to siblings, and to other potentially supportive persons.

When Connie returned for the follow-up evaluations, she reported a sustained reduction in the pathological aspects of her grief reaction. This good symptomatic outcome had been apparent by the fourth therapy session. Her self-report scales reflected a decline in such symptoms as stress, anxiety, and depression.

MODIFICATION OF STATES

The *despair* and *highly pressured* states were now absent. These state changes can be related to nine specific state-related complaints, as summarized in table 4.6.

TABLE 4.6
Connie's State-Related Problems

Pre-therapy	Follow-up
1. Sudden uncontrolled crying spells	1. Not present
2. Inability to control thoughts such as fear of death	2. Feels in control of thoughts
3. Excessive daydreaming	3. Not present
4. Difficulty in concentrating	4. Not present
5. Fading out of conversations	5. Not present
6. Out of touch with feelings and frightened by them	6. Able to experience and accept feelings
7. Inability to concentrate on work	7. Able to concentrate
8. Excessive sleeping	8. Not present
9. Inability to initiate or complete tasks	9. Ability to focus on and complete most tasks

ALTERATIONS IN SELF–CONCEPT AND ROLE RELATIONSHIPS

The "messy emoter" and other defective self-images were of reduced importance as current organizers of mental life. Connie experienced increased self-confidence, even during periods of emotionality. She could cry and feel sad without simultaneously feeling out of control. She had an increased but still marginal ability to experience hostile affects, while still feeling competent, worthwhile, guilt-free, and in control. The main shift, then, was away from organization of her experience by the role relationship model of herself as the undesirable "messy emoter" in relation to a scornful other. This stabilization remained even though she was rejected by the man with whom she had become involved during therapy.

Connie had clearer and more realistic views of her relationship with her father. To some extent, she had mourned the loss of an idealized relationship, although this process was incomplete. The residual model of trying to recapture this fantasy in her relationships with men was still evident in her recent repetition of the pattern. She did indicate insight into this problem, but at the moment it was intellectual insight without demonstrated change toward a new behavior pattern.

Before treatment, Connie was working on plans for retraining in a new field of her own choice. After her father's death and before therapy, she was unable to concentrate on this effort and had a reduced sense of purpose. After therapy she completed projects related to her studies. The evaluator did not note new self-concepts or role relationship models, but there seemed to be restabilization of Connie's previously present, more competent self-concepts. Further, there was an increase in her self-esteem that appeared to derive from a stronger sense of identity manifested as an increased sense of continuity between various memories and attitudes. Dissociation was reduced.

Connie's sense of greater self-confidence was shown in the following excerpts from the first follow-up interview, which was conducted five months after she terminated therapy (thirteen months after the death of her father).

Connie: Well, I felt like my therapy here was extremely valuable.

Evaluator: Yes?

Connie: I'd never been in therapy at all [before], and I was really afraid of a lot of my emotions, to express them, you know. And so, just that experience alone, just having the chance to express them. I mean, if only to come here and cry for an hour, which is something I don't or didn't do, you know. And to think about things, I mean, I feel like I got some tools from the way therapy worked. I mean, the ways of looking at things and trying to work out some things for myself.

Evaluator: So you got a new experience with your sadness, which freed you up. Maybe with some other feelings, too?

Connie: Well it . . . it gave me a feeling of more self-confidence. You know, that I could take control. . . .

Evaluator: So that hasn't been such a current concern, about your feelings being as out of control as they were when you first came here.

Connie: No, no.

Evaluator: Has there been a change in your feelings about your anger, as well as your sadness?

Connie: Um (*pause*). Well, I don't feel as much anger. I felt a lot more anger before. And now, when I feel it, it's kind of really related to the sadness. I mean, it's like I go along feeling sadness and every once in a while I'll have a spurt of anger, you know, just a quick one, because it doesn't seem like it's important. I mean, it's important and I recognize that I feel the anger, but it doesn't get me anywhere to feel it. I mean, like I recognize that I am angry, you know, about certain things that I didn't get from my father or the way he treated me.

Evaluator: Yes.

Connie: But that's the way it was, and I don't know just why, you know, he did all the things that he did, but it just seems that bits and pieces just kind of became clear, and I'm most of the time just content to wait and see, how my feelings about him change, as I learn more about myself. My feelings about him change in terms of just being a human being. I mean, I can rationalize or give him all those reasons why he didn't treat me the way I wanted to be treated, and still be angry.

In the above dialogue ideational continuity was increased. Connie would think of her father as lost without also feeling intense pangs of sadness, panic, or anger. She experienced modulated forms of these emotions. The ideas that led to such feelings were more clearly represented and available to contemplation. She was still mourning her father, but the process was free from major entry into intrusive or avoidant states of mind.

Connie showed no sign of fundamental change in her defensive style. She had advanced in terms of working through some particular themes about her father and so was less defensively vague and inhibited on that topic. But she was still thought to be likely to use inhibition, disavowal by countering ideas, vagueness, and surface associations when other conflicts occurred.

In summary, the brief therapy had a major impact on Connie's working through a pathological grief reaction, markedly reducing her anxiety and depression. The therapy helped in some areas of social functioning, but did not produce extensive changes in schematizations or defensive style. The therapist's understanding of these schematic patterns and of Connie's defensive style was very useful in accomplishing the working-through process that restored her to a sense of stability and control.

5

THE MORE DISTURBED HYSTERICAL PERSONALITY

S DESCRIBED EARLIER, within a given character style there is variation in the degree to which an individual has a stable self-organization. Connie, in the case illustration in the preceding chapter, only rarely regressed to states in which she conceptualized herself as incomplete, empty, or severely damaged. The more disturbed hysterical personality style is one in which such regressions are more likely to occur despite the person's use of all of his or her coping efforts.

This observation—that persons with a hysterical personality style differ in their vulnerability to regression into disorganized or chaotic states of mind—has been made over several decades. In the clinical literature, this phenomenon has been given various labels, some of which we now consider inappropriate, such as the "good" versus "bad" hysterical personality type. Gradations in organizational level of self and object concepts have been thought to arise from developmental fixations. This theory has led to the distinction between a "genital" rather than "oral" hysterical personality as well as to the distinction between an oedipal rather than pre-oedipal character structure (Abraham 1921, 1924; Reich 1949; Marmor 1953).

Easser and Lesser (1965) separated hysterical personalities into two categories, based on the level of psychosocial development. Distinguishing between the mature, better integrated hysterical personalities and hysterical personalities that are more pregenitally fixated, these authors called the more disturbed individuals "hysteroid." They suggested that major difficulties had arisen for this group because of early emotional deprivation by the mother. Though seeming to look like the "true" hysterical personality, these individuals were thought to have higher levels of dependency and higher frequencies and intensities of irrational states of mind.

Zetzel (1968) described four subtypes of hysterical personalities, ranging from "good" to "bad" on the basis of their prognosis and suitability for psychoanalysis. Those who were categorized as "good" had oedipal-level conflicts; those who were "bad" had pre-oedipal conflicts and ego deficits. Lazare (1971) posited that the more disturbed group defended not against the anxious and guilty threats of sexuality, as was the case with the healthier group, but against passive and childlike orality, with rage responses to frustration, as well as anxiety and guilt over aggression.

The greater pathology in the more disturbed hysterical personality may also be related to instability of self and object organization. The more disturbed hysterical personalities at times may be unable to stabilize an acceptable self-concept; they may incorporate others into their self-organization as if they were extensions of the self, using them as what Kohut (1971) has called "self-objects." Such people have a reduced capacity to contain multiple self-concepts within an overarching self-schematization, and instead dissociate or split apart aggregates of experience. As with narcissistic or borderline personalities, state lability and explosive emotional expressions are prominent.

Because of state lability, dependency on self-objects, and unstable self-conceptualization, these patients, when they seek therapy, are so caught up with a sense of neediness that they may be unable to recall times when they were less needy. Hope is hard to maintain, and a therapeutic contract difficult to develop.

Diagnosis

The *DSM-III* description of the histrionic personality as outlined in chapter 4 may apply to the more disturbed hysterical personality as well. When under stress, persons in the more disturbed range are likely to become both depressed and disorganized. Devalued images of the self often alternate with grandiose concepts and expectations. There may be a history of relationships that are swiftly intense, then chaotic and unpredictable, then abruptly terminated. The person's relationships are often characterized by intense jealousy, possessiveness, and aggressive assaults.

Associated Features and Impairment

The more disturbed hysterical personality shares traits in common with persons who have impulsive character disorders. Under strain, substance abuse may become a prominent problem. Sexual behavior may be promiscuous, and general behavior impulsively erratic. Hypochondriasis, panic attacks, conversion symptoms, severely depressive moods, hypomanic flights, or psychophysiological disorders may also be prominent. Such individuals present a high suicide risk.

Observation of Style

General patterns of the hysterical personality were described in chapter 4. Only aspects of style that pertain specifically to the more disturbed hysterical personality will be added here.

The inhibition of ideas may become quite pronounced, leading to states in which there is severe confusion or state lability so extreme that the observer may be unclear about what is going on. More rigid (and also less successful) defenses are used to ward off the experience of certain emotions. Most feared are feelings of intense sadness, hopelessness, and rage at abandonment. High-risk behavior may occur when the person is under strain and makes desperate attempts to gain attention. There may be adherence to different and conflicting value structures, depending upon which individuals, groups, or ideologies might provide support for the moment.

Typical Problems for the Therapist

The therapist is likely to feel overwhelmed by the intensity of the person's needs and demands in the face of limited time. On the other hand, a time-limited brief therapy can help to restabilize the vulnerable patient who has shifted to chaotic states because of stressful events. The current crisis situation may help therapist and patient to focus the treatment toward particular aims.

Tactics in Therapy

As noted in chapter 4, the aim of the therapist is to counteract the hysterical style sufficiently for the person to work through a selected set of problems, deal with a life event, or make life-planning decisions. Global, diffuse, short-circuiting styles are counteracted by reconstruction of the meaningful sequences of behavior that led to particular consequences, by requests for details, and by reconstruction of the events that led to problematic states of mind. The therapist might proceed at a slower-than-usual pace, necessitated by the vulnerable patient's inability to simultaneously maintain varied self-concepts and role relationship models. This is especially true of the quantity of information given in transference interpretations. The therapist cannot interpret warded-off ideas as rapidly as would be possible with a more mature patient, because the more disturbed patient is likely to enter mental states where there is a lack of awareness of the therapeutic alliance. In such states, the patient is caught up in self-concepts and role relationship models characteristic of the transference relationship; aspects of the reality-based working relationship may be temporarily lost to awareness.

A supportive stance can help the patient to tolerate contemplation of otherwise overwhelming topics, but care should be taken to avoid appearing seductive. If the patient acts out (for example, abusing drugs or alcohol), limit-setting is appropriate, but structuring should not be heavy-handed or offer the promise of extended external regulation. The therapist should convey a sense of support without appearing intrusive, critical, or controlling. The patient should be encouraged to take responsibility for himself or herself.

While brief treatment with a less disturbed hysterical personality may aim for insight and some revision of unconscious attitudes, goals for the more disturbed hysterical personality are generally less ambitious. Helping the patient to gain a sense of continuity and linkage between already *consciously* experienced memories, fantasies, wishes, fears, and plans may be sufficient to restore some stability.

The following case will illustrate some of these issues.

Marilyn, a Representative Case

PRESENTING COMPLAINTS

Marilyn, a twenty-year-old woman, came to the clinic five weeks after her mother's death in a hotel fire. After two weeks of insomnia, intrusive images, nightmares, repeated car accidents due to reckless driving, and finally a suicide attempt, she agreed to her sister's urgent plea that she seek help. She had been trying to control her symptoms by use of drugs and alcohol, but this only contributed to her chaotic feelings.

Marilyn was an attractive-looking, seductively dressed young woman who smoked cigarettes frequently throughout the evaluation interview. Soon after it began, she stated that she "had a good attitude about death" and "wasn't upset" over the loss of her mother, but was more disturbed by her inability to maintain relationships with men.

Her ambivalence about her mother's death was evident in two statements she made within the first five minutes of the evaluation session. She first described herself as not bothered by her mother's death. A few minutes later she described "freaking out and crying hysterically" when she was bringing her mother's belongings back to her own house.

It was only during the past five years that Marilyn had established a rewarding relationship with her mother, although her mother was more like a "buddy" than a parent. Losing this relationship was difficult for Marilyn because this was, in effect, the second time they had been separated. The first time occurred a year after her parents' divorce, when at the age of five, she was sent to live with her father and stepmother. Before age five, her life with her mother had been quite turbulent.

In the initial evaluation session, Marilyn attempted to define her difficulties as a series of rejections or abandonments by men, rather than focusing on the early abandonment by her depressed mother and her subsequent search for the loving relationship she had never had. Marilyn did receive support from Trudy, an older sister who stayed with her and tried to comfort her, until Marilyn's neediness had so depleted Trudy that she brought her to the clinic. For Marilyn, however, this kind of support was not enough. She described her inability to be alone, her need for a man to love and to be loved by, and her constant disappointment over termination of each new relationship.

Since her mother's death five weeks earlier, Marilyn had spent most of her time seeing lawyers and comforting her grandparents. She was also trying to sort out her feelings about a recent impulsive separation from a male friend. This man had said he didn't believe that her grief was real and had told Marilyn that she "didn't know what caring was."

In discussing her current depression, she noted that she had experienced other depressions before and compared her present state with how she had felt a year ago. At that time she had taken a crayon and written the words "I want to die" on the wall of her room. She described her current feelings as "wanting to give up" and recounted how, as a child, she had had a closet she sat in, with the door closed, when she felt this way. She expressed a wish that she could do that now, "to make the world go away."

BACKGROUND

Marilyn was the youngest by far of four children. Her parents divorced when she was five. She had lived with her mother for a year after that, and described it as a very bad time. Her mother was deeply depressed, never knew or cared where Marilyn was, and had brought a man into their home who, she said, "hated and yelled at me all the time." Before the year was up, the mother realized that she wasn't able to care for Marilyn, gave her to her father, and moved away. Her mother's lover left shortly after that; her mother subsequently married again, and that man left. Several years before her death, the mother had again remarried a man with whom she had a good relationship. Marilyn lived with her father and stepmother for the next thirteen years in an Italian neighborhood in New York City, where many of the children, including Marilyn, attended strict parochial schools. Marilyn received considerable criticism during this period of her life, which contributed to the defective self-image that remained with her as an adult.

She described her stepmother as lacking in affection and her father as distant and supportive of the kind of treatment she received from her stepmother. The consequences of these individuals' attitudes were evident in the following statements.

Marilyn: Well, let me explain probably why I've got the low opinion of myself, although I can't blame it all on my stepmother. For thirteen years I heard nothing but bad things about myself, that I was no good, that I was lazy, that I was never going to amount to anything. My stepmother's idea of raising children was "You put 'em down and they'll prove you wrong," which didn't work with me. She put me down all the time. When she was angry she wouldn't talk to me for like three days at a time. One of my big problems is my opinion of myself is based on what other people think of me. So if other people are not thinking good things about me, then I'm not good.

Evaluator: You can switch to a bad image of yourself right then?

Marilyn: Yeah. And that's one of the recurring nightmares, that I'm being replaced by somebody better.

She noted that her relationships with her father and stepmother had improved in recent years and that they all got along well now.

Marilyn went to college as an art major. She briefly entered psychotherapy during her freshman year, at a time when she was confused about herself, her goals, and her only relationship—with a boyfriend whom she had dated since she was fifteen. She dropped out of college, although the therapist tried to discourage her from doing so. She had secured a part-time job in a large advertising agency, began to meet people whom she felt liked her, decided to shift her goals to getting ahead in this field, and quit school. She worked at her job for two years, moving through various positions, and had recently been transferred to a different department in a branch office. She looked forward to this as a challenge she felt she could meet.

Marilyn had an intense craving to attach herself to a man, almost any man, and would then use that man as an extension of her self-image. Without a man she felt bereft, abandoned, and lost. At times she felt intensely enraged and frustrated by men who had deserted her, and had been unable to maintain a long-term, mutually satisfying relationship. Until recent years, her relationship with her mother had been disruptive and painful. She saw her mother as responsible for the initial loss of her father; for subjecting her to a surrogate stepfather who was angry, hostile, and alcoholic; and for abandoning her to her father and stepmother, who showed her neither understanding nor affection. In recent years the relationship between mother and daughter had improved. The mother had become more stable while living with a man with whom she had a good relationship. She and Marilyn had become "pals," until the mother's abrupt death.

Marilyn's relationship with her sister seemed to be solid and rewarding for her. She described her sister as "her lifeline," but one wondered whether she was capable of reciprocating, maintaining, and mutually engaging in this relationship.

IMPORTANT STATES OF MIND

Marilyn had serious problems with states in which she felt and seemed out of control. If she had been a less disturbed patient, her chief complaint might have been an extended mood of intense, needy sadness. Instead, she presented as completely distraught and overwhelmed. In this *severely distraught* state she experienced piercing pangs of sadness, fear, shame, and rage. These emotions were jumbled, chaotic, and confusing even though one or another affect might predominate at a given time. She also had other problematic states in which she vacillated between feeling hurt, feeling disgusted with herself, and being angry at unfair criticism by others. She also suffered from a pining, grieving, empty feeling state we labeled, for brevity, as *sad-needy*. These states of being *sad-needy* or feeling *hurt-criticized* were overshadowed by the *severely distraught* state.

Series of States. Marilyn felt most out of control during the *severely distraught* state, with its affective variations and lability. Sometimes, in a sudden and unpredictable way, she entered the *severely distraught* state, which frequently was preceded by the painful *sad-needy* or *hurt-criticized* states. These latter states contained some of the self-concepts of the *severely distraught* state. For example, in the *sad-needy* state Marilyn felt like an empty, helpless, yearning waif, pining for full attention from an unavailable or inadequate caretaker. In the *hurt-criticized* state she felt as though she was inadequate, disgustingly demanding, and also a perpetrator of wrongs in relation to a disgusted critic (she alternated between viewing others as critics and playing the role herself).

Defensive Organization of States. In a not always successful effort to escape from the danger of entry into the *severely distraught* state, the kind of state in which a narcissistically vulnerable hysteric might attempt suicide, Marilyn attempted to enter into avoidant states, one important one being the *excited-giddy* state. This state occurred when she was able to experience herself as a star attraction in relation to some admirer or potential rescuer. To enter this state, she drank, drove too fast, or engaged in impulsive and potentially dangerous sexual encounters. When this didn't work, she numbed herself to an even greater degree with alcohol, or loud music. Sometimes the *excited-giddy* state would spiral out of control, as in a hypomanic exaggeration of enthusiasm.

Manifestations of Marilyn's sadness ranged from the *sad-needy* state to the overwhelmingly sad variant of the *severely distraught* state. This continuum reflected a grieving state in which Marilyn contemplated and mourned her loss. Had she been functioning at a higher developmental level, her sadness would have been contained within tolerable limits. An early maternal loss, without sufficient replacement figures, is thought to be prominent in the histories of more disturbed hysterical personalities and may leave an individual extremely vulnerable to subsequent losses. This appeared to be true in the case of Marilyn. Her grief reached overwhelming proportions because she was experiencing not only the loss of her mother as an adult but also the reactivated pain and fear of having been abandoned as a young and emotionally conflicted child.

In addition, despite desperate attempts to ward off any expression of anger, Marilyn's *distraught rage* sometimes broke through outside of therapy. Although she was frightened by this lack of control, she was unable to stop herself from expressing fury toward others, regardless of how inappropriately timed or misdirected the outburst was.

Marilyn wanted to be in adaptively controlled states in which she would be an authentic caretaker of a needy or reciprocally caring other person, who would minister to her needs. For her, this was a *tender* state. The desire to be mutually caring and compassionate was complemented by another adaptive state in which she would feel competent and capable, the *composed-authentic* state. In approaching this goal, as noted in the later therapy sessions, she had a *fragile-communicative* state where the anxiety evoked by telling of her real concerns was unpleasant but tolerable. The goal of the treatment with a more disturbed hysterical personality is to help stabilize the patient in a state such as this, in which she can process the implications of stressful events, and arrive at new decisions and plans on life problems.

As already noted, there were overcontrolled states, described in the summary of states in table 5.1 Histrionic behavior is sometimes especially blatant in the more disturbed hysterical personality, and seems to be contrived as well as overcontrolled. Marilyn's *as-if authentic* states were marked by a superficial, playacting quality in which she talked about and acted out various emotions, with no indication that these feelings were being personally experienced. The *excited-giddy* state was her most extreme example of this kind of playacting. It was characterized by vigorous attention-seeking behavior (for example, giggling, making faces, and acting "cute" in an overanimated way). It seemed as if she were on an

TABLE 5.1
List of Marilyn's States

Label	Description
Undermodulated States	
Severely distraught	An overwhelmed state with extremely labile changes in emotional qualities of rage, sadness, and fear, occurring separately or as a mixture of jumbled emotions. Usually tense, anxious, confused, verging on or entering panic. Feels overwhelmed and vulnerable, acts on impulse. May include weeping or rages. Is impulsive and reckless, feels out of control.
Hurt-criticized	Vulnerable, frightened, self-disgusted. May have nonverbal component of looking as if okay but self-protective (for example, smoking, drinking, curling inward) with breakthroughs of anxious, hurt facial expressions.
Well-Modulated States	
Sad-needy	Grieving.
Fragile-communicative	Direct communication but frightened, worried, head down. May get confused in oscillation with *severely distraught* state.
Composed-authentic	Similar to the *fragile-communicative* state, but without fear or confusion.
Tender	Caring for another, with reciprocity.
Overmodulated States	
Excited-giddy	Histrionic, attention-getting behavior. May include apologetic denials of distress, masquerade quality, "cute" behavior, forced laugh or giggle, making faces. While usually a contrived presentation to others, this state could turn into a hypomanic type of undermodulated state.
As-if authentic	Seemingly composed but with intrusion of momentary elements of *severely distraught* or *excited-giddy* state.

emotional roller coaster, using broad gestures and dramatic behavior that a spectator could not avoid noticing. The defensive organization of Marilyn's various states is shown in table 5.2.

IMPLICATIONS OF DEFENSIVE LAYERING OF STATES OF MIND FOR THERAPY

In psychotherapy, adaptive states of mind are those during which the patient is able to modulate and regulate her actions and is able to contemplate problematic thoughts, feelings, and decisions. An appropriate relationship with another person can be maintained, with the other indi-

TABLE 5.2
Defensive Organization of Marilyn's States

State	Self	Aims	Concept of Other
Problematic Role Relationships			
Hurt-criticized	Inadequate; disgust-ingly demanding; wrongdoer	← Scorn ———————	Critic
Sad-needy	Waif ———————	Yearning ————→	Unavailable or inadequate caretaker
*Dreaded or Warded-Off Role Relationships**			
Severely distraught*	Dangerously defective or out of control		
	Waif ———————	Yearning ————→	Abandoner (sad)
	Victim ←———————	Hurting ———————	Destroyer (fear)
	Exposed as selfish ←	Humiliating ———————	Scornful (shame)
	Avenger ←———————	Hurting ————→	Betrayer (rage)
Desired Role Relationships			
Tender	Caretaker ←———————	Reciprocal providing → and receiving	Needy
Compromise Role Relationships			
Excited-giddy	Star (self-concept as sexy, attractive, powerful)	— Gain attention ———→	Admirer
		←— Adoration, rescue —→	

* These role relationships are so threatening that they cannot be consciously contemplated without loss of control. Marilyn tries to ward off awareness of these relationship models, but defensive failures lead to breakthroughs of overwhelming despair.

vidual experienced as potentially helpful. Marilyn's problem was that she had great difficulty in staying within this zone. When she was able to enter such a state, there seemed to be a delicate balance, one vulnerable to sudden disruption. That is why the state was labeled as *fragile-communicative* when it was observed on videotapes of her treatment.

Marilyn's extreme state lability posed a serious dilemma for the prospective therapist. When the therapist tried to help her move from an overcontrolled (for example, *as-if authentic* state) to a more adaptive *fragile-communicative* state, the result was sometimes a *severely distraught* state. When Marilyn was helped to modulate her expressions during a *severely distraught* state, the result was sometimes an *excited-giddy* state rather than the *fragile-communicative* state.

Of most importance, when Marilyn entered an undercontrolled *severely distraught* state, she might feel so overwhelmed with rage, shame, or grief that she would kill herself. That was her situation at the onset of therapy.

MODELS OF ROLE RELATIONSHIPS AND SELF-CONCEPTS

A major difference between the less disturbed and more disturbed hysterical personalities is the level at which relationships are organized. While both types of people struggle with issues of sexual competition as well as dyadic concerns involving separation-individuation, the emphasis in the more disturbed hysterical personality is on intense dependency, fear of loss, and rage at frustration. Other people are not always viewed as separate individuals with emotional lives of their own, but rather as extensions of the self that are used to stabilize an acceptable self-concept.

Marilyn depended on others, particularly men, to provide a sense of self-cohesion, self-stability, and self-esteem. She tended to view herself as a helpless, defective child who needed someone to rescue and take care of her. She would behave in a sexually provocative manner in order to elicit such care. As long as she was attached to an admiring man, she felt temporarily safe.

She was extremely vulnerable to rejection or abandonment by another, and when this occurred, she went into a downward spiral and wound up feeling so worthless and empty that she could not tolerate her anguish. At such times, she resorted to any behavior that could alter her mood, regardless of how dangerous it was. In order to counteract an image of herself as ugly, worthless, and abandoned, Marilyn shifted to a view of herself as a "star," the most attractive, sexiest, most talented woman around. To achieve this, she drank more or drove faster than anyone in her crowd, risking her life in order to secure attention and a sense of relatedness to others. As is typical, she appeared to be "too available" and attached herself to the first man she could find, without adequate appraisal of his real characteristics.

In addition to images of herself as unrealistically defective, victimized, or hostile and her compensatory self-concept as a "star," Marilyn had more realistic views of herself and others. In these role relationship models, she was bereaved in relation to a lost other or was a student in relation to a sympathetic mentor. She might feel mildly criticized, but the criticism was within an acceptable range. In general, each of Marilyn's self-concepts was part of a role relationship model in which she was being either cared for or abandoned by another. She wanted to relate to others in a mutually caring way, but did not feel sufficiently self-sustaining and stable to achieve this goal.

When her mother gave up her care, Marilyn must have felt bitterly disappointed. From a child's perspective, she probably explained the abandonment as due to her own defects and unworthiness, setting the stage for her self-image as being worthless. She relied on external self-

121

objects to counteract this image of herself and to restore a sense of wor-thiness. Her stepmother may have helped, but at times she reinforced Marilyn's sense of defectiveness by denigrating Marilyn's wish to look attractive.

From mid-adolescence until her mother's death, Marilyn enjoyed a renewed, positive relationship with her mother, in which Marilyn tried to please her and the mother responded in an approving manner. Thus, a more positive role relationship model was provided, but it could be main-tained only as long as her mother was physically available. With her death, the earlier role relationship model was reactivated and Marilyn reverted to feeling like an abandoned child.

People with hysterical personalities tend to use cardboard-type stereo-types in their concepts about others. The more disturbed hysterical per-sonalities, however, tend to compartmentalize their stereotypes into dis-sociated combinations of bad self with bad others, and good self with good others. They have difficulties with continuity, and tend not to ac-knowledge the good traits when in a state of badness, or the bad traits when in a state of goodness.

Even at a less extreme level, varied self-concepts, object concepts, and role relationship concepts are not organized into an overarching schemat-ization. Thus the person is not actually ambivalent, having pleasant or unpleasant beliefs about self and others at the same time, but is univa-lent, having either pleasant or unpleasant beliefs at any given time. This means that the displeasurable states cannot be softened by acknowledg-ment of the positive attributes of self or others at another time. These discontinuities between self and object conceptualizations mean that states change abruptly, leading to the well-known phenomenon of labil-ity of mood.

The varied self-concepts and object concepts, as related to Marilyn's most important current states of mind, are listed in table 5.3.

DEFENSIVE ORGANIZATION OF ROLE RELATIONSHIP MODELS

These themes of self-concepts and role relationship models can be for-mulated in the conflictual relationship schematization shown in table 5.4.

IMPLICATION OF ROLE RELATIONSHIP MODELS FOR THERAPY

Marilyn presented special therapeutic dilemmas because of the inten-sity of her neediness and the degree to which she mistrusted any care that could be provided. Because she felt so defective and incapable of caring for herself, she was likely to make unreasonable demands on the therapist and would be expected to form an excessively dependent rela-

TABLE 5.3
The Example of Marilyn: Relating Role Relationship Models to States

State	Self	Other
Undermodulated States		
Severely distraught	Dangerously defective or out of control	
(Sad)	Waif	Abandoner
(Fear)	Victim	Destroyer
(Shame)	Exposed as selfish	Scornful
(Rage)	Avenger	Betrayer
Hurt-criticized	Inadequate; disgustingly demanding; wrongdoer	Critic
Well-Modulated States		
Sad-needy	Empty, helpless, yearning waif	Unavailable or inadequate caretaker
Fragile-communicative	Vulnerable	Potentially supportive
Composed-authentic	Worthwhile, pleasing adolescent or young adult	Sympathetic, approving mother
Tender	Caretaker/needy	Needy/caretaker
Overmodulated States		
As-if authentic	Interesting peer (inadequate peer)	Interested peer (potential critic)
Excited-giddy	Star (self-concept as sexy, attractive, powerful)	Admirer, rescuer

tionship. If the therapist gratified her needs, the dependency would intensify, a situation that could create increased difficulty when the therapy was terminated. If the therapist set limits, however, she might be perceived as critical or rejecting—Marilyn's model of caretakers based on experiences with her biological mother and stepmother.

Given Marilyn's dependency on men to provide a sense of self-cohesion, she was likely to view a woman therapist as being insufficiently sustaining. She might also feel competitive with a woman and would anticipate abandonment. On the other hand, if she saw a male therapist, she might escalate sexy, provocative behavior in an attempt to secure care.

Of greatest concern was Marilyn's sense of hopelessness and despair vis-à-vis potential caretakers. If she were to experience the therapist as insufficiently empathic, supportive, or admiring, Marilyn might flee from therapy or become so disappointed and distraught that she would attempt suicide. This possibility might make the therapist understandably worried and could result in a reluctance to broach painful issues.

TABLE 5.4
A Conflictual Relationship Schematization for Marilyn

Aim:	I want love and care from a man or a mother.
But I have these impediments:	
Personal deficiencies	I am empty without my mother and therefore impulsively grab onto anyone in order to feel cared for.
Environmental deficiencies	My family is too unavailable or preoccupied; my lover has withdrawn; my sister feels unable to help me any further; my co-workers are competitive; I am experiencing financial strains.
If I get what I want, then:	
Internal positive responses	I will feel whole and capable of functioning. I will feel capable of tolerating the rage, fear, and grief activated by my mother's death.
External positive responses	By showing that I matter, he will replace my mother. Also, he will provide the controls I lack.
But if I get what I want, then:	
Internal negative responses	It still won't be enough and, if I get frustrated and angry, I may fail to sustain the relationship.
External negative responses	I will be used and then rejected, at the mercy of others.
So I will use these coping strategies:	
Interpersonal attitudes or behaviors	Act childlike and helpless so that others will feel they should take care of me; act flamboyant to get attention and as a way of denying the serious reality of my situation.
Intrapsychic attitudes	View myself as childlike so that I can deny my hostility, which might otherwise drive others away.
Intrapsychic styles	Deny rage over rejection; externalize blame onto others who refuse to accept my care or loving attention.
And the results will be:	
Recurrent states of mind	Intense despair with fear, shame, and rage when rejected or abandoned.
Patterns of state transition	Emotional lability ranging from giddy excitement when I feel admired and loved to empty depression and rage when others abandon me.
Likely life course (accomplishments in working, relating, experiencing):	
Short-range	Impulsive suicide or accidental death due to reckless behavior.
Long-range	Increasing loneliness, leading to chronic use of alcohol.

Marilyn's extreme neediness and demanding behavior, as well as the very disruptive changes in her state of mind, might increase the possibilities for both transference and countertransference reactions. The self-concepts and views of the therapist that the patient holds in a given state of mind will also provoke the therapist into certain states of mind, organized by his or her own separate, even if complementary, concepts of the patient and himself or herself. These potentials for Marilyn are indicated in table 5.5.

INFORMATION PROCESSING

In the more disturbed hysterical personality, severe stress leads to disorganized thinking and impulsive action rather than to life planning. These patterns were noted in Marilyn's bereavement response, as the death of her mother and the subsequent breakup with her lover evoked problematic themes.

THEMES PREDISPOSING TO PATHOLOGICAL GRIEF

Bereavement was experienced as too overwhelming for Marilyn to handle because she had an enduring attitude that if she did not have someone to relate to at all times, she would fall apart. She believed that she could not function unless she was in a relationship with someone who could serve as a self-object. With the losses, Marilyn felt frighteningly alone and helpless.

Ideas that she was now hopelessly alone and incapable of managing autonomously became very threatening. Thus, she inhibited representation of these ideas. Rather than dwelling on thoughts of herself as worthless and alone, she facilitated grandiose thoughts of herself as a star who would be admired by others. Grandiose fantasies and frenzied activity allowed her to feel the *excited-giddy* state instead of feeling deadened, suicidal, confused, or intolerably anxious. When failure of this defense occurred, she was plummeted into the *severely distraught* state of mind.

STYLE OF COPING AND DEFENDING

Marilyn was very much aware of her sadness over losses. She was cognizant of feeling defective each time she was abandoned, but the intensity of her rage over abandonment was restricted from awareness whenever possible.

During her more recent reparative relationship with her mother, Marilyn was able to keep in check and to hold dormant an early model of her mother as rejecting and abandoning. This dormant and then reactivated concept of her mother as abandoning her had variations as a role rela-

TABLE 5.5

Summary of Key Relationship Potentials for Marilyn's Therapy

Potentials for Relationship Patterns in Therapy	Patient's View:		Therapist's View:	
	Of Self	Of Other	Of Patient	Of Self
Potential negative transferences and countertransferences	Defective, deprived, needy, critical	Critical, abandoning caretaker	Demanding, unreliable, excessively out of control	Depleted or unappreciated victim of overwhelming demands (incompetent helper)
Potential positive transferences and countertransferences	Needy, admired star	Omnipotent rescuer, admiring audience	Adorable but incompetent child	Parent surrogate
Potential therapeutic alliance	Vulnerable but worthwhile	Supportive and sympathetic	Vulnerable but worthwhile	Supportive
Potential social alliance	Interesting peer	Interesting peer	Engaging, potentially capable	Friend

tionship model, depending on which of Marilyn's self-concepts was associated with the abandoning person. When Marilyn conceptualized herself as unworthy of care, she felt mortified. The betrayed version led to rage.

From a child's perspective, caretakers are omnipotent beings who are capable of providing adequate care if they so desire. Within such a mental set, the death of Marilyn's mother and the loss of her lover were experienced as deliberate, hence as betrayals. Thoughts about them as uncaring and even evil and selfish were activated and led to her rage.

In the other variation of the role relationship model, she conceptualized herself as worthless, and hence as rejected and abandoned. This enduring attitude of her own worthlessness and emptiness, except in relationship to a continuously approving and supporting other, led to another intolerable train of thought.

As depicted diagrammatically in figure 5.1, this enduring attitude was related to ideas immediately triggered by Marilyn's learning of her losses. She concluded that things would never improve, and that she was now and forever alone. Since Marilyn had the enduring belief that she had to have a reflecting other, or self-object, the aftermath of a loss was intense, fearful, empty sadness—that is, her *severely distraught* state of mind in its frightened variant. To ward off this distressing state of mind, various controls were instigated. These included inhibition of the thoughts about her loss, and of the enduring attitudes that made the loss so painful to bear. In order to avoid the warded-off state, her "worthless waif" self-concept had to be inhibited as well, and that could be done by facilitating a contrary self-concept—that of the star who could readily gain (or regain) admiration.

The shift from the waif to the star self-concept accomplished the change in state of mind from *severely distraught* to the *excited-giddy* state. This coping strategy was unstable, since it depended on the undependable: the continued admiration of others (in Marilyn's case the imperatively sought male figure) as she used her charm and attractiveness to obtain attention.

IMPLICATIONS OF THEMES AND INFORMATION-PROCESSING STYLE FOR THERAPY

Marilyn was feeling out of control when she agreed to enter treatment. Until then, she had been relying on her sister for support, and it was her sister who urged Marilyn to seek professional help. While Marilyn was able to acknowledge that she did have problems and wanted to feel better, it was difficult for her to conceptualize what would help. She was

Figure 5.1
Marilyn's Sadness Theme

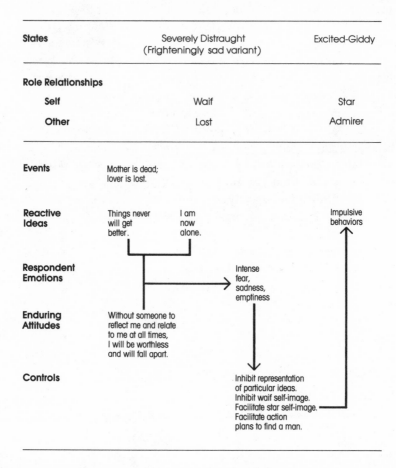

States	Severely Distraught (Frighteningly sad variant)	Excited-Giddy
Role Relationships		
Self	Waif	Star
Other	Lost	Admirer

not optimistic about psychotherapy. Rather, she was desperately hoping for some magical restoration of the lost relationships.

She acknowledged that she had left a previous psychotherapy as soon as her symptoms were relieved. In retrospect she realized that dropping out had been premature, but it seemed likely that she might repeat that pattern. It also seemed likely that she would treat a woman therapist as a surrogate mother and a male therapist as a surrogate lover. Themes of sadness, separation anxiety, rage at abandonment or slights, and shame over self-exposure would also be expected to complicate the establishment of a therapeutic alliance and clarification of a focus. Marilyn displayed inhibition of thought and devaluated thoughtfulness, decision-making, and preplanning as ways of adapting to life challenges. Therefore, she would be inclined to disparage or be unable to readily use the suggestions, focusing, confrontations, clarifications, and interpretations that were likely to be involved in psychotherapy.

The Process of Therapy

ESTABLISHING A THERAPEUTIC ALLIANCE AND A FOCUS

Marilyn's emotional lability became an immediate therapeutic issue. In the first hour, she explicitly asked the therapist, a woman older than she was, for help in controlling her mood swings:

Marilyn: I was thinking if we could work something out where you could see me more than once a week, because lately my moods have just changed so drastically. I would like you to be able to see everything that I'm experiencing so that maybe you could help me cope with these different moods.

The dilemma for the therapist involved finding a way to help the patient to confront painful ideas and feelings without entering the *severely distraught* states of either engulfing rage or despair. This task is especially complex because such patients cannot imagine that a person who simply listens, understands, and interprets could really help; they wish the other to take over active decision making. In addition, Marilyn yearned for a figure who would admire her and who would magically stabilize her as a grandiose star with her self-concept in the *excited-giddy* state. She wanted someone to function as a self-object, a replacement for her mother and lover. Marilyn tested the therapist to see if she would go beyond the ground rules of therapy to satisfy her neediness, or criticize her for being too demanding. When Marilyn felt admired, she entered overcontrolled states; if criticized, she might feel demeaned or worthless, and might enter undercontrolled, *severely distraught* states.

The therapist used a variety of techniques to reduce the frequency and intensity of Marilyn's dangerously impulsive behavior, as occurred in *severely distraught* or *excited-giddy* states. She advised Marilyn to refrain from alcohol, set limits, and complied with Marilyn's request for medication to reduce states of excessive anxiety. An anti-anxiety medication was prescribed to be taken on a "pill at a time" basis only when she felt about to be overwhelmed by panic in the *severely distraught* states. Providing the prescription demonstrated concern on the therapist's part and meant that the proscription against alcohol and other drugs was not simply criticism and deprivation. The therapist wanted Marilyn to see that she could benefit from controls rather than only be deprived because of them, as she had felt with her critical stepmother.

Interventions that included reassuring Marilyn that her reactions were expectable, rather than aberrant or distasteful, reduced the threat of entry into *severely distraught* states. The therapist also helped Marilyn to organize her thoughts, by questioning her, clarifying what she had said, focusing on specific topics, and reconstructing sequences of behavior. This assistance enabled Marilyn to regain a sense of coherence, and reduced her sense of depersonalization.

It is important to remember that concepts of the self can become so easily devalued in these patients that entry into states of extreme self-disgust and loathing present a danger. To counter this, Marilyn's therapist focused considerable attention on bolstering and stabilizing Marilyn's positive self-images before presenting her with potentially threatening information in the form of interpretations, clarifications, or confrontations.

Nonverbal communication may be as important as the content of specific comments. Patients with greater narcissistic vulnerability are sometimes closely tuned in to nonverbal aspects of the therapeutic relationship, even though they may misinterpret them. Such patients are likely to interpret any sign of fatigue, boredom, or irritability in the therapist as a personal rejection or as an indication of their poor prognosis. Maintaining an optimistic and empathic demeanor is reassuring. The therapist's attitude of optimism countered Marilyn's sense of hopelessness and convinced her that her situation was not as desperate as she had feared.

When in her demanding and *severely distraught* state, Marilyn would probably evoke frustration, helplessness, or anger in other people. Friends or acquaintances might feel overwhelmed by her neediness or irritated by her provocations. A likely behavioral response on their part would be to react with hostility or withdraw. In contrast, Marilyn's therapist displayed calmness and consistency, serving as a model of relaxed control whom Marilyn could emulate. The therapist's poise, comfortable posture, slow speech, and well-modulated voice tone all helped to provide a reassuring atmosphere. The soothing sounds and rhythms of the treatment were experienced as a kind of nurturant "holding" or cradling, which reduced Marilyn's oscillating feelings of frenetic excitement and despair.

It may also make sense to change the ground rules of the therapy to adapt somewhat to the special needs of the more disturbed person with a hysterical style. In a brief therapy, the therapist can establish an initial contract for a specified period of time instead of holding to a specific number of allotted sessions. In this way, additional sessions can be scheduled should the patient enter out-of-control states between therapy interviews, without the treatment agreement being broken. Knowing that the therapist can be reached between sessions may be sufficiently reassuring to counter entry into states in which the patient feels frighteningly alone and helpless to deal with overwhelming feelings.

At the beginning of therapy Marilyn attempted a defensive posture, a social rather than therapeutic alliance. As shown earlier, in table 5.5 depicting the potential therapy relationship, Marilyn defensively tried to establish an "interesting peer" status, not a patient role. She tried to present herself as a humorist, parodying rather than experiencing hurt, needy feelings. She also displayed an *as-if angry* state in which she presented herself as nobly tolerant of, rather than enraged at, the defects of others. The therapist was expected to overtly admire her for this attitude and to covertly side with her. Sometimes Marilyn also presented herself as a star—the sexiest woman, best musician, most robust drinker, or most outstanding worker. In this model, the therapist was viewed as an admiring audience, impressed by superlative ability.

Had the therapist allowed Marilyn to develop and maintain the social alliance, manifest in her displays of the *excited-giddy* state or *as-if authentic* state, Marilyn might have felt temporarily gratified. Therapist and patient would have enjoyed a pleasant, friendly interaction, but therapeutic progress would have been stymied. Marilyn might have concluded, covertly, that her real thoughts and feelings were too overwhelming for the therapist to handle or else that she had fooled the therapist into believing that her problems were not serious. The therapy would be experienced as another transient, superficial relationship, leaving her vulnerable and distraught at its end.

Movement from a social alliance to a therapeutic relationship pattern was difficult because of the high potentials for intense transference reactions. As already described, Marilyn's repertoire of concepts for self and others contained two models for relationships that had the potential to evoke negative transference reactions. One of these models was based on a perception of herself as a defectively bad person being criticized by a scrutinizing therapist. This model was developed during Marilyn's earlier relationship with her disapproving stepmother, and could be activated by any acts of the therapist that Marilyn might perceive as judgmental. On the basis of her experience with her stepmother, who had scorned outward displays of emotion or sexuality, Marilyn expected the therapist to react negatively to information about her out-of-control feelings, her sexual behavior, and her substance abuse.

Rather than risk criticism that could lead to her feeling totally worthless, Marilyn preferred to withhold "incriminating" information about her current lifestyle. However, this defense still risked criticism. If she withheld information, only to reveal it later, the therapist might then view her as either dishonest or deliberately retentive. Marilyn might then feel forced to maintain the illusion that her life was stable, even after learning to trust the therapist, and could become increasingly worried that she might slip and reveal the truth. Rather than risk the criticism that could ensue for being a "bad" patient, she might prematurely leave therapy. This theme generally occurs with any patient who exhibits extensive narcissistic vulnerability.

In instances where the above potential is present, the patient is likely to appraise a particular facial expression, a glance at the clock, or any harshness in the therapist's voice as criticism. In Marilyn's case, this could have led to a rapid devaluation of self-esteem. Considerable testing of whether the therapist would indeed be critical was present throughout the therapy. An example of this can be seen in the following excerpt from the sixth session.

Marilyn: Well, my sister said, "Look, you know, people can't handle hysteria. They just don't accept it, and maybe you should just try calming yourself down." Then I just started getting really angry, because I thought she was trying to tell me, "You've got to hide your feelings. Don't be upset now." And then I just got really mad at her. (*Marilyn is testing, through the example of her sister, whether the therapist will be critical of her labile emotional expressions, or "hysteria."*)

Therapist: So when somebody puts some kind of limit on you, it feels like a rejection, from what you're saying.

Marilyn: Yes, and all of a sudden my stomach tightened up and I had to go in the bathroom and I thought I was going to throw up and I just got upset very quickly. It's not when somebody puts a limit on me—that makes me sound like a spoiled brat. It was just, just too much sounding like, well, you can't let your problems show. (*Marilyn probably interpreted the therapist's comment as suggesting that she thought*

Marilyn was a spoiled brat. Marilyn may have interpreted this as meaning that the therapist was threatened by her expression of intense feelings.)

Therapist: So your feelings just welled up inside you then.

Marilyn: Yeah, but things have gotten better this week for some reason. I don't know why, though. (*Here she withdraws from the therapist, presenting only her positive, more controlled facade.*)

Therapist: Yes, well, when I said that to you, about the limits, you almost reacted as if I had said you were a spoiled brat. I'm wondering if that was the feeling you got.

Marilyn: I'm sounding rather, ha ha, off the cuff, ha ha, or whatever. That's the way I feel. (*Marilyn laughed nervously because a covert view she had of a relationship had been made explicit by the interpretation.*)

The second role relationship model that had a potential for negative transference was Marilyn's conceptualization of herself as needy and dependent on another person who had the role of a defective or ambiguous caretaker. We infer that Marilyn developed this model during early transactions with her biological mother, whom she felt had inadequately cared for and then abandoned her. Marilyn's subsequent experience with caretakers recapitulated her earlier views. Her stepmother did not abandon her, but Marilyn recalled her as imposing infantilizing restrictions which implied that the stepmother could not tolerate Marilyn's independence. Marilyn repeatedly chose men who used and then discarded her, who were themselves too immature to provide sustained care and nurturance; thus, this model was frequently reinforced. The demands made on her sister after her mother's death were experienced as so formidable that the sister, too, urged Marilyn to turn elsewhere. In the following excerpt from the seventh session, Marilyn's sensitivity to possible rejection and abandonment on the part of the therapist is evident, as well as the therapist's expectation of negative transference reactions.

Therapist: I think that as time goes along, one of the things that we ought to talk about is kind of both planning for that ending [of the brief therapy in five more sessions] because I know endings are something that you have a whole lot of feeling about, and even talking about it, I think, would be of some use to you. Also, there is the question of what you'd like to do beyond that, whether you'd like to see somebody else, settle down and do a more long-term consideration of your life. I don't throw that out for an answer now.

Marilyn: Uh-huh.

Therapist: But for something for you to keep in the back of your mind and think about.

Marilyn: Okay. (*faint*) Can I go?

Therapist: No, I'm not kicking you out (*laughter*).

Marilyn: Oh, I thought I was being booted out. (*The hour was not over, yet Marilyn surprised the therapist by taking the latter's remarks as if they ended it and the therapy at once. Marilyn interpreted the therapist's offer of further help as a sign that the latter could not care for her and wanted to fob her off on someone else, as her biological mother had done.*)

Therapist: Sounds like that's the feeling. I know that for you, stopping feels like rejection, and I think that's one of the things we can talk about some together.

Marilyn: Yeah. That's true. That's why I was really surprised I was going to tell this guy to take a hike. (*Marilyn, feeling threatened by the therapist's focus on the immediate relationship between them, shifted to discussion of an outside-of-therapy interaction. She reversed roles by presenting herself as the rejecting person who was needed by someone else. With such patients it is sometimes useful first to clarify a relationship pattern, including its roles and story line, with regard to an outside relationship. Then the therapist can tactfully and gradually offer further clarification of the views that appear to be present in the in-therapy relationship.*)

There were also numerous occasions when the therapist might actually have felt critical of or annoyed with Marilyn. For example, Marilyn was frequently late. After missing one appointment in order to have her hair done, she indicated to the therapist that she valued external over internal change. She "invited" criticism by coming to sessions hung over, sleepy, or drugged, and expected the therapist to take care of her.

POSITIVE TRANSFERENCE ISSUES

A common role relationship model in patients with a hysterical personality is that of a needy self in relation to an omnipotent rescuer. Because of this view, the patient transfers power to another who is perceived as capable of fixing everything. Personal responsibility is disclaimed. In the positive transference, Marilyn saw herself as a needy, helpless waif in a dependent relationship with an omniscient, omnipotent parental surrogate who would assume responsibility for her life and magically make everything better.

The countertransference danger lies in the possibility of the therapist accepting this role, and enjoying the power and adulation of being viewed as godlike. Through any show of gratification, this unrealistic relationship could be encouraged. It would prove destructive to the patient, however, since it fosters a sense of helplessness and dependency instead of facilitating autonomy and self-reliance. This is especially true in the context of a brief therapy.

THERAPEUTIC ALLIANCE ISSUES

Establishing a therapeutic alliance with a more disturbed hysterical personality requires patience and persistence. Where time is limited, there is a need to rapidly formulate the potential pitfalls and dangers inherent in interpersonal relationships. Patients like Marilyn may seem warm and engaging at the outset, and may engage in a social charade of rapport. It must be remembered that they usually have experienced tumultuous relationships in which they have been rejected, abandoned, or emotionally deprived. These experiences have left them deeply distrustful and wary, regardless of their intense need and desire to latch onto someone.

Unlike the developmentally more advanced patient, the person with a more disturbed hysterical personality style will not expect the therapist to be a helpful expert capable of guiding them through stormy emotional waters. Such patients hope that the therapist will be an admiring audience who will make them feel whole, but their fear and expectation are that the therapist will turn out to be a sham. They expect that behind the therapist's kindly facade is a potentially critical, evil, rejecting person whom they will secretly disgust and who will be eager to get rid of them.

As noted earlier, Marilyn was habitually late for therapy sessions— usually by fifteen or twenty minutes. This behavior not only indicated reduced self-control but was evidence of Marilyn's devaluation of the therapist. Marilyn let her know early on that she regarded help from a woman as inadequate. As she put it, "I need a man." She conveyed the message that she put little stock in the value of talking during therapy. Yet, despite extreme provocations, the therapist remained firm, understanding, and consistently supportive. Marilyn's provocations, which theoretically might cause the therapist to become angry or rejecting, were regarded as an ongoing test to see whether the relationship potentials for negative transference reactions were appropriate or not in this context. As her therapist "passed these tests" by remaining supportive and empathic, Marilyn felt safer and expressed the more threatening ideas and feelings that she had experienced as too overwhelming to face alone. (See Weiss et al. 1981 for a discussion of transference tests.)

Some techniques for supporting a therapeutic alliance are illustrated in the following excerpts from early therapy sessions.

> Therapist: Yes, and I think the other thing that you're going to hit is that you are going to have waves of sadness. You probably do have some crying to do. It's been our impression that people who kind of let the feelings come can handle them and work them through. (*Here the therapist helps Marilyn to anticipate painful feelings, gives her permission to experience those feelings, and provides a sense of hope that things can and will work out.*)
>
> Marilyn: If I want to cry, I cry, you know. I don't hold back that way, but I just. . . .
>
> Therapist: You had apologized to me at the beginning of the hour when you started to cry. (*Again, the therapist repeats that Marilyn's feelings are acceptable and no cause for shame or discomfort.*)
>
> Marilyn: Oh, did I? I'm always apologizing for myself. That's another one of my problems.
>
> Therapist: I was thinking about your stepmother, who always said "no tears," and it's almost like you expected that from me. (*Here the therapist identifies a negative transference potential and lets Marilyn know explicitly that she is different from her critical stepmother, who scorns her for outward displays of emotion.*)
>
> Marilyn: Oh, I'm doing it again, I guess. I always . . . my sister is always pointing out to me that I'm always apologizing for myself.

Interventions were delivered in a warm, supportive manner, in a vocal tone characterized by a soft, holding quality, and with facial expressions that indicated positive regard and concern. While the therapist established herself as a noncritical, nonjudgmental figure, she also set limits and was concerned about Marilyn's safety. This kind of patient feels too isolated and out of control if the therapist simply clarifies and interprets.

There is a need for limits because of the patient's lack of control and inability to process insight-producing information. However, it is most helpful if the therapist can oscillate between the interpretive approach and the use of professional advice. Interpretations of how the patient perceived the therapist's suggestions, and intentions, can then be made to correct inappropriate transference attributions.

The educative stance, when necessary, may be aided by direct questioning and by giving simple, matter-of-fact (rather than heavy-handed) advice, as in the following passage. Note that the therapist advised Marilyn to desist from mood-altering, state-destabilizing drugs, in a way that differentiated her from Marilyn's authoritarian, prohibitive stepmother. Rather than criticize Marilyn for being self-destructive, the therapist invited her to observe for herself her potentially dangerous behavior.

Therapist: Do you ever get suicidal thoughts?

Marilyn: Oh, yes. In fact, my sister made the initial appointment here, because she was worried about me. It's not that I really want to kill myself; it's just that I wish that I could just die.

Therapist: Uh-huh.

Marilyn: I don't think I ever would, but I came close once. I took some heavy-duty pills and a lot of times I just think, "Oh, all right. This is it. I'm gonna do it. I'm tired of fighting." But then I chicken out.

Therapist: How about drinking? Is that much of a problem for you?

Marilyn: No, not really. I like to drink, but I don't do it all the time. I did last night and I'm still not quite together yet.

Therapist: That's something to watch out for, because alcohol is a real downer, and if you're feeling down to start with, and you drink much, it's apt to really slide you further down. It also dissolves your judgment some. (*Note that the therapist refrains from criticizing the patient for coming to therapy "not quite together." Rather, she emphasized the dangers to Marilyn's well-being, conveying a sense of interest and concern.*)

Early in treatment the therapist also identified Marilyn's pattern of grabbing onto the first available man. She advised Marilyn to try to delay reattachment during this vulnerable period, as this problematic behavior generally led to subsequent rejection and emotional distress. The therapist addressed Marilyn's negative self-images, but she linked these with positive traits and abilities so that Marilyn would not feel so deflated.

It can be dangerous to overemphasize positive self-concepts, since this may suggest that the therapist either is fooled by the patient or cannot tolerate hearing negative information. As a result, the patient may withhold revelations about her "worst" feelings and behaviors in order to protect the therapist and her own self-esteem. In spite of this risk, the therapist needs to support positive self-concepts. This kind of patient finds it hard to sustain a good self-concept when she is feeling critical of herself or is denigrated by others for some behavior or attribute. Boosting the patient's self-esteem in realistic ways makes it more tolerable to proceed to those topics that deflate her self-image. Another aspect of this oscillating technique is to couple "good" and "bad" information so as to *dose* the latter. The goal is to help the patient to accept all attributes of herself, negative as well as positive.

During the session, it was repeatedly emphasized that the therapist was different from the stepmother and would not be cold, critical, and depriving. The therapist backed up her words with actions. She expressed concern about Marilyn's suicidal ideation and impulsivity, and asked Marilyn to call if she needed to between sessions. Emergency sessions were scheduled when necessary, and the therapist provided a low-level anti-anxiety medication, to be taken one dose at a time, as an alternative to the use of alcohol. Despite Marilyn's provocative acting out, the therapist stayed with her, offering warmth, comfort, and support. The therapist was firm, insisting that Marilyn assume some responsibility for her own behavior, but her manner was gentle, hopeful, and comforting. She gave Marilyn permission to let her know how badly she felt, but conveyed the message that, despite Marilyn's distrust and disregard, she would stay with her for an allotted period of time, bolster her self-esteem in a realistic way, and help her figure out ways to put her life back in order.

PROBLEMS IN ESTABLISHING A FOCUS

Marilyn began the first therapy session with a denial and then an acknowledgment that she was "falling apart" because of the death of her mother. When the therapist tried to focus on her reactions to the death, Marilyn denied that she was troubled by the event. She changed the subject to the related, but less disturbing, issue of the lover's rejection:

Marilyn: Death is—I think I can cope with that a little more because it's something that's inevitable. It's something that's final. Whereas I really can't understand why people keep not caring about me—that just keeps really blowing me away.

Marilyn offered a possible area for further exploration:

> Marilyn: I just keep getting rejected, and I think I'm setting myself up for it and I want to find out why. I've just about had it with being rejected. And another thing is that I have a bad habit of basing my opinion of myself on what other people think of me. You know, like if other people think badly of me, then I'm lousy.

Yet when the therapist began to pursue this line of reasoning, Marilyn shifted to complaints about how others were defective since they could not accept her caring for them.

These rapid reversals alerted the therapist to the fragility of Marilyn's coping ability. Marilyn's avoidant behavior, plus the intensity of her denial regarding the impact of her mother's death, suggested to the therapist that Marilyn was not yet ready to focus on this issue. Had the therapist insisted on doing so, Marilyn might have felt too flooded with emotion and might have dropped out of treatment. Instead, the therapist suggested that they focus on the more recent loss of the lover. This loss involved many similar themes (for example, issues of rejection and abandonment), so it could eventually be linked to feelings about the mother's death. The therapist planned to realign the focus during a later session when a therapeutic alliance might be more firmly established.

TACTICS IN THERAPY

It is important to remember that although patients such as Marilyn display an exaggerated emotionality, they actually have an extremely low tolerance for some feelings. They are likely to experience interpretations as criticism even though that is not the therapist's intent. When the patient feels criticized there is danger of entry into states of despair or rage, which are habitual responses to abandonment or injury. Thus, the therapist needs to progress tactfully and pay special attention to the timing, dosage, and phrasing of interventions. Empathic comments, indicating support and concern, help the patient to tolerate ideas that lead to uncomfortable feelings. The therapist may also need to provide more structure than is necessary with others, because of the more disturbed patient's tendency to become conceptually disorganized.

The therapist's major focus was on the meanings and implications to Marilyn of the loss of her mother and lover. The objective was to help Marilyn shift to more positive self-concepts in which she could view herself as capable of tolerating the emotions of mourning. This view of herself, in turn, would lead to state stabilization and a sense of greater mastery over herself and her situation. To achieve these goals, the therapist offered reassurance and a sense of hope. She reminded Marilyn of her positive traits and abilities, while exploring negative self-images. She identified Marilyn's pattern of impulsively grabbing onto any man, and encouraged delay so that Marilyn could avoid relationships that would inevitably lead to feelings of despair. The therapist structured the sessions by talking more than was usual. She showed Marilyn how to solve problems through contemplation and step-by-step planning.

CHRONOLOGY OF THE THERAPY

The following account of the therapy illustrates how the therapist suggested that Marilyn give more prior thought to actions she was considering. The therapist also helped counter Marilyn's vagueness by conceptually labeling the latter's feelings.

The Sessions. At first, Marilyn focused on the recent rejection by her lover and complained of a general pattern of rejection by others. She externalized blame for this pattern, angrily criticizing people for "not caring." The therapist acknowledged how hurt Marilyn must have felt when her boyfriend failed to provide support after her mother's death, but clarified that it was Marilyn who had actually made the final break from him. Marilyn then described how worthless these rejections made her feel. In the following excerpt, the therapist indicated that she, unlike Marilyn's harsh stepmother, could tolerate expressions of her grief.

Marilyn: I just can't handle it (*referring to her rejection by a lover*).
Therapist: To be hurting the way you were, after the loss of your mother, and to have somebody turn away from you then, must have been very difficult for you. . . .
Marilyn: (*Slight laugh*)
Therapist: It's a familiar feeling. (*Underlines recurrent life pattern.*)
Marilyn: It's just. . . . I don't understand.
Therapist: Yes. (*Indication that therapist understands Marilyn's pain and confusion, and that the therapist is there to support her.*)
Marilyn: I don't understand why people are that way. Oh dear, I'm going to cry.
Therapist: Yes. That's okay. You probably have some crying to do. (*Suggests that feelings are expectable and can be experienced safely.*)

It was striking in the first session that Marilyn was anticipating that the care she would receive might be inadequate. The therapist was firm in offering her more availability, but not so much that she promised to take over total responsibility for Marilyn. These actions somewhat countered Marilyn's feeling of being frighteningly alone and abandoned.

Marilyn came to the second session after a week of heavy drinking. She had used alcohol to block entry into a *severely distraught* state. During the week she had been so overwhelmed with grief that she had been sent home from work. The therapist noted the *severely distraught* state in therapy and reacted to Marilyn's sense of pervading disorganization by structuring the session. The therapist also emphasized her availability and provided Marilyn with phone numbers where she could be reached between sessions. Marilyn asked for advice, but indicated that she had ignored the therapist's previous suggestion to give her sleeping pills to a friend for safekeeping. The therapist helped Marilyn to think more clearly about her immediate situation by organizing memory fragments into sequences and labeling major concerns. She emphasized Marilyn's wish to latch onto a new man as a replacement for her losses, and suggested that Marilyn try to delay such reattachment until she could work through the meanings of the current losses.

Marilyn had a phone call from her old lover before the third session. The shift to a more positive self-image and the increased state stability that this brought enabled her to contemplate the painful loss of her mother. Marilyn discussed her childhood conflict of having two mothers, and the pain of losing the one with whom she could have fun. The therapist helped Marilyn explore the tug she felt to reattach to her lover, despite serious reservations about his capacity for a relationship. This was an effort to help her avoid another rejection. The therapist also explored Marilyn's feelings of loss and ambivalence regarding her mother.

Marilyn was depressed and disorganized when she came in for the fourth session, after being rejected by a new man the night before. This experience was used to explore her negative self-images as well as the link between being rejected and plummeting into states of despair. The therapist labeled grabbing onto people as "neediness" and expressed understanding of the intensity of these needs. She interpreted Marilyn's tendency to turn every encounter with a man into a major test of self-worth, explaining that Marilyn did this repeatedly because she was so unsure of herself. The therapist also pointed out that the pattern of impulsive attachments intensified Marilyn's self-doubts and self-disgust because it led to equally impulsive separations.

The Middle Sessions. Despite the therapist's efforts at tact, it was likely that Marilyn experienced her suggestions as critical of her neediness and her rapid, sexualized attachments. The therapist's suggestions of thought-filled delays probably seemed, to Marilyn, impossible to follow. In the period before the next appointment, she experienced a second rejection by a man and called her sister in a *severely distraught* state, indicating that she was having intense suicidal thoughts. When phoned by the sister, the therapist was unable to reach Marilyn and was sufficiently alarmed to notify the police. They found Marilyn crying in her apartment. She spoke with the therapist at length on the phone, but declined an immediate appointment or hospitalization.

Marilyn came to the next session twenty minutes late, looking pale and tearful. The therapist noticed that Marilyn seemed blocked in her thinking and commented that it looked as if she felt bad; the therapist used a technique of labeling affect to clarify the patient's vagueness. Marilyn explained that her mood had shifted following a call from her lover the night before. He had told her that he cared for her, but would not be calling again because he could see that their relationship would not work out.

The therapist helped Marilyn to explore the pressure she felt to reattach to her lover in the face of many reasons why she should wait. She interpreted Marilyn's fear of relinquishing a relationship in which she had experienced some caring. The therapist saw a link between the experience with the lover's call and Marilyn's difficulty in grieving over a mother who had been alternately accepting and rejecting. The therapist did not directly interpret Marilyn's conflict over ambivalent relationships, but did help Marilyn to organize her thoughts so that she could assess the relationship more realistically.

The therapist linked Marilyn's sense of desperate longing for attachment to her feelings about her mother, whom she was more able to think about by this time. She interpreted Marilyn's wish to have her mother's approval as she developed new relationships with men, and indicated how empty Marilyn felt without the repeated approval of another. The therapist encouraged Marilyn's active contemplation of her own good traits so that she could rely more on herself to regulate self-esteem.

Marilyn canceled her next appointment because of illness. Then she called the therapist at home on the weekend, demanding a prescription for codeine for an earache. The therapist firmly indicated that she could not prescribe without seeing her, and suggested a local emergency service. Marilyn was able to accept the limit without hostility.

She appeared on time for her subsequent session. She was in a more *composed* state. She said she no longer felt such a desperate need for attachment; she felt capable of rejecting men who treated her badly. She observed that she no longer automatically assumed that she was defective if a relationship failed to work out. The therapist praised her new abilities and reinforced the need for circumspection. This encouragement allowed Marilyn to feel safe enough to discuss her mother, entering the *sad-needy* state as she did so.

The therapist urged Marilyn to review her past relationship with her mother as a way to work through conflicts. She conveyed the message that Marilyn could do this gradually, without losing control. In the following excerpt, the therapist pointed out how Marilyn could incorporate the approving, nurturing characteristics of her mother. In this way she could become her own caretaking person rather than having to so desperately seek nurturance and validation from others. These interventions were aimed at stabilizing her self-esteem.

Therapist: You had talked about the sense of doing some things and knowing that she would have been proud of them; your work or. . . . (*Encourages internalization of positive self-image.*)

Marilyn: Uh-huh. Well I can't call her [the mother] anymore (*slight laugh*). In the last letter I got from her, she wrote saying, "show them what you can do at the agency." I wish I could call her and tell her what I am doing.

Therapist: Yes. There's some feeling that you're doing for yourself what she would have done for you, giving yourself strokes sometimes. (*Tells her to comfort herself actively instead of invariably being self-critical.*)

Marilyn: Yes. The only thing now is that I just know there's gonna be more bad times, but I'm not really afraid of them. If they come they'll come, but I'll just try to get through them as best I can. Like Monday is not going to be too easy, because it's my birthday and the highlight of my birthday was always hearing from my mother.

Therapist: So you have a sense that there are going to be ups and downs and there are going to be periods when reminders or waves of feelings are going to come in on you, but you are already not as overwhelmed by sadness. (*Helps her to anticipate, with a suggestive reassurance that things will get better.*)

Marilyn: Yeah.

Therapist: So you know that you'll be able to get through it. (*Repeats the suggested attitude of being able to tolerate negative emotions.*)

Midway through this therapy period, the therapist introduced the subject of termination, explaining that Marilyn could anticipate and plan for the ending. Termination was linked to the sadness theme (as shown earlier in figure 5.1, p. 128), with the therapist noting that "endings are something that you have a whole lot of feeling about." She encouraged Marilyn to think about this issue and to contemplate what she would like to do (for example, get a referral for time-unlimited treatment). The therapist explored Marilyn's interpretation of termination as a rejection, and suggested that she could plan for the anticipated ending.

Marilyn failed to come to her next appointment, probably because the therapist had introduced the threatening subject of termination, and she was "leaving first." A subsequent phone call indicated that she had had two minor car accidents.

The Later Sessions.　In Session 9, Marilyn's attitudes toward the impending loss of the therapist were clarified and related to the sadness theme as it pertained to the loss of her mother and lover. The therapist again repeatedly stated that Marilyn could think thoughts about sad topics without necessarily plummeting into despair, as in the following excerpt:

Therapist: So you've been reflecting some on yourself, on what's going on, then? You were afraid that if you did that you would be overwhelmed.

Marilyn: But I haven't, (*laughs*) at least not the last couple of days. My birthday was kind of bad for me. Tom wasn't there and my mom wasn't there. I keep having a lot of feelings about my mom, and then I kind of take a deep breath and wait till it passes. What else can I do?

Therapist: What kind of feelings?

Marilyn: Just very depressed, like I want to talk to her. I really miss her.

Therapist: So there is a real awareness of her loss, then.

Marilyn: Yeah, I just have to wait it out until it passes.

Therapist: Do you ever find that you have kind of mixed feelings about her, remembering some of the times that weren't so good? (*This is a repeated exercise in contemplating both positive and negative thoughts in order to establish continuity be-*

tween dissociated views of her mother and the relationship with her.)

Marilyn: No, not at all. I just miss her, and I just miss being able to talk to her. (*Marilyn declines the exercise.*)

Therapist: But you've been able to experience that sense of loss without being totally overwhelmed by the grief? (*The therapist is being clearly noncritical as Marilyn declines the exercise, in this instance by bolstering a more competent self-concept.*)

Marilyn: Yeah. When I started getting really depressed, it's only about once a week now that I get feelings of total depression, and I say, "Well, that's the way it happens. I just need more time." It's been the time, I think, that's helped me.

Therapist: So you've been able to feel the pain and still stick with it? (*The therapist is continuing the above tactics.*)

Marilyn: Yeah.

Marilyn went on to describe a recent experience in which another woman was "bad" in the way that she sometimes saw her mother or herself as "bad." After telling the story of this other woman, she "owned" the pattern.

Marilyn: Well, I told you about the guy who is my new friend. He just became manager of the office, and suddenly every girl in the building is trying to seduce him. So we're getting a big kick out of it, but there was a woman in his office last night. She is only thirty-one, and I called him for something and he said, "You've got to help me get rid of her!" So I went up and I was being really catty and I was trying to get her to leave, because he didn't want her there. She's wearing a low-cut dress, showing off her breasts and she was very drunk, but she is a very flighty type person. And I just sat there and watched her. *I just started to think that was going to be me if I didn't slow down pretty soon, and I don't want to end up like that, so I did a lot of thinking about that.*

Therapist: So you really have a choice of where you end up.

Marilyn: Yes.

Therapist: In terms of who it is you're going to be. (*The therapist repeatedly reminds Marilyn of the possibility of choice by thinking rather than by impulsively acting.*)

Marilyn: Yeah. I'm not going to end up like her, (*laughs*) a basket case, throwing herself at him. It was so funny (*laughs*) any-

> way. (*Marilyn defensively enters a mild variant of the* excited-giddy *state.*)

Therapist: Funny but sad. (*The therapist counteracts the shift to the excited-giddy* state, *and Marilyn resumes a* fragile-communicative *state.*)

Marilyn: She was very lonely, and she kept repeating herself every five minutes. She is the kind that has lived a very fast life and it hasn't gotten her very far. In fact I'd say that it has gotten her nowhere at all.

By this time Marilyn's sister had withdrawn from her in order to spend more time with her own boyfriend. Facing the loss of her therapist as well, Marilyn felt a pull to return to her earlier lover, although the imperative aspect of her need to reattach to a man had diminished. It remained difficult for her to deal directly with her ambivalence about people who had been supportive but were inadequately available to her now (mother, sister, therapist).

The therapist aimed to stabilize a positive self-concept in Marilyn by praising her increased tolerance for emotion. When the therapist remarked, "I liked your ability to let yourself experience the sadness," Marilyn was able to praise herself for her sensitivity to feelings and her improved ability to think the emotion-activating ideas that she had previously inhibited. The therapist once again reinforced the idea that Marilyn was a worthwhile person who deserved a caring relationship. She praised Marilyn's increased ability to assess the other person before throwing herself into a new relationship, and advised delaying reattachment until her "old wounds" healed.

Keeping her pattern of prematurely leaving therapy in mind, the therapist helped Marilyn to anticipate negative feelings about termination. She recommended dealing with the feelings in therapy rather than defensively avoiding them by dropping out.

Impending termination led to a continued emphasis on loss of relationships. The therapist helped Marilyn to explore the "tug" she felt to return to her lover as "a wish to be close to someone." She again clarified Marilyn's pattern of impulsively "plugging in a new person" to handle the loss of another. Marilyn's yearning for her lover was linked again and again to her loneliness because of the mother's death and her subsequent fear of losing the therapist.

The therapist suggested that Marilyn's relationships could be different if she could keep thinking in ways that improved her respect for herself. Perhaps now that a more positive self-image was dominant, she could work out a more satisfactory arrangement with her lover. If the relationship failed, she could handle that without spiraling down into a *severely distraught* state.

In the next-to-last session, Marilyn reported bad dreams and intrusive images regarding themes of loss and the gruesome nature of her mother's death.

Marilyn's recent discussion with her stepmother about the division of her mother's estate led to thoughts about the memories of her mother that she wanted to keep. The therapist helped her to sort out these themes, to evaluate her current responses to her losses, and to confront her sadness over termination. Together, they discussed plans for a transfer to long-term therapy.

Marilyn came to the last session twenty-five minutes late. She reported sadness over termination and increased pangs of yearning for her mother. Despite her increased feelings of sadness, however, Marilyn felt in control. She said that she did not think of herself as helpless. The therapist helped her to plan for the future by telling her what to expect regarding the continuing natural course of grief. She also discussed some possible difficulty in starting and staying with a new therapist, to whom Marilyn was being referred for long-term work on personality-related issues.

Marilyn ended the session by handing the therapist a note on a card with a utopian scene on the front. The note expressed gratitude for the therapist's help and expressed the wish for a friendship with her.

THE EXPLORATION OF ANGER

It was clear from the beginning of therapy that Marilyn was struggling with feelings of anger as well as sadness. During her pre-therapy evaluation, she had reported an outburst of *distraught rage* at a rude stranger on the street. Hostile reactions to others were motivated by wishes to retaliate for the injury of abandonment. As with any vulnerable and disturbed patient, it was difficult to focus on Marilyn's anger. She felt she was bad for having it and wished to conceal it. The early process notes of the therapist indicated a concern that emphasis on Marilyn's anger might only reinforce her loathing of herself as hostile and vengeful, and could prove more disorganizing than useful.

The therapist chose not to confront the anger with head-on or in-depth interpretations, even though Marilyn's anger at her mother was an important theme of mourning. This judgment relates to many discussions of similar patients in our clinical case conferences. The issue of whether or not to, or when and how tactfully to, confront anger in difficult patients is a recurrent and vexing issue. Often, clinicians can be divided into two groups on the basis of their viewpoints. One group favors direct interpretation of the hostility, the other a more gradual and gingerly approach because of the threat of conceptual disorganization when angry emotions are excited. To us, this means that the risks are high with disturbed patients, and that anger is an important issue but one not easily mastered. If it is addressed, much may be gained or lost. Sometimes the best approach is an oscillating technique of a direct approach alternating with a more structuring technique when conceptual disorganization begins to occur.

An example of addressing anger early in its evolution with more disturbed patients is found in the following excerpt related to termination, and taken from the eleventh session:

Therapist: One of the things that we talked about before is that at times of leavetaking you tend to feel rejected. Separations tend to make you feel both hurt and angry. I guess that those very same feelings are going to come up around our stopping, with the difference being that maybe we can talk about them beforehand.

Marilyn: Yeah.

Therapist: You find that you have some angry feelings?

Marilyn: Not really, nothing to be angry about.

Therapist: You said once that you felt like you were getting kicked out.

Marilyn: Well, that was before, that was three weeks ago. Maybe next week I will. No, I don't know. It's a long time.

Therapist: That would be a very usual kind of feeling to have.

Marilyn: Ah. Morose. (*Tries to switch to a sadness theme, denying her anger.*)

Therapist: What came up that kept you from coming last time? (*The therapist explored the failed appointment as a possible expression of anger.*)

Marilyn: Uhm, I got off my hair appointment at about 2:15 and being the vain person that I am, I had to go do my hair, 'cause I was in a state of shock, anyway, so I looked at a clock and it was about 2:35 and I felt so bad, 'cause I knew you'd walked all the way over here [to the clinic], and I just didn't feel like calling you and making an excuse. But I should have, I know, but I didn't. I do that a lot. (*Rather than express anger, Marilyn became apologetic, as if she had been criticized by a disapproving stepmother-therapist.*)

Later in the session, the therapist tried to explore potential anger again. Marilyn evaded this effort by bringing up past associations to the theme that had occurred outside of therapy or by shifting the focus to her weak rather than enraged self-images. Marilyn showed that she was unwilling to deal with anger in the immediate relationship, even when the roles were reversed, as in the excerpt below. The therapist was gently trying to explore Marilyn's anger further with regard to the issue of not calling the therapist.

Therapist: So I guess you were afraid I would have been angry with you [for missing the appointment]?

Marilyn: I don't understand (*laughs*). I just don't like people being angry with me. It upsets me greatly.

Therapist: I wonder why.

Marilyn: Probably because my stepmother was always mad at me (*laughs*) all the time. She wouldn't speak to me for days and I couldn't handle that. There were a lot of times I would come home from school, really excited, to show her something and (*she roars like a lion*) rrrr—— the minute I got in the car she'd start yelling at me.

Therapist: What did you do then? Can you remember what you felt like or how you reacted?

Marilyn: Yeah. I'd just go sit in my closet and cry (*laughs*). I had a walk-in closet. I used to hide in there (*laughs and sighs*).

Therapist: So they were very painful kinds of feelings.

Marilyn: Yeah. Sometimes I would be able to open up to her and talk to her and tell her about some of my feelings, not about her necessarily, but just about things, and then feel really good. Then when she'd get mad at me, she'd throw them back in my face and make me sound stupid, so that's why it took me a long time to even be able to express my feelings, 'cause I was so used to not being allowed to. I couldn't laugh aloud, couldn't cry. It took me a long time to work that out, to be able to say "I want" or "I feel" or "I need." It took a long time. I guess sometimes I still feel guilty when I have those feelings.

These excerpts convey the impression that one obtains from reviewing more of the therapy process. Marilyn was able to contemplate and work on the sadness theme, as synopsized earlier in figure 5.1 (p. 128).

The therapist broached a related theme of anger over abandonment. This theme was partially examined but not fully confronted because of both Marilyn's defensive resistances and the therapist's sense that exploration of anger would be too disorganizing. As had been planned, brief therapy was terminated at the end of the stipulated three months. During the termination phase, Marilyn's continued pattern of behavior problems was summarized. And, as a consequence of that discussion, long-term therapy aimed at personality change was recommended.

Marilyn went for a single session with the new therapist, a man this time. She then left town, and dropped out of therapy, as part of a decision to reunite with her previous boyfriend.

Outcome

Marilyn reunited with Tom and obtained a job but went through a turbulent period for several months. She resumed drinking and quit working. She felt abandoned by her sister, who was spending more time with her lover, and by her stepmother, who was preoccupied with Marilyn's father. During an argument with Tom, she impulsively smashed a vase she had cherished as a gift he had given her.

Following this period, things began to change as Marilyn became increasingly introspective about her own role in precipitating turbulent life events. She returned to ideas of becoming more responsible, thinking through life choices on her own. Using money inherited from her mother, she bought a new wardrobe. She took courses in preparation for a new career in public relations. She spent her spare time returning to her painting (an activity that had elicited maternal approval) and began to take an interest in homemaking.

Marilyn was then able to achieve a better relationship with Tom, and at the time of a follow-up interview one year after therapy termination, they were contemplating marriage. She had begun to insist that they talk together about problems instead of becoming enraged and acting impulsively and she gave up alcohol.

The Patterns of Individual Change Scale scores by clinicians reviewing the videotapes of evaluation sessions before and after treatment are shown in figure 5.2. Improvement was noted in all scales except for the Relationship with Female Friends, which was already at adaptive levels, and Work Identity, which represents the recent career change without a

Figure 5.2
The Pattern of Change: The Case of Marilyn

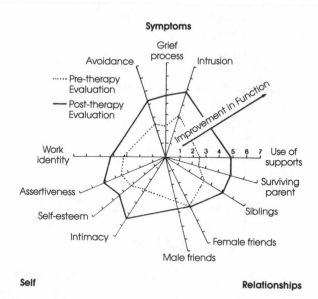

firm new role established at follow-up. The greatest change was in the area of Intimacy. This is of interest because, as noted previously, much of the therapy focused on Marilyn's relationships with men as well as on the presenting stress of her mother's death.

MODIFICATION OF STATES

Marilyn maintained a stable *composed-authentic* state throughout most of the follow-up interview. She appeared poised and confident, and maintained direct eye contact with the evaluating clinician. She had clearly spent great effort on her hair, makeup, and clothing in order to present an attractive appearance. There was no evidence of *severely distraught* states, and considerable reduction in the occurrence of *as-if authentic* states.

Marilyn reported an increased ability to have periods of contemplation during which she tried to figure out what she was thinking and feeling. She sometimes entered the *sad-needy* state and felt in better control during this mood. She noted that she could remain sad and needy without spiraling down into a *severely distraught* state. These feelings no longer consumed her. She said, "I do something to get my mind off it. I don't feel scared anymore."

When asked about periods of "getting blue," she said, "I have 'em, but I realize that I'm going to have them, and that possibly in the future, there may be another real crisis; maybe Tom and I will break up or something. Sure, it will hurt, and it will bother me, but I will get through it."

Marilyn dealt actively with her tendency to feel ugly and self-disgusted. She had gone on a diet, and the purchase of a new wardrobe made her feel more attractive. Her anger did not escalate into explosive rages, and she no longer displayed self-destructive behavior. In her words, "I don't get so hysterical anymore."

With regard to anxious states of mind, Marilyn said that she still tended to become "a little hysterical at times when I shouldn't. Just in small ways, like our dog hurt her foot the other day. I practically went through the roof, and said, 'Oh, my God, what am I going to do?'" But Marilyn added that, in those kinds of situations, she talked to herself as the therapist had done. She would tell herself to "stop and think about the situation and come to a solution rather than just going 'aaaahhhh!' and going off the deep end." She added that she had "gained a lot more control of myself in that way."

To summarize, state stabilization had been achieved. Marilyn was functioning primarily in adaptively controlled states and was able to exert conscious control over state transitions. She felt vulnerable to entry into *severely distraught* states, but could avoid becoming consumed by them. Her increased control over undercontrolled states decreased the need to facilitate states such as the *excited-giddy* one.

External changes helped account for some of Marilyn's increased sense of stability. While she demonstrated increased restraint and greater mutuality in her relationship with Tom, we wondered whether a separation from him might precipitate another crisis. However, we felt relatively sure that Marilyn was better able to accept her mother's death. Mourning was less intense, although it was still a continuing, attenuated process. She retained memories of the good times she had had with her mother, and was able to internalize some of her mother's approval. Marilyn felt that her mother's spirit was guiding her and believed that her mother would approve of the way she was leading her life. She had some pangs of sad feelings but chose to actively call up memories of her mother, even when painful, rather than taking the risk of forgetting her. In contrast to her previous avoidant behaviors, she had visited the cemetery and returned to areas associated with her mother, "choking back a tear or two." She acknowledged continued symptoms relating to her mother's death, particularly a rare but repetitive and violent dream of fire, but said that she had not experienced any of these nightmares recently.

ALTERATIONS IN SELF-CONCEPT AND ROLE RELATIONSHIPS

Marilyn's relationships with her sister and with her stepmother had improved. Her friendship with her sister was characterized by a greater sense of mutuality, in which the two could now focus on the sister's problems as well as Marilyn's. Because Marilyn's neediness was not as great, the relationship became less one-sided.

A related theme that emerged at follow-up involved Marilyn's thoughts about herself as a caretaker. She expressed the wish to be a nurturing person who cared for others and was able to reverse the relationships of being needy and abandoned by others. Although she felt some resentment toward her stepmother for being preoccupied with her own problems at just about the time that Marilyn was terminating her therapy and shortly thereafter, Marilyn had been able to help her stepmother cope with some of the difficulties she was experiencing with Marilyn's father. Closer feelings were established between Marilyn and the stepmother. At the time of follow-up, Marilyn was also caring for puppies, learning to cook, growing an herb garden, and taking pleasure in these activities. She commented playfully to the evaluator that maybe by the time they got together for the second follow-up she would have five kids. She then quickly added, "Better not." This shift seemed to indicate that she felt that she could now experiment with the idea that she herself could be a caretaker.

Although her relationship with her stepmother had improved, it seemed to function at this point as a replacement for the lost good relationship with her mother. While this relationship helped Marilyn to feel worthy of attention in the short run, we hypothesized that Marilyn would probably reexperience intense grief if her stepmother became critical or when she died.

Marilyn reported that she and Tom had reconciled when he started saying the kinds of things that she wanted to hear. For example, he said that he did care about her and wanted her to come back. It was not clear to what degree his renewed interest may have been based on the money she inherited from her mother. However, it was evident that some of the changes that Marilyn herself had made helped to stabilize the relationship.

ATTITUDINAL AND STYLISTIC CHANGES

Marilyn's increased ability to think things through and to make decisions helped her to feel more in control and less needy. This, in turn, contributed to the improved relations with Tom. As she was able to think about her feelings, she could label them and speak to him about them.

This change allowed Marilyn and Tom to negotiate about their different needs. If Tom was critical, she was able to weigh his comments, sometimes accepting them as constructive suggestions.

For example, one incident that she described as a turning point occurred after her therapy was over and she had returned to live with Tom. She got drunk at lunch with Trudy and couldn't drive herself home. She was able to accept Tom's criticism of her as a "lush," take stock, make a decision to stop drinking, and then adhere to it. Marilyn reported that she was more able to tolerate some emotional withdrawal on Tom's part, without automatically feeling hurt and abandoned. She also appeared to be more aware of the variability in the emotional states of others, and to realize that such states could be caused by events for which she was not entirely to blame.

Furthermore, when Marilyn did enter a *sad-needy* state, she was not as likely to move on to a *severely distraught* state because she no longer felt totally abandoned and helpless. She was less preoccupied with being rejected, and was less inclined to prematurely reject Tom as a way of protecting herself against being potentially hurt. When she encountered an image of herself as physically unattractive, she reported that she no longer immediately generalized with a plethora of other negative thoughts about herself.

The money that she had inherited helped facilitate the shift to a more positive self-image. The inheritance enabled Marilyn to quit a job where she frequently felt that her self-esteem was being challenged, and allowed her to take time to prepare for work in a new field where she could potentially "earn what I'm worth." She was able to limit her spending and invest some of her money. Her ability to spend her money more sensibly, something not in evidence before she started therapy, led to a greater sense of self-control and pride in herself. Improved finances allowed her to upgrade her wardrobe, which also helped her to feel physically more attractive. In contrast to many other patients, Marilyn did not seem to feel guilty about enjoying her inheritance.

PERCEPTIONS OF THERAPY

Marilyn felt strongly that her therapy had been a great help in altering her self-image. She noted that:

Marilyn: The therapist helped me to see things for what they really were, rather than the distorted picture that I had at times. She really supported me. I would come in here, I was always late (*laughing*). Every time I was late, and I'd always feel really guilty, like: "Oh, she's going to be mad at me. I'm late, I shouldn't do this." And she'd say, "Well, relax. Don't worry about it. If you're late, you're late." And that was just one aspect of me that was always feeling guilty, and she helped me to get over that by realizing sure, I should try to be on time, but I don't have to feel so bad about it.

Marilyn indicated some awareness that she had, in a sense, repeatedly invited the therapist to criticize her for being late for appointments. When the therapist did not, in fact, criticize her, Marilyn felt less negative about herself and less vulnerable to abandonment.

She also seemed to have benefited from the therapist's emphasis on her need either to be the best or to feel totally worthless. Marilyn reported considerable change in this area. She no longer had to engage in extreme self-destructive behavior, such as grandiosely drinking the most in her group of friends. She was able to confine her wish to excel to more realistic and adaptive functions. Similarly, she no longer had to be the "champ" in her career and could be satisfied by trying to perform ordinarily well. This attitude was encapsulated in her remark: "I'm really looking forward to my new job and I'm going to do a good job, but it's not like I have to be the best this time."

During therapy sessions Marilyn had seemed more attuned to the process than the content. Yet it is clear that she had retained particular comments of the therapist, such as the labeling of her all-or-nothing patterns. She clarified how she felt the therapist had helped her to feel less worthless.

> Marilyn: I would just think about things that she said. I had problems feeling guilty because I was so out of control. I felt guilty about that, like I shouldn't allow myself to be in this condition. And that was adding to my problems. And she made me see that—that I *was* going through a crisis, and that naturally I was going to have these kinds of feelings. I was *going* to feel bad, and that I shouldn't make myself feel *worse* about it.

It also seemed likely that the therapy was responsible for Marilyn's newfound ability to discuss her shortcomings with Tom without becoming enraged. She described how she could tolerate this process now because they confronted each other using humor, just as the therapist had tempered potentially threatening information about Marilyn's self-concept with humor. It is possible that the role relationship model developed with Tom was based on identification and modeling learned in Marilyn's relationship with the therapist. In any case, the therapist's noncritical limit-setting provided a paradigm for a more adaptive way of handling personal criticism. Marilyn was now better able to tolerate criticism without feeling that the critical person was about to abandon her for being bad. She could experience herself as wrong when criticized and could view the other person as helpfully critical.

The main changes were in the reestablishment of more positive self-concepts and role relationship models that had preexisted but had been lost during a period of intense stress. Marilyn's defective self-concepts still existed; they seemed to have returned to a latent status and might be reactivated again during some potential future regression, as after some new abandonment. Nevertheless, Marilyn's ability to survive her period of suicidal despair had increased her confidence in her capacity to sustain losses and to plan her life. Marilyn was no longer entering *distraught anger* states and said that she was able to tolerate the frustrations in her everyday life. This was in contrast to her pre-therapy status, when her anger was experienced as intense and out of control. We nonetheless inferred that hostility, fear of guilt over aggression, and repression of both themes remained an unresolved conflict. Evidence for this hypothesis was her experience of continued violent nightmares about her mother.

One possible clue as to Marilyn's current means for dealing with "abandoning" caretakers was the manner in which she coped with feelings about her therapist. She reported that she had absolutely no negative feelings about the therapy, her therapist, or the clinic. She felt that her therapy experience had been completely helpful and in no way harmful. She gave superlative ratings on a client-satisfaction scale. The striking absence of any negative attitudes about the therapy or therapist recapitulated her view of good caretakers and may have in part expressed a denial of ambivalence. Her difficulty in reattaching to a new therapist, who may have seemed potentially critical ("he looked at me funny"), might have represented a fear of abandonment or a categorization of therapists as "good" and "bad." In her relationship with her stepmother as well, Marilyn dissociated "good" and "bad" attributes; both mother and stepmother were described as being all good, and the memories that Marilyn reported were solely positive. We believe that this split in thinking remained an area of potential vulnerability.

In summary, Marilyn had accomplished state stabilization by the time of the follow-up interview. As with Connie, the result seemed to be due to working through some of the more difficult aspects of mourning. Unlike Connie, however, Marilyn did not exhibit full stabilization of states during the brief therapy period. Stabilization occurred later, as a result of both gains during the therapy period and major situational gains.

This combination of gains resulted in a shift in Marilyn's self-concepts from less competent to more competent ones. A shift also occurred from impulsive (yet defensive) actions to improved coping by use of rational thought and planning. There was little evidence of personality change during the therapy, but rather some shift in those elements of personality which were used to appraise incoming stimuli and to organize responses. There was evidence that a given process, that of mourning her mother, had been facilitated although not completed. The result was a reduction of stress.

These changes resulted in a major decline in self-reported symptoms. Before therapy, for example, Marilyn had scored very high on measures of depression and hostility. These scores could be viewed as reflecting two aspects of the sadness theme and her resulting *severely distraught* states of mind. The initial mean score of 3.3 for depression, on a four-point scale for the Hopkins Symptom Checklist (HCL) items, declined to a mean of 0.2 at follow-up. Equivalent scores for the hostility set of symptoms on the HCL-90 were 3.0 at pre-therapy evaluation and 0.7 at follow-up. Anxiety scores also declined, from 2.6 before to 0.6 at follow-up. Clinician symptom rating scales reflected the same pattern. Some specific problems present before therapy were not present: she was no longer suicidal, but rather invested in the future; her self-esteem was improved; and she had no difficulty sleeping.

Conclusion

Connie and Marilyn had both depended in part on the deceased parent for self-confidence, self-esteem, attention, interest, praise, and support. The news of the death set in motion a mourning process in which giving up that dependency would play a prominent part. Both Connie and Marilyn felt that it seemed intolerable to no longer rely on the parent, and both used various maneuvers for inhibiting painful ideas and feelings. Therapy countered their inhibitory styles and provided a temporary, controlled level of experience, one sufficient to permit hesitant but progressive contemplation about the real implications of the loss.

In Marilyn, with her higher degree of narcissistic vulnerability, a sufficiently sustaining therapeutic alliance was more difficult to establish, and her variations in state were more turbulent and threatening than in Connie. But, in both cases, careful attention to clarity of ideas seemed to be a valuable facilitator of the mourning process, and progression in the grief work led to marked reduction in stress. With that reduction, with some new conceptual tools learned in therapy, and with some new modes of relating also learned in therapy, both patients were no longer derailed by recent traumas.

Brief therapy helped both patients to grieve in a way that reduced dependency. Further changes in their personality styles would require more life experiences. Some personality differentiation and development would take place in the course of living through new loves and work experiences. If the hysterical style interfered with such learning through living, then a time-unlimited therapy aimed at character change would be indicated.

6

THE COMPULSIVE PERSONALITY

LTHOUGH the compulsive personality style is one of the most common, it is least adaptable to the emotional accessibility and centrality of focus desirable for effective brief therapy (Malan 1979; Sifneos 1966). The characteristic rigidity of this style may also conceal a considerable degree of vulnerability to deflation of self-esteem. The therapist will generally try to probe beneath the shell of overcontrolled emotions, but this effort may well have negative effects if it is perceived as criticism by the patient. In contrast, a therapist who is very sensitive to this issue may approach such patients so gingerly that after a brief therapy they are left untouched. This is the dilemma illustrated by the case that will be discussed in this chapter.

Diagnosis

The cluster of behaviors typifying this style have often been referred to as "obsessional," but we will use the current nomenclature of compulsive personality. The following statements are part of the standard, generalized definition of the disorder as it appears in *DSM-III*:

An individual who has restricted ability to express warm and tender emotions; perfectionism that interferes with the ability to grasp "the big picture"; insistence that others submit to his or her way of doing things; excessive devotion to work and productivity to the exclusion of pleasure; and indecisiveness.

Individuals with this disorder are stingy with their emotions and material possessions. . . . Everyday relationships have a conventional, formal, and serious quality. Others often perceive these individuals as stilted and "stiff."

Preoccupation with rules, efficiency, trivial details, procedures, or form interferes with the ability to take a broad view of things. . . . Time is poorly allocated, the most important tasks being left to the last moment. Although efficiency and perfection are idealized, they are rarely attained.

Individuals with this disorder are always mindful of their relative status in dominance-submission relationships. Although they resist the authority of others, they stubbornly insist that people conform to their way of doing things. . . . Decision-making is avoided, postponed, or protracted, perhaps because of an inordinate fear of making a mistake. For example, assignments cannot be completed on time because the individual is ruminating about priorities (*DSM-III*, 1980, pp. 326–28).

Observation of Style

The information-processing style of the compulsive is often characterized by a seemingly sharp focus of attention (Shapiro 1965). The word "seemingly" is used because while there is pointed detail, often presented at great length, the *center* of the theme is seldom reached. The *periphery* is dealt with in detail instead.

Rational ideas pertaining to a theme are overemphasized in an effort, often sensed by the clinician, to jam conceptual channels so that the possibility of emotions or surprises is excluded. When confronted with these patterns, the compulsive person will often indicate a hope that adequate knowledge of the rules for coping with the theme will lead to mastery of it. Often, there are endless scene-setting descriptions and concern over general issues that avoid disclosure of the real emotions at the heart of a theme. Emotional connotations are omitted to avoid shame or weakness and the possibility of loss of control. The result is an arid, intellectualized communication.

When ideas threaten to lead toward the heart of an aspect of a conflict, the patient with a compulsive style seeks to shift away from that aspect in order to avoid strongly emotional states of mind (Nagera 1976). Very often, a given theme has opposite poles of conflict, and the patient shifts rapidly from one to the other and back again. This leads to a phenomenon that Salzman (1968) calls "verbal juggling." Oscillation to a pole that contains fear is used to undo the anger or guilt evoked by the opposite pole. The ideas communicated usually reflect shifts between assertions as to who is strong or weak, right or wrong, dominant or submissive, clean or dirty. For example, a sense of impending guilt over being too strong is undone by a quick shift toward a sense of impending fear over being too weak and vulnerable. For the person who makes such shifts, one emotional propensity undoes another. Since oscillation occurs rapidly, no strong emotion is experienced. The result may be prolonged indecisiveness or confusion. To avoid this experience, some compulsive patients make impulsive decisions. However, these choices are not based on rational completion of a train of thought. Accordingly, the decision itself may then become a focus for further undoing operations.

It is difficult for any strong or weak position to be maintained because the compulsive often tends toward various degrees of magical thinking, in which ideas are equated with actions. Thinking of submitting to the aims of another is tantamount to lying prone and waiting to be assaulted; thinking of disagreeing or being angry is tantamount to unleashing severely destructive behavior. To avoid a sense of foolishness, the compulsive constantly conceals his irrational ideas, even from himself, and cloaks them in a shell of logical control.

A review of the history of the prototypical patient with compulsive style will often reveal the person's wish to avoid failure at all costs. Constant self-doubt fuels this effort, and has often caused interpersonal actions to be restricted to those patterns known to be safe, secure, and routine. Spontaneity and risk are found only in the occasional moments of impulsivity noted above, moments that contain seeds of their own defeat in self-fulfilling prophecies.

To ward off reproach, the prototypically compulsive patient may make intense efforts to be neat, clean, contained, and proper. Such intellectual control, evidenced by orderliness, parsimony, and organization, has an obstinate quality that indicates a fear of being controlled. The patient may attempt to argue, quibble over the meaning of words, or "naively" ask for instructions in an effort to remain remote from emotional engagement. These behaviors are also part of an overt or covert effort to uncover the "rules" of therapy (Nagera 1976; Shapiro 1981). The mind and even the body are regarded as machines that should always function perfectly and according to known rules. Any aberration is regarded with dread, as a sign of impending loss of control. The compulsive person systematically masters the "words" of life, but is far less free to dance to the "music."

Typical Problems for the Therapist

The compulsive patient may approach therapy as an intellectual exercise during which he will find out what he "really" thinks, so he can direct himself to act accordingly. Intense scrutiny of the therapist is used to find out what the therapist "really thinks" and expects. The resulting fantasy may precipitate a dominance-submission struggle as the patient alternately tries to comply with the projected expectations or rebels to prove his independence. Therapy can become an adversarial procedure in which any interpretation is viewed as shedding doubt on the patient's omniscience. An interpretation may be strongly rejected by the patient, only to be "owned" by him as his personal insight at a later time.

A person with this style experiences the therapeutic task as a new kind of pressure, and feels a compelling duty to carefully orchestrate each hour, presenting countless details that are intended to satisfy the "good patient" role. The patient may bring a written agenda or elaborately detailed dreams in an effort to protect himself against the emotional risks of spontaneity. Although he appears to be working hard, intellectual insight into an irrational attitude underlying a behavior does not alter the pattern of actions.

The patient may bring up concerns about several themes and be unable to choose any single focus. Further, the patient, as he experiences increasing anxiety about the exploration of a given theme, may switch to a less threatening version of that theme or to a completely different theme. As a result, no theme is fully explored and the therapist finds the focus puzzlingly diffuse. The feeling tone of such sessions often remains socially appropriate, with a notable lack of expression of either positive or negative feelings. The patient hopes to maintain the status quo while eliminating unpleasant symptoms and developing a set of guiding principles. As in all of his potentially intimate relationships, the patient possesses a covert sense of limited involvement (Shapiro 1965, 1981).

Emerging feelings of warmth and dependence toward the therapist are fearfully experienced as a loss of control and may precipitate a flight from treatment. Any sexual component of the patient's responses is particularly worrisome because of the potential humiliation if the feeling were exposed. Hostile feelings are experienced as dangerous because of the perceived magical links between thought and action. The therapeutic alliance develops very gradually as the essential blocks to an emotionally open, trusting relationship are uncovered.

When the patient presents in crisis or the therapist chooses to become more active, the tone of the hour changes. The authority vested in the therapist is accentuated. He is usually seen either as a parental figure who demands perfect behavior and may criticize or reject at any moment when such behavior is not forthcoming, or as a parental figure who has failed to provide the correct rules of behavior and so is responsible for the crisis.

Tactics in Therapy

As Salzman (1980) has pointed out, even in an open-ended treatment "the obsessional defensive structure tends to make the process of therapy difficult, arduous, tedious, and sometimes unrewarding." Ferenczi (1920) attempted to speed up the process by forcing the patient to cease undoing or switching from one aspect of a theme to a less threatening one, and by evoking strong emotion. While some rapid changes were noted, the technique seemed to intensify transference issues of struggles for control. More recently, Davanloo (1980) has advocated a firm approach in which the patient is shown how stubbornly and covertly he is resisting an important chance to use therapy productively.

An important issue concerns the patient's ability to maintain a view of the relationship between himself and the therapist in the context of a therapeutic alliance, even at the same time as he experiences a firm confrontation in the context of the transference. The risk of unworkable negative transference reactions is somewhat reduced if the therapist maintains a neutral stance. This neutral stance should be empathic and should display understanding, so that the patient is gradually assured that he has found a safe place for self-disclosure.

The therapist himself must guard against frustration and hostile countertransferences because of the patient's general use of intellectualization, isolation, endless undoing, and procrastination. In a social relationship, these qualities evoke irritation. Countertransference feelings, leading to sarcasm, are particularly noxious for such patients. Humiliation and competition are avoided by presenting interpretations not as elementary or obvious, but as interesting observations upon which the patient can usefully elaborate. Continued emphasis on the emotions as a barometer to use in decision-making adds value to elements that the patient has regarded as irrational or unimportant.

163

In a brief therapy with such patients, the therapist needs to be active and directive, holding to the focus and avoiding irrelevant excursions into detail or history. Establishment of an early, clear treatment contract provides a structure to which both patient and therapist can consistently refer.

The therapist must counter switching of topics away from threatening material by slow, step-by-step unraveling in which habitual side-stepping maneuvers are brought to the patient's attention and countered by volitional effort (Horowitz 1974, 1976). Identification of the switching pattern allows the patient to contemplate his resistance to developing an interest in why this pattern occurs. The therapist should suggest to the patient that the anxiety he experiences is not an "alarm" signaling the need to cover up. Rather, it is a signal pointing to an area that is in need of exploration and is an essential component of the change process. Painful themes can be approached in "doses" so that the anxiety level remains tolerable and the patient becomes increasingly bold in addressing warded-off concepts. The therapist repeatedly acts as an anchor, holding to the issues presented before the switching away occurs.

An adversarial stance can be circumvented by enlisting the patient's interest in the process, often allowing increased contemplation of a train of thought by repeating what the patient has said just before a switching-away maneuver. Sometimes, however, this action does lead into an adversarial stance and the therapist is confronted with the dilemma of whether to proceed firmly nonetheless or to draw away. This predicament is illustrated in the following case.

Ann, a Representative Case

PRESENTING COMPLAINTS

Ann was a twenty-four-year-old married social work student. She sought help seven months after her father's death because of a marked denial of the reality of the loss and of its implications. In spite of this numbing and avoidance, Ann had intrusive breakthroughs of a shattering, painful sense of despair.

Since the death of her father, she had repeatedly suggested to friends that he was alive. She became frightened by her "irrationality," and a state of panic broke through the numbness as she thought of the potential humiliation she would feel when others learned the truth.

Ann also worried about the increased constriction in her activities as she forced herself to avoid any external reminder of her father. This pattern included a phobic response to a particular street because on it was a house in which Ann's father had attended a party for her on the day of his death. She reacted with profound anxiety to passing by the area, even in a car.

At the evaluation interview, Ann was pale and fidgety, alternating between nervous laughter and tears. During the hour, she began to choke and cough as she described her father's death from viral pneumonia, secondary to chronic lung disease.

In discussing her difficulty with the grief process, Ann said, "I feel that he is alive in me, but somehow I am stuck and can't deal with his being gone. I'm not going to say goodbye. I want to hang on to him." This inability to "say goodbye" made it particularly difficult for her to review her relationship with her father as part of a mourning process in which gradual acceptance would alternate with grief. Among troublesome thoughts that she hoped to dispel were the guilty idea that she could have saved him by taking better care of him, and the opposite idea that his death was just another example of his abandonment of her when she needed him.

Ann was the youngest of five siblings. Her father worked in an institutional setting where he felt that his potentially productive work had been destroyed by bureaucratic and routine requirements. He counterbalanced his job dissatisfaction with intense dedication to physical fitness, particularly long-distance running. His wife designed her life around her children and, according to Ann, assumed a role of "weakness" in order to emphasize the role of her husband as head of the family.

Three older siblings went on to professional schools. Ann was a good student but juggled her career choice between ambivalently held alternatives. She attended several colleges, changing her mind back and forth between two possible vocations. She had recently married a dental student who was seriously involved in his own work, but had episodic doubts about whether she had been ready to marry.

During the course of her father's increasing incapacitation, Ann and her father had mutual difficulty in acknowledging the terminal nature of his chronic lung disease. He felt antagonistic about his illness and therefore was sometimes sarcastic and hostile. She described going to visit him in the hospital during the last three months, thinking that she could share with him an acceptance of his condition. However, when she got there, he was so actively denying his problems that she avoided the discussion. He had been hospitalized with a second attack of pneumonitis for these three months, but was discharged from the hospital one week before his death. As mentioned earlier, shortly before he died he attended a luncheon party in Ann's honor. That night he succumbed to respiratory complications of his illness.

This sudden and unanticipated death left Ann stunned and reticent to give up a residual sense that her father was still alive. Her preparations for his funeral reflected both a wish to honor him and a lack of acceptance of his death. She and her mother chose the grave site carefully, with conversation about how the father might enjoy the view. In contrast to other members of the family, Ann preferred an open casket because she wanted a chance to be with her father for a few more hours.

Ann went to the mortuary the night before the funeral. She had prevailed against her mother's wishes, and followed through on her plan to bury her father in the clothes that he had liked best when he was alive. She dressed him in his favorite jogging suit and shoes, with a map of the place where he had planned his own marathon tucked in the pocket. When she viewed her father, she was suddenly shocked that he did not move. Having a sudden, out-of-control urge, she shouted at him and expressed anger at him for leaving her.

Ann got up early on the morning of the funeral and returned to visit her father. She said she had a desperate feeling that her time with him was running short. When other family members came into the room unexpectedly, she said goodbye and slammed down the lid of the casket.

From the time of the funeral on, Ann's main response to the death was to deny its implications. She had some breakthroughs of painful emotions which, like her shout, she felt to be out of control. She reported that her husband had tried to be good to her for a brief period, but that it had not lasted. He had said, "You're acting like your father's daughter and not like a wife," an indication that he was jealous of the strength of her feelings toward her father.

Since the funeral, Ann had kept herself busy with work. Over the summer she worked at two jobs and regimented her time so that she almost always had an essential "duty"-type task to do. This method of avoiding ideas and feelings that were pressing toward representation broke down when she was driving to work. By the time she pulled out of the driveway, she would start to cry angrily and continue crying the whole way to and from work. She felt that these outbursts were shamefully uncontrolled emotional expressions, ones to be avoided strictly even when she was with close companions.

Ann had promised her father that she would be kind and supportive to her mother, but found this difficult to do because she felt so needy herself. It was her older sister who actively comforted the mother during the funeral, so that Ann felt both respect for and envy toward her sister. Later, her mother hinted that Ann had lost opportunities to please her father, highlighting Ann's frustration at not having had the opportunity for a deathbed scene in which she would finally tell her father of her love for him. Ann's contemplation of the reality of her father's death was complicated by her worry that she had been a faulty caretaker, her anger at his abandonment, and her recognition that his future caring was now lost.

When Ann's mother had first informed her of the father's medical difficulties, Ann's response was that she wanted him to live long enough to support her in completing her education. With the father's untimely death, she felt that he had lived just long enough to do his duty, without being able to enjoy the years afterward. She therefore felt that she had exploited him.

When Ann was an adolescent, her father was withdrawn and responded minimally to his children, except for caustic criticism or angry outbursts. In efforts to please him, she described herself as seeking but never finding perfection.

When Ann's father died, she and her mother colluded to hide the "bad parts" by sweeping away dirty laundry and putting his professional books prominently on display. During the funeral period, they cleaned house together to overcome their senses of helplessness. They also carefully selected information to tell the minister, who was a stranger, so that there would be no social criticism of the father. Ann's husband and her siblings urged her to continue to cope without undue emotional display, thus supporting her compulsive style.

Formulation of Ann's problems by the evaluator suggested that her difficulties were multiple and each multifaceted, and that it would be difficult for the therapist to hold her to a topic. Ann's avoidance of her grief seemed tied to her anger at her father for abandoning her, and to her guilt over demanding financial support until she had a career. She was blocked in her expression of anger by a sense of omnipotent responsibility for his illness and death; she also feared that recognition of her anger would concomitantly erase all positive memories of their relationship. The evaluator felt that strong identification with her father caused her exaggerated concerns about being as mortal and flawed as he. In general, her difficulty with expressing affection and experiencing intimacy was illustrated by earlier distancing from her father and by current relief when her husband left on one of his frequent trips. Intense emotions of any kind made Ann feel out of control and vulnerable. She viewed both herself and her body as defective. Finally, she was having problems with her ambivalence about choosing a career.

IMPORTANT STATES OF MIND

Most Problematic States.   The dichotomy of problematic states for Ann reflects both the compulsive's fear of intense emotion and the compensatory entry into states of mind so rigidly controlled that numb immobilization may result. Ann's response to the death of her father potentially contained both a frightening entry into states of explosive rage and the despairing sadness of a helpless child. These states were mostly blocked from Ann's conscious experience, but leaked through in the form of intrusive bitter crying when she was driving by herself.

More frequently, Ann avoided such intense emotional experiences by entering a frozen, deflated state in which she felt defective and unable to act. When she was in this state, her inability to confirm the reality of her father's death led to a humiliating distortion in front of her friends. More importantly, her own life choices had become restricted because she wanted to avoid contemplation of a future bereft of her father. She also blocked the needed reevaluation of her actual past relationship with her father. Her compulsive tendency to feel exaggerated responsibility often led her to enter a state of searing guilt. Since the most problematic states contained both undermodulated and overmodulated experiences, Ann had been unable on her own to stabilize a productive state that gave her flexible access to the emotions and controls instigated by her father's death.

Series of States.   Ann's states of mind are labeled and described in table 6.1. The states are presented along a gradient of modulation from undercontrolled to overcontrolled. Ann's overmodulated *artificially engaging* state was the most prominent one in her presentation to the evaluator and then to her therapist. This state enabled Ann to present herself as an emotionally controlled individual, although this state was punctuated by brief, uncontrolled entries into the *frightened yearning* or *numb immobilization* state. These latter undermodulated states were like general stress-response states of intrusion (frightened yearning) and denial (numb immobilization).

Defensive Organization of States.   As shown in table 6.2, Ann's problematic undermodulated states, *numb immobilization* and *frightened yearning*, contained views of a significant other as either scornfully critical or absent. Intrusive crying and the *frightened yearning* state occurred when the therapist attempted to hold her to themes of loss and abandonment. The state also occurred when she was alone, without the fantasized po-

TABLE 6.1
List of Ann's States

Label	Description
Undermodulated States	
Frightened yearning	Waves of sadness, weakness, and shame. Feels alone; fears that if she starts to cry, she may not be able to stop. Sometimes intrusive crying occurs.
Numb immobilization	Deflated, vaguely hurt, inattentive to others, unproductive. Eyes downcast.
Explosive rage (warded off)	Accusatory complaints. Feels dangerously impulsive and "crazy."
Searing guilt (warded off)	Sees herself as a hurtful assailant or failed caretaker; fantasies devastating criticism.
Well-Modulated States	
Vulnerable working	Has tolerable anxiety; looks thoughtful, worried, or hurt. Abrupt, jerky movements.
Assured productivity (ideal)	Calm problem-solving, productive; feels wise and strong.
Overmodulated States	
Artificially engaging	Coyly ingratiating, play-acting, blustery.
Sniping	Indirect criticism of others; challenges with convoluted undoing by vague praise and submission. Maintains overall distancing.

tential social critic/observer, and was accompanied by a sense of herself as a bitterly resentful, weak, and abandoned child. When in this state, she was intensely aware of the loss of her father, and refused in an almost omnipotent way to accept the death as real. She worried about the unbidden entry into her thoughts of these ideas and feelings, and was frightened by the possibility that when she began to cry she would lose control and be unable to stop.

Ann fought against *frightened yearning* because in this state she felt alone in the world and overwhelmed by waves of sadness, weakness, and shame. In a reversal of roles, Ann could enter another, even more disliked and undermodulated state, *explosive rage*, in which she experienced herself as being "ugly" in her strong hostility and reactive guilt. In this state she took on the role of a powerful critic, seeing herself as someone who had injured or deprived another. The rage took the form of destructive accusations directed toward a willful abandoner, and that set

TABLE 6.2
Defensive Organization of Ann's States

State	Self	Aims	Other
	Problematic Role Relationships		
Frightened yearning	Abandoned child	Supplicate ———————▶	Gone
Numb immobilization	Weak and defective	Conceal self ———————▶ Scorn ◀———————	Strong critic
	Dreaded or Warded-Off Role Relationships		
Explosive rage	Dangerous assailant	Hurt ———————▶	Willful abandoner or weak victim
Searing guilt	Dangerous assailant	Punish ◀———————	Strong critic
	Desired Role Relationships		
Assured productivity	Wise and strong	Benefit and approve ◀——————— ———————▶ Do and show	Wise and strong
	Compromise Relationships		
Artificially engaging	Ingenue	Perform ———————▶ ◀——————— Encourage	Mentor

in motion a sequence of feelings. The person who was perceived earlier as a strong, willful abandoner would be seen later in Ann's train of thought as a weak victim, whom she had unjustly harmed by rage. She would then feel another dreaded and generally warded-off state of *searing guilt*, in which she saw herself as evil and harmful to the victim.

As shown in table 6.2, the *explosive rage* and *searing guilt* states were painful but rare, warded off usually by defensive operations. Ann's most frequent problematic state was *numb immobilization*. In this state she felt constricted, vaguely hurt, and deflated. Although she felt driven to do her work, she made no progress and was withdrawn and dulled. She viewed herself as a defective woman trying to conceal her lack of progress or productivity from a strong and scornful (rather than supportive) other. In therapy, she entered the state of *numb immobilization* when she struggled with concepts of herself as helpless and defective.

In contrast, Ann entered a desired state of *assured productivity* when she felt safe from criticism. She was able to sit erectly and speak firmly to the therapist, feeling that there was a peer relationship between two professionals. She became more reflective and bold, and could present her thoughts and feelings without disavowal. In this state she was competent, calm, wise, productive, and admirable, in relationship to an appreciative companion.

When discussion led toward themes of sadness and defectiveness, Ann often entered a *vulnerable working* state, in which she looked more thoughtful, worried, and a bit hurt. Signs of the tensions that were building showed in her abrupt, jerky movements, and one had the sense that she feared entry into out-of-control states. When this happened, she either stayed in the *vulnerable working* state, or compromised by entering the inauthentic, overcontrolled states labeled in tables 6.1 and 6.2 as *artificially engaging*.

In the *artificially engaging* state Ann acted the ingenue, coyly performing for an approving mentor, a role that she assigned to her therapist. Constant monitoring of her own and others' responses, with subsequent shifting of ideas and subject changes, contributed to Ann's sense of emotional distance. In this state, she told sequential stories that were greatly detailed but were not moving toward any resolution or decision point. Her mode of presentation was to describe instances or general principles rather than to experience any feelings. She did this in a singsong voice, using sweeping hand gestures.

Her father's personal criticism of her had been devastating, and her obsessive attempts to avoid failure in his eyes had often led to paralyzing indecision. However, Ann had also learned a coping style from listening to her father's chronic harangues on the ineffectiveness of workers in his institution. As unconscious protection against a possible attack on the self, Ann would encourage the interviewer to join with her in criticizing an absent third person. This occurred in a pattern that we came to refer to as the *sniping* variant of the *artificially engaging* state. If the criticism was challenging to the therapist, it was much more indirect and was undone in a convoluted manner through phrases that conveyed praise or potential submission.

IMPLICATION OF DEFENSIVE LAYERING OF STATES FOR THERAPY

From the outset, it was clear that Ann would be a relatively difficult patient. Her predominantly compulsive character style was characterized by control, indecisiveness, and the avoidance of emotional expression. Underlying these defenses was a considerable sensitivity to potential criticism of herself as weak, selfish, hostile, or a career failure. In order to get help, however, Ann had to risk exposing these areas of vulnerability.

The major pattern in therapy, as indicated in figure 6.1, was an oscillation between the *artificially engaging* and *vulnerable working* states. These were relatively stable and not particularly intense emotional states. When the therapist would attempt to hold Ann to a focus, with its potentially painful ideas and feelings, she would sometimes enter the *vulnerable working* state to explore that focus. The mounting threat of the emotions aroused would then motivate her to switch back out of this state into the *artificially engaging* state. If the therapist would then continue to hold her to the painful themes, she would shift back into *vulnerable working* and would return to *artificially engaging* when she experienced an emotional threat, and so on repetitively.

It was clear that the *vulnerable working* state would be threatened by any hint of perceived criticism. This could shift Ann to overmodulated, socially contrived states or ones that would frighten and humiliate her. Interpretations of areas of maladaptive functioning would seem like criticism to Ann, and could provoke her to facilitate a role reversal. When this occurred, she would guardedly reverse roles, enter the *sniping* state, attack the therapist and devalue the therapy, or try to join with the therapist in criticizing a third party. The latter type of collusion would be provoked by Ann, since her strong wish to work through her problems was in conflict with her wish to establish a social relationship between comfortable peers who were united in criticism of an uncaring world. At times, the supportive aspects of such a relationship encouraged symptom relief. However, Ann's detailed storytelling did not address her problems in dealing with anger and despair. Any experienced clinician will recognize this problem with a compulsive patient: a great deal of "interesting material" is discussed, leading to "fascinating insights" and restabilization of a rigid defensive style that had been threatened by stress-induced breakthrough phenomena.

MODELS OF ROLE RELATIONSHIPS AND SELF-CONCEPTS

The key constructs for the compulsive personality are strength and weakness relative to other persons. This is associated with issues of dominance and submission; and control in interpersonal transactions is seen as being one up or one down, not in terms of mutual cooperation. These issues are blended with universal constructs such as activity and passivity, and good and bad in reference to values. The additional construct of clean and dirty, often present in compulsives, was not a conspicuous issue in the case of Ann, and so was not an aspect in the formulation of her case.

Individuals with compulsive personality styles show characteristic os-

Figure 6.1
Ann's Potential for Main States in Therapy

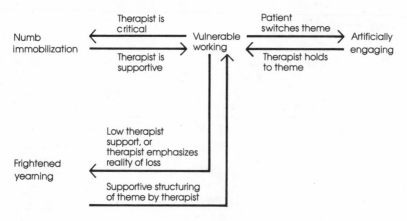

cillating shifts on bipolar dimensions (act–do not act, dominate–submit, approach–avoid, like–resent). As an example, to be in control through domination is a desired aim up until the point at which the domination is felt to be menacing to another. When domination is felt to be dangerous, there is a counterpull to be submissive and undo the perceived hostility of domination. Unfortunately, as this countermovement progresses, it carries the risk of humiliation and degradation as well as arousing a fear of being controlled. Accordingly, the person undoes the submission by reactivation of the aim to dominate. Instead of constant active conflict, the compulsive personality may create a structure of rituals and rules that is so entrenched that no domination or submission surfaces. Ann had not reached this level of rigidity.

In therapy relationships, as in all relationships in life, the issue remains one of control. The compulsive cannot be too dominant because then he feels that he is damaging the therapist. He also cannot be too submissive because he either feels too degraded or feels under threat of domination by the other. The struggle over control may be concealed behind a veneer of niceness, as in Ann's *artificially engaging* state. Such a veneer preserves distance and provides an insulation against the feelings of aggression or attraction, which might then lead to control struggles. Such inauthentic states as the *artificially engaging* one interfere with frank self-exploration and insight, and may prevent experimentation with new forms of intimate communication.

Important constructs for Ann were polarities between activity and passivity and between strength and weakness. These basic constructs led to four combinations in which Ann would be actively or assertively strong or weak, passively strong or weak. Furthermore, these polarizations had good or bad versions. These combinations are shown as different self-concepts in table 6.3.

TABLE 6.3

Organization of Ann's Self-Concepts by the Basic Constructs of Activity, Strength, and Valuation

Active/Passive; Strong/Weak	Good	Bad
Assertively strong	Producer	Destructively dominant
Passively strong	Preserver	Contemptuous critic
Assertively weak	Ingenue	Inadequate caretaker
Passively weak	Openly needy and close	Deflatingly submissive

Ann often externalized her own critical function of assessing good or bad. Her major control operations were directed at the avoidance of a relationship in which she would experience herself as deflatingly defective, weakly submissive, or in which she would view herself as destructively assertive. In any of these three roles she imagined herself as seen and scorned by another person in the role of a superior critic. This painful model of a relationship was developed in childhood and adolescent experiences with her father, and reactivated as she responded to his death.

Ann's father had been unable to acknowledge and accept his own weaknesses as tolerable human frailties, and had experienced his terminal illness as final proof of his defectiveness. He covered his own chronic concerns about inferiority at his institutional workplace with bluster and by openly denigrating women as "second class."

To counteract her self-concept of defectiveness, Ann attempted to stabilize a strong, assertive self-concept. She would be the one to dominate and control others. She wished to be "first class" in this way, but when she experienced herself as superior she began to feel that she was threatening her husband and developing too much of a masculine identification. Because of her fear of being too strong, she could be upset by achievements such as receiving a college degree.

In general, Ann feared strong feelings as dangerously out of control. She had feared this in her father as well, and described a hug from him as being of "rib-cracking" intensity. For Ann, spontaneous expressions of affection or annoyance were related themes, since both meant out-of-control excitement. She did not really see how people could be very close without hurting or overwhelming each other.

In her early relationship with her father, Ann wished for closeness but easily confused this with forbidden incestuous sexuality. Currently, she and her husband readily tolerated frequent physical separations, ostensibly related to their dual careers. Weeks would pass without sexual intercourse in this recent marriage, with the lack being attributed to scheduling difficulties. Once Ann caustically described her husband as having a "drooping libido," but it seemed clear that they shared rationalizations to avoid the anxieties of intimacy. Even with regard to her mother, the possibility of a new closeness after the father's death brought up fears of dangerous intimacy and of not being able to be fully self-assertive again.

Within a relationship, especially a new one, Ann scrutinized both parties for evidence of the degree of each other's worth, power, productivity, reliability, and potential destructiveness. The feared negative traits were always in the air and could be applied to either the self or the companion. When Ann experienced the negative traits as located in herself, she felt that her value was lowered and that punishment would potentially occur; these traits were so worrisome that Ann would defensively externalize them onto others.

Ann often described a three-person story line in which one person was weak and defective, one was a strong and scornful critic, and one was reasonably competent. This combination could be expressed as a threesome with any of various roles for the different family members. Ann could see her father as weak and defective, and could take the role of his scornful judge while also being critical of her own similarities to him. She sometimes repeated the role of scornful judge with her mother, as she had joined with her father in criticism of the mother as well. Separation from her disappointing parents would temporarily promote a distant sense of superiority, but this also led to anger at the loss of attachment.

DEFENSIVE ORGANIZATION OF ROLE RELATIONSHIP MODELS

Ann had a conflictual relationship with her father. Early in life she probably idealized him, but over time she became disappointed by his withdrawal and concerned over his too ready criticisms of others. Blame shifted among family members as to responsibility for evoking the father's hostile outbursts. Ann conceptualized her mother both as a quietly strong preserver of the family security and as weakly submissive to her father. Ann was not clear on whether her mother's failure to confront her father regarding his faults was due to her unempathic obliviousness or a resolute, even heroic determination to make the best of a difficult situation. At the same time, her father appeared strong, productive, and assertive, but much of his presentation had a quality of bluster to compensate for perceived inferiority. He was self-enhancing, but often at the price of the well-being and esteem of others.

Ann wanted to become independent of her father, and because of contempt for him that she warded off, she also wanted to become better than he was in terms of perceived weaknesses. She too could be strongly assertive, and when she saw herself as strong she then became worried that she had harmed her father or some substitute figure. As a defense, she could then switch to a weakened, depleted self-concept. This would be safe but contemptible.

There was potential self-criticism with regard to both the dominant and submissive stances. For example, as Ann entered a dominant role in describing her work successes and career ambitions to her husband, she immediately became worried that she was too aggressively controlling for a woman and that he would be hurt and critical. She would then rapidly reverse roles, praising her husband's work and establishing her work as second-class, just as her mother had "supported" Ann's father. However, the submissive role reminded her of the father's criticism of the mother and of her own fears of incompetence, and she had to switch to dominance.

Table 6.4 summarizes some aspects of this defensive organization. The table deals with Ann's aim of wanting to be independent and superior to her father—that is, superior to what she sometimes viewed as his weak traits.

IMPLICATIONS OF ROLE RELATIONSHIP MODELS FOR THERAPY

Ann's role relationship models constituted potential transference relationships during psychotherapy. The most important potential positive transference involved Ann in the role of a patronized daughter, with the therapist seen as an idealized parent who would replace the bad attributes of the father and thereby restore the connection to an idealized early father concept.

The most likely potential negative transference would be a recapitulation of Ann's experience of herself as a defective daughter in relation to a critical parent. These aspects of the transference are shown in table 6.5. In addition, her student-mentor relationship would probably be the one upon which she would organize a potential therapeutic alliance. The potential social alliance would be a competitive one in which there would be a low key, basically amiable struggle for superiority.

TABLE 6.4
A Conflictual Relationship Schematization for Ann

Aim:	**I want to be independent from my father.**
But I have these impediments:	
Personal deficiencies	I feel weak and defective.
Environmental deficiencies	My father is dead, leaving me no further opportunity to get him to agree to (permit) my independence.
If I get what I want, then:	
Internal positive responses	I will feel competent.
External positive responses	Others will respect and admire me as a model of how to be assertive.
If I get what I want, then:	
Internal negative responses	I will lose the hope of a close relationship with my father and I will feel selfish and guilty for hurting him.
External negative responses	Others, including my father, will see me as a selfish abandoner of him.
So I will use these coping strategies:	
Interpersonal attitudes or behaviors	When I experience too much submission, as in being a caretaker, I will strike out independently. When I feel that that is too aggressive, I will emphasize my caretaker (submissive) roles.
Intrapsychic attitudes	If I keep my accomplishments minimal and am insufficiently caring, I can prevent the danger of being either too caring or too accomplished.
Intrapsychic styles	By switching attitudes back and forth, I can avoid the threat of any one position.
And the results will be:	
Recurrent states of mind	Overcontrolled states such as *artificial and engaging* ruptured by breakthroughs of frightened yearning or of irritation at others.
Patterns of state transition	Stabilizes overcontrolled states for a long time. Experiences any emotional states of mind as dangerous or embarrassingly out-of-control.
Likely life course (accomplishments in working, relating, experiencing):	
Short-range	Inability to progress in career or in relationships with husband.
Long-range	Absence of career development or close interpersonal attachments, leading to embitterment or depression.

TABLE 6.5
Implications of Role Relationship Models for Ann's Psychotherapy

	Patient Role	Therapist Role
Potential negative transference	Defective daughter	Critical parent
Potential positive transference	Patronized daughter	Idealized parent
Potential therapeutic alliance	Earnest student	Caring mentor
Potential social alliance	Competitive competent peer	Competitive competent peer

INFORMATION PROCESSING

The Theme Predisposing to Pathological Grief. Ann's experience of her father's death dashed her hopes that she could resolve the relationship with him. She had especially hoped that he would eventually acknowledge in a proud, loving way her growing competence and independence, a theme found also in Connie's case in chapter 4. The news of his death intensified three major conflicts, which will be dealt with in sequence under these headings: the conflict between closeness and independence; the conflict between her wish for and her fear of identification with her father; and the conflict between her anger at her father and her guilt over thinking that she had harmed him.

The Theme of Conflict Between Wishes for Closeness and Wishes for Independence. Ann's loss of her father through death produced a reactive yearning to get closer to him. Yet, when she began to experience closeness to another person, she sometimes feared that she would be overly controlled by that person. In addition, Ann had to accept the fact that she and her father could never be close again, except in memory: she could not ever tell her father in some final and unambivalent way of her love. This loss was so painful that she had to defensively enter a prolonged denial, manifested as her *numb immobilization* state.

When Ann was able to contemplate that her father was really dead, a major association was to the idea that he had abandoned her prematurely. Before her father's death, Ann had been advancing steadily in her career training and personal life. She had anticipated a gradual improvement of the relationship with her father to the point of mutual esteem based on pleased recognition of her growing independence. Now that he was gone, Ann felt frightened that she might not have the ability to cope on her own. This sense of weak defectiveness conflicted with her ideal of being an assertive, independent, competent young woman. The conflict generated feelings of shame and anger, quickly avoided by her defensive use of denial, isolation, rationalization, and undoing.

The Identity Theme. One aspect of closeness or separation concerned the degree to which Ann could allow herself to experience self-concepts developed by identification with her mother or her father. She was especially frightened of being weak or defective or of viewing her father in that way. Yet, as part of the mourning process, she would have to review such concepts about one of them as weak. Instead, as at his funeral, Ann attempted to remember only strong, capable traits of her father. She set rigid, perfectionistic standards for both her father and herself. Her continued need to avoid any evidence of his shortcomings made her unable to realize that people can and do live their lives with limitations and may die before they have full productivity or achieve total success and mastery.

A particularly problematic meaning of the father's death for Ann was the confirmation that he was sick and vulnerable, a frightening recognition of his all-too-human frailty. Her enduring attitude was that she and her parents should be invulnerable and their bodies strong enough to master all threats. The father's inability to master his physical deterioration in illness made Ann feel that this weakness must be terrifying. She also believed, as part of an identifying process, that she would be unable to cope any better with bodily vulnerability than had her father. In a familiar pattern of switching from fear to anger, she asserted that the doctors could and should have rescued him and made him strong again. Ann's anger at the physicians also shifted blame away from herself. This emotion defended against guilty ideas that she had been an inadequate caretaker because she was not able to omnipotently prevent his death.

Further aspects of Ann's difficulty in evaluating her competence in relation to others were highlighted by her continuing ambivalence about career choice. She felt that in contrast to her father's choice of psychology, one of her career choices was second-class. The idea that her father had wanted her to advance was seemingly contradicted by other evidence that Ann cited: she said that both her father and her husband seemed to prefer nonthreatening women and might value the more "feminine" choice. This career choice involved being like her mother, who acted weak to make the father look strong.

When considering her alternative higher-status career training options, Ann was equally conflicted. Even when she imagined encouragement from her father for her achievements, Ann believed that she could not meet her own rigid and perfectionistic standards in the more demanding career choice.

Related to her career conflict was the thought of adopting a parental role, both identifying with her mother and hopefully replacing the father with her own baby boy. Ann felt guilty about this wish, in part because she believed that children should be wanted in their own right rather than as replacements for other people. The guilt over her potential self-ishness was handled through obsessional rumination about possible infertility. Such thoughts were both a replay of many concerns regarding somatic defectiveness and a reminder that her feminine identification was conflictual.

The Harm Theme.   For Ann, the harm theme included prominent role reversals, so that she was both aggressor and victim in terms of blaming or being blamed (see figure 6.2). One of her immediate responses to the father's death was anger at him for abandoning her, both in death and in his previous emotional unavailability. In life the father had been sniping and judgmental, and Ann now feared magical retaliation for her angry criticism of him. His death represented a failure of her caretaking actions when these were compared with her sense of omnipotent responsibility for his fate. Further, Ann knew that physical weakness and vulnerability to death would be intolerable for her father, even as they were frightening for herself.

An aspect of the harm theme was Ann's obsessional concern over the power of negative thoughts and her need to maintain perfectionistic standards of altruism. Ann feared that she had hurt her father and would have to live with her own self-blame and a fantasied angry retaliation from him. As is frequent when a parent has a chronic illness, Ann found herself occasionally wishing that her father would die in order to relieve the tension of anticipating the death and end the suffering of illness—especially since, in her own words, "he was such a lousy invalid." However, Ann knew that her father would experience death as a deprivation and felt guilty that she had not always "wished him the best." She quickly displaced her anger onto the "inept doctors" as well as denying her momentary death wish toward her father. The rapidity with which she clamped control over her thoughts did not give her sufficient time to process, revise, or accept the death wish as ordinary, nonmagical, and only part of her overall loving feelings toward him.

Ann had a related set of guilty ideas that she had been selfish by wanting to complete her career training before her father died and by not paying a complete farewell tribute to him. Her guilt was related to the enduring belief that *taking care of yourself deprives others*. An unfortunate coincidence, in which a party for Ann was followed by her father's death, reinforced her characterological tendency to feel that her own achievements were a dangerous triumph over her parents as rivals, a frequent source of work inhibition in the obsessional. Finally, the expectation that the father would be angry led to a role reversal, in which she became the one angry that the father had deprived and hurt her when she deserved more. Ann continued to shift between these roles, alternating dominant and submissive aspects of the theme or crossing back and forth to the closeness and identity themes.

Style of Coping. Ann habitually coped with threats by a strategy of heightening intellectuality and a sense of mental planning of details; meanwhile she dampened emotional excitement by deflecting from the affective heart of conflictual themes. Denial, rationalization, isolation of affect, intellectualization, and generalization were repetitive defensive patterns, to the point where they constituted a cognitive style.

An especially prominent aspect of this style was the use of rapid switching of ideational and emotional meanings within a theme, achieved by shifting concepts of the self and other. Role reversal was a major feature in these defensive operations. By switching roles and sets of ideas, Ann switched between types of emotional arousal. This meant that no one emotional system was continuously excited, because other emotional systems could be aroused to reciprocally inhibit it. Fear, guilt, and anger (as observed by Jones in 1929) were the major emotions that Ann sought to dampen through her switching and role-reversing maneuvers. In figure 6.2, these emotions are outlined in relation to the ideas comprising the harm theme.

Implications of Themes and Information-Processing Style. The probable frustration of the reader at this point with the many-layered and shifting context of the thematic material mirrors the dilemma of the therapist who works with the compulsive patient. It was difficult for Ann to work through the meanings of the three themes of closeness, identity, and harm without therapeutic help because she was unable to tolerate staying with any of the pertinent trains of thought. Focus on a given theme tended to arouse negative affects, and Ann judged such emotional experiences to be potentially out of control and harmful to her relationships and personal productivity. Instead of focusing on difficult themes after her father's death, Ann had tried to ward off feelings and devote herself to work. But she was painfully blocked in the mourning process and felt helpless to proceed.

Figure 6.2
The Harm Theme

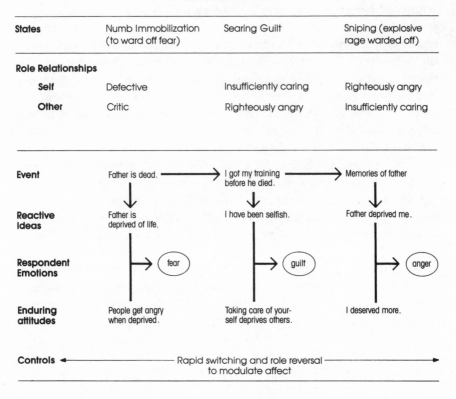

States	Numb Immobilization (to ward off fear)	Searing Guilt	Sniping (explosive rage warded off)
Role Relationships			
Self	Defective	Insufficiently caring	Righteously angry
Other	Critic	Righteously angry	Insufficiently caring

Event	Father is dead. →	I got my training before he died. →	Memories of father
Reactive Ideas	Father is deprived of life.	I have been selfish.	Father deprived me.
Respondent Emotions	→ fear	→ guilt	→ anger
Enduring attitudes	People get angry when deprived.	Taking care of yourself deprives others.	I deserved more.
Controls	◄————— Rapid switching and role reversal to modulate affect —————►		

The Process of Therapy

Ann's major motivation for therapy was to complete her grief work, if possible, without experiencing a loss of emotional control or feeling criticized. She had positive feelings about the intellectualization provided by the research process and wished to have a peer relationship with the therapist. The limited intimacy and guaranteed escape hatch of a brief therapy contract were comforting to her. She could envision a safe procrastination through detailed storytelling, and felt that in this way she could get through therapy without painful self-revelations. A major therapeutic task was to counteract Ann's defenses and help her to tolerate her negative affects so that self-revelation was not perceived to be so dangerous.

ESTABLISHING A THERAPEUTIC ALLIANCE AND A FOCUS

Ann was assigned to a therapist who was a woman just a few years older than she. Ann initially liked this match, because she was anticipating with dread an older, critical male therapist. Yet, even with a more peerlike match, Ann had to struggle for superiority and to maintain rigid emotional control through the social alliance as indicated in table 6.5.

Establishment of a therapeutic alliance required focus on potential areas of change. However, whenever Ann and the therapist agreed about the existence of maladaptive personal patterns, Ann felt that such agreement amounted to an acknowledgment of her own imperfections. If the therapist appeared too strong, Ann could view her as a critic who could demolish her fragile self-esteem; if too weak, Ann could continue intellectual rationalizations or invite the therapist to join with her in criticism of some other person rather than herself. This is a dilemma typically found with the compulsive patient where the working zone in therapy is quite narrow.

DEALING WITH RESISTANCES

Ann began the therapy with the projected expectation that the therapist either would be rejecting or would demand that she meet rigid standards to gain the therapist's esteem. Within the first hour, Ann tested to see whether she could deviate from the focus on the meanings of her father's death that had been suggested in her pre-therapy evaluation. Instead, she wished to discuss her present and future career plans. A struggle for dominance occurred in the opening minutes, as Ann responded to the therapist's inquiry about the grief process by insisting instead that the career issue was focal. The therapist relented because of the need to establish a working alliance before instituting vigorous holding maneuvers. At this point, Ann entered the *artificially engaging* state.

Once this tentative focus was established, Ann entered a *sniping* state of mind and attempted to have the therapist join her in criticism of a third party. The therapist's partial acquiescence to this safe but nonprogressive gambit led Ann to complain near the end of the first hour that the session had not been as helpful as anticipated. She then carefully observed as the therapist accepted the remark, continuing to reiterate her interest in working with Ann. Relieved that the therapist seemed both intact and nonretaliatory, Ann softened her distant manner and more submissively or pseudo-submissively asked for some parting advice.

At first the therapist apparently felt a need to proceed gingerly because of Ann's feelings of vulnerability and her dread of strong affects. The therapist seemed to partially share a defensive posture in which she and Ann agreed that Ann did not have the bad attributes of the father. The danger of Ann entering a state of *searing guilt* motivated the therapist to deliver serious statements with a light manner, both softening the intervention and transiently siding with the patient to keep Ann a safe distance away from weak self-images. At a later point, a secure therapeutic alliance permitted greater boldness in addressing negative images.

In the early sessions, when the therapist was silent Ann became uneasy and shifted toward her *artificially engaging* state. If the therapist made an interpretation in which she clarified her nonjudgmental attitude and identified Ann's fear of criticism, there seemed to be increased movement toward a *vulnerable working* state. In contrast, interpretations of Ann's style of switching from one attitude to another were experienced as critical and tended to precipitate Ann's entry into a *numb immobilization* state early in therapy, but this technique of interpreting defense was tolerable later in therapy.

For Ann, the social alliance was reinforced by the fact that her therapist was an attractive, competent, peer-aged woman. In the second session, Ann tested for the therapist's reactions to material about women being assertive. She talked in detail about the changes she had observed in her mother's behavior since her father's death. Ann compared her mother's previous behavior with her current ability to act in a stronger fashion and appear more confident now that the father was dead.

> Ann: What my mother wanted to talk about was the fact that she always appeared weak to make him look strong—and all my other brothers and sisters are extremely angry at her for allowing that to happen. I guess the girls are angry because they feel she was a lousy role model as a result; and some of the others are just as angry because they don't think she should have lowered herself to that, and somehow they dream that if she hadn't, maybe things would've gone okay.

The therapist's presentation as a comfortably assertive married woman seemed to help Ann, through modeling, to be bolder, but it also stimulated a competitive response. During the third session, Ann reported her fear that her own success would threaten her husband. Ann's difficulty in handling contradictory expectations and evaluations regarding the therapist remained an issue throughout the treatment. Ann often polarized the therapist's feared and idealized responses, and projected both onto the therapist. In the post-therapy evaluation, Ann said, "There were times when I would go home and I would think, 'She keeps up such a good front.' Then I would think to myself on one extreme, 'I bet she has a lousy life at home. She gets to keep a front and I don't.' " Ann also said, "I'll bet her life's really in control and I resent that." And, "The end result of those ideas was the worry that she has it all together and I don't, therefore she doesn't respect me."

The shifting role relationship models held by Ann gradually stabilized in a more uniform and predominantly positive pattern as the therapist established her steady trustworthiness, a unique relationship experience for Ann. Ann stated, "She was always very consistent and never seemed to be truly shocked at anything. I had to say that by near the end, you know, it took that long, that I really got the attitude that it was okay, everything I was saying was okay, and that she did respect me, because of those two little minor things: that she was always on time and that she never appeared shocked and she was always calm and consistent. But I felt sad that it took me all those twelve sessions to need to come to that conclusion because her role felt so standoffish to me."

As Ann gradually developed a trusting relationship with the therapist, the role relationship shifted from social competition of peers to that of a trusting student learning from a more experienced mentor. This was the role relationship underlying the *vulnerable working* state in her treatment, and the basis for the therapeutic alliance.

TRANSFERENCES AND COUNTERTRANSFERENCES

Obsessional patients often worry that any of their interpersonal responses might be either too soft or too tough. Therefore, potential negative transferences with the obsessional patient focus on the fact that any response by the therapist is likely to be experienced as either too tough or too soft. If one person is soft, the other must be hard, for the obsessional has difficulty in developing a role relationship model in which both persons have the same rather than the opposite quality.

Ann and the therapist struggled together to evolve a relationship in which both persons could be perceived as strong or vulnerable, independent or dependent, directive or receptive, at the same time. Issues of being rejected and defective remained primary, but Ann gradually became more tolerant of criticism, and it was experienced as focal and issue-centered. As the most positive role relationship developed—that of a caring mentor and earnest student—the working alliance continued to improve. The therapist directly interpreted the distortions inherent in Ann's projection of a negative model of a defective self and critical other; such interpretations helped Ann to experience the therapist in a more positive way. Also, when Ann, inviting criticism, was actively provocative, the therapist deliberately and manifestly remained neutral, concerned, and caring.

Ann studied the therapist's response to her provocations and appreciated the latter's stability and the professional expertness that this repetitive neutrality signaled. The therapist was firm about maintaining a focus without trying to go so far as to dominate and control the patient. Ann learned that she could tolerate closer attention to the heart of conflictual themes without becoming emotionally overheated.

Ann then wanted to see if the positive transference would be realized. In her idealized positive transference, the therapist was viewed as very emotionally close and eternally constant. Later in the therapy, Ann entered a somewhat excited *titillated* state produced by the empathic closeness that followed an accurate interpretation. There appeared to be an element of flirtation in Ann's behavior; neither patient nor therapist was ready to consider the subject. It was anticipated that maintenance of a positive transference through the rest of the sessions would be difficult because the fragile imprint of the student-mentor experience would be threatened.

As already emphasized, the most problematic negative transference occurred when Ann felt she was defective and was being criticized by a scornful judge. This response was particularly precipitated when, early in therapy, the therapist would make direct interpretations about Ann's defenses, particularly her style of switching back and forth. These interpretations of defense as resistance were experienced by Ann as what she called "character assassinations." A further extension of the negative transference occurred when Ann appraised herself as being defective because she was too demandingly needy. But, in contrast to her previous experience with her father, the therapist did not criticize her for needing and asking for care. The encouragement to be open and not frightened of expressing her needs allowed Ann to bring up new material in a safe way within the context of the therapeutic alliance.

Several crucial episodes in the therapy suggest the progression in Ann's ability to contemplate weak or defective self-images. Using her frequent tactic of mastery of a difficult issue by distancing (in the fourth session), Ann discussed an episode with her husband in which he had done poorly in providing expert-witness testimony. For the first time,

Ann and her husband were able to look at his sense of feeling defective in failing to meet his high standards for himself. This was a role reversal in which Ann identified with the therapist and wished to observe someone else experience, cope with, and master the feeling of vulnerability. Such an experience made it easier for Ann herself to be vulnerable. There was a kind of synergistic relationship between this experience with her husband and the experience Ann herself was having in treatment, where she was also beginning to let her guard down and expose feelings of vulnerability. The two experiences acted together to make it safer for Ann to view herself as having problematic traits without expecting to be attacked and humiliated. Some relevant dialogue went as follows:

> Ann: When he got up there (*when her husband got up to give his paper*), he really freaked out, and . . . apparently, anyway . . . he practically whispered the whole time—so he tells me—the audience couldn't understand him. And the reason why it was so upsetting to him was because he likes to think of himself as very articulate, and it was a huge blow to his self-concept to have that happen. (*Ann shows some recognition of the danger of damage to his perfectionistic, in-control image of himself.*) And the way in which it was so important was . . . just having him to be human, too. The way in which it really helped us was . . . just for the last month or so *I've* been so vulnerable and everything, and looking in a way bad to him, but still having him most of the time accept me. The big change is that he was terribly vulnerable, because I could see this really had a lot of significance to him, and it was really kind of surprising to him that he was willing to share it with me, and then we just talked about all sorts of things that he was scared of and I was scared of. (*Ann notes that she has encouraged her husband to be open about painful topics, as she was learning to do in therapy.*)

The therapist responded to this material:

> Therapist: So when you saw he was not fully in control, then it made it easier for you to let down some of your tight controls. (*The therapist implies that Ann has excessively regarded being in control as paramount and that some reduction in rigidity of control would be desirable. This is conveyed by a supportive*

statement indicating that Ann has already moved in this direction with her husband and found it relatively successful. Such an implication reduces the patient's sense of being criticized by the interpretation of rigidity of control as a maladaptive trait.)

The therapist focused on the defensive aspects of the exaggerated need for control rather than more directly on the warded-off feelings of defectiveness and the subjective anxiety that, without rigid control, a dangerous explosion of impulses might occur. This technique, in which the patient's defensive avoidance of feared relationship potentials is addressed prior to exploration of the underlying threats and impulses, permits safety and increases the likelihood that the patient will later relax rigid and stereotyped defensive maneuvers. This approach is to be contrasted with a front-line attack on the patient's main unconscious defenses with direct interpretation of the warded-off content. For example, a therapist's statement that "you fear you will destroy me if you express the anger you have bottled up inside you" is likely to increase rather than diminish defensiveness in the early phase of treatment, prior to firm consolidation of a therapeutic alliance.

In the fourth session, the therapist made an explicit linking interpretation comparing Ann's fear of being defective in the eyes of the therapist to her fear of being criticized by her father as well as to her father's fear of appearing defective to Ann. The therapist consistently sought to have Ann contemplate the way in which her rigid expectation of criticism colored all of her current responses. A clarification of perfectionistic, archaic standards is essential for the compulsive patient, who has difficulty in appraising the irrational demands imposed by some values.

THE THERAPIST'S CONCERN ABOUT POSSIBLE DISORGANIZATION

The most problematic countertransference issue was the therapist's early concern that Ann's obsessional defensive style might cover over a more profound vulnerability. This dilemma is frequent in brief therapy, when the limitation on time forces the therapist to move boldly and without a carefully elaborated developmental history as a guideline for identifying potential fragility of self-concept.

The therapist's tactic in mid-therapy was to be supportive but exploratory while emphasizing Ann's strengths in order to stabilize her self-esteem. The therapist repeatedly suggested, as well, that a version of "switching," i.e., choosing to think about less upsetting ideas when in danger of becoming upset by problematic themes, could be used as a deliberate, conscious coping strategy rather than an automatic unconscious defense, as discussed by Weiss (1967). Here is a sample bit of such dialogue in mid-therapy:

> Ann: The thing that I focus on more is uhm . . . namely that I'll miss him [father] so much that I won't be able to function, you know. I sometimes start thinking about things like that and I think that I can't afford to get upset, "I have to leave in five minutes for an appointment," you know. So that's what I tend to focus on.
>
> Therapist: Well, I think that you'd be able to think of him a little bit at a time and then if you felt that it started to get overwhelming you could start thinking about other things.

Ann's concern about becoming overwhelmed was addressed again later in that hour:

> Ann: Well, you know I think you're probably right, I know you're right. One of the things is, it's just hard to know how to do that . . . well, how to do that without it being a whole crisis situation where I'm completely unable to function for, say, a week.
>
> Therapist: What makes you think it would get to that extreme? (*Gently challenges the patient's exaggerated fears.*)
>
> Ann: My feelings. Just that . . . I don't know. I don't know how to do it a little bit at a time only have it be a real, well, I don't know how to do it in blocks, that would really be enough, I mean the barriers, the barriers are so much there and then if it weren't there I assume that . . . it would just be a flood. I . . . I . . . in actuality things are often time-limited. I might spend an afternoon feeling like that and then I would feel better and I . . . and that has happened sometimes, mainly more like the time when I was first coming to see you.
>
> Therapist: And so your experience in fact actually has been that when you need to, you can pull yourself back together again and go on functioning. (*Emphasizes patient's view of herself as capable of mourning without becoming overwhelmed.*)

Compulsive patients may dissect in detail the faulty behavior of others. They are also likely to provide a detailed genetic history, although the plethora of material will be curiously devoid of associated emotion. In this treatment, the therapist concluded that Ann could tolerate more incisive work and actively countered her obsessional style, holding her to contemplation of affect-laden themes and commenting on her experience of the relationship within the hour. The therapist interpreted Ann's resistance, eventually labeling her pattern of being tangential during the first part of sessions and getting down to serious business only in the latter half of sessions.

As the therapist firmly held her to topics, Ann was able to stabilize a state of *vulnerable working* and there was the emergence of a *titillated* state in which she seemed excited by the new intimacy that resulted from shared knowledge of her real capacities. Ann was then able to experience gratitude toward the therapist and express that feeling. She began to consider the possibility of more emotional openness with others. Ann actively modeled both the therapist's assertiveness and openness within her marital relationship, becoming able to enter an *assured productivity* state in which she felt competent and wise.

ROLE CHANGE EXPERIENCE

The stability of the therapeutic alliance was most severely tested with regard to Ann's fear of losing control of her anger. In the first two sessions, Ann repeatedly brought up the issue of being angry at her mother for acting weak to make the father look strong, all the while checking to see the therapist's responses. As frequently happens in early therapy sessions with a compulsive person, Ann switched away from this anger to another problematic area, and it was difficult for the therapist to focus her back. Early in therapy, the therapist was not as firmly persistent as she would be later on.

In the third session, Ann told her therapist that her father would have been threatened by her annoyance with him and most likely would respond by becoming aloof. The therapist responded with a clarifying restatement of the hostile-critical relationship pattern with her father, and said that Ann might expect the pattern to repeat itself if she were to express any annoyance with the therapist. The therapist added that this was not the case; she would not be critically reactive to or harmed by Ann's angry feelings as the father might have been. The patient brought up the idea of closeness and of aggressive closeness. She told about the rib-cracking hugs her father had given her. The therapist commented that people could be close without hurting each other.

There was a progression in Ann's understanding of this relationship theme: she risked the expression of both positive regard for the therapist and annoyance, and then found that her fantasied expectations of being hurt or ridiculed by the therapist did not come to pass. However, at termination, Ann considered skipping the last hour because it might be emotionally close and so uncomfortable. She did not act this out. The experience of the emotional safety of the therapeutic alliance permitted her to go to the session and deal with her feelings about the therapist and therapy without feeling that she was losing control.

PROCESSING OF IMPORTANT THEMES

The information-processing style of the compulsive personality poses difficulties in brief therapy. Tangentiality and overinclusion of detail make any focus fuzzy. Even the apparently cooperative patient can provide a quagmire of historical background. An ever widening chain of associations provokes inexact interpretations by the therapist. Even when a topic is selected, there is difficulty in establishing a sequential flow of ideas leading toward a decision on changing an attitude or plan. The patient's vulnerability to defective self-images and fear of strong affects are defended against by the use of switching mechanisms. The patient shifts from the emotional tone and meaning, and changes the subject, in an avoidant hopscotching pattern that serves to confusingly intertwine themes as the therapist struggles to attain a focus.

An ideal for Ann would be to allow herself conscious contemplation of a limited number of central themes, including the experience of the emotions involved, without her feeling that the emotions were out of control and without a shift to her more defective self-images. For example, on the yearning-for-closeness theme, an ideal route would be for Ann to realize that she fantasized a better relationship with her father in the future, to acknowledge his death, to accept the limited real relationship, and to mourn the longed-for but now lost idealized relationship. With the brief therapy as a catalyst for work on the developmental issues of young adulthood, Ann would then think about the idea that her father had not reached the level of social maturity that she wished for herself. She would examine her own life and, by experiencing a new kind of relationship (with the therapist), she would develop herself without setting perfectionistic standards. She would contemplate her belief that wanting to be close implied either inevitable sexual attraction or submission, and through a rational examination of this attitude, she would develop a more realistic counterbelief that closeness was possible without forbidden sexuality or loss of personal initiative.

The themes of closeness with her father versus independence, identification with her father versus a wish to be unlike him, and the fear of guilt over harming him were all unified because they related to his death. Nonetheless, it was hard to establish the focus of therapy as being the

191

meanings to her of his death. Instead, Ann initially regarded the topic of her father's death as something that the therapist wanted her to focus on, at variance with the topic of her career choices on which she wanted to focus. She viewed the onset of therapy, therefore, as a competitive struggle over whose focus would be the dominant organizer of the communication between her and the therapist.

The struggle over the focus and the complex defensive switching across themes are illustrated in this transcript from the first session.

> Ann: Uhhh . . . . (*sighs*) (*ten seconds' pause*) I have a hard time starting (*sighs*). Well . . . yesterday I was upset, and I'm only just coming down off it right now. And uhm . . . I'm real tired . . . and . . . *I don't want to be here!* Uh, and another thing that's going on is that, uhm, I'll explain it [one word inaudible], but another thing that's going on is that I have some other problems that aren't . . . that are probably related, but aren't (*note switching from "are" to "aren't"*). . . . I'm not sure how narrow this study is . . . this counseling is supposed to be. So one thing at some point that I'd like to know is . . . is . . . whether you can help me deal with my other problems or whether or not I should get a different type of counselor, 'cause these problems are career problems. (*Note switch to career issues, though the implicit contract by the very nature of the study is to focus on grief over the parent's death. Also she believes that "psychotherapist" is a higher status or more powerful position than counselor, and is seeing if the therapist will "insist" on being called "therapist."*)
>
> Therapist: Mmmhmm.
>
> Ann: But my life is not really too much divided (*laughs slightly*), but it . . . but it is a serious problem for me right now.
>
> Therapist: Well, if you feel that it's related to, uh, to the loss of your father in that everything's interconnected, then it might be appropriate to talk about it. (*The therapist tries to maintain the focus, while avoiding power struggles by permitting Ann to shift away from grief-related issues.*)
>
> Ann: (*Sighs*) I'm not sure how much I . . . I can most . . . (*sighs*) . . . somewhat. I mean, but it definitely aggravates everything, 'cause when I'm upset about career decisions I don't want to think about the others, and when I think about the others I use it as an excuse to not think about career. . . . (*Ann*

describes how she uses switching as a defense to avoid staying with problematic themes.)

Therapist: Mmmhmm.

Ann feared that if she faced the reality of her father's death in discussions with the therapist, then she would have intolerably painful affects. The therapeutic situation caused her to worry that she would have to place herself in the needy role (weak and defective self, critical other) or risk becoming absorbed in the therapy rather than pursuing her career goals, a risk analogous to the danger of being sidetracked by her father and his terminal illness. The therapist, by working to establish a therapeutic alliance, was signaling that it would be possible to agree mutually on a topic, with both persons cooperating by being independent yet jointly responsible for how the sessions proceeded.

Even after the firm establishment of a working alliance, the therapist had to struggle to keep Ann on a theme. Repetitive holding maneuvers were used to slow her switching, as can be seen from the following series of excerpts from the eighth session. After an initial discussion of appointment times, Ann stated that she had not been thinking about her father. The therapist repeated this remark, and the patient continued as follows:

Ann: Shall I tell you what I have been thinking about? I'm not sure it's related . . . (*The therapist does not respond when Ann pauses, so Ann launches into a complex series of historical and medical details relating to her concern over possible infertility. Here Ann seems to be covertly asking for active focusing by the therapist, a tactic that appears to be appropriate by the eighth session, when themes and information-processing style are well known. After about ten minutes, the therapist attempts to intervene, speaking with some exasperation, and also shifting the focus of discussion away from what the patient actually said initially, a deflection commonly provoked by the obscurities of the compulsive style.)*

Therapist: You prefaced this story by saying maybe this is somehow related to your feelings about your father or about your mother.

Ann: No, I said I'm not sure it is. What I'm saying is I've been thinking about this all week, and . . . and . . . it's really crowded out any other thoughts, except for one thought that I had last night. And that is to go to this clinic. They might insist that I be trying to get pregnant now. And the thing is, I don't really want to try now, so I have this decision.

(After about five minutes of Ann's rumination over possible outcomes, the therapist intervenes again, even more firmly.)

Therapist: What do you make of the timing of this, that at a time when you're not thinking about your parents, you've suddenly started thinking about the possibility of becoming a parent?

Ann: Well, that's the other thing I was thinking about last night (*Ann signals acquiescence, but gets increasingly tangential*), gee, how could I, if I got pregnant at really the wrong time, then I'd probably want an abortion, and the odd thing about that would be, several odd things, one would be here I'd be going to an infertility clinic, and then I'd be wanting an abortion.

Ann then continued with a rambling discussion of the problems of abortion, saying that wanting a child was somehow a "deception." She associated to the fact that her sister had not named her new baby boy after the deceased father. The therapist now repeated the interpretation made earlier, trying to maintain a focus on reactions to the death of Ann's father.

Therapist: And then again, I wonder if the timing of your interest right now, the prospect of your becoming a mother and your husband becoming a father, is linked to the recent loss of your father.

Ann: Well, it isn't (*now disavows interpretation*). I mean, when he died it wasn't something that I wanted right away, uhm . . . it's hard to say. Another thing (*switches*) is that even now I have a keen interest in knowing what the statistical chance is. . . . . But I feel really uncomfortable about the idea of getting pregnant, and uhm . . . (*At this point she pauses, probably in response to the therapist's effort to keep her focused on the implications of her father's death, as she continues on that topic.*) But when I do think about that whole business, I do think about him. How good it feels to be able to feel like you're carrying on something, you're replacing something. (*She tentatively takes as her own the therapist's view of her recent motivation to have a child.*) And that is one of the reasons why it makes me think that a pregnancy could come out of what I would call a perverse sort of deceptive situation. (*"Deception" refers to both her substitution of a baby for her father and her substitution of a focus on pregnancy for contemplation of the loss of her father.*)

In the face of the therapist's persistent holding operations, Ann continued to more clearly link her concern about infertility to a worry that she selfishly wanted a child in order to replace her father, and to replace him symbolically instead of and rather than mourning his loss. In the initial struggle over a focus, Ann wished to use the topic of career choice in opposition to the therapist's intention to focus on the meanings of the father's death. As is often true with the compulsive personality, the oppositional stance contained kernels of thematic material that had general significance but were not immediately relevant to the deepening exploration of the paramount theme. The patient was not countering the therapist with "nothing," but usually with an important "something." The choice of a career was an aspect of the closeness versus independence theme. When the therapist brought up the topic of the father, Ann felt a sense of danger: she not only feared too much closeness but wanted to avoid the frightened yearning associated with her father now that he was dead. The wish to focus on the career theme (which included the issue of career versus or with motherhood) was part of her aim to become independent from her father. This included a wish to separate without mourning, by not thinking of the father's death.

Because the switching of topics was an important defensive maneuver, it was difficult for the therapist to be clear early in the therapy regarding which themes were central. By following the patterns of defensive flight from particular issues to other issues or to subfacets of the same one, the therapist was gradually able to develop a sense of what would be an appropriate major focus. By mid-therapy this focus was the closeness versus independence theme.

Once the therapist had decided on the closeness theme as a focus, she began to hold Ann to that theme when she tended to switch away from it. At times the therapist directly interpreted the defensive switching. Ann experienced this as criticism. However, when the therapist first stabilized the patient's positive self-image, by stating that Ann had good feelings toward the father, or emphasizing her competence in being able to take care of other persons as well as herself, *then* Ann showed an ability to stay with the closeness versus independence theme for a longer time.

Within her current relationship, Ann was struggling with the same closeness and independence issues. She wished to be close to her husband, but he was impatient with her neediness and emphasized independence. Ann's mother was now needy herself, and closeness with her carried the perceived risk of great responsibility. Ann had inhibited concepts that might lead to the *frightened yearning* state, but the reality distortion required by her denial that her father had died was worrisome. Ann turned to a brief therapy as a place to work on these issues without feeling frighteningly close to or dependent on the therapist. (The time-limited contract, when focused treatment is indicated, is helpful to the compulsive patient as a protection against the regressive dependence that would become a major transference issue in extended treatment. However, the briefness of the treatment can also be used as a rationale for limited emotional engagement and therefore may promote a truncated, intellectualized experience.)

In the early therapy (Sessions 1–4), Ann tested the therapist to discern her attitudes about closeness and dependence as the therapeutic alliance was established. In Session 1, after the therapist specifically said that it was all right to have the wish to be close, Ann switched and displayed her opposite wish in a way that could have provoked criticism from the therapist.

> Ann: I'm not a caretaking person. I enjoy being productive. I enjoy looking at a problem and looking at the factors and independently being able to make a solution and acting on it. . . . I've never taken care of people in my life. I never want to, at this rate!

By mid-therapy (Sessions 5–8) Ann was able to reintroduce her compulsive perception of exaggerated responsibility. She was attempting to master this concern over responsibility by being able to be supportive to her mother while setting some limits. Ann had an ideal for herself in which she and her mother could be helpful to each other, meeting both of their needs through the supportive aspect of their relationship. However, Ann feared that if she allowed her mother to meet some of her needs, she would be dragged back into a childlike, infantile-dependent position and would lose her sense of autonomy. Ann, during a session, said, "It worries me, not that I feel dependent now, but it worries me that just being close to her [the mother], if there's any possibility of going backwards. I don't think that complete separateness is most mature; what's mature is to have a good, close friendship, but to maintain enough of a separate identity and to be able to do things separately as well as together. But you know, I feel almost overwhelmed by the responsibility."

For the compulsive patient, the therapeutic modeling of a particular behavior may be as effective as a more intellectual interpretation. Such modeling allows the patient to study and identify with the therapist's behavior, eliminating the threat of humiliation or submission, a potential danger with interpretations that may lead to intellectualizations. The therapist was able to allow Ann to be needy and not to make her feel ashamed or guilty about this, and at the same time did not foster a relationship in which Ann would give up her sense of independence in order to be cared for by the therapist. As a result of thinking about this theme, Ann decided on a clear plan. She tried to regulate the degrees of closeness and of responsibility for her mother, rather than abandon the mother altogether or rush in and feel she was totally responsible.

By Session 7, Ann had generalized her experience of safety with the therapist by talking to her close friend about her father's death. The fact that the friend was not upset by this news, up to now withheld from her by Ann, was very reassuring. In the eighth session, Ann told the therapist that she was beginning to feel she could handle feelings about her father's death without being overwhelmed by emotions. As Ann considered the degree of attachment between people and the responsibility of one person for another, she was also able to realize more clearly that she resented her mother's dependency on her. She reviewed the issue of her degree of responsibility for rescuing her father and, with the therapist's repetitive factual questioning, became able to differentiate reality from fantasy in realizing that overall she had not *behaved* badly during his illness, even though she had had selfish *thoughts* at times.

In the treatment, Ann scrutinized the therapist as a potential alternate role model in contrast to her parents. The therapist encouraged exploration of Ann's doubts about her future career. The fear of identification with each parent was interpreted and related to her ambivalence. The emphasis was on Ann's fear of being flawed like her father if she tried to take on too much, or of being too limited like her mother if she took on too little. There was evidence pointing to the theme of Ann's fear of identification with her father, but the therapist did not select that theme as a major focus. It was dealt with occasionally in connection with specific traits in herself and in her father, as Ann and the therapist explored the general issue of her ambivalent reactions to his death. In this way, there was some processing with regard to the fear-of-identification theme.

Compulsive patients frequently have an almost magical fear of the consequences of expressing anger. They may require the repetition and security of a long-term therapy to fully work through ambivalence involving aggressive themes. In the case of Ann, work on ambivalence was necessary in order to deal with the ideas that she had deprived her father or he had deprived her.

In the following excerpt, Ann expresses ambivalence toward the therapist whom she resents for being in a position which is emotionally more protected than Ann's.

> Ann: I was about to say that one thing that's . . . well, one thing that's bothered me is just that because of the nature of my coming here, that I make myself more vulnerable than you do, and . . . that doesn't encourage me to feel quite so affectionate. I mean, it's not much . . . as much a suffering-through-together feeling. (*Ann is hinting that she feels something other than affection. The hint is that she feels something in reaction to being in an uncomfortable vulnerable position in relation to the therapist. She may feel reactively angry. The therapist picks up on the vulnerable stance and emphasizes it in what follows.*)
>
> Therapist: You feel vulnerable?
>
> Ann: And sometimes . . . and sometimes *angry* that you don't have to put yourself in the same situation. (*Ann has more boldly stated the feelings she was only hinting at earlier, in order to clarify issues for both herself and her therapist. It might be more useful at this point to have asked Ann if she could go on and say more about this anger, but possibly the therapist already knows that Ann will not do so in response to such a statement. Instead, the therapist tries to clarify and show empathic recognition of the anger, and indicate that she is not critical or guilt-provoking in response to its expression.*)
>
> Therapist: So it sounds like you're saying that you're feeling both close to me and angry at me for the same reason—that I'm not overwhelmed. And that makes me a safe person, and that makes it safe to feel close and talk about those feelings. Yet at the same time, you feel it's easy for me to be calm because I'm not suffering as much as you are.

Later in the hour, Ann showed that the working through of the harm theme was incomplete by commenting that the therapist might be able to handle Ann's anger but that others would not. The therapist stated that she was not unique; Ann acquiesced, but switched to discussing her husband's discomfort with her career success.

This switch from discussing anger as it related to the therapist to issues of hurting her husband by her career success is a typical one. The shift of subject served to reduce the intensity of currently experienced emotions. The outside relationship between Ann and her husband can be discussed more dispassionately. Concentration on such a subject is sometimes useful in order to identify the attitudes that distort perceptions of interpersonal relationships. But once such a clarification occurs, it is useful to bring the matter back into the therapy situation. This may involve a major focusing effort if the patient is reticent and has been switching away to an outside relationship more as a defensive maneuver than as an exploratory one.

Midway through the discussion of anger and harm themes in this hour, Ann seemed to experience a fear that her father would angrily retaliate for harm she had done to him by pursuing her own career with relative success. At the moment that she had seemed to be experiencing these emotion-laden ideas more vividly than earlier, she abruptly reversed roles and began taking a kind of therapist-like stance in which she described her husband's problems of inadequately working through his relationship to his own father. The therapist did not clearly interpret the defensive shift and the degree of Ann's own concerns about envy, jealousy, and rage. Nonetheless, by the end of the hour, in spite of the lack of comfort of both parties in contemplating the harm theme, Ann had an increased sense of safety. She said, "You know, it's really funny. The first time I came in this room (*depersonalizes the therapist to avoid critical retaliation*) it seemed to have all these dark colors . . . somber, dangerous colors . . . and now it's sort of like I know the room well."

As with the identification component, the harm theme, an aspect of the relationship with Ann's father, was not dealt with by persistent and direct interpretation. Nonetheless, there was work on it, sometimes in displaced and sometimes in direct communicative form. In the relationship itself, there was a repetitive transaction in which the patient tested the therapist to see whether the latter would respond to Ann's competitive strivings with some kind of retaliation. The therapist repeatedly indicated that there would not be criticism or rejection. Even when there was minor leakage of exasperation or a small amount of sarcasm, the therapist would counteract these countertransference lapses by clarification and compassionate acceptance. The therapist's ability to respond evenly in a noncritical manner over time defused much of the intensity of Ann's fears of potential harm, even though she had difficulty in clearly present-ing her warded-off self-images of being dangerously selfish or righteously angry.

Outcome

Ann was seen in two follow-up evaluations, four months and thirteen months after her therapy. Each time she seemed more carefully groomed and had a more feminine, sprightly appearance. She openly expressed strong pangs of emotion when discussing her father's death without signs of defensiveness. She felt able to consider both good and bad as-pects of her father without overidentifying with him, but her repetitive switching in this area suggested continued discomfort with ambivalent feelings.

Ann had grown closer to her mother and was proud of being helpful to her in a recent medical emergency, a successful reworking of her failure to save the father. Ann now advised her mother about dating and sexual-ity, using a role reversal reminiscent of her efforts to counsel her husband during treatment.

Communication with Ann's husband had improved as she became more able to see him as "human and insecure." She had shifted to de-scribing her career choice as "a means to an end," deferring to her hus-band's geographical choice and focusing on child rearing. These changes underlined Ann's growing identification with her mother.

MODIFICATION OF STATES

In the period during and after the therapy, Ann had achieved better state stabilization so that she was able to spend a longer time in *working* states in which she could contemplate the many meanings of her father's death. On the first anniversary of the father's death, Ann offered empathic support to her mother. Once again she seemed to have incorporated the therapist role, and now Ann was able to advocate emotional openness to her mother without the avoidance that had been evident earlier.

> Ann: We talked to each other on that date, and she said how she'd had several social engagements she could have gone to but she turned them all down. She isn't sure why or if she should have, but she did. So she's all alone and a little

> bit depressed, and I said well, that I thought that maybe that it was better to have turned things down than to have filled her day so much that she didn't have a chance to think about him.
>
> Evaluator: So it was difficult for you to share her sadness, but you stayed with it.
>
> Ann: Yes.
>
> Evaluator: I have more of a sense that you let feelings come now without having to be uncomfortable about strong waves of emotion.
>
> Ann: That's because they don't go past what's acceptable.

Dealing with anger remained a problem for Ann, and she was apt to withdraw to avoid entry into an *explosive rage* state. In particular, she experienced some anger toward her siblings, but felt that she had to inhibit these sentiments in her mother's presence because the mother so strongly wanted all of the children to get along. At work she was very annoyed by the attitudes of superiors but did not manifest her feelings in any self-impairing ways.

In summary, Ann was less vulnerable to undermodulated states and experienced her continuing grief in a *vulnerable working* rather than *numb immobilization* state. Anger was still perceived as potentially dangerously close to an *explosive rage* state, and Ann's need for overcontrol probably inhibited her ability to be appropriately assertive as part of an *assured productivity* state. Her powerful sense of self as "saving" her mother and her claim that she now felt "120 times better" than prior to the onset of therapy suggested that she had entered an *elated* state. The use of excessive controls was most clear when Ann discussed her sexuality, at which time she tended to enter the *artificially engaging* state. In general, there was a reduction in undermodulated states and increased emotional richness within modulated states. Ann still used overcontrolled states prominently when under stress.

ALTERATIONS IN SELF-CONCEPT AND ROLE RELATIONSHIPS

There was a change in terms of the relative predominance of self-concepts and role relationship models within Ann's preexisting repertoire. The major change was from weaker to stronger self-concepts in terms of which available schemata were most active in organizing states of mind. As shown earlier in table 6.3 (p. 174), eight self-concepts could be organized by Ann's principal constructs of goodness and badness, assertiveness and passivity, strength and weakness. Her father's death, while creating conflicts along all these dimensions, tended to heighten her tendency to feel weak, passive, and bad. Her efforts to focus on career choices during the therapy were part of an attempt to counteract a negative self-concept by feeling, with the help of the therapist, more active, stronger, and "good." In the follow-up sessions, Ann indicated that she was not emphasizing her career development but instead was attempting to work on her relationships with her husband and with her mother. She was helping her mother during the mother's own distress, and so was stabilizing a competent self-image as a caretaker. Ann had also come to identify with her mother's earlier and familiar role of being a passively strong caretaker. This shift was made possible in part by the mourning work, in which she was less preoccupied with the idea that she, after the death of her father, was now too needy (passively weak) or had been an inadequate caretaker (an active but weak person).

There was also circumscribed modification of Ann's feeling of being dangerously active vis-à-vis her father. She was increasingly able to differentiate real from fantasied consequences of their mutual hostilities. These insights did not generalize well with regard to Ann's current relationships, in terms of enabling her to be more comfortably self-assertive. However, she was less prone to the self-image of being a dangerous and blameworthy aggressor.

INFORMATION PROCESSING

Ann had not radically changed her habitual cognitive style but was able to specifically modify it in order to more fully contemplate the meanings of her father's death. There had been a learning process in which she had taken more risks and found herself successful in expressing negative emotions. She could also encourage her husband to express his doubts and worries without becoming too defensive. Ann's sadness about her father's death was experienced as tolerable, so she no longer had to switch from or deny themes regarding sadness as she did with regard to her ambivalence over anger. Ann's continuing fear of imperfection and criticism seemed reflected now in her concern over the "normalcy" of her reproductive functions.

> Ann: I was really having an emotional crisis about not ovulating, and it was too bad I had to focus just on that. But it was sort of like I didn't like the word "sterile." In fact, I don't like the word "infertility." I used to tell my husband "I'm going to the fertility clinic," 'cause that's the goal.

Evaluator: You were worried about having something wrong with you.

Ann: Especially that one, and to not have known it all that time, to not be normal.

The need to be perfectly functioning and in control was repeated in the experience of therapy, as Ann described how she both had feared exposure as defective and was competitively threatened by the therapist's modeling of a high, desirable standard of behavior. In the following dialogue, Ann described her struggle with the negative transference expectation that the therapist might attack her at any moment.

Evaluator: Did you have special feelings about her as a therapist?

Ann: Oh, yeah. As time went on, she was so consistent, that towards the end was the worry that she has it all together and I don't. Therefore, she doesn't respect me. That was the thing that was really behind it all. Obviously we couldn't spend all our time commiserating together, but still I felt it was just a little on the extreme side for my needs. The question of respect . . . I mean, there were times when I was late, and really the reasons why I was late a lot of the time were real good. But she was always on time and she was always very consistent and never seemed to be truly shocked at anything I had to say. So that, by about near the end, you know, it took that long, that I really got the attitude that it was okay. Everything I was saying was okay, and that she did respect me because of these two little minor things. She was always on time and she never appeared shocked and she was always calm and consistent. I felt sad that it took me all those twelve sessions to come to that conclusion.

Evaluator: And somehow what looked like perfection on her part made you feel less perfect, then. Is that right? Somehow, in contrast.

Ann: Well, absolutely. After all, one person in those sessions, you know, really pouring it out and falling apart, as far as I'm concerned, and not having her to have to do anything on that side.

FOLLOW-UP SCALES

The scale data at follow-up reflected the clinical picture of steady improvement with some residual symptomatic areas. On self-report, Ann noted a decline in both intrusive and avoidant symptomatology related to the father's death on the Impact of Event Scale (Horowitz, Wilner, and Alvarez 1979). By the second follow-up, she was experiencing only mildly intrusive thoughts of the father with some disturbing imagery, and had no avoidant symptoms. Her overall score on the Hopkins Symptom Checklist was now within the normal range. Anxiety and depression, as well as anger and obsessive-compulsive thoughts, had also diminished to asymptomatic levels. Ann indicated 80 percent adjustment to her father's death, and the evaluator gave her a much higher global adjustment rating score than at entry. Between the first and second follow-ups there was only slight further improvement, since symptoms were already at a minimal level at the first follow-up. This suggested that Ann was maintaining the improvement that she had gained during the period of therapy and immediately afterward.

This rapid change in self-reported symptoms was reflected by clinical judgments made after review of pre- and post-therapy evaluation interviews. The evaluators used rating scales for Patterns of Individual Change. In most of these scales Ann was rated as more symptomatic than the average patient in the series, and at follow-up she was rated as less symptomatic than average for patients in the series. The most marked change was found on scales that indicated pathological grief and her course toward resolution of it. Both self-report and clinician ratings as well as our review indicated that Ann had an excellent response in terms of working through her father's death.

The Patterns of Individual Change Scale for this representative patient is shown in figure 6.3. There was improvement noted on the various scale points, the most prominent (beyond the reduction of symptoms) being Ann's improved ability to relate to her mother, the surviving parent; her increased use of supports; and her increased capacity for intimacy with her husband. Work identity, assertiveness, and self-esteem, all of which reflected Ann's thematic concern of being second-class in the therapy, showed positive but less robust change.

Figure 6.3
The Pattern of Change: The Case of Ann

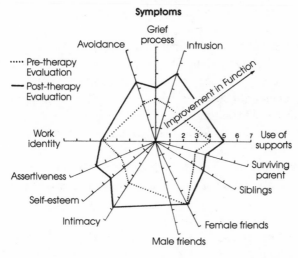

Conclusion

Ann had presented a dilemma for the therapist that is frequent in work-ing with persons having a compulsive character structure: her rigid style and avoidant defenses concealed a considerable degree of vulnerability to deflation of self-esteem. In such a situation, the therapist must broach the patterns of switching topics by consistently holding to a focus but avoid-ing humiliation or intellectualization. The usual competitive struggle for dominance between the compulsive patient and the therapist was modi-fied by Ann's fear of the other as a scornful critic. Early clear identifica-tion of this role relationship model was essential for progress in working through major themes. By actions as much as words, the therapist pro-duced a climate of safety in which Ann could turn to considering the painful loss. Ann's continuing discomfort with ambivalence promoted a marked alternation of self-images in which self and/or other could be viewed as good or bad, weak or strong. Negative self-images threatened

205

to precipitate undermodulated states, and the characteristic defensive switching maneuvers made the process of therapy tedious.

Within the context of a brief therapy focused on a loss, aspects of Ann's character continued to be prominent if less problematic. Her difficulty in balancing appropriate assertiveness versus threatening anger and her fear of intimacy suggested that a longer therapy oriented toward broad-based characterological change would be helpful in the future. Such a referral would now be more possible because Ann had felt successful in this therapy and had not been criticized or pushed to a level of feeling out of control. Within the therapy experience, she had mastered the sadness and anger about her father's death, as well as terminating the treatment without becoming too dependent. In the follow-up evaluation, Ann acknowledged the centrality of the grief work and indicated that the brief therapy had had the catalytic function of helping her to approach developmental issues.

> Ann: Well, it seems . . . seems so incredible that I could feel in such a good place. I mean, I was in such a bad way on numerous issues at the beginning of the year. I was really torn up about my father, hated school, didn't know what I wanted to do with my future, and then the infertility thing came up near the end and I was torn up about that.
>
> Evaluator: So coming back for evaluation has allowed you to take stock of yourself, then, in terms of what's changed.
>
> Ann: Yeah. Although I knew by the end of the sessions that the question of my father was somewhat pulled together, I just had to prove it by working on it on my own after therapy. On the school issues I felt better, and over the summer I just felt better and better because I just have the sense that if I have a kid, great, and if I don't have a kid, that'll make me sad, but I'm so active that I can just see myself doing a lot of other things.

The compulsive personality trait of avoiding failure by procrastination and ambivalence generally continues to be an issue in Ann's life. However, the crisis of pathological grief was past, and Ann had used the novel experience of therapy to adopt a more hopeful and flexible approach to her future.

7

THE NARCISSISTIC
PERSONALITY

T HIS CHAPTER will focus on a character style in which vulnerability to deflation in self-esteem, with a compensatory trend to display superiority, represents a key set of traits. An important intrapsychic component of the style is protection of self-esteem through
manipulation of the meaning of actual events.

Diagnosis

In defining narcissistic personality disorders, *DSM-III* describes an individual who has:

... a grandiose sense of self-importance or uniqueness; preoccupation with
fantasies of unlimited success; exhibitionistic need for constant attention and admiration; characteristic responses to threats to self-esteem; and characteristic disturbances in interpersonal relationships, such as feelings of entitlement, interpersonal exploitativeness, relationships that alternate between the extremes of
overidealization and devaluation, and lack of empathy.

The exaggerated sense of self-importance may be manifested as extreme self-
centeredness and self-absorption. Abilities and achievements tend to be unrealistically overestimated. Frequently the sense of self-importance alternates with
feelings of special unworthiness. For example, a student who ordinarily expects

207

an A and receives an A-minus may at that moment express the view that he or she, more than any other student, is revealed to all as a failure. (*DSM-III*, 1980, p. 315)

The therapist will find elements of this *DSM-III* description in the patient's response to observations communicated to him by the therapist during psychotherapy. For example, the therapist may tell the patient about a change in attitude noted in the patient during the course of therapy. This comment may be intended to sharpen insight about positive changes, provide realistic encouragement, promote reflection by the patient, and communicate recognition of the progress being made. But the patient may hear the remark as implying that "your grade is A-minus," an indication that the patient is not yet perfect and was not always perfect in the past. Instead of bolstering self-esteem, the therapist's action may evoke an angry response.

Features of entitlement, excessive expectations, disregard for the integrity of others, and a low level of positive regard for others (except during times of idealization) mean that there may be less than the usual gratification for the therapist in treating this type of patient. Rationalization and outright lying, as well as the faking of feelings in order to impress others, are likely to occur in therapy and may impede the therapeutic work. There may be unrealistic goals regarding what the therapist can provide, as well as unrealistic goals established for the self (Kernberg 1975; Kohut 1977; Ornstein 1978). There is almost always a lack of planning—that is, step-by-step skills are not acquired—in relation to achievement of the unrealistic goals. These characteristics of the narcissistic personality will be illustrated in the case material of this chapter.

Observing Patterns Characteristic of the Narcissistic Personality Style

During the flow of expressed thought and emotion on a given theme, a narcissistic patient often distorts information that might damage his or her self-concept if it were communicated realistically. This type of distortion is often accomplished through a "sliding of meanings" (Horowitz 1975), in which information that enhances the self is exaggerated, and information that might reflect poorly on the self is minimized. Similarly, people, institutions, or ideals that foster a positive self-image may be protected by idealization or exaggeration. Those that insult the self are blamed or denigrated by minimization of their good attributes and by contempt for their bad ones.

Sliding of meanings recurs from theme to theme. Since the distortions are sometimes conspicuously self-serving, the patient conveys a sense of being unusually self-centered or acting as if he or she were especially "entitled." To make matters a bit more complex, the grandiose overestimation may be cloaked in pseudo-humility, which may have a cloying impact on a listener. Note here the layering effect of inferiority, masked by grandiosity, cloaked by the appearance of humility.

Despite the clinician's efforts to secure a well-rounded picture, the patient avoids certain themes to prevent confrontation with the self-deflating meaning of his actions. If and when such themes are expressed, a conspicuous variability in demeanor may be observed, as the patient displays great sensitivity to loss of self-esteem. Signs of shame may be observed, with compensatory bluster aimed at covering defectiveness. If the clinician probes for information in sensitive areas, deflated or enraged states may suddenly emerge. Short of such occurrences, the patient may display charm or vivacity to win over the therapist, or to show his poised superiority and lack of need for the therapist.

Narcissistic patients may have a long history of a lack of empathically intimate relationships (Kohut 1971, 1977). Instead, they use others for particular purposes and then discard them. They avoid criticism of themselves by goading others to criticize them unfairly. They then become self-righteous, enraged, or remote, and fracture the relationship. For such reasons, narcissistic patients tend to have an unstable network of social supports. This problem predisposes them to a vicious cycle in times of strain. As they become more needy, they feel more threatened, display regressive behavior, alienate others, feel more strained, regress further into selfish preoccupation, and damage their already tenuous support system.

Typical Problems for the Therapist

In contrast to narcissistic patients, those with less narcissistic vulnerability tend to enter therapy with some trust in the therapist, and with a capacity to establish what Kernberg (1976) has called "mature dependency." They recognize and present their need for the therapist to act as a catalyst in accomplishing the goals of therapy. This differs from "immature dependency," where patients expect the therapist to assume the role of parent and rescue them from distress.

The narcissistic patient has conflicts about dependency and tends both to experience and to disavow "immature dependency" (Kernberg 1976). If confronted by his dependency needs, even those of a "mature" variety that are appropriate to the strain he is currently under, the patient may feel rage or even envy. This hostility is directed toward the therapist as caretaker, and is often mixed with sadness and shame at harboring such irrational responses. To avoid this dilemma, the patient pretends to have no need, devalues his potential helper, and guards against displaying neediness, strain, or irritation.

Alternatively, the patient may attempt flight into a "restorative fantasy" based on his interaction with the newly met therapist. By fantasizing a combination of himself and this new, idealized person, the patient restores the ideal self-concept that became lost during the evolution of the symptoms that motivated him to seek help (Goldberg 1973). This may restore morale and allow the patient to discuss recent disappointments. On the other hand, the patient also may become demanding, to prove how very special he is and to assert his difference from "ordinary patients." When the therapist follows usual procedures such as exploring problems, this sense of special entitlement may be jeopardized. The patient may then retaliate by premature termination or by an attempt to triumph over or depreciate the therapist's efforts, theories, and techniques.

These patterns may coexist—that is, the patient may use dissociative mechanisms so that he simultaneously but separately views an action by the therapist *both* as a sign of idealized status *and* as a sign of his defectiveness. For example, when the therapist maintains a "ground rule" for therapy in the face of the patient's demand for special status, the patient may interpret this action on the one hand as a sign of the therapist's sturdy, ethical reliability, and on the other as proof that the therapist is critical, rejecting, unempathic, and selfish. These dual attitudes may be accessible to consciousness and communicated to the therapist, but the patient does not recognize their incompatibility.

Tactics in Therapy

Because of the extreme vulnerability of such patients, the therapist must focus unusual degrees of attention on both tact and timing. In general, the pace of therapy seems slower than usual to the therapist, and very firm, persistent confrontations are sometimes necessary. The therapist may gradually approach the confrontation and, when it actually occurs, may need to be quite firm. Thereafter, the therapist may have to patiently repeat and review what was meant and what was not meant.

Usually it is helpful to counteract probable exaggerations and minimizations by reexamining the detailed sequence of events in a transaction. Tact involves not forcing the patient into a corner so that he might have to lie. The therapist may allow room for changes in the report of the event during a reconstruction, rather than pinning the patient down. During such retelling of a memory, the patient will often focus on evaluating who was responsible, in the sense of who was to blame for each aspect of the chain of events. Such constant blame appraisal may be interpreted as a general preoccupation. The therapist may then try to help the patient to modify his distortions in the attribution of blame.

Repetition of the story, or its events, needs to be done patiently, without creating either a classroom "evaluation" atmosphere or boredom. This tactfulness requires close attention to the optimal degree of confrontation, nuance of delivery, and timing in the sense that any challenges to the patient are made in a palatable context. Such therapeutic work is difficult because these patients usually provoke countertransference reactions such as self-protectiveness, anger, contempt, sarcasm, or boredom.

The therapist faces a dilemma with respect to the type of relationship that is established with the patient. On one horn of the dilemma, the patient is frightened of and expecting criticism from the therapist. Revelation of problems will quickly seem like an exposure of the patient's bad attributes. The patient expects withdrawal of interest, criticism, or even persecution by the therapist. His natural response is to reduce exposure of his problematic traits.

The other horn of the dilemma is one in which the patient fears he will present such a good picture that the therapist will be fooled into not focusing on maladaptive or pathological themes. This is dangerous to the patient because he then feels that he cannot get help because the therapist is not capable of understanding him through his facade.

This two-horned dilemma is present in nearly all psychotherapy pa-

211

tients. In less narcissistically vulnerable patients, there is a middle zone for safe work within which the patient can present problems. With the narcissistically vulnerable patient, there is less of a safe or "tolerably anxious" zone for therapeutic work. Such a patient is both in danger of fooling the therapist (and so feeling misunderstood) and in danger of informing the therapist (then feeling ashamed). Awareness of both dangers is advisable for the therapist in working through this dilemma.

Harold, a Representative Case

PRESENT COMPLAINTS

Harold was a twenty-five-year-old single man when he sought psychotherapy. Six months earlier his mother had died. Before the first evaluation interview he had experienced a gradual increase in feelings of frustration, depression, and loneliness, as well as an increase in impulsive and self-impairing actions.

Harold was an only child. He had social contacts but few close relationships other than that with an aunt. He had difficulty at work, and viewed his future as bleak. He had major career goals but had impairing lulls in his efforts to train himself to meet them. This experience led to listless periods in which he felt dull and despondent. All of these problems were present before the death of his mother, and had intensified following the loss of her support. Yet, Harold had remained aloof from the idea of seeking psychotherapy. It was only because of insistent urging by his aunt, who had benefited from psychotherapy earlier in her own life, that he agreed to a brief therapy.

He presented himself at the evaluation interview in a poised, graceful manner. However, in spite of his attractive appearance, he nonetheless had a "chip on the shoulder" quality. He presented his complaints but depreciated their importance.

BACKGROUND

During the evaluation interview, Harold described the death of his mother, the latest in a series of stressful life events, as "the proverbial straw that broke the camel's back." These events included the much earlier death of his father in childhood, difficulties with superiors during a recent period of voluntary military service, and troubles with a girlfriend. Feelings of low self-esteem and emptiness were episodic. It appeared as though, in losing his mother, he had lost his major and perhaps sole source of unconditional support and approval. He said:

I know Mom gave me some of this feeling of being able to do things, being able to accomplish whatever, and I know with her illness and death a lot of that disappeared. All of a sudden I was put into a situation where, instead of Mom always being there to go to and talk to, boom, she wasn't. At the time of Mom's death I feel that I did not get one-hundredth of the moral and emotional support that I wanted and needed from my girlfriend. Most of the friends I had in the military are elsewhere, and the ones here are more just acquaintances and so I can't say I have any friends to talk to about it either.

Due to turbulence in the marriage of his parents and then his father's unexpected death in an automobile accident, Harold had painful but vague memories of his childhood years. He was very close to his mother, but there were ambivalent and remote periods with his father, toward whom he had often been rebellious. In adolescence he began to boldly seek out thrills (and danger) in order to counteract feelings of being dull or useless. In contrast to angry exchanges between Harold and his father, his mother tended to be more forgiving and continuously supportive, finding rationalizations for Harold's disruptive behavior. Sometimes she indulged him with gifts and increased permissiveness.

When Harold left home for college and then a period in the military, his mother pursued her own career. Harold courted his present girlfriend and they had a turbulent relationship, with separations, for several years. Recently, his mother had become ill and had died within a few months.

The period of his mother's illness began with Harold visiting her frequently. He felt helpless and his visits became infrequent. He began to regret his withdrawal, and, at the time when he sought to make amends, she died. His relationship with his girlfriend, already deteriorating, floundered after his mother's death. He turned for support to his aunt and felt that she was sometimes helpful, but also was sometimes too critical and made too many demands that he change his behavior patterns (which she said were too self-centered and demanding).

Harold enrolled in college and then dropped out to get special technical training on a "deal" with the military. He worked his way up in the ranks but had some trouble with superiors. Upon discharge he returned to college and again dropped out of several courses, at about the time therapy began, because of his own failure to keep up with the course requirements. He supported himself by night work as an advanced mechanic. His goals at school, described during therapy, were to prepare for a career in forestry management, specializing in fighting forest fires. This career choice indicated his preoccupation with excitement and his movement from "being rebellious" toward a more positive relationship with society. He held four different jobs as a mechanic in a short time, from which he quit or was fired.

IMPORTANT STATES OF MIND

Most Problematic States. One of Harold's complaints was lack of initiative and productivity: he was unable to keep a job or to complete the training program that would qualify him for a better career. These problems hereafter will be referred to as the "procrastination theme." This theme was associated with Harold's frequent entry into a *dulled, listless, and inactive* state of mind. Although this state resulted in impairment, he found it preferable to more unpleasant states that ranged from a *panicky emptiness* state dominated by sad and empty feelings to *remorseful self-disgust.* He drank excessively at times to ward off both of these painful states.

Series of States. These problematic states could be compared with his desired state of mind, an *active engagement* in productive work. This ideal state was seldom achieved, but a variant of it occurred, in which he was *anxiously and tentatively engaged* in productive tasks and could recognize some of his own faults without deflation of self-esteem. This state was much preferred over the *dulled, listless, and inactive* state.

Sometimes, Harold would pretend to be in a productive state. This was usually a *social chitchat* state, in which another person would find him somewhat engaging but also veiled in his self-presentation. In addition, there was a state in which he engaged in unauthentic posturing that we will label as *mellow display.* Sometimes Harold displayed his sadness in these contrived states through a pretended poignancy or pretended remorse.

Harold displayed hostility in a variety of ways, with expressions of aggressivity ranging from undercontrolled rage, to adaptive anger, to overcontrolled "pseudo-angry" states. At one extreme was a relatively intense, undercontrolled state of *self-righteous rage.* There were sudden transitions into this state. A related state contained a mixture of emotions that were often experienced as confusingly blended feelings predominantly of shame, rage, and fear, as described by Kohut (1971) and by Horowitz (1981). This mixed state lacked the exhilaration of "pure" anger found during *self-righteous rage,* or the clearer emotional signals of *panicky emptiness* or *remorseful self-disgust.*

Harold also expressed anger or irritation in the *anxiously and tentatively engaged* state. In comparison with the explosive, impulsive qualities of *self-righteous rage,* this state was experienced by him (and recognized by others) to be more easily regulated and more modulated in its display of feeling.

A similar range of states from undercontrolled or overcontrolled affectivity was found with feelings of shame. There was the undercontrolled state of *remorseful self-disgust* in which shame was experienced as intense, searing, and out of control. Tolerable recognition of faults was experienced in the *anxiously and tentatively engaged* state. A pretended self-blaming took place in the *social chitchat* state. All of these states are described in table 7.1.

TABLE 7.1
List of Harold's States

Label	Description
Undermodulated States	
Remorseful self-disgust	Searing pang of shame
Dulled, listless, and inactive	Brooding unproductivity with a sense of meaninglessness, low initiative, and mild depression
Panicky emptiness	A piercing, momentary anguish and sense of loss followed by a feeling of being empty and damaged, with a sense of anxious dread
Self-righteous rage	Indignantly hostile and volatile
Well-Modulated States	
Active engagement	Working, concentrating, feeling interested
Anxiously and tentatively engaged	Communicative but in a somewhat halting and vulnerable manner
Overmodulated States	
Social chitchat	Pseudo-amiable and superficial conversing, sometimes with feigned positive feelings, mourning, or pretended remorse
Mellow display	Feigned good-fellow cheerfulness, sometimes with blustery lecturing

Defensive Organization of States. Harold wished to avoid rage, shame, fear, and sadness and to feel competent and productive. Unfortunately, there were many times when the closest that he could come to this ideal was a contrived state of *social chitchat* or *mellow display.* His habitual use of contrived states, or his withdrawal during the *dulled, listless, and inactive* state made it difficult for others to relate to him. Loss of a relationship then made him feel sad, hostile, ashamed, or scared in confusing oscillation.

In his *self-righteous rage* state, Harold behaved in a manner that was perceived by others as very arrogant and disdainful. These traits seemed apparent in the hard edge to his voice, his smug demeanor, and his complaints about others or about society as the source of evil. This externalized contempt was sometimes accompanied by a sneering demeanor, with gestures that indicated indignation and hostility. At other times, however, he would use a cranky, whiny tone of voice to express a feeling of outraged virtue at being unfairly deprived, controlled, misunderstood, or exploited. This resentment at forces outside of himself often occurred when he was being forced into what he saw as a conventional position, rather than one that would have allowed his full competence to blossom. Such behavioral patterns tended to bring about a vicious cycle of counterhostility or withdrawal by others, leading to his sense of isolation.

In contrast to the angry variants, Harold's contrived states, ranging from *social chitchat* to *mellow display*, often took the form of pseudo-earnestness. He was expansive, gestured widely with his hands, and dramatized any idea or feeling that was being expressed. There was a fluctuating vocal rhythm characterized by a kind of singsong inflection and fullness of tone. This was accompanied by steady eye contact and a general attitude of superiority. During these states, Harold often expressed himself with poster-like slogans about his ideas, and gave intellectualized position statements, sometimes even about his own painful emotions.

At such times he did not seem to be feeling the painful emotion, but only to be talking epigrammatically about it. For example, he would describe sadness as "a piercing arrow" or talk about how he "worked himself to the bone," or about how he had "a burning desire within me." However, the emotion displayed in his voice and facial expression seemed inauthentically reflective of such feelings. In the less emotionally colored aspects of the *mellow display* state, he lowered his voice, appeared relaxed, spoke in an even and measured tone, and seemed to be exuding reasonableness and an appearance of total control over any potentially upsetting feelings.

Harold also tended to rationalize and justify himself. He disavowed various behavior patterns that, if contemplated, might lead toward feelings of shame.

At times he was able to maintain a working state, the one labeled as *anxiously and tentatively engaging*. This state was choppy and accompanied by frequent silences. When Harold was in this state, his facial expression flickered from moment to moment, reflecting various emotions.

His vocal tone also reflected these emotions, with irritation. anxiety, shame, disgust, and sadness all expressed in a halting manner. When in this state, he hesitantly exposed his problems about work, self-control, and relationships, even though there was some defensive distortion.

Harold's *social chitchat* state was a defensively overcontrolled state aimed at preventing entry into the state of *remorseful self-disgust* or *self-righteous rage*. When the *social chitchat* state could not be stabilized, he entered the *dulled, listless, and inactive* state which also had its defensive properties. When situations allowed externalization of blame, the *self-righteous rage* state was preferable to *remorseful self-disgust*, the most dreaded state.

The warded-off states were antithetical to a desirable *active engagement* state. The defensive states, *social chitchat* and *mellow display*, were also antithetical to *active engagement*. This simplified defensive arrangement of states is shown in table 7.2.

TABLE 7.2
Defensive Organization of Harold's States

State	Self	Aims	Concept of Other
	Problematic Role Relationships		
Dulled, listless, inactive	Insulated and self-sufficient	None	Unnecessary
	Dreaded or Warded-Off Role Relationships		
Remorseful self-disgust	Bad or defective son	Exposure ⟶ ⟵ Punishment or shaming	Critical parent
	Desired Role Relationships		
Active engagement	Competent	⟵⟶ Communication	Competent
	Compromise Role Relationships		
Social chitchat	Pseudo-competent	Display ⟶ ⟵ Acceptance	Admirer

IMPLICATIONS OF DEFENSIVE LAYERING OF STATES OF MIND FOR THERAPY

Harold's vulnerability to state transitions created a dilemma for the therapist. If the therapist interpreted the defensive posture contained in the *social chitchat* state and urged exploration of themes that threatened self-esteem, Harold would not necessarily enter the desirable *active engagement* state but might instead be triggered into an uncontrolled *remorseful self-disgust* or *self-righteous rage* state. In the latter state, he might stalk out or act in a way that, later on, he would recall as shameful. In either state he might feel so exposed that he would drop out of therapy. Two independent clinicians who reviewed his evaluation tape before therapy predicted premature dropout as a likely possibility. On the other hand, if the therapist only joined the *social chitchat* state, it would be difficult to develop therapeutic communication.

MODELS OF ROLE RELATIONSHIP AND SELF-CONCEPTS

Harold was vulnerable to experiencing himself as incomplete, unworthy, incompetent, and damaged. His self-organization might have been more stable if he had had someone to reflect him, a self-object as described by Kohut (1971, 77), Ornstein (1978), and Horowitz and Zilberg (1983). The other person did not need to be physically present, but was conceptualized unconsciously as available and "in the world." When Harold had no reflective self-object and perceived himself as incompetent, he entered the state of *panicky emptiness*. When he thought of himself as more competent, he could tolerate sadness about the loss of his mother.

Harold was also vulnerable to experiencing himself as a bad person, one who either had exploited others or, because of his defectiveness, had failed to sufficiently help them. When that role relationship model dominated Harold's thoughts, he experienced the *remorseful self-disgust* state. The associations between his various self, object, and relationship concepts and the prominent states of mind are shown in table 7.3. Note the reversal of the role of exploiter in the states of *remorseful self-disgust* and *self-righteous rage.*

DEFENSIVE ORGANIZATION OF ROLE RELATIONSHIP MODELS

Ideally, Harold would maintain a competent self-concept, as shown in table 7.3, in the *active engagement* state of mind. Since this was difficult for Harold to manage, he had to utilize the next best views of himself—a variety of pseudo-competent or grandiose self-concepts in which he felt admired and supported by others (as existent rather than lost "self-objects").

Because of his motive to present himself to others as worthy of admiration, Harold frequently functioned in the range described as *social chitchat* and *mellow display.* Unfortunately, these states of mind also reflected

TABLE 7.3
The Example of Harold: Relating Role Relationship Models to States

States	Self	Other
Undermodulated States		
Remorseful self-disgust	Exploiter Bad Defective	Exploited victim/ ambiguous critic
Dulled, listless, and inactive	Insulated and self-sufficient	Unnecessary
Panicky emptiness	Bereft and incomplete	Needed but absent (self-object)
Self-righteous rage	Heroic avenger	Exploiter/ambiguous critic
Well-Modulated States		
Active engagement	Competent	Competent
Anxiously and tentatively engaged	Tolerable mixed image: part faulty and part competent	Part critic and part helper
Overmodulated States		
Social chitchat	Pseudo-competent	Admirer
Mellow display	Grand (pseudo-competent)	Admirer (taken in or fooled)

inauthenticity and contrivance. They carried seeds for their own failure as maneuvers of defense or restitution. Knowing this preconsciously, Harold constantly scanned the environment for signs of approval or disapproval. This search reflected his need for others, a need he found humiliating. For this reason, the scanning had to be muffled by a display of indifference to others.

Real accomplishments could help Harold to stabilize his self-esteem. Any kind of achievement might be useful: work productivity, acquisition of status or power, commitment to a sexual relationship, a secure and enduring friendship, or assumption of a caretaking role himself. Steps toward any of these goals were impeded when his aims were organized by either bad and incompetent self-concepts or compensatory, grandiose ones. Feelings of either deficiency or omnipotence led to poor planning and low commitment. Harold had the fantasy that he would be *instantly* loved, admired, accomplished, wealthy, and heroic. Therefore, he did not carry out the step-by-step procedures that were needed to achieve his aims.

This recurrent but conflicted story line is outlined in table 7.4.

TABLE 7.4

A Conflictual Relationship Schematization for Harold

Aim:	**I want to make a solid accomplishment in my own estimation and to be seen as competent by others.**
But I have these impediments:	
Personal deficiencies	I feel incomplete or helplessly weak. I have an inability to form and stick to a plan because of low hope and lack of confidence.
Environmental deficiencies	I have no steady work or social support system, with both my parents dead.
If I get what I want, then:	
Internal positive responses	I will be proud of myself as an authentic man.
External positive responses	I will get admiration.
But if I get what I want, then:	
Internal negative responses	I will still fall short of my exalted ideals.
External negative responses	People will feel they don't owe me any support. They will envy me for doing better than themselves.
So I will use these coping strategies:	
Interpersonal attitudes or behaviors	I will pose as competent and be contemptuous of others. I will demand things and will then show that what I get is unfairly deficient.
Intrapsychic attitudes	I will maintain an illusion of self-sufficiency.
Intrapsychic styles	I will externalize blame, exaggerate my own good traits, and minimize my bad ones.
And the results will be:	
Recurrent states of mind	I will display social chitchat. I will have states of remorseful self-disgust or listless inactivity when my pose of competence and illusion of self-sufficiency fail. I will feel enraged when I can blame others, and depression when I feel alienated from them.
Patterns of state transition	Labile changes from exhilaration to deflation.
Likely life course (accomplishments in working, relating, experiencing):	
Short-range	Tendency to procrastinate or impulsively quit work; impulsive entry into excessively challenging or romantic projects; grandiose but actually self-impairing actions as desperate attempts at compensation.
Long-range	Lack of accomplishment.

DEVELOPMENT OF A REPERTOIRE OF SELF–CONCEPTS AND ROLE RELATIONSHIP MODELS

Harold's self-concepts had been established through a variety of relationships during his childhood and adolescence. We had only limited information about his background. Between the ages of ten and twelve, he felt confused, anxious, and angry about his parents' separations and divorce. He subsequently engaged in a series of rebellious actions, motivated primarily by disappointment in his father. His father, in turn, criticized Harold for his rebellious, lazy, and disorganized behavior, and called him "a loser." After a period of years with little communication, Harold was making efforts to mend their relationship when his father died, largely due to neglect of his car's safety features, becoming himself "a loser" as far as Harold was concerned.

At times, Harold experienced himself as a bad, defective person or as a bad exploiter in relation to his father (whom he saw as the critic) or his mother (whom Harold felt he was exploiting). The mother may have also felt that her husband's defectiveness had led him to exploit her. Harold's various "bad" roles were related to the state of *remorseful self-disgust*.

At times Harold reversed these roles. The other person was the exploiter and he took on the role of the heroic avenger, as in the *self-righteous rage* state. Or, in another role reversal that occurred in a mixed state of shame, rage, and fear, the other person was the exploiter and Harold became the defectively weak victim.

Such states involved a third party, the ambiguous critic noted in table 7.3. This critic was viewed as assigning blame for being bad or being an exploiter. The word "ambiguous" is used to signify that the critic was undependable, sometimes blaming one party and sometimes another (Horowitz 1981). It is also used to indicate that value judgments are not quite self-owned and not quite social conventions nor attributions of others. The ambiguous critic role was related to Harold's defensive use of externalization of bad traits. He could ward off the *remorseful self-disgust* state if he could find someone else to contain bad traits, and he would then experience feelings of rage or contempt directed at that person and not himself.

Harold described a close, loving adolescent relationship with his mother. He reported how she had gone out of her way to accommodate his wishes. For a time she apparently treated him as though he could do no wrong. He may also have experienced her as an unreliable critic, since she seemed taken in or fooled by him. For example, she continuously rewarded him for bad as well as good behavior, possibly in an effort to restore his self-respect. This led to the development of an enduring attitude that people should unconditionally love, admire, and respect him, but it also made him distrust the ability of people to understand the motives and intentions behind his behavior. One can see how this attitude might impede therapy. The need for him to become considerate and helpful to others was not fully emphasized by his parents. He retained magical expectations of getting without giving, of advancing to a position of high status without having to pay the price of sustained efforts.

Harold also recalled his father as being quite critical. But this was also ambiguous, since his father did not himself consistently follow his own major injunctions, and was criticized for this by the mother and Harold. For example, the father told them to be careful, but neglected his car and drove heedlessly. The issue was clouded because Harold also appreciated his father's efforts to be helpfully critical. These efforts, however, sometimes degenerated into harsh, vindictive, or irrationally critical dialogues.

It was difficult for Harold to anticipate that his own self-evaluation would change for the better in the future, because he tended to experience himself as an imposter rather than a stable, worthy adult. He was aware that he presented a contrived self to the world. As a result, he had an enduring attitude that he would not be able to obtain love or admiring acceptance in the future, no matter what he did. Yet he yearned for these responses from others.

Harold externalized the blame for his lack of success onto others, claiming that they had used coercion which caused him to rebel, or that they had not provided him with enough support and thereby had caused a drain on his energy. He oscillated between seeing himself as the critic, as an unsupported and overcontrolled person, and as an exploiter, or seeing others in the same roles. Sometimes, in an effort to communicate his feelings and gain sympathy without losing control, he became safely remote from these feelings by presenting himself *as if* angry, *as if* hurt, or *as if* remorseful, using the *social chitchat* state of mind as a vehicle.

As already mentioned, the painful humiliation of having to acknowledge this kind of need for another was warded off by Harold's attempts to conceptualize himself as self-sufficient. In doing so, he entered the *dulled, listless, and inactive* state. He felt listless because of his real need for other people in order to feel enlivened. His angry states, ranging from *self-righteous rage* to a more subdued but chronic embitterment, were a way out of this state because they gave him a sense of having a higher level of energy.

IMPLICATIONS OF ROLE RELATIONSHIP MODELS FOR THERAPY

Social Alliance Potential. A social alliance would be likely to be grounded in the role relationship for the *social chitchat* or *mellow display* states of mind in which Harold presented himself as pseudo-competent, while viewing the therapist as an admiring but unreliable observer. Even if the therapist appeared to respect Harold, it would be respect that was not based on "true" knowledge of him. Later, the therapist might withdraw his respect. If he did not, it might mean only that the therapist was too unobservant to be of much help. Either alternative would thwart Harold's hope that therapy might be useful.

Therapeutic Alliance Potential. From Harold's repertoire of role relationship models, the one best fitted for a therapeutic alliance was the role in which Harold conceptualized himself as partly faulty and partly competent (as in the *anxiously and tentatively engaged* state). The therapist could then be tolerated as a helper as well as a potential critic.

Potential Negative Transferences and Countertransferences. Harold presented with the potential for three negative transference reactions, ones that might motivate him to flee the therapy. These three potentials concerned the relationships (1) between a bereft and damaged patient and an indifferent helper, in which (2) an enraged patient lashed out at a malicious exploiter, and in which (3) a demanding patient harmed a vulnerable therapist.

A Damaged Patient and an Indifferent Helper

In this role relationship model, states ranged from *sadness* to *intrusive sadness* to *panicky emptiness.* Harold might be expected to test the situation with the therapist, to see whether this model of the relationship was applicable. If the therapist was late, absent, unresponsive, rigidly adherent to the perceived role, extremely passive, or unempathically parsimonious, then Harold could shift toward viewing himself as incomplete or damaged and the therapist as indifferent. Such a reaction might disrupt treatment. For example, Harold could have begun with complaints of being too weak for the kind of treatment, insisting that this type of help was not "enough" or not the "right kind" for him. The therapist might have reacted by seeing Harold as a "demanding" patient, one "insufficiently motivated" to benefit from insight.

An Enraged Patient Lashing Out at a Malicious Exploiter

Using this role relationship model from his pre-existing repertoire, Harold could see the therapist as an unfair or malicious exploiter of his needs. In the story line evolving from this model, he could then view himself as an indignant "heroic avenger," calling the therapist to task for his utilization of Harold for his own aims and his failure to provide nourishment and help. In an effort to test the therapy situation for fit to this model, Harold might have criticized the therapist, his office, or his technique. This could have provoked the therapist into feeling that Harold was hostile, and he might have become reactively self-protective or enhancing. Harold might then have recognized signals of the countertransference and intensified his use of this negative view of the relationship.

A Demanding Patient Harming a Vulnerable Therapist

Like many narcissistically vulnerable or traumatized patients, Harold might have demanded special treatment and exhibited the sense of entitlement discussed earlier. The combination of demanding behavior, expectation, and vulnerability provokes some therapists to be especially soothing and hoveringly attentive. At its extreme, Harold might feel that he was draining the therapist.

This relationship view might be activated if the therapist were to feel depleted and unappreciated (because of all the one-way attention required by such patients) and allowed himself to complain. This role relationship model had already been activated in the relationship between Harold, his mother as she was dying, and his aunt, who criticized him for taking from his mother but then not giving.

Positive Transferences and Countertransferences. Kohut (1971) has described two positive transference reactions common in patients with narcissistic vulnerability. Both are attempts to compensate for the sense of self-damage. In one, the therapist is regarded as a mirror, reflecting idealized traits exhibited by the patient. Admiration is projected onto the concept of the therapist and used to stabilize self-esteem. In the other transference reaction, the therapist is regarded as having ideal characteristics, and the patient is restored to self-esteem through bonding with the therapist. Damage to the self is obscured by reflected radiance.

One aspect of these transference potentials has already been emphasized in the discussion of Harold's state of *mellow display*, during which he presented in an idealized way. If, in order to bolster Harold's self-esteem, the therapist indicated that he was receptive to such an ideal, Harold could have construed the therapist as joining with him in mutual values. As a result, Harold might have adopted role relationship models that were either mirroring or idealized. If the therapist indicated empathy for Harold's traumatic history, and for his courage in attempting to master it, then Harold might take this as a sign that he had been granted special status, different from that accorded to other patients.

If the therapist regarded Harold as a traumatized child, he might have made comments that would stimulate Harold to activate a role relationship model in which the therapist was a replacement figure, substituting for his lost mother and father. The related countertransference would cause the therapist to feel that he was a surrogate parent, making up to Harold for all of his bad times in the past.

Recapitulation. The social alliance, therapeutic alliance, and transference reaction potentials have all been described in terms of the available repertoire of self-concepts and role relationship models that Harold had as he entered treatment. The social alliance and even the relatively more realistic therapeutic alliance were, in part, "transference phenomena" in that they were based on preexisting schemata. For reference to the various possible transferences and alliances, see table 7.5.

INFORMATION PROCESSING

Themes Predisposing to Pathological Grief. We infer that Harold had an unconscious enduring attitude that verbally could be expressed in this way: "Without another person to see me as special, I am incomplete." When his mother died, he felt sadness over the loss, but he also had a fear of losing a sense of his own completeness.

The constellation of his losses was large: now both of his parents were dead; his aunt had become critical; he was episodically separated from his girlfriend and from familiar friends; and he was let go from his work. The result was an increased tendency toward *panicky emptiness* states or, as a result of defensive operations, the state of *dulled and listless* inactivity. Figure 7.1 provides a model of this sequence.

The Sadness and Comfort Theme

Because of the frighteningly painful possibilities associated with the dreaded *panicky emptiness* state of mind, Harold had to shift from his self-concept of being a bereft and incomplete person to another concept in his repertoire, that of himself as insulated and self-sufficient. This shift allowed him to enter the less painful *dulled, listless, and inactive* state. He felt leaden because he was not really self-sufficient. Rather, he was understimulated as a result of lack of human contacts and insufficient reciprocal interest on the part of others.

As shown in table 7.1, the configurational analysis teams inferred that a different enduring attitude gained prominence during this listless state. It could be verbalized as "comfort for me is all that counts." Harold provided succor for himself by eating and drinking, watching television, and avoiding work. He also avoided social contacts to prevent any possible rejection by others.

TABLE 7.5

Summary of Key Relationship Potentials for Harold's Therapy

	Patient's View		Therapist's View	
	Of Self	Of Other	Of Patient	Of Self
Potential negative transferences and countertransferences	Bereft and damaged	Needed but absent	Excessively demanding and/or unmotivated	Indifferent helper
	Heroic avenger	Exploiter	Vindictive	Innocent victim
	Exploiter	Exploited victim/ambiguous critic	Selfish	Depleted, unappreciated
Potential positive transferences and countertransferences	Grand	Admirer	Special	Guru
	Bereft and damaged	Replacement self-object	Traumatized child	Kindly parental surrogate
Potential therapeutic alliance	Tolerably part faulty and part competent	Part critic and part helper	Tolerably part faulty and part competent	Part critic and part helper
Potential social alliance	Pseudo-competent and seemingly engaged	Admirer (taken in or fooled)	Competent man	Competent man
Avoidance of any relationship	Insulated and self-sufficient	Unnecessary	Glossed over	Hampered in relating

Figure 7.1
The Sadness and Comfort Theme

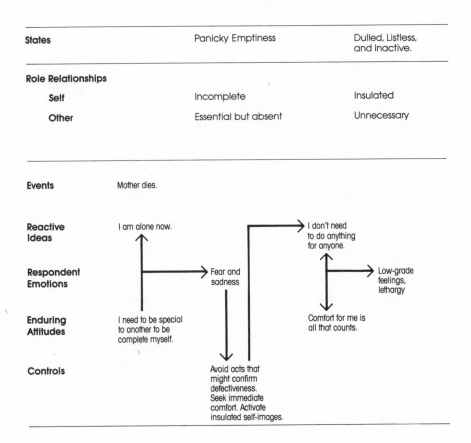

States	Panicky Emptiness	Dulled, Listless, and Inactive.
Role Relationships		
Self	Incomplete	Insulated
Other	Essential but absent	Unnecessary

Events	Mother dies.	
Reactive Ideas	I am alone now.	I don't need to do anything for anyone.
Respondent Emotions	Fear and sadness	Low-grade feelings, lethargy
Enduring Attitudes	I need to be special to another to be complete myself.	Comfort for me is all that counts.
Controls	Avoid acts that might confirm defectiveness. Seek immediate comfort. Activate insulated self-images.	

Blame Attribution Theme

There was another important theme in his grief reaction that we label as "blame attribution." In this theme, he thought of himself as an abandoner who had neglected his mother when she was dying in order to maintain his own comfort. We infer that this idea conflicted with an enduring attitude that could be stated as "family members should support each other."

The comparison of the "comfort" and "blame attribution" ideas tended to lead to feelings of humiliation, shame, or guilt, depending on whether blame was attributed internally or was seen as a potential external accusation. It was the discrepancy between the two ideas that led into the state of *remorseful self-disgust* in which Harold saw himself as a selfish exploiter, viewed his mother as an exploited victim (deprived of support during a crucial moment in her life and death), and conceptualized another person (his aunt) as accusing him of blame.

Another Defensive Maneuver, One Related to the Blame Attribution Theme

Harold's defensive response was to reverse roles, externalizing blame by attributing his shortcomings to others. This behavior tended to evoke thoughts about how his mother had deliberately abandoned him in the past, and again by her death; how his girlfriend criticized him instead of comforting him; and how his father had criticized but not taught him, and had abandoned him by death. A heightening of these memories and fantasies led to the reactive idea that they (his girlfriend, mother, and father, and not he) were the selfish exploiters and abandoners.

When this idea was compared with the enduring attitude that family members should support each other, Harold's indignation increased, leading into the state of *self-righteous rage*. In that state the roles were again reversed so that he was the exploited victim and also the heroic avenger of such crimes, for which others were to blame. There was an intervening state of *mixed shame, rage, and fear* in which Harold oscillated among roles as the exploiter, the victim, and the ambiguous critic who attributed blame first to one and then to another person.

Procrastination Theme

Harold complained about the *dulled, listless, and inactive* state, calling it his "trait of procrastination." His chief complaint early in the therapy was this state. The danger of rousing him from this state, or of too directly confronting him with the implications of his mother's death, was that he might then enter the dreaded *panicky emptiness* state. On the other hand, continuation of the *dulled, listless, and inactive* state had its own consequences, in that it impeded completion of the mourning response, and reduced Harold's sense of rewarding gains in career training, or progression.

The *dulled, listless, and inactive* state was, then, the surface manifestation of Harold's pathological grief reaction. In a way, he was procrastinating in the resolution of his mourning process, just as he tended to procrastinate concerning the development of skills that would enable him to attain his high ambitions. Procrastination represented one of his major conflicts and can be conceptualized as follows.

Harold had very high ideals for his future, but he did not plan realistically for the steps that were necessary to achieve his ambitions. Instead, he tended to fantasize about high accomplishments. Rational appraisal of the fantasies caused him to recognize that they were unlikely to succeed in reality. Unfortunately, at the same time, Harold viewed commitment to smaller, yet more realistic, steps as plodding, uncomfortable, and humiliating. As a way out of this impasse, he took exciting physical risks to gain a momentary sense of omnipotence.

Style of Coping and Defending. Harold's coping and defensive styles were dominated by efforts to stabilize acceptable self-concepts and thus bring about desired states of mind as described above. In terms of the flow of information within a train of thought, he used the type of sliding of meanings discussed earlier in this chapter. This included externalization of blame by describing bad traits that he (often accurately) detected in others, traits he unconsciously disparaged in himself. For example, he avoided the shame of procrastination by blaming others for their failures to act on his behalf. In addition, Harold used intellectualization and generalization to reduce emotional reactivity.

Implications of Information-Processing Style for Therapy. It was predictable that Harold would approach his therapy in the same way he approached life, wanting either the thrills of an emotionally explosive and rapidly powerful therapy, or procrastinating in order to avoid step-by-step thinking and the gradual working through of feelings that might be part of a brief therapy. A specific problem was Harold's inability to directly present his concerns, because to do so would activate feelings of shame. Instead, he tended to stabilize himself in the state of *mellow display* or *social chitchat*. This made it difficult for both the evaluator and the therapist to assess whether or not Harold was sufficiently motivated to arrive at an appropriate focus for a brief therapy. The evaluator, indeed, raised the possibility of referral for long-term therapy, as did the therapist in early sessions. Harold indicated his decision to continue with the research-based brief therapy to see if anything at all might help him as well as a lack of intent to try anything other than this.

The Process of Therapy

ESTABLISHING A THERAPEUTIC ALLIANCE AND A FOCUS

Instead of establishing a therapeutic alliance, Harold tended either to oscillate between overconfidence and excessive self-devaluation, or to impose a shell of indifference between himself and the therapist. He presented himself as if he were at the therapist's disposal in an amiable *social chitchat* state. There were also some nonverbal signals of an incongruent sort, indicating that a mixed affective state (shame, fear, and anger) was just beneath the surface.

At the same time, Harold signaled a "chip on the shoulder" attitude. It seemed that Harold sensed that he was under some kind of attack, and felt anger at the aggressor and shame because of those personal defects that prompted the "attack."

Awareness of Harold's opening attitude placed the therapist in a bind. If he was soothingly supportive of Harold's self-esteem, Harold might feel an increase in confidence but might remain remote and not focus on emotional issues. If the therapist confronted him with Harold's own problems, the therapist could be perceived as challenging and critical. Harold was preconsciously aware of this dilemma, and at this dim level of recognition was curious about whether and how the therapist could approach him in spite of it.

Focus. Harold began the therapy by complaining of lack of support, emphasizing difficulties with his girlfriend. These complaints involved others, and did not contain aspects of his own functioning. The therapist attempted to explore the meanings of his mother's recent death and the increase in problems since that event. The therapist suggested to Harold that he felt less supported because he no longer had his mother. Harold rejected this possibility, and this theme as a focus.

The therapist tactfully persisted, summarizing the various interpersonal situations that involved lowered levels of support: Harold and his girlfriend, Harold and his aunt, Harold and his boss, Harold and the therapist, and Harold and his lost mother. None of these topics was chosen by Harold as a potentially useful theme. The therapist then mentioned procrastination, and Harold displayed interest in working on that theme. The following excerpts illustrate this process.

THE FIRST THERAPY SESSION

As the first session began, Harold, in a challenging manner, asked whether the therapist had watched the videotape of his evaluation interview. He referred to the evaluating clinician by her first name, which is unusual for our patients.

> Harold: . . . Did you watch the tape from when Pauline and I were talking?
> Therapist: No, I didn't, so I don't know a great deal about you.

> Harold: Yeah. Well, do you just want me to start, uh, start talking?
> . . . or, like I've never been in a situation like this before. . . .
>
> Therapist: Well, you'll have to find out what it's like now.
>
> Harold: (*Laughs*) Yeah. Uh, I really don't know where to start or what to say.
>
> Therapist: Well, let's just review where we are. You came in for some reason.
>
> Harold: Right.
>
> Therapist: And you talked with Mrs. Jones and she recommended treatment, and you and she kind of agreed on it.
>
> Harold: Yeah.
>
> Therapist: And now it's up to you and me to see what we think.

Harold asked the therapist how to proceed. The therapist recognized a kind of pseudo-naiveté as Harold said, "I've never been in a situation like this before." Such remarks are often authentic, but Harold delivered this one ingenuously. For that reason, the therapist made a somewhat "tough" statement: "Well, you'll have to find out what it's like now." While not directly critical, this remark was moving in the direction of a negative transference–countertransference potential. The comment was provoked by Harold's "chip on the shoulder" demeanor. Harold responded with a laugh. He maintained his position by saying, "I really don't know where to start or what to say."

Recognizing Harold's vulnerability to criticism, and the initial confrontational feeling of the session, the therapist reconstructed what had happened in order to keep the confrontation from becoming too intense. He said, "Let's just review where we are," and did so without fully giving the directions that Harold had requested. The therapist concluded by saying, "And now it's up to you and me to see what we think." This was an offer in the direction of a therapeutic alliance.

Harold responded by laughing, then gave a genuine complaint. He quickly moved away from this commitment, using generalization and intellectualization.

> Harold: (*Laughs*) Well, uh, I've just been very, very sad and depressed for a little over a year. Uh, a conglomeration of many things, uh, problems with my girlfriend, uh, my mother's sudden illness and, uh, death had a rather shocking effect. Uhm, my loss of values or goals, you might say. I started questioning my basic attitudes when my relation-

ship with my girlfriend started deteriorating, and uh, I'm just really trying to get ahold of myself, you know, and, uh, not knowing which direction to go or anything like that.

Therapist: So had you been thinking about therapy? What actually led you to think about therapy?

Harold: I had been thinking about it for quite a while, and various friends and acquaintances said, "Harold, why don't you go do some sort of therapy?" I had toyed with the idea of seeing a school psychologist but never got around to making the phone call more than anything else. Then a relative told me about the, the set-up here.

Therapist: Mmmhmm.

Harold: And so, the price was right more than anything else. (*He disavows his motivation and tests to see whether the therapist is easily provoked into one of the potential negative counter-transferences.*)

Therapist: Yeah. So it's kind of like a trial for you, to see what kinds of things might happen. (*The therapist answers the provocation in the direction of setting up a tentative alliance by agreeing to see the onset of therapy as a test.*)

Harold: Yeah. I mean I, I've talked to friends, I've had sounding boards. My aunt highly recommended some sort of treatment. I guess that's all I was thinking about, mm, you know, give it a try, and maybe it'll help me out, give me some direction, give me further insight into myself, or something or other (*pause*).

Therapist: Well, I'd be happy to tell you what I think when I know more about you.

Harold: Yeah.

Therapist: First, I'd have to, you know, hear from you, who you are, and where you're at, and what's been happening.

Harold: Yeah. Uhhmmm. (*Laughs*) I assume you know my name (*said sarcastically*).

Therapist: Yes.

Harold: Yeah. Uhh, well, I'm twenty-five years old. I was in the military for a while. I've had a girlfriend for some time, but it may be coming apart. I want to branch out, uhmm, explore other avenues of life, to learn more about what's going on in the world. I feel like I've been in a shelter for years, in a little cubbyhole, and, uhm, I've been trying to break out of this cubbyhole, and of course making new friends is a very difficult thing to do. (*While the therapist does not know it, in retrospect this aim, to break out, and its opposite, remaining sheltered, are aspects of the procrastination theme that became a focus.*)

Therapist: Hmmm, well.

Harold: And when you find very little support from the friends and acquaintances that you've had for a number of years— they've been siding with my girlfriend in our difficulties— and so I've been very lonely, which when I think back has really been a basis of a lot of my feelings. Loneliness, being alone, I really don't have any support for the things I do, finding skepticism amongst friends and acquaintances. When I set out to do something and I find skepticism on their part about my desire, my ability, my capabilities, then I find it discouraging, and I don't complete these goals or these tasks, which again is very discouraging to me because I say "I know I can do it" but "Look, you haven't done it in the past, what makes you think you can do it?" and I go into a self-pity type of thing. (*This combines the themes: the message is, "I procrastinate, but it is their fault for not sustaining me." Harold's comments predict a negative transference in which he procrastinates in terms of working in the therapy, but this is viewed as the therapist's fault for being nonsustaining.*)

The therapist picked up on the very last comment about self-pity as one of the more directly personal remarks yet made, and asked Harold to expand further on the topic. In response he became vague, and the therapist asked him for some example of how he had been feeling. There were further references to Harold's problems in working and his attitudes toward his girlfriend. The therapist asked Harold how the death of his mother fit into all of this. Harold was able to talk for quite some time about his relationship with his mother. Later, the therapist pointed out that Harold was feeling a loss of support from his mother, from his girlfriend, and from people at a job he had recently ended.

There was a discussion of the issue of support as it related to the therapy, with the therapist pointing out that the work would be time-limited and would end within three months. Harold reacted to this by a brief expression of bitterness and then masked this with a version of the *social chitchat* state that had an "as if sad" emotional coloration. He sniffed, sighed, and said, "You know to me. . . . I just . . . I chuckle at it for the simple fact that . . . mmmm . . . rather than cry, because it seems . . .

that . . . you know . . . here it starts going good, and then *bam!* The story of my life, so to speak."

The intention of this statement was to make the therapist feel bad for offering a brief therapy. An interesting shift then occurred. Harold moved into the *mellow display* state, and made a "stiff upper lip" comment. He said, "I vaguely recall my Dad telling me something along the line of 'grinning and bearing it' and 'playing your cards as they lay.' "

It was very interesting to note that in the *mellow display* state of mind, Harold indicated that there had been a positive relationship with his father. The therapist did not yet know about Harold's feelings of contempt and anger toward his father. Instead, reacting to the generally positive statement, the therapist repeated the father's phrase, saying: "Well, let's say we play it as the cards lay. Let's see what we want to play. I think this is an issue that you might want to work on with me, the issue of who you are, what are the different ways you're capable of feeling about yourself in relation to support that is both present and absent, and how you work to get or lose support."

Harold reacted to this suggestion of a focus, which involved issues of support, in a remote manner, staring blankly at the therapist, perhaps because the therapist repeated a phrase of his father's. After some halting remarks back and forth, the therapist stated directly that he wanted to know Harold's thoughts about possibly focusing on support and on his self-concept during their work together. The therapist said, "I just want to know what you think right now, tentatively, about us talking on that issue of you and support." It is quite usual in examining transcripts to note that sentences are not grammatical. Also, the words and subordinate clauses that are selected all carry meanings that the therapist did not realize as he spoke. However, in microanalysis, the meanings of some of the phrases can be inferred. In the above remark, the therapist added the phrase "right now" followed by "tentatively." The phrase "right now"— especially coupled with the emphatic beginning of the sentence, "I (just) want to know"—was a sign of a firm stance, meant to probe Harold's remoteness. Preconsciously realizing this, the therapist undid the firmness by adding the words "just" and "tentatively."

Harold remained within the range of states between *social chitchat* and *mellow display*. With intellectual remoteness from any emotion, he said, "Well, I know for me [support is] . . . that is, a very big thing that. . . . I don't know how much I need it. But I do know how much I want it."

He then went on with peripheral associations, talking about how much monetary support he would like to have. Harold presented an idealized image of himself as willing to work ten hours a day in order to feel that he earned the money that in fantasies he wanted to accumulate by "wheeling and dealing." He said he wanted people to support him by saying, "Go on, Harold, you can do it."

The therapist then described a brief therapy that would not supply the kind of support that Harold requested in his wish to have someone say, "Go on, Harold, you can do it." Instead, the therapy would focus on understanding some issue, such as the meaning of his mother's death or the relationship between himself and his girlfriend. The therapist added that by the end of the brief therapy, nothing would be "fixed up and finished. You won't be getting ongoing support from me because both of us will be aware that we're going to stop." He distinguished between that and seeing somebody for a long time in therapy, and said that Harold might see such a person as supportive because the person would stick with him through turbulent periods. The therapist added that Harold had not sought that long-term kind of therapy, but had come to a place where he knew brief therapy was offered. The therapist pointed out that long-term therapy was available at other clinics and he could refer him to it if Harold wanted it.

Harold indicated that he understood., He said immediately that he preferred the brief therapy:

Harold: I understand that. Well, like I mentioned earlier, playing the cards as they lay or whatever, I've always been under the impression that you're not going to get anything out of anything unless you give it a go. Going through the therapy here for twelve weeks and then having it stop . . . uhm. I think not going through it for myself would be more detrimental.

Therapist: Yes. It makes sense for you to go through it. I just want you to see you have the choice now. You'll have a choice then after termination, too.

Harold: Yeah. Well, this is how I look at it. I mean, I can go through it now, and if I really think it's done me some good, great, and if it hasn't, and if maybe I feel that I would need some more, well okay, this would be like a stepping-stone for me, or the first rung on the ladder.

Therapist: Yes. You could check out what it's like, because you haven't had experience with it.

Harold: Yeah, exactly. And uh, as you probably gather, I am very confused right at the moment. My life has been very complex and I need someone to talk to to help me straighten it

235

out—like you said, to help clarify it, to help me put it in a different perspective.

Therapist: You're feeling it would be a good idea for us to go on.

Harold: I definitely do.

Therapist: Well, I'm agreeable.

At this point, Harold and the therapist had agreed to go on seeing each other, but they still had not established a focus. This interchange may have indicated to Harold that the therapist would not accept unrealistic goals and that there were ground rules for giving and taking opinions that might eventually build the therapeutic alliance.

THE SECOND THERAPY SESSION

The second therapy session began with Harold saying he had "screwed up his school semester by not attending class, doing projects or homework." He then revealed that what had "hit it off" (made him angry) was that one of his professors had mentioned that morning that Harold had an incomplete grade. This was stated vaguely: "The professor mentioned this morning about the incomplete grades." Harold did not use the pronoun "my" before "grade." When describing the situation to the therapist, Harold indicated that he did not want to change his behavior at school but rather wanted to have his incomplete grade erased. He said, "I'll have to talk to him about working that out. There is, you know, the possibility of getting that erased, too, you know, some sort of passable grade that is acceptable to me."

The therapist responded to Harold's implication that the problem resided within the professor by asking, "How come you didn't do the term paper, go to class, read, and study?"

Harold responded, "I think a lot of it is just that I didn't get around to it. Hmmmm. Procrastination, motivation. As much as I was interested in it, and the few times that I did sit down and study, I really enjoyed it."

Harold's use of the term "procrastination" indicated an aspect of his behavior that was causing him problems, although it was not presented clearly as something he wished to work on. After asking a few questions about the class that was involved, the therapist directly took up the topic of procrastination.

Therapist: So—is procrastination . . . is that a new thing for you, or is that a pattern?

Harold: Uhmm, no, it's not a new thing for me. It's something that I've had for as long as I can remember.

Therapist: Yes, and, does it cause you impairment?

Harold: Impairment in what way?

Therapist: In your success?

Harold: Uhhmm, I really don't know. I mean, it's caused uhmm, my own bitterness towards myself, 'cause I know I can do better.

Therapist: Uh, that, I'd say that counts. If you dislike yourself, that's a knock.

Harold: Yeah. Exactly. I know the few times I can think back where I have completed something, and I'm referring to school-work in particular, uhhh, successfully, how good I felt, and how much I did like myself for it.

Therapist: Yeah. So you can get pleasure really. . . .

Harold: I can get satisfaction out of it.

Therapist: And then get pain when you don't.

Harold: Right.

Therapist: So then it's a real, it's a real problem that you reflect on.

Harold: Uh-huh. I've talked to my aunt a couple of times. I was mentioning to her how hard I found it to sit down and study. . . .

Therapist: Mmmhmm.

Harold: And uh, but thinking back on it, it's a problem that I can, you know, think back on throughout my school years.

This interchange indicated a tentative focus. Harold's state of mind, however, was still within the *social chitchat* range. Next, the therapist experimented to see what interventions might have helped Harold to enter a closer, allied working state.

The first context for this followed after Harold described how he had never developed a plan for reading his textbooks. Instead, he "sat around, listened to the ball game on the radio, or whatever." He added that he found it hard to occupy his time. He thought of all the things that needed doing, but found it difficult to get up and do them. Harold presented this situation in a provocative manner, testing to see whether the therapist would criticize him instead of asking the therapist to help him to understand the procrastination.

In order to respond to the test, the therapist offered to take on the critical role in an "as if" manner. He said, "I am going to challenge you, but I want to see if you agree with the challenge." The therapist then changed his tone of voice and conspicuously role playing a critical manner said, "That's a hell of a way to go about it [studying]." Harold's response was to laugh and say, "I'll agree with you there! I mean I should be able to have the motivation, the self-control, the discipline needed to just—you know, stop what I'm . . . I'm doing." He then emulated the therapist's critical, role-playing tone of voice and said to himself, "You've got to spend this time. You've got to sit down and study."

The therapist then said in an ordinary tone of voice, "You'd like to be able to do that?" Harold assented and then went on to enter an *anxiously and tentatively engaged* state of mind. He described his procrastination further. The therapist then attempted to see whether the procrastination theme was related to the abandonment-versus-support theme. When the therapist asked if the procrastination was related to support or criticism from others, Harold disavowed this possibility and called the problem an internal one. He repeated the following statement with various rewordings: "But it keeps coming back to this dislike of myself for not getting up and doing it, whether I have the support or not."

The therapist reflected this by saying, "You're now disgusted with yourself." Harold was able to speak a bit more directly, telling the therapist that he was indeed discouraged.

The same basic dilemmas and difficulties in establishing working states emerged again and again during the therapy. However, there was one indication of a transition from the social alliance states (*mellow display, social chitchat*) toward therapeutic alliance states (*anxiously and tentatively engaging, active engagement*).

In the foregoing passage the therapist took on the role of a critic, through mimicry, which both clarified and repudiated the negative-transference role relationship model. The therapist indicated that he could be critical and was being provoked to criticize, but that he was not going to do it. Rather, the therapist contrasted the role relationship model in which he would criticize Harold for procrastination, with one in which he attempted to help Harold clarify and grapple with this problem. The shift in emphasis enabled Harold to step back, temporarily, from the negative transference of being criticized for wrongdoing or defectiveness, and suggested that Harold could be seen as both partly faulty and partly competent.

The purpose of this example is not to advocate such a role-playing technique for patients with narcissistic personality styles. We are simply giving a retrospective analysis of what happened in this therapy at this particular moment. If the role-playing technique had been carried out repetitively, it probably would have been countertherapeutic. This approach could have meshed with Harold's tendency to use isolation of affect as a defensive maneuver. Role-playing could have easily become just another intellectualization and isolation maneuver. The therapist, in the next transcript, attempted to clarify the potential transference impasse in which Harold would provoke him to criticism and to react with anger. This occurred as Harold revealed his impatience, his inability to wait for long-term benefits, and his anxiety over whether the benefits would be gained at once. The therapist attempted to label the feelings that led Harold to adopt a "chip on the shoulder" attitude. The session continued in this way:

Therapist: You don't want to be pushed around.

Harold: I would need that pushing.

Therapist: . . . In a therapy, that's going to end, you'd be procrastinating and procrastinating and you won't work on a topic that's really important to you. You'll work on something else that's easier or looks important, but it really isn't. And if I were not a good therapist and did not catch onto this, I might be fooled. But if I were good and caught on to it then I'd say, "Come on, Harold, let's move on this therapy and stop procrastinating." And then you'd feel like I was pushing you around, and you'd be angry with me. You'd feel deprived of support because I was pushing you, and I'd be belittling you. Then you'd stubbornly drag your heels, and this wouldn't help you in any way. And I wouldn't enjoy that.

Harold: Mmmhmm.

Therapist: And I wouldn't feel like I was being helpful. But here I'd be trying to be, on the surface I'd look "real helpful," you know.

Harold: (*Laughs*)

Therapist: So we'll have to watch out for that.

Harold: Right. I, I can see the point, the dilemma there.

The therapist then asked Harold again how he felt at this point about the time limit. Harold was able to say, albeit in a somewhat remote way, "I'll tell you. One of my initial reactions is negative, for the fact that a time limit is put on it. I personally feel that maybe some people can get maximum benefit out of such a time limit, maybe even a shorter period of time, but then again others can't. Maybe they need another three weeks, or four, or fifteen. Ummmm . . . I feel a little bit of pressure, knowing that there is that time limit there." (Here he is signaling his need to be seen as special and not just another research patient.)

Harold told the therapist that he felt awkward and uncomfortable, as he often did while he was with people, and as he often did before he withdrew from people. The therapist told Harold that he was aware that he was feeling awkward. The therapist was also aware that Harold wanted him to talk more when either one of them was silent. The therapist added that he was not being silent to make Harold feel uncomfortable, but rather to allow him to bring up whatever needed to be brought up, and to indicate the direction that they might have to go together.

As the session continued, the therapist again clarified and interpreted Harold's fear of being criticized, through the positive statement "You'd like me to think well of you." The therapist also interpreted another potential for a negative transference, in which Harold would reveal his sense of personal need to the therapist but the therapist would not be available to him or would be too defective to help him. If that were to happen, Harold would defend himself by going into the *dulled, listless, and inactive* state, in which he felt that other people were unnecessary. The dialogue was as follows:

Therapist: I was thinking that if you really try, you have to also test me out.
  Harold: Mmhmm.
Therapist: If you really try, uhhh, then you would be admitting to me and to yourself that you really want someone to help you with yourself. And it's like taking off a mask to do that. You're then just saying, "Will you help me, please?" And, then if I can't do it, either I don't want to or I don't like to deal with people like you, or I do it poorly, then you're left in a very bereft position. I think you'd. . . .
  Harold: Being left in a lurch.

Harold was then able to bring up a few of his reservations and negative thoughts about himself. He stated that he had come into the clinic knowing that it had to do with life stresses, and that he was "qualified" for it because of his mother's death. He felt that this focus was hanging over his head. He wanted to come in for therapy, but he did *not* want to talk about his mother's death. He wanted the therapist to tell him that it was all right to talk about other things. This would include the relationship with his girlfriend and what he expected to get out of therapy in general, as well as school and his financial problems. He didn't like the idea that the therapist would always say, "How does this relate to your mother's death?" The therapist tried to clarify this in terms of Harold's expectation of being criticized:

> Harold: Uhmm . . . I just don't want it to be, you know, this narrow path that you have to follow.
>
> Therapist: If I had a narrow path, if I wanted to talk only about your mother's death, and if you talk only about these other things, like school, then I'm going to, in my mind or overtly, tell you that you're bad. Then we wouldn't get anywhere (*pause*). On the other hand, I think we should struggle towards an *agreement* about some issues about yourself that *you* might want to change. What do you want to know more about so you can be in a position to work it through and live it through after we're done?
>
> Harold: I know one of them that I can think of right offhand is having the self-discipline to be able to do the things that, you know, interest me, rather than just sit back and think about them.
>
> Therapist: Yes.

This was Harold's restatement of a focus on the procrastination theme. The therapist was well aware that this statement did not guarantee smooth sailing. He understood Harold's continuing vulnerability to criticism, and thought it possible that he might drop out of therapy. In order to reduce that possibility, the therapist wanted to further clarify the therapeutic relationship using a less threatening "as if" stance, and sought to present a new context for Harold's tendency to experience others as critical.

After the ramifications of Harold's personal problems became more evident, the therapist explored the cycle of Harold's feelings with him. Harold would first tell himself that he was stupid. Second, in an effort to avoid the feelings of humiliation, he would become indifferent to his own goals. This feeling of indifference would then allow him to procrastinate. In response, Harold said:

> Harold: You know, I can see it so plain—that exact thing—you know, you try, or I try and try and try and it seems like I'm not getting anywhere, uhhh, and I just give up, say, "Why, why bother trying anymore?"
>
> Therapist: Well, that's why I want to challenge the "stupid" idea first.

Because if you're going to feel stupid here with me, if we don't challenge that judgment of yourself as stupid, we won't be able to do our work.

Harold: Well, I, I don't think I'm challenging our relationship here, with my seeking help from you as being stupid.

Therapist: No, no. But here's a mistake we could make.

Harold: Okay.

Therapist: You and I, we'd listen to a little bit of your talking, would see some concrete examples of this behavior and this pattern, and then we'd both agree, "Isn't that stupid. Let's just you stop it." That would be a mistake. Because you can't "just stop it." Those patterns don't "just stop." They don't go away. They don't evaporate. And a decision or willpower does not usually get rid of them. That doesn't mean you shouldn't try, but I can't hold a lot of hope for it.

Harold: It's something that takes work.

Therapist: But rather we're going to have to really work on that. Now we have to agree that it's not stupid, in order to work on it without you feeling humiliated and ashamed and then stopping our work.

Harold: I think that humiliation and that shame is just within myself about myself.

Therapist: Yes. So we'd have to be patient with that and be willing to look at that. If we start working on this. . . .

Harold: Be willing to overcome that and, and, you know, as much as I may feel, you know, why work with this dumb fool. . . .

Therapist: Yes.

Harold: . . . yet continue to work.

Therapist: And to, and to. . . .

Harold: And to overcome that feeling.

Therapist: Right. And to report it to me.

Harold: Yeah.

Therapist: Or to accuse me when you think I'm feeling it. Right up front, just tell me that I'm criticizing you or I don't like you, or whatever . . . you're going to feel that sometime if we work with this, I would guess, if we're right on the track. That's just the way that it works psychologically. We'll have to examine it together, and see. Maybe I'll do that and maybe make some mistakes, but they'd be mistakes. This is a serious problem. It has to be taken seriously. . . .

Harold: I think it, it boils down to wanting to overcome it more. . . . I mean, the easy thing to do is just give up.

Therapist: Yes.

Harold: You know, rather than fighting what seems like an uphill battle, rather than just continuing to fight, continuing to try to overcome this. . . .

Therapist: Yes.

Harold: . . . this problem, this feeling, or whatever. And I think it's hard for me, you know, working on it myself to see, you know, that I have climbed up on Step A, and that I'm climbing up onto Step B. Uhhh, it'd be so nice to be able just to be at the top of the ladder, you know.

Therapist: Sure.

There was further discussion of Harold's impatience, and how it led him to impulsive actions. Again, the therapist related this to the therapy. Harold agreed that he was hoping for a quick solution. The therapist indicated that this would not be possible.

Therapist: So, this, our work together will have. . . . One of its features will be disappointment.

Harold: Mmmhmm.

Therapist: You are going to be disappointed with me and our work and yourself because in the time given to us we may see the road more clearly, and walk a step or two down the path, but we won't arrive at the marvelous city of. . . .

Harold: Of Oz.

Therapist: Yes. Do you think you'll be able to tolerate that?

Harold: I'm willing to give it a try.

The therapist has clarified potential negative transferences and attempted, in doing so, to build a therapeutic alliance. By predicting a likely impasse, he hoped to arm Harold beforehand against impulsive, premature termination. He also attempted to indicate that direct communication of these negative ideas and feelings was acceptable and desirable in this context, even though such communication was not socially conventional. Because Harold was insulated and prone to disavowal, intellectualization, and isolation, the therapist repeated each facet of this effort several times during the second therapy session.

243

WORKING THROUGH CONFLICTS: GENERAL CONSIDERATIONS

Working through is especially difficult with the narcissistically vulnerable personality because interpretations and clarifications are a double problem. Such patients experience both the threat to themselves of the warded-off information and the threat that the therapist will learn of the warding-off process that is taking place. That is why interpretations and clarifications have to be given in small doses. This sometimes means proceeding slowly as compared with the rate of working through with less vulnerable patients. Repetition of segments of work is valuable to counteract the patient's tendency to slide meanings, and to minimize damaging information about the self even after such information has just been directly confronted and "accepted." Some of these general tactics can be seen in table 7.6.

WORKING THROUGH CONFLICTS: SPECIFIC CONSIDERATIONS

Two themes, procrastination and abandonment, occupied the majority of effort in the therapy process. Each theme surfaced in the early hours as a potential focus of concern for the brief therapy. Procrastination was agreed upon first as the focus, and so will be discussed first.

The Procrastination Theme. We pause here to recapitulate briefly what has already been said about this theme. Harold thought about his life plans along these lines: "I would like to achieve my goals, but as I am incapable (without others to support me) I will fail in that effort. Therefore I have two options. I will pull in my horns and procrastinate in order to avoid the pain of wanting, striving, and failing, or being anxious about failure. My other option is to remain comfortable and make episodic efforts at big success. My sense of grandeur tells me that this will solve the problems at once, and I will be relieved of the necessity of making step-by-step efforts."

Harold presented his state of *mellow display* to the therapist to ward off a feared relationship in which the therapist would criticize his activities and his nature, and in which he would thus feel incompetent. In order to find a focus, the therapist had to see through the facade of the *mellow display* state. He had to have at least a hunch about the above formulations. Most important, and useful, was the therapist's recognition of the *mellow display* state as a sign that this patient was extremely vulnerable to an opposite state, one of *remorseful self-disgust.*

For the task of exploring real problems without being too critical for Harold to accept, the use of a single acceptable term, "procrastination," proved helpful. The trait did not sound too bad to tolerate. The establish-

TABLE 7.6
Some "Defects" of Narcissistic Style and Their Counteractants in Therapy

Function	Style as "Defect"	Therapeutic counteraction
Perception	Focused on praise and blame	Avoid being provoked into either praising or blaming but be realistically supportive
	Denial of "wounding" information	Tactful timing and wording to counteract denials by selective confrontation
Representation	Dislocates bad traits from self to other	Repeated review in order to clarify who is who in terms of the sequence of acts and intentions in a recalled interpersonal transaction
Translation of images into words	Slides meanings	Consistently define meanings; encourage decisions as to most relevant meanings and how much to weight them
Associations	Overbalanced in terms of finding routes to self-enhancement	Hold to other meanings: cautiously deflate grandiose beliefs
Problem solving	Distortion of reality to maintain self-esteem	Point out distortion while (tactfully) encouraging and supporting reality fidelity
	Obtain illusory gratifications	Support patient's self-esteem during period of surrender of illusory gratification (helped by the real interest of the therapist, by identification with the therapist, and by identification with the therapist as a noncorrupt person). Find out about and gradually discourage unrealistic gratifications from therapy
	Forgive selves too easily	Help develop appropriate sense of responsibility

ment of a therapeutic alliance and focus, with this term as a conceptual label, helped Harold to proceed. There was a change in Harold's state frequency pattern. The *mellow display* state of mind decreased and his state of being *anxiously and tentatively engaged* increased. In general terms, this was a shift from an overcontrolled state to one that was more conducive to therapeutic work and that was itself an analogue to working rather than procrastinating.

This movement from a nonworking state to a working state could be qualified by state analysis (Horowitz, Marmar, and Wilner 1979; Marmar, Wilner, and Horowitz 1983). Minutes fifteen to twenty-five of the video-tape of each hour of therapy were viewed by three clinicians who scored the states that were present. Working states, associated with development of the therapeutic alliance, increased over time. The overcontrolled states that were associated with the social alliance, such as *mellow display*, declined after the first three hours.

Therapist Aims. The aim of work on the procrastination theme was to go as far as possible toward reaching an ideal goal, which would be stated as follows: Harold "should have" reduced his grandiose expectations and increased his ability to work toward more realistic goals, learning to accept the step-by-step plans that were necessary to achieve them. With feedback from each successfully undertaken step, he would have more external and internal support for his worthwhile self-concepts. As he progressed and gained distance from his defective self-concepts, he would take further steps. This would result in less time being spent in the *dulled, listless, and inactive* state and more time spent in a working state. At first, this working state, because of Harold's vulnerability, would probably have some qualities of anxiety and hesitation as in the *anxiously and tentatively engaged* state.

Tactics in Therapy. The therapist proceeded gradually, attempting to find language that would be acceptable to Harold. He reconstructed sequences of Harold's actions by slowly summarizing what the latter had said and by questioning cloudy reports. The therapist listened sympathetically, encouraged realistic step-by-step planning, and contrasted short-range objectives with Harold's grandiose goals. The progress of the therapy can be examined session by session as it concerned this theme.

Session 1

The therapist was empathic with Harold's sense of vulnerability regarding the lack of support from his girlfriend. The anger underlying Harold's "chip on the shoulder" attitude was tentatively clarified. The therapist also confronted some grandiose plans. "You're kind of ambitious," he said in a matter-of-fact manner. Harold's pride was not injured because the therapist's vocal tone did not insinuate that he was *too* ambitious. The expanded meaning was that the therapist agreed to align himself with this goal: to help Harold be realistically ambitious.

Session 2

In the second session the therapist persisted with this theme of realistic versus grandiose plans. He sympathetically stated that it was depressing for Harold to feel so far from realizing a goal, and used the following wording: "You want to be master of the long-range course of your life."

Session 3
During the third hour, Harold's "chip on the shoulder" attitude was again addressed and linked to his father, with this interpretation: "It's possible that you had a certain amount of contempt for your father" (an affect noted by the therapist in Harold's attitude with regard to the treatment relationship).

In his process notes, the therapist observed that whenever he commented on Harold's impatience in viewing his life plan, Harold had a startled reaction (apparently surprised at being understood) and then responded with a franker display of sadness and anxiety. He was in the *anxiously and tentatively engaged* state, in which he was more willing to present self-critical information than when he was in the *social chitchat* state. The therapist also emphasized that Harold's feeling of loss of support after the death of his mother had increased his procrastination.

Session 4
The therapist addressed the theme of yearning for and envying high status by concentrating on the nature of the immediate therapeutic relationship. He framed a question in the following manner: "Let's say that five years from now you're delivering packages [an example from one of his part-time jobs that Harold had used disparagingly]. What do you think I might say about that?" Reading Harold's facial expression (because Harold would otherwise have isolated, disavowed, and misused emotional descriptors), the therapist said, "Scorn would come down on your head and you would feel resentful." Harold responded, calling his feelings in this context "anxiety." The therapist firmly contradicted him: "That's not anxiety, it's anger. Let's look at it clearly, it's bitterness and anger, isn't it?" The therapist balanced the confrontation by commenting on Harold's forward movement: "You just told me something for the first time that you've skirted around before."

Prediction of the stubborn, angry, deflated, or withdrawn states reduced the likelihood of defensive or undermodulated responses and increased Harold's hopefulness that he would be understood enough to be helped. Yet he still did not know how to counter his procrastination. It was necessary to continue the theme and connect it to recent and current relationships, especially with men, and the past relationship with his father. An episode of angry crying about losing his father surfaced in an intrusive way during a momentary *self-righteous rage* state during this session.

247

Session 5

Harold again returned to the procrastination theme during this hour, attributing blame for the trait to his support system. He said that he procrastinated because others gave him inadequate support. The therapist first bolstered Harold's competent self-concepts by remarking on his determination to go ahead and become an independent and capable person instead of being buffeted about by not having support from his mother, father, or girlfriend. Harold's inclination to terminate therapy if the therapist was not supportive was predicted in order to increase his control over this impulse. Despite the therapist's efforts, Harold canceled the next hour on short notice.

Session 6

The missed hour was discussed, and was included as one of the twelve sessions offered (that is, no makeup session was offered). The therapist raised the issue of threatened loss of support in terms of past, current, and in-therapy relationship patterns.

The procrastination theme was seen as made worse by loss of support after Harold's mother died and, later, by the activation of mourning for his father. Similarly, missing the session constituted Harold's procrastination over confronting the therapist with (as he saw it) the low support he was receiving from others.

Harold described current work problems and the lack of support even when he had tried, during the week, to improve matters with his girlfriend.

Session 7

The therapist said that Harold's present procrastination was potentially reversible if he could endorse a patient, step-by-step approach to counterbalance his own grandiose insistence on immediate arrival at a high-status social position. The therapist also made several concrete suggestions about how Harold might improve communication with his girlfriend. We infer that the therapist was somewhat worried about premature termination and reacted by giving fatherly "how to do it, son" kind of advice.

Harold indicated that he had been aware of all the ideas provided but felt that they "came together for him" during this hour (a view about this session that he repeated many months later in the follow-up interviews).

Session 8

Harold spoke of himself as procrastinating less. He said that he was practicing his music and working on long-overdue college papers. When the therapist asked persistently for step-by-step details, it turned out that Harold had not yet worked on his paper but was "intending to do so at once." The misinformation was probably an attempt at furthering the idealized father-son positive transference relationship—a transference that had been activated by the therapist's "helpful advice" in the previous hour.

Session 9
There was then an unforeseen break of four weeks when the therapist, while on a short vacation, became unexpectedly unavailable for a longer time. In the ninth session, Harold spontaneously discussed termination and the deaths of both parents, themes that had probably been activated by his warded-off feelings about the therapist's absence.

Session 10
The theme of procrastination was again dealt with in regard to the concrete topic of Harold's doing a paper that would help him progress in his training plans. His high ideals were clarified, and the discrepancy between such goals and the absence of step-by-step plans to reach them was again emphasized. Some role-playing was done to differentiate Harold's unrealistic plan for writing necessary papers from a realistic plan that was gradually suggested by the therapist. Harold took this as encouragement during the session, but may have then experienced it as criticism after the session, when he was no longer directly involved in a relationship with the therapist. He may also have tried to be "the first to leave" before the last session. He did not appear for Session 11, nor did he call before or after that session. The therapist called him and established a time for what would be the final session.

Session 12
In the final session, Harold announced in an offhand manner that he had completed and turned in one of the two papers he needed to erase an incomplete at school, and had done work on the other one. He communicated in both *active engagement* and *mellow display* states, thanking the therapist casually for his help.

The Abandonment Theme. As already mentioned, the intensification of problem states after the death of Harold's mother meant that the theme of abandonment was potentially an important topic, although he disavowed its importance early in the therapy. The therapeutic alliance and

more working states occurred as a consequence of dealing with the procrastination theme, as has been described. It then became possible to
make more of an effort to confront the abandonment theme. This theme
was disavowed in the earlier sessions and accepted as important in the
later ones. The shift is illustrated by summaries of several sessions.

Session 1

Harold indicated indifference to the therapy; in part, he did so to ward
off expressions of anger and sadness. The therapist remarked on this and
connected it to deflated self-images, but he did not present these ideas
clearly and did not stick to them.

Harold expressed indignation when he spoke about how his girlfriend
did not give him support. In contrast, he had received support from his
mother. Then he spoke of how his aunt criticized him for neglecting his
mother. He remained indignant, using this stance to indicate the aunt's
current lack of support.

The therapist clarified the relationships between Harold's self-image
and the various degrees of support in his current environment, suggesting that such relationships were a possible focus. This focus was also
discussed in terms of the relationship with the therapist, since the therapist expected to be gone for a time during the therapy period. The therapist asked Harold to what degree he would feel unsupported during his
own anticipated absence and whether Harold might prefer to begin therapy with another therapist in view of this planned gap. Harold made the
active choice of continuing with the same therapist. But the suggested
focus was not clearly accepted.

Session 2

The issue of support emerged again, this time as related to the procrastination theme. The therapist pointed out that Harold would be stubborn
toward someone who cajoled him to work but who did not support him
totally, and that he would be angry if he experienced this person as
abandoning him.

When Harold came to understand this series of reactions in terms of his
relationships, the therapist then linked such a pattern of reactions to the
immediate context of therapy. If the therapist did not push Harold to
develop a focus and make progress in therapy, then he would procrastinate because he was not supported. If the therapist pushed him, he
would become angry and feel shoved about rather than supported. The
therapist also interpreted Harold's tendency to make a defensive display
of self-sufficiency in order not to display his need for support.

These interpretations helped to prevent an excessive positive expectation based on Harold's idealized mother transference (of being totally supported and always forgiven for his actions). At the same time, the therapist showed that such problems could be addressed without excessive criticism from the therapist.

There was a revision of focus when Harold agreed to work on the procrastination theme, as discussed above. This focus was established through unusually active interventions by the therapist. He wrote in his process notes: "The reason for this unusual activity was my feeling that he had very brittle self-esteem, that he was impatient, and that he would otherwise be unable to tolerate the degree of self-exposure that might allow him to confront core conflicts."

The therapist also indicated awareness of the theme of Harold's remorse for his lack of support to his mother, and related it to Harold's susceptibility to depressive episodes. The therapist felt that Harold had not become truly independent from his parents, and instead had a brittle pseudo-separation. He was stubbornly independent while being critical and envious of them. Because of traumatic upheavals between his parents, Harold saw his pseudo-separation as precocious and premature. He still had dependency needs, and a periodic sense of hopelessness prevented him from progressing in his own development. The therapist reasoned that it was important to support Harold's self-esteem, by indicating ways in which Harold was once again embarking on a purposeful life, before contemplating closer confrontation with the theme of remorse.

Session 3
In subsequent sessions, the remorse aspect of this theme emerged in associations, but the therapist continued to focus mainly on the procrastination theme already discussed. During the third hour, Harold was able to bring forth memories of bad thoughts toward his father, for which he now felt remorseful. He described his remorse for neglecting his recent work, which had led to his being fired. There was then some work on the theme of remorse for Harold's insufficient support of his mother. A major intervention was the therapist's assertion that understanding Harold's reactions to the death of his mother was important in explaining his current *dulled, listless, and inactive* state. The use of exciting and impulsive actions to counteract this state or a state of *remorseful self-disgust* was interpreted. Aspects of the abandonment theme (his or their abandonment) did not recur in any clear way until Session 7.

Session 7

As this session began, Harold talked about how bad he felt about being cool toward his girlfriend when she conveyed that she needed him in some way. The therapist made a general remark, one that might have been linked with Harold's mother, as he spoke of "taking the responsibility to stay with someone through thick and thin." Harold responded, "I don't know whether there are guilt feelings or what, but I do feel bad about it."

In comparison with earlier discussions, Harold was able to contemplate this theme for a longer time. The therapist attempted to clarify both sadness and remorse in relation to Harold's girlfriend and mother. He interpreted that Harold seemed to prefer the role of being an active abandoner to the experience of feeling sadness and anxiety over being abandoned.

Session 8

Harold knew that the therapist was going on vacation, causing a longer than one-week interval between sessions. The *mellow display* state was more prominent. He said he used to be much angrier in the past than now about losing support. He also praised the therapist, maintaining the *mellow display* state: "Without having talked to you or another therapist, I really don't think I would've been able to see it as clearly." But when the therapist said, "How will it sit with you when we stop?," Harold went from a *mellow display* state to a *struggle with vulnerability* state and came closer (however transiently) to experiencing his own feelings about being abandoned.

Session 9

After the therapist returned, he and Harold talked again of the abandonment theme. Harold stated that his thoughts had been returning to his mother. "It hurts to think that I can't show her love now." The therapist then made a more focused interpretation that was related to the remorse aspect of the abandonment theme: "Well, how about when she was dying? It seems to me you felt guilty about not seeing her more in the hospital." Harold was able to say, "I wish I had gone to visit her more often." But shortly after that, he began to shift blame to his aunt, saying that she was in part responsible for his lack of attention to his mother. Harold said, "I remember wanting to be involved as much as I could," implying that his aunt did not take him up on his offer to visit on some occasions.

Harold then continued to talk about his mother's death and how much he missed her. He described how she had bought him expensive presents. The therapist used this as an opportunity to move back to the topic of Harold's remorse for neglecting her. His aunt's criticism and his self-blame were slowly reviewed through a sequence of clarifications. Harold was asked about how much remorse he thought he ought to feel, how frightened he was by death, and how upset he was over not having been able to be independent of his mother. The therapist also interpreted Harold's fear of being drawn into the illness with her.

Outcome

Harold had follow-up interviews fifteen months and twenty-four months after the death of his mother. The first interview took place four months after the brief therapy was terminated. We will discuss each interview separately.

FOLLOW-UP INTERVIEW

During the interview, Harold conducted himself in the context of the social alliance described earlier. His states of mind were overcontrolled and ranged from *social chitchat* to *mellow display*, with occasional evidence of vulnerability. Harold seemed to have a strong need to present himself as in control and doing well. He had not sought a longer-term therapy.

In some ways, Harold had come to terms with the death of his mother and had a better understanding of the implications of this event for him and for his life.

> Harold: Well, when Dad died, uh, Mom was there to take care of me. Now with Mom dying, I was really on my own. I mean, "She's not there, Harold, if you get into any trouble, if you get into a bind or whatever. She's not there anymore. You've got to deal with it yourself." So I really think that it's encouraged me or prompted me to get a firmer grip on myself with my own direction in life. I think it's helped me realize that, uh, you gotta grow up and you gotta take care of yourself 'cause there's not always going to be somebody there to do it for you.
>
> Evaluator: Mmmhmm. So it sounds like you've experienced your fa-

ther's death as very disruptive, but in a way your mother's death has helped you grow up a little bit and take care of yourself like she used to.

Harold: Uh-huh. I think so.

The fact that Harold and his mother had reconciled briefly shortly before her death was comforting to him. However, he was still occasionally prone to think of himself as a selfish exploiter and to experience feelings of remorse at not having given to her as much as he would have liked. Harold seemed less preoccupied with feelings of shame and self-criticism, and reported that he identified with his mother's "lively, friendly, and involved personality." He did not report any disruptive, intrusive, or avoidant symptomatology in relation to her death.

The reactivation of mourning for Harold's father was not yet worked through. He described feelings of confusion and anger at the time of his father's death, and continued to have feelings of anger, emptiness, guilt, and frustration at not having completed his effort toward reconciliation.

The Procrastination Theme. Harold had recently begun holding down two jobs in order to pay his debts. "I couldn't keep putting the bills off and putting them off. I've got to pay for what I've done." He reported a plan to go to school at night as well. It seemed unrealistic to the evaluator for Harold to plan on two jobs and school.

Harold described therapy as having helped him to understand his tendency to put off work-related tasks.

Evaluator: Can you be specific on that?

Harold: Uhm . . . I was thinking we talked a lot about the procrastination that I have. I have a tendency to put things off. Uhhh, and I really found that I was just making excuses rather than honest reasons. . . .

Evaluator: Mmmhmm.

Harold: . . . for putting things off. And it helped me to realize that I don't have to go out and do whatever it is all at once. I mean, a little bit here and a little bit there and a little bit following that, and it adds up and gets done.

Working at two jobs seemed to be an indication of Harold's effort to progress in one area of his life. However, he discussed his long-range plans for a career with some vagueness. This made it difficult to evaluate his progress. In addition, aspects of the problem remained:

Evaluator: Getting back to procrastination, that you brought up, that you said was a big focus in therapy. Do you find that you're able to put that into practice also? That you're not procrastinating now? Or. . . .

Harold: (*Sigh*) Oh, I'm still procrastinating. Uhhh, but I don't think as much.

Evaluator: Mmmhmm.

Harold: I would say there has been improvement in that. Not an extreme amount, though.

The Abandonment Theme.   In the interval between termination and the first follow-up interview, Harold continued to feel a sense of abandonment by an unavailable, admiring, supportive mother. He indicated, however, that he was coping with the feeling better than he had before therapy began.

Harold: . . . a couple of months ago . . . something was going on . . . and I said, "Mom, where are you now that I need you?" And I feel even more so that way now because of all the rapid changes that are going on in my life. Uhmmm, she is not there to help me get a grip, she's not there to lean on. . . .

Evaluator: Mmmhmm.

Harold: Uhh, not there for the moral and emotional support that I could . . . it would help. I'm trying to cope without it, and it's uh, it's not easy. It's not as hard as I think I would imagine it to be if Mom was there to help me out, if that makes sense to you.

Evaluator: Mmmhmm.

Harold: Uhhmmm, but I do miss my Mom very, very much.

Evaluator: Do you find yourself feeling angry that she's not there?

Harold: Not at her, no. No, because I mean, it was just one of those things that happened. I mean, there's nothing I can do about it now, nothing I could do about it then.

Evaluator: When you feel you need support from somebody, is there somebody that you have now that you can go to, in the same way that you used to go to your mother, for example?

Harold: No. I have to rely on myself.

Evaluator: Mmmhmm.

Harold: And I think that's, I honestly think it's helping to build . . . helping to make me stronger emotionally.

Harold reported feelings of anger toward the therapist for having "interrupted" the therapy by his absence. He felt that the therapist had a responsibility to be there for him. While the therapist was absent during the therapy period, Harold reported that he felt worthless and let down.

Harold's ratings of the degree to which he was currently upset, as related to his mother's death, decreased from 95 out of a maximum possible of 100, at the pre-therapy evaluation, to 35 at the time of the first follow-up interview, with 0 being the lowest possible level. At the pre-therapy evaluation, Harold's self-ratings on the Hopkins symptom checklist had indicated high levels of depression and anger (each was rated 2.2 on a 4-point scale, with 4 as the highest possible score), and both affects had declined by the time of the first follow-up (0.6 for depression and 0.5 for anger). Anxiety symptoms were present (1.1) before therapy and had also declined (to 0.5). The evaluating clinician had rated Harold as highest on depression, and this score declined from a high to a lower (but still symptomatic) level (6 at pre-evaluation, 3 at first follow-up).

The Patterns of Individual Change Scales, as judged by six clinicians for this patient at the time of first follow-up, is shown in figure 7.2. Improvement was noted on most scales, but there was some reduction of functioning in Harold's capacity for intimacy. Work identity, assertiveness, and self-esteem were rated as much improved. While some improvement occurred, there was a continued tendency toward avoidance, and Harold still did not relate well to male authority figures.

SECOND FOLLOW-UP INTERVIEW

As at the next follow-up interview, Harold presented himself in a state of *mellow display*, with unruffled optimism over what was happening in his life. In fact, he had been having a stressful and turbulent time since the first follow-up. He was again experiencing feelings of loneliness and emptiness. This situation, combined with financial and other pressures, contributed to his increased drinking and seeking somewhat risky diversions.

The Procrastination Theme. While Harold reported improvement in his self-esteem, there was a continuing pattern of instability in his career goals. Since the first follow-up interview he had had several different jobs and had not yet reached his educational objectives.

The Abandonment Theme. Harold was experiencing a bittersweet mixture of sad, remorseful, and warm memories of his mother instead of denying these themes as he had before therapy. The feeling of regret for

Figure 7.2
The Pattern of Change: The Case of Harold

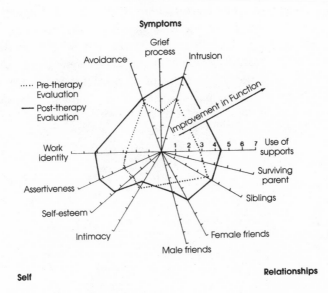

not having done more, considering how much she gave him, continued. His grief process seemed to be proceeding without impediments.

On the Hopkins Symptom Checklist, his depression had gone up slightly from 0.6 to 0.9; anxiety and anger stayed down at the same levels as in the earlier follow-up. A time-unlimited therapy, in which there would be further work on characterological issues, was discussed. Harold then sought out a person whom he later described as a kind of "friendly big-brother" type for additional therapy.

In summary, symptomatic reduction and working through of the mother's death seemed to have been substantially accomplished. The character trait focus, on issues related to the procrastination theme, had the salutory effect of developing a therapeutic alliance. This enhanced Harold's working states of mind and prevented premature termination. The topic of procrastination led to the opportunity to work on the abandonment theme, and Harold was able in turn to overcome his avoidance of grief-related processes. However, resolution of the procrastination character trait was not achieved. While insight and self-esteem had increased, there was insufficient change in behavioral patterns related to productivity to indicate that self and relationship schematizations had been altered.

Rather, there was a shift, because of stress reduction, from less to more competent self-concepts within Harold's existing repertoire.

With stress reduction, due in part to work on the abandonment theme, there was decreased defensiveness. However, Harold's defensive and cognitive style seemed otherwise unchanged. His characteristic defenses were like a filter; recognition of them allowed him to work on the recent loss of his mother. Nonrecognition would have prevented such therapeutic activity. Had he not become aware of his defensive maneuvers, he most likely would have engaged in a pseudo-therapy or would have dropped out of treatment.

8

THE BORDERLINE
PERSONALITY

Diagnosis

Whether there is a specific entity of "borderline personality disorders" or several characterological and phenomenological syndromes under this one rubric has been the subject of therapeutic controversy (Knight 1953; Grinker, Werble, and Drye 1968; Mack 1975; Green 1977; Hartocollis 1977; Stone 1981; Modell 1983). While much remains unresolved, a current working definition of a sample entity has been provided in *DSM-III* as follows:

The essential feature is a Personality Disorder, in which there is instability in a variety of areas, including interpersonal behavior, mood, and self-image. No single feature is invariably present. Interpersonal relations are often intense and unstable, with marked shifts of attitude over time. Frequently there is impulsive and unpredictable behavior that is potentially physically self-damaging. Mood is often unstable, with marked shifts from a normal mood to a dysphoric mood, or with inappropriate, intense anger or lack of control of anger. A profound identity disturbance may be manifested by uncertainty about several issues relating to identity, such as self-image, gender identity, or long term goals or values. There may be problems tolerating being alone, and chronic feelings of emptiness or boredom (*DSM-III*, 1980, p. 321).

Observation of Style

The personal vulnerabilities noted above manifest themselves in a variety of ways, depending on the interpersonal context and the time frame of the observations. In short-order patterns observed during an interview, there may be sudden, disjunctive shifts in states of mind with associated abrupt changes in the person's perception of self and others. There is a caricatured view of the self and the interpersonal world, with the latter being seen as populated by all-good or all-bad characters. Gratifying experiences lead to positive moods and to all-good images, while frustrating or stressful experiences may precipitate a collapse of the sense of goodness. When this occurs, the person may perceive the world as dangerous, toxic, and chaotically lacking secure refuge (Kernberg 1976; Horowitz 1977a; Grotstein 1981; Adler 1977; Masterson 1981).

These rapid shifts in affect reflect the inability of the person with a borderline personality to achieve a stable, simultaneously occurring ambivalence. Such an individual has difficulty construing self or a companion as having a balance of both affectionate and hostile feelings and intentions. Instead, when there is a threat of simultaneous recognition of these usually segregated good and bad representations, a state of flooded anxiety may occur (Volkan 1976). Because experience is subject to such sudden disjunctive transformations, there is a disturbance in the sense of temporal continuity. This difficulty contributes to a sense of confusion, disorientation, and derealization. As a result, errors may be made in the perception of the locus of thoughts, feelings, and intentions. The person may also have difficulty discriminating among bodily sensations, an experience that leads to a sense of depersonalization. As an example of these undermodulated swings in state, the person may shift from a state of unrealistically excited appreciation to hate-filled vengeance or despair.

Once a particular affect tone and relationship view are established, associations are overly driven by this affective valence. The result is often a cascading pattern of overgeneralizations. For example, when the feeling tone is predominantly positive, the evaluation of self, others, past accomplishments, and future prospects may be seen in a globally optimistic perspective. When the feeling tone is negative, the person's expectations are uniformly pessimistic: past valued accomplishments and relationships are transiently annihilated from memory, and future prospects may appear catastrophically bleak. While these latter negative perceptions are frequently found in nonborderline patients who are in entrenched depressive states, it is the short-order shifts among views that is characteristic of the borderline personality organization.

In the borderline personality, such short-order patterns are manifested in especially prominent maneuvers, including splitting, projection, and projective identification. Splitting is the segregation of role relationship models and their concomitant emotional states into loving and hating aspects (Kernberg 1975; Horowitz 1977a; Grotstein 1981). E. R. Shapiro (1978) differentiates splitting from the inhibitory controls characteristic of neurotic-level hysterical character structure as follows: "Splitting as a defense is to be distinguished from denial, which is the disavowal of whole percepts and the substitution of wish-fulfilling fantasies, and repression, which is the repulsion of mental content from consciousness due to a linkage of that content with a conflicted memory. In splitting, the positive and negative fantasized relationships remain alternatively within consciousness, with the complementary side dissociated" (p. 1307). Splitting can be differentiated from the defensive switching maneuvers described earlier with regard to the compulsive personality. In switching, there is an active mulling over of one and then the other side of the ambivalence, and the person attains at least a partially integrated view.

In the second prominent defense of borderlines, projective identification, there is a disavowal of unacceptable aspects of the self, with projection of these onto another person and then identification with the projected view. This process results in a heightened sense of familiarity with the other person because the other functions as a receptacle for the disavowed aspects of the self (Klein 1952; Kohut 1971; Grotstein 1981). There is often an unconscious effort to evoke these qualities in the person who is the object of the projections, as well as a disregard of certain real differences that are inconsistent with the projective expectations. There may be an attempt to vicariously experience and control aspects of the self through involvement with their real and imagined manifestations in others.

When the borderline personality is viewed from the perspective of history, particularly with attention to long-term relationship patterns, certain characteristics emerge. There is often a pervasive if warded-off sense of loneliness and emptiness. Concomitant difficulty in tolerating being alone motivates an intense hunger for interpersonal contact. However, this yearned-for intimacy creates as many problems as it is intended to solve. Intimacy may be experienced as intrusive and suffocatingly close, threatening the sense of self as separate and autonomous. Or, it may lead to fears of being dangled like some helpless puppet on a string. The

261

tendency to defer to others because the assertion of needs is viewed as dangerously aggressive, in combination with an exaggerated sense of responsibility for others' safety and happiness, leads to progressively increasing resentment. Such resentment is usually unexpressed until it reaches the boiling point, at which time it spills over in poorly controlled tirades that may threaten a relationship.

These difficulties in closeness and separation are related to a pervasive identity disturbance, in which an inner sense of cohesiveness, worth, direction, and meaning is not stably maintained. There is often confusion about gender identity, gender role, work identity, and long-term relationship commitment.

In the borderline personality, multiple conflicts and deficits acting in concert with unstable controls result in pervasive anxiety. Depressive states are a problem, in which feelings of emptiness are more prominent than they are in the guilty depressive states more typical of neurotic-level character structure (Grinker, Werble, and Drye 1968). Many shifting neurotic symptoms may appear, producing a "pan-neurotic" picture: that is, obsessions, compulsions, panic attacks, depressions, dissociations, and conversions may occur at different stress points. This tendency toward pan-neurotic symptomatology further reflects the lack of well-differentiated, stable utilization of cognitive controls.

Painful affects—particularly fear, anger, loneliness, and disappointment—are poorly tolerated. When they do occur, there is a rapid attempt to seek alleviation of such feeling states through impulsive flight into activity, drug and alcohol abuse, promiscuity, and related efforts to drown out or deflect attention from such painful affects. Interpersonal stressors such as rage at abandonment, fear of attack or merger, and out-of-control sexual excitement may trigger transient psychotic states. Evidence of irrational thinking may occur in unstructured tasks, such as projective testing (Gunderson and Singer 1975; Singer 1977). In contrast, most borderlines exhibit coherent, well-organized thinking in structured, nonthreatening situations.

Typical Problems for the Therapist

The relationship with the therapist reflects the predispositions of the borderline patient. The relationship is typically intense and unstable, marked by shifts of attitude. Idealizations give way to painful disillusionments, often following disappointments in the therapist that are objectively minor. As compared with the reactions of more stable persons, the transference reactions of the borderline patient shift abruptly in a way that may jar the therapist. In contrast to neurotic-level patients, who have a better capacity to recognize the subjective origins of their distorted views of the therapist, borderline patients have much greater difficulty engaging in a simultaneous comparison of an unrealistic transference view with a relatively more realistic therapeutic-alliance-based view of the relationship with the therapist.

This difficulty in differentiating what is real from what is imagined is heightened by a generally diminished capacity for self-observation and reflection. The therapist is frequently not attended to as a real person with strengths, vulnerabilities, imperfections, and a personal existence outside the therapeutic setting. Instead, the patient attempts to maintain a positive affective connection with an entirely good and often omnipotently endowed figure. The therapist is perceived as a powerful, ever present force whose purpose is to intercede in the troubled world of the patient. That view is threatened whenever the patient perceives the faulty human qualities of the therapist, and there may be a shift to an all-bad view and a rage-filled response.

Because the patient feels on the verge of evil actions or chaos, the therapist "must" be seen as an invincible figure who serves as a protector and stands between the patient and threats from inner or outer sources. Even when the treatment alliance seems secure, there is an undercurrent of fearful expectation. Therapists, sensing this fear, feel precarious, especially because lapses in this idealized view may trigger fantasies in which the therapist is seen as aligned with threatening forces. When a frightening metamorphosis of the therapist from benevolent to malevolent caretaker overwhelms the patient's capacity for reality appraisal, delusional concerns about the therapist may transiently occur.

Tactics in Therapy

With such patients, the therapist needs to continue to clearly communicate the nature of the therapeutic alliance by putting the "obvious" into words. This is especially important when the patient has manifested irritation, contempt, hostility, or disinterest in the therapist. At such times, the therapist needs to demonstrate to the patient that the compassionate approach will remain in spite of the patient's reproaches. The patient may be reminded of previous helpful interchanges with the therapist in order to counter the collapse of perspective that commonly occurs at times of disillusionment. With repeated enforcement, the therapist can then help the patient to assess issues of self-esteem. Here the issues are similar to those touched upon in the preceding chapter, in the section on tactics with the narcissistic personality disorder (pp. 246–49). Especially important in deflations of self-esteem will be the patient's periodic experiences of feeling too inadequate to merit attention from the therapist.

At times it is necessary to gently counter both the overidealization and the unrealistic devaluation of the therapist. However, in working with the borderline patient, interpretation of the defensive needs for idealization and devaluation may not be as necessary in a brief, stress-focused therapy as they are in long-term psychotherapy aimed at characterological change.

A brief therapy, if and when used at all with a borderline patient, should have focal aims of working through problems relating to a particular stressful event or dealing with a particular symptomatic situation. Such therapy may be utilized after the person has had a long period of psychotherapy but has a regression due to current stress, or may serve as a bridge to help convince a mistrustful and skeptical patient that long-term psychotherapy might be beneficial. Work on the specific focus will be slow and require patience because of the time and attention needed to keep the relationship as realistically based as possible.

As mentioned earlier in this chapter, a spectrum of disorders are associated with a borderline prototype. In persons with less severe forms of borderline pathology, recognition of the condition itself may not occur during early evaluation and psychotherapy sessions. In fact, such recognition may not take place until several years into an extended psychodynamic psychotherapy. When such recognition does occur, some modification of technique may then be useful.

In persons without such vulnerabilities to disordered self and object concepts, it is generally sufficient for the therapist to interpret transferences and resistances. In contrast, a different tack is needed with patients who are vulnerable to states of mind in which some aspects of interpersonal schematization either are lost or are dissociated into all-good and all-bad categories. In such cases, it is desirable for the therapist not only to point out the irrational warded-off contents and the patient's defenses against their expression but also to clarify a more rational and integrative way of organizing ideas.

It is frequently necessary to spell out immediately what is real and what is imagined, particularly when transference-based misperceptions of the therapist threaten the therapeutic alliance. By contrast, in working with neurotic-level patients, the technique of permitting misconceptions regarding the therapist to deepen by delaying reality feedback often permits a richer elaboration of the transference and more convincing interpretations. Working through occurs in this latter case because the patient has the capacity to tolerate the elaboration of the transference while he is simultaneously sustaining a more realistic view of the therapist.

For the borderline patient, comparison of a realistic view of the therapeutic relationship with the transference view is often difficult to accomplish. What is indicated here is a modulated strategy of prompt and repeated reality testing instead of allowing progressive deepening of feelings based on the transference relationship. The process will move more slowly than that in higher-level neurotic patients, who can retain a memory of the therapist's interpretation, recall their own experience at the time the interpretation was made, and contemplate it on their own. In patients in the borderline category, such capacities are unstable, so that the therapeutic continuity is fragmented by periods of confusion and by periods during which only one aspect of a situation can be retained.

Borderline patients may have some states in which they think of their therapist as bad, other states in which they think of the therapist as an omnipotent rescuer, and a third set of states in which they maintain a realistic appraisal of what transpired in the preceding session. Because of potential embarrassment, patients may not want to expose these diverse between-session thoughts. Instead, they will present only the more idealized view of the treatment and appear ready to tackle their difficulty. However, this will have an "as if" or contrived quality, masking over the more serious concerns about the relationship with the therapist.

In such instances it is helpful for the therapist to acknowledge the possibility of such transitions between "good" and "bad" images, and to indicate a compassionate acceptance and a willingness to repeat previous episodes of therapeutic work numerous times in order to gradually help the patient build a new integrative structure. Unfortunately, the time required for the repetitions necessary for such development is usually not available in brief therapy. But the brief therapy may provide a temporary restorative relationship in which the patient is calmed from states of stress and may be able to work through a life event.

In brief therapies, the problem of counteracting the patient's avoidances may be as prominent or even more prominent than the problem of major swings in affect. The result is that the therapist is faced with the dilemma of either accepting the avoidant defenses, in which case working through may not take place, or using confrontation to penetrate these resistances, with the danger that disorganizing affective storms, marked by rage, may occur. Adler and Buie (1976) have discussed the advantages and disadvantages of utilizing uncovering clarifications and interpretations with persons manifesting a borderline style. They caution especially against confrontation motivated in part by the irritation of the therapist with the patient's avoidance of intimate communication.

Ellen, a Representative Case

PRESENTING COMPLAINTS

Ellen was a thirty-two-year-old divorced woman who sought psychotherapy nine weeks after the death of her mother because of intense feelings of sadness, rage, and guilt. Of these feelings, anger predominated, and Ellen related this emotion to resentment of her mother's excessive dependency on her. She felt that her mother had attempted to manipulate and control her and had tried to avoid her parental responsibilities by exploiting recurrent illnesses and somatic complaints. Ellen was especially outraged that her mother had at times threatened to commit suicide if Ellen abandoned her in order to pursue her own autonomous self-development.

At the time of the pre-therapy evaluation, Ellen was living in an apartment with a female roommate and was enrolled in a graduate program in European history. She was referred to the clinic by a private psychologist with whom she had been in treatment pertaining to her marital difficulties. The patient and her therapist had mutually agreed to termination of this treatment approximately ten months prior to her mother's death. The therapist had no available openings at the time Ellen requested help following her mother's death.

Ellen's mother had been ill with cancer for twenty months prior to her death. The disease appeared to have been in remission for the ten weeks prior to her death, and yet she chronically complained to Ellen about pain and weakness, complaints which Ellen labeled hypochondriacal and which led her to resentfully withdraw from her mother. Ellen subsequently experienced intense and painful pangs of guilt when a relapse led to her mother's rapid deterioration and death.

While intrusive pangs of anger and guilt were most troublesome, Ellen also reported moments of "tremendous compassion and sadness" for a mother who had been ill and frightened much of her life. Further, she felt helpless and desperate when she thought of coping without her mother. This grief for her mother disrupted Ellen's academic functioning. She could not concentrate on her preparation for the oral preliminary examinations, felt confused about the value of pursuing this goal, and felt guilty about using her inheritance to support her academic work. She experienced an intensification of conflicts in dealing with her roommate, whom she resented as being critical rather than supportive during her time of need. Ellen was prone to angry outbursts, which further alienated her roommate and accordingly increased her feelings of abandonment. This perception of lack of support was compounded by the unavailability of her previous therapist. Additionally, Ellen felt called upon to provide emotional support to her younger brother, who was himself bereft and was struggling to both establish an architectural practice and cope with his own marital difficulties at the time of his mother's death. Her brother's demands were experienced as burdensome to her, as she already felt depleted, yet efforts to limit her caretaking toward her brother were highly guilt-provoking. Ellen was divorced two years prior to her mother's death, after eighteen months of marriage, and had not established a satisfactory love relationship with a man in the interim. This situation led to further feelings of isolation and failure.

BACKGROUND

Ellen described her early childhood as containing two "good mother" periods. One occurred during the first three years of her life, the other between the ages of seven and ten. Between the ages of three and six her mother was bedridden with a series of illnesses following the birth of Ellen's younger brother. For this period of time, she and her brother were cared for by a housekeeper and by her maternal aunt and uncle.

Ellen's early memories of her father were of a "sarcastic, critical, and defensive" person who could not protect her or provide emotional support. This pattern of behavior was always painful for her, but was particularly hurtful during the period of her mother's unavailability. There was considerable marital strife, and Ellen recalled her father's angry tirades about her mother's nagging physical complaints. Ellen saw this as the reason for his final decision to leave her mother for a woman he had been involved with for several years prior to the separation. Since this woman had been Ellen's ballet teacher, and since the father had accompanied Ellen to her dance lessons, Ellen felt guilty about her father's involvement in the affair. Ellen was ten years old when her parents' divorce occurred.

The period following her parents' separation was highly problematic. Ellen claimed no regrets and even some relief when she and her critical father became more distant from each other. However, she also recognized the traumatic effect of the divorce on her mother, whose psychological deterioration had been triggered by the separation. Her mother was markedly distraught and demanded that Ellen care for her and for her then six-year-old brother, a responsibility that simultaneously frightened and infuriated her. At the age of eleven, Ellen went away to a Quaker school for one year, and recalled her relief at being freed from her caretaking role. When she expressed a wish to return to this school for a second year, her mother threatened suicide.

This excerpt from the pre-therapy evaluation interview illustrates Ellen's feeling about the reversal of roles that characterized her relationship with her mother.

> Ellen: So our relationship was kind of normalized by the last visit. The only part that I guess I was thinking of was the left-over part, was that she clearly felt both before and right at the time of her death that I didn't need a mother. That was sort of one of the things that I realized when I first got back, was that (*sniffing*) that my mother has really never thought I needed a mother. From the time I was ten or eleven years old (*voice breaking*) obviously, or she wouldn't have let *me* be *her* mother. And— really—ignored—my need for a mother. And her response when I wanted to go for that year, you know, back to the Quaker school, was not—anything around *my* needs, but *her* needs. And, not whether I was a child too young to—to do this, but whether (*voice very low*) she was a mother too, you know, too dependent to let me.

Ellen tended to stifle her resentment toward her brother and mother because of feelings of guilt but was subject to breakthrough tantrums. At these times her mother would chastise her for a "shameful lack of control."

Ellen remained at home and attempted to compensate for the emotional unavailability of both of her parents by forming surrogate parental relations with several teachers and by "adopting" herself into her girlfriends' families. Her relationship with her father continued to be strained, with Ellen, rather than the father, initiating all contact. Ellen felt humiliated at having to beg for her father's attention in this way, and rationalized that she was doing it for her brother's sake. She was further insulted when her father responded to these overtures in a cool, rejecting manner.

For three years after her graduation from high school, Ellen majored in fine arts at a Canadian university. She then moved to Chicago, where she finished her undergraduate work and found employment as an art history librarian in a large gallery. However, she hated her living situation. She felt lonely and alienated in Chicago, and after an unhappy sexual liaison became ill with severe cluster headaches that forced her to be bedridden for repeated periods of time. Despite this, she was grimly determined to establish herself in that city, a decision that she saw as tantamount to "locking herself in an institution." She felt eerily identified with her mother during this period of suffering.

Ellen finally left Chicago after five years, returned to her hometown in southern California, and subsequently married an attorney after a relatively brief courtship. The decision to marry was impulsive, and occurred during a phase when she was idealizing her fiancé. The marriage lasted eighteen months, until Ellen became disillusioned with her husband. She experienced him as "superficially warm, but cold, domineering, and critical, like my father, when I got to know him better." Sexual intimacy only occurred after both partners drank, and was often not remembered the next day. Around the time when Ellen left her husband, her mother suffered a fractured hip in a domestic accident, and exerted pressure on Ellen to be available to her. This conflict divided Ellen's loyalties and was a further strain on her marriage.

For the past seven years Ellen had pursued studies in European history. The topic chosen for her dissertation was a study of adolescence in relation to cultural standards of child rearing practices in various historical epochs. Her main interest was in exploration of the roles assigned to mothers and fathers during the adolescent's emancipation from the family. Ellen was consciously aware of the relationship between her choice of a dissertation topic and her own unhappiness during childhood and adolescence. She felt blocked in organizing her thesis, a state that reflected a long-standing problem that had been intensified by her mother's recent illness and death.

IMPORTANT STATES OF MIND

Ellen presented an unusually complex array of states, with a number of variations and shadings in state quality. For that reason, the task of modeling these states is difficult. In addition, it was hard for Ellen to tolerate her conflictual feelings, which tended to rapidly escalate to frighteningly disorganized and out-of-control proportions. She preferred to maintain overcontrolled states that appeared compulsive in style in order to prevent entry into out-of-control states. However, she was subject to defensive failures that were experienced as overwhelming waves of feelings. Her most commonly experienced states are shown in table 8.1.

TABLE 8.1
List of Ellen's States

Label	Description
Undermodulated States	
Furious rage	Towering rage in which she feels destructive toward others, whom she sees as exclusively evil. There is a cascading overgeneralization of resentments toward others, who are seen without qualification as deceitful, exploitative, disloyal, and persecutory. Crosscurrents of shame and remorse color the rage.
Flooded despairing sadness	A predominantly warded-off state of panicky, out-of-control sadness and hopelessness. It is a piercing, nearly unbearable experience in which the outpouring of grief feels like "vomiting." There is a loss of perspective, an inability to remember past sustaining ties, and a pervasive painful sense of loneliness and emptiness.
Chaotically jumbled	Appears perplexed, confused, struggling with a disordered array of competing thoughts and images. Emotions are not clearly differentiated but instead are experienced as jumbled, with intensely vivid images and impaired concentration. This may be manifested behaviorally by poor eye contact, lowered voice, blocks in communication, or silences.
Well-Modulated States	
Open crying	Sad, tearful, authentically expressing the inwardly felt emotions of sadness and loss; slow but not halting cadence to speech; stillness with restricted range of movement. Alternately looks toward and away from listener as though searching for someone else. State may be preceded or followed by an anxious variant in which a struggle to control crying is manifested by facial and postural tensions.
Irritable anger	Anger toward others manifest in vigorous outward gestures, raised voice, and clenched fists. There is a staccato-like quality of open expression alternating with motoric inhibition of the feeling.
Needy martyr	Frustrated deferral of needs to others. Self-pitying display of own neediness without assertion of anger. Dejected manner evidenced by tremulous voice, hesitation, disparaging laughter, and sighing.

TABLE 8.1 *(continued)*

Label	Description
Struggle with vulnerability	Experiences self as vulnerable, feels criticized, and adopts a "there, there" self-comforting attitude.
Overmodulated States Controlled communicating	Presents a distanced, intellectualized report of difficulties as though describing someone else's experience. Voice has conspicuously measured inflections and clear sentence structure; voice is also pedagogical, with deep, slow intonation and strong underscoring of words, creating the impression of a rehearsed presentation. In general, appears composed and restrained, creating the appearance of mastery over frightening concerns so that there is an air of contrivance reflecting the inconsistency between outward display and inner uncertainty.
Artificial and engaging	Cordial, jovial display as in animated social conversation. The up-tempo spirit appears exaggerated, and even caricatured, with wide gestures, sudden loud tonalities, rapid head nodding, bouncy postural movements. Struggle to conceal anxiety which is, nonetheless, manifested in tremulous laughter and shifts to higher voice pitch. A lighthearted play-acting of emotions that are inwardly threatening contributes to a "laughing it off" quality.

Most Problematic States. One of Ellen's most disturbing out-of-control experiences was entry into a *chaotically jumbled* state, in which she felt out of control. Ideas and feelings were experienced as jumbles of intensely vivid but disconnected sequences of imagery, resulting in a frightening sense of confusion and distracted blocks in communication. An extreme version of this state was noted in her report of occasional, though rare, hallucinatory experiences earlier in her life.

Ellen's anger toward her mother was a chief complaint. She could tolerate manageable states of *irritable anger*, but these could rapidly escalate to *furious rage*, in which Ellen was flooded by profound anger with or without crosscurrents of shame or remorse.

In addition to the *chaotically jumbled* and *furious rage* states, there was a third relatively uncontrolled state, that of *flooded despairing sadness*. This state contained an element of panic, with a piercing and unbearable quality that the patient described as "like vomiting" her grief.

Modulated States. Also included in table 8.1 are a series of relatively more modulated states. These included a state of *open crying* in which

Ellen's sadness, while still conflicted, was not experienced as out of control. There were also an *irritable anger* state, a *struggle with vulnerability*, state, and a rather unusual *needy martyr* state. Ellen oscillated confusingly between self-pity, anger, compliance, and anxious and disparaging laughter.

The threat of entry into the *furious rage* state was countered by a state in which Ellen outwardly projected assurance, assertiveness, or hostility. However, she was usually role-playing rather than authentically experiencing these feelings. The *needy martyr* state, in which she was angry at having to suppress her needs because others were even more needy, also served to ward off intense rage. In this state, anger was not directly experienced.

As with anger, Ellen experienced a sadness that was authentic and of tolerable intensity. This could be seen in the *open crying* state. Her sadness might, however, rapidly advance to *flooded despairing sadness* or might be defended against by mimicry, in an *"as if" pensive* state.

Overmodulated States. The predominant overcontrolled state is labeled *controlled communicating.* In this state Ellen was an intellectualizing reporter of her feelings, presenting her troubles to the therapist as though she were a colleague discussing another case rather than a patient who was experiencing difficulties. There was movement back and forth between this state and the *artificial* and *engaging* state, where conversation was polite and superficially congenial, as between cordial acquaintances. Ellen was frequently in one of these two states, which protected her against entry into states of mind in which she felt flooded with disorganizing levels of affective intensity.

For completeness, several minor states are noted here. These include a wished-for state of *warm mutual engagement,* which was ideal, seldom realized, and mimicked in a *social chitchat* state. There was also a state of *numbed withdrawal,* and a state of *fearful sexual arousal,* which characterized efforts at sexual intimacy. This occurred in place of a wished-for state of *joyous sexual excitement.*

Defensive Organization of States. The defensive layering of five of these states is shown in table 8.2. *Flooded despairing sadness* and *furious rage* are listed as the most problematic states. The most dreaded and so warded-off state was that of being *chaotically jumbled.* Ellen's most desired state was one of *warm mutual engagement.* However, because of her inability to stabilize such a state, Ellen used a compromise of being *artificial and engaging.* This allowed her to maintain contact and thus avoid the intense feeling of chaotic aloneness. She also was able to avoid the close-

TABLE 8.2
Defensive Organization of Ellen's States

State	Self	Aims	Concept of Other
Problematic Role Relationships			
Flooded despairing sadness	Abandoned waif	Cries in vain ⟶ Deserts ⟵	All good: hope-lessly lost
Furious rage	Wounded avenger	Seeks revenge ⟶ Deceives ⟵	All bad: selfish betrayer
Dreaded or Warded-Off Role Relationships			
Chaotically jumbled	Floundering, incoher-ent, and fragmented	Seeks structure and coherence ⟶ Ignores ⟵	Remotely indiscernible
Desired Role Relationships			
Warm mutual engagement	Competently caring	⟵⟶ Mutual give and take	Competently caring
Compromise Role Relationships			
Artificial and engaging	Cheerful (but unreli-able) companion	Appear friendly ⟶ Circumscribed interest ⟵	Cheerful (but un-reliable) companion

ness that might lead to an outpouring of rage, sadness, or fear that she might be either abandoned or betrayed.

IMPLICATIONS OF DEFENSE LAYERING OF STATES OF MIND FOR THERAPY

Ellen was afraid to enter states of sadness, anger, tenderness, or neediness because of the danger of being carried into one of the confused, jumbled, or flooded states. Instead, she retreated from authentic feeling into overcontrolled states, such as *controlled communicating*. In such a situation, if the therapist does not counter the overcontrolled stance, the patient will be too affectively distant from relevant themes to progress. But if the therapist does counter these avoidant trends, the patient may be threatened with entry into states whose intensity and complexity may overwhelm her capacity to process these feelings. As a result, she may not be able to adaptively explore important themes.

When Ellen entered states of real but tolerable affective intensity, anticipatory anxiety built up because of her past experiences of loss of control. When she feared criticism for being too controlled and lacking feelings, she mimicked her real emotions in an effort to gain social approval and to practice mastery of emotions without losing control.

MODELS OF ROLE RELATIONSHIPS AND SELF-CONCEPTS

Ellen sometimes viewed herself as an omnipotently responsible care-taker who had to suppress her own autonomous needs in order to accommodate the demands of others, particularly her mother. This problematic self-image was intensified during the period of her mother's recent illness and especially with the mother's death, but was not unique to this recent event. It had been Ellen's enduring view that she must sacrifice herself to accommodate extreme demands on the part of her mother, a view that was repeatedly exacerbated at every life transition. Variations of this role relationship occurred across a spectrum of states. For example, in the *needy martyr* state Ellen experienced herself as being needy but also felt forced to provide for the other person, who was overwhelmed, depleted, and extracting care from Ellen. In the *irritable anger* state she experienced herself as frustratedly struggling and the other as self-absorbed and unavailable. In the *furious rage* state she experienced herself as suffocated and misunderstood in relation to a destructively needy, controlling, selfish, and trust-betraying person.

During the initial interview, Ellen related her angry feelings, which had been intensified by her mother's death, to her reactions at the time of the parental divorce.

> Therapist: Can you say more about what did get stimulated by your mother's death?
> Ellen: Uhm, well—one thing is a lot of—a lot of anger. I have, uh, I had uh, a very complex relationship with my mother, and since I was about ten or eleven, when my parents were divorced, we basically reversed roles. . . .
> Therapist: Mmmm?
> Ellen: . . . and I was her caretaker for a while. I wanted to get out of that. I also wanted some support for myself, and that wasn't forthcoming, and I couldn't get out—she threatened

suicide. And by getting out I mean I had spent a year in a Quaker school while she was getting her business degree in San Diego and living in an apartment, and I *loved* it.

Therapist: This is when you were ten or eleven years old?

Ellen: Eleven—eleven or twelve.

Therapist: Mmmm?

Ellen: Seventh grade. And I said I wanted to go back, and that was when she basically cried and made threats of suicide— and said that if I didn't stay that there wouldn't be any reason for her to live, and so on. . . . There's a lot of old anger around not having been able to get out; and some things I've never dealt with in my therapy, and that suddenly seemed very . . . well, important in some way. I don't remember—what it felt like—to, uhm, during that time that I was (*clearing throat*) that she was leaning on me so tremendously when I was ten and eleven.

The guilt that Ellen felt in relationship to this theme was complex and central to her conflicted grief reaction. Because of her mother's threats, the wish to be separate and independent from her mother was extremely guilt-provoking. This could be seen in the guilt that she now felt for having failed to keep her mother alive, as well as her guilt for harboring murderous rage because she was forced to be the caretaker and minister to her mother's childlike needs. The mother's threats of suicide, should Ellen abandon her, led Ellen to the partly realistic, partly fantasy-based belief that she had the power of life and death over her mother. Ellen believed that if she had expressed her feelings of intense hatred, she could have driven her mother to suicide.

At a later developmental period, this theme was replayed again. Ellen broke off her marriage in part because her mother had sustained a fractured hip after a fall. Her mother insisted that Ellen care for her instead of spending so much time with her husband. The mother had disliked Ellen's husband from the outset, and was intensely jealous of his hold on her daughter. She covertly sought to undermine her daughter's marriage, and Ellen was particularly sensitive to this pressure.

Shortly before her mother's death, when it appeared that the cancer was in remission, Ellen withdrew, making fewer telephone calls and visits, and inwardly berated her mother for being a cranky, hypochondriacal complainer. Ellen was now worried that her hostility and withdrawal had contributed to her mother's ultimate demise.

DEFENSIVE ORGANIZATION OF ROLE RELATIONSHIP MODELS

Ellen's central wish was to be independent and separate from her mother, and not to be forced into the role of caretaker. An associated but antithetical wish was to be close to her mother—to be nurtured and cared for without strings attached, and without having to feel greedy about taking from someone who was already depleted. Ellen wished to be able to receive from her mother without surrendering her own autonomy in the process. While this is not an uncommon pattern of conflictual wishes, the negative consequences of expressing these wishes were, for her, relatively extreme. Instead, she canceled out one wish with the other, stifling the full expression of either to avoid threats.

What were these threats? If Ellen left her mother, she would risk intolerable guilt and anxiety that her mother would either kill herself or eventually retaliate by disowning her. If, on the other hand, she did not place distance between herself and her mother, she might become engulfed by the insatiable quality of her mother's emotional and physical neediness, and might sacrifice the precarious structure of her autonomy. It is the extremity of the alternatives—as conceptualized by Ellen, and at least in part acted out in reality by her mother—that had made development difficult for her, in spite of valiant struggles toward maturation. At the age of thirty-two she was deeply preoccupied with issues of separation-individuation, identity formation, and stabilization of a realistic, positive self-concept. This is reflected in the self and object concepts that characterized her varied states of mind as shown in table 8.3.

Following her mother's illness and death, there was a definite intensification of the core relationship pattern, which is summarized in table 8.4. The illness afforded her mother an opportunity to assault Ellen yet again with her neediness. Ellen experienced an intensification of her feelings of responsibility toward her mother and also toward her younger brother, who was struggling with career and marital pressures at the time of the mother's death.

An unfortunate experience with Ellen's previous psychotherapist tended to further reinforce this role relationship pattern. Her psychologist was unable to offer her immediate treatment because of realistic time constraints. Ellen subjectively interpreted this to mean that her former therapist was, like others who had disappointed her in the past, unable to tolerate her stormy demands. Ellen felt that this "rejection" was punishment for her appeal for help.

Finally, the fact that Ellen did experience moments of an incredible sense of freedom following her mother's death, especially freedom from the possibility that her mother would eventually commit suicide, was a

TABLE 8.3

The Example of Ellen: Relating Role Relationship Models to States

State	Self	Other
Undermodulated States		
Flooded despairing sadness	Abandoned waif	Hopelessly lost
Furious rage	Wounded avenger	Selfish betrayer
Chaotically jumbled	Floundering, incoherent, and fragmented	Remotely indiscernible
Well-Modulated States		
Open crying	Bereft child	Lost, scornful critic
Irritable anger	Frustrated protestor	Self-absorbed
Needy martyr	Resentful caretaker	Demanding exploiter
Struggle with vulnerability	Vulnerable child	Tentative parent
Overmodulated States		
Controlled communicating	Professional	Colleague
Artificial and engaging	Cheerful (but unreliable) companion	Cheerful (but unreliable) companion

mixed blessing for her. The thought that she had benefited from her mother's death was guilt-inducing—a final ironic twist to Ellen's lifelong sense that her personal growth was at her mother's expense.

THE MULTIPLICITY OF SELF-CONCEPT AND ROLE RELATIONSHIP MODELS

In the face of deprivations, criticisms, and other frustrations, Ellen was prone to very negative self-concepts without a tempered awareness of her positive qualities. Her images of her mother were subject to swings of idealization and devaluation, leading to "all good" or "all bad" representations. The segregated negative views of herself and others frequently precipitated entry into *chaotically jumbled, furious rage,* or *flooded despairing sadness* states. Attempts at control led to contrived self-images and a sense of distance from others, since vulnerabilities and needs had to be kept in check. Closeness had to be mimicked rather than felt.

Ellen's presentation was further complicated by variations in role relationship models when a third person was introduced. When Ellen had a view of her mother as bad and herself as wrongly betrayed, she felt righteously enraged. But if a third party implied that she had only gotten the treatment she deserved because she was a bad daughter, she entered a mixed state in which shame, rage, and fear of loss of control all occurred together. Similarly, when Ellen struggled to risk presenting her vulnerability to someone who at the moment appeared sympathetic, she

TABLE 8.4
A Conflictual Relationship Schematization for Ellen

Aim:	I want to be independent from my mother so that I am separate from her and am free to satisfy my own needs (for love, autonomy, sexuality, power).
But I have these impediments:	
Personal deficiencies	I lose my sense of self and feel dangerously engulfed in the other's presence, a feeling that is intensified during any joint excitement.
Environmental deficiencies	My family does not support my independence. My roommate exploits my difficulty in asserting my own needs by dominating me. I don't have a lover who can help me over my fears of intimacy.
If I get what I want, then:	
Internal positive response	I will feel whole and proud. I will be relieved of the anger I feel for subjugating my needs to the needs of others.
External positive response	I will be respected and others will want to care for me in a mutually giving relationship.
But if I get what I want, then:	
Internal negative response	I will feel guilty that I have hurt others by selfishly pursuing my own aims. If I allow myself to believe that I am cared for in a mutual relationship, then my trust will be betrayed, or I will be so totally possessed that I will lose my sense of identity.
External negative response	Those I leave out will retaliate or shun me. I will be criticized as selfish and punished by abandonment. At the extreme, others will kill themselves to show me how I destroyed their lives by excluding them in the pursuit of my own interests or by extracting too much from them.
So I will use these coping strategies:	
Interpersonal attitudes or behaviors	I will defer my needs to those of others, placate them, and then believe that they will always reward and protect me. I will present myself as if not needy or vulnerable and I will avoid exciting intimacy. I will vacillate between being remote and being close in order to control excitement or loneliness.

TABLE 8.4 *(continued)*

Intrapsychic attitudes	If I disavow aspects of my competence I can reduce the danger of punishment. If I denigrate those things I strive for (love, career), I can protect myself from intolerable guilt if I should succeed and intolerable disappointment if I should fail.
Intrapsychic styles	By constant vigilance and self-regulation I will attempt to stabilize an unambiguously positive view and distance myself from any sense of badness. I will evacuate my dysphoric states by evoking them in others and then helping others to manage them.

And the results will be:

Recurrent states of mind	Artificial and engaging or controlled intellectualizing states.
Patterns of state transition	Sudden entry into furious rage, overwhelming despair, or disorganization, with disappointments, resentments, and losses as triggering events.

Likely life course (accomplishments in working, relating, experiencing):

Short-range	Failure to make career decisions or to consolidate important relationships.
Long-range	Shifting feelings or signs of anxiety, depression, somatization, dissociation, and compulsive behavior.

was fearful that the person might become a scornful critic of such displays of neediness (her mother had berated her for "messy tantrums"). This shifting view of others motivated Ellen to both display and conceal her vulnerability.

A variation of this ambiguity was Ellen's experience of herself as open, hopeful, and misunderstood in relationship to a seemingly empathic and loving, but actually tricking, mother. Ellen's mother would make promises that things would go well if they could be close, and would woo Ellen into greater intimacy. This would stimulate hope, and Ellen would let her defenses down somewhat, particularly the defense of denigrating her mother to maintain distance and protect against disappointment. Her mother would betray this trust by inevitably presenting her pressured demands, and would extract care from Ellen.

Ellen responded to her mother's self-absorption with resentment, and withdrew emotionally with an even greater resolve to be independent. She had to avoid raising her hopes for an excited reunion because she also anticipated that there would be a betrayal, and that she would become flooded with shame or hard-to-control angry impulses. In her present life, Ellen was caught on the horns of a dilemma. Her wish for intimacy led her to initiate relationships. However, she was paralyzed by her ambivalence: she felt that growing closer would mean risking disappointment, exploitation, and abandonment; alternatively, if she moved away from the person, she would feel empty and lost.

This difficultly in appraising the risks and benefits of intimacy was also repeated in Ellen's sexual relationships with men. She experienced excited involvement, but then became frightened and acted disinterested when a desirable man reciprocated her overtures. Ellen's problems with sexuality had complex origins. She was aware that both her mother and her aunt had had bisexual strivings. Her aunt had covertly influenced Ellen's belief that a woman was either a competent, strong, and masculine careerist or a weak, submissive, feminine housewife and mother.

Ellen's relationship with her father further intensified her difficulties in establishing a sexual identity. Her father was overtly critical and rejecting, yet it was inferred from Ellen's history that her father was covertly seductive. A probable distortion of the meaning of her parents' divorce is that she was a sexually interested, guilty, and punished daughter, whose attraction to her father had contributed to his decision to leave the family. The loss of her father was both frightening and enraging, since he had abandoned her for another woman. This event contributed to Ellen's sense of defectiveness and left her without protection in the smothering, possibly sexual, closeness with her mother. The impact of these events was intensified because the divorce had occurred during the sensitive developmental period of Ellen's early adolescence, and because her father's lover was Ellen's ballet teacher.

Therefore, for Ellen to become close to a man, multiple threats were involved. There was guilt for separating from her mother, guilt for surpassing her mother, anxiety about committing symbolic incest, anxiety about the loss of Ellen's identification with her aunt and mother, and fear of an engulfing sexualized merger with a lover who might woo her only to subsequently abandon her.

Finally, there was an important triadic role relationship in which Ellen experienced herself as critical of a second party. That second party was in relationship to a third person who evaluated the appropriateness of Ellen's feeling that the second person, usually her mother or father, was in the wrong. If the third person supported Ellen's feelings, she was able to maintain a good image of herself and could feel contemptuous or hostile toward the second party. However, if the third person should turn against her, she might feel subject to self-blame and might react with shame and guilt over inappropriate and destructive hostility.

IMPLICATION OF ROLE RELATIONSHIP MODELS FOR PSYCHOTHERAPY

As suggested by this variety of encapsulated, poorly integrated self-images, Ellen was vulnerable to rapidly fluctuating swings in her assessment of herself and others. There were frequent role reversals regarding who was powerful and who was weak, who was good and who was bad, and who was to blame and who deserved credit. At times she floundered between these contradictory views; this led to a confused state that could range from fleeting lapses to sustained entry into the disorganizing *chaotically jumbled* state. The complexity of such role relationship models, combined with the fragility of Ellen's positive view of herself in relation to a caring rather than critical and depleting person, would be expected to create difficulty in establishing and sustaining a therapeutic alliance. This problem was likely to be intensified both by the time limit of a brief psychotherapy and, in the case of our bereavement study, by the recording of the therapy for research purposes, with its imagined audience of judgmental third parties.

As indicated in table 8.5, there were several very likely negative transferences. Ellen could see herself again as the wounded avenger in relationship to the tricky betrayer if she perceived that the therapist was not meeting all of her needs, or when the therapist wished to stick with the time limit of the brief therapy. Ellen could also experience herself as the abandoned waif in relation to the hopelessly lost caretaker. This was most likely to occur following the end of therapy, at times when Ellen anticipated the end of therapy, or on weekends during the therapy period. Such transferences could lead into the *chaotically jumbled* state, in which Ellen had no clear view of the object. On the other hand, she might feel that the therapist was moving too close, and could feel engulfed by an invasive and smothering mother figure.

These negative transference themes could lead to countertransferences, in which the patient was seen as dangerously explosive or in which the therapist felt like an inadequate, neglectful caretaker. The extent of Ellen's needs might lead the therapist to see her as hopelessly needy and so feel either depleted of energy or too withholding of care. If clarifications and interventions seemed to lead into the *chaotically jumbled* state, then the therapist might feel guilty for overstimulating or damaging the pa-

TABLE 8.5

Summary of Key Role Relationships for Ellen's Therapy

Potentials for Relationship Patterns in Therapy	Patient's View:		Therapist's View:	
	Of Self	Of Other	Of Patient	Of Self
Potential negative transferences and countertransferences	1. Wounded avenger 2. Abandoned waif 3. Jumbled, fragmented 4. Engulfed	1. Tricky betrayer 2. Hopelessly lost 3. Remotely indiscernible 4. Invasive, smothering	1. Dangerously explosive 2. Hopelessly needy 3. Confused, fragile, and disturbed 4. Disorganized	1. Bad caretaker 2. Depleted or withholding 3. Helpless 4. Intrusively seductive
Potential positive transferences and countertransferences	1. Worthwhile, lovable child 2. Titillated student	1. Selfless, nurturing parent 2. Exciting mentor	1. Lovable but weak 2. Exciting student	1. Super-nurturant 2. Titillated mentor
Potential therapeutic alliance	1. Vulnerable child 2. Student	1. Potentially harmful parent 2. Mentor	1. Vulnerable but worthwhile 2. Worthy student	1. Sympathetic and concerned 2. Facilitator
Potential social alliance	1. Professional 2. Friend	1. Colleague 2. Companion	1. Colleague 2. Interesting peer	1. Professional 2. Friend

tient, with the result being negative consequences rather than positive gains. If warded-off contents were frequently interpreted, the therapist might also worry that Ellen was being flooded by more insights than she could tolerate. Potential therapeutic relationships between Ellen and the therapist are summarized in table 8.5.

Potential therapeutic alliances would also have some transference aspects, perhaps with Ellen viewing herself as a vulnerable child in relation to a potentially helpful parent. Another possibility is that she might carry over her academic role, that of a student to a mentor.

INFORMATION-PROCESSING

Ellen's complex and often contradictory wishes and fears with respect to her mother, as well as her limited capacity to contemplate both positive and negative feelings, predisposed her to pathological grief. Many variations of role relationship models with the mother carried the threat of entry into affectively flooded, disorganizing states in which a sustaining and balancing perspective was transiently lost. Ellen's posture of overcontrol, designed to ward off a pervasive sense of badness and danger, led to avoidance of feelings and thus impeded realistic adaptation to her loss. Several important constellations of experienced and warded-off ideas and emotions, which are centered around the meanings of her mother's death, are modeled here to illustrate the structure of Ellen's grief reaction at the time of the pre-therapy evaluation.

Despair and Rage Themes. The thoughts that provoked the disturbing affects in the pre-therapy period began with Ellen's conscious recognition that her mother was dead. This idea set off various trains of thought that led toward *flooded despairing sadness* and *furious rage.*

The sequence leading to *flooded despairing sadness* began with Ellen's belief that she needed closeness with her mother, whom she viewed as all good. She experienced sadness as she recognized that the death once and for all time had closed the door on the yearned-for intimacy. The experience of having initially tolerable levels of sadness set off anticipatory anxiety that she might become overwhelmed with grief and become disorganized. She was fearful of the suicidal extreme of her despair, a worry that in part reflected an identification with her mother.

In order to ward off these frightening ideas leading to *despairing sadness,* she attempted to disavow her need for her mother by facilitating ideas about how her mother was totally bad, abandoning, uncaring, and demanding of Ellen's caretaking (as shown in figure 8.1). These ideas, however, led potentially to the state of *furious rage.* From these ideas of mother as bad, Ellen oscillated defensively back to the mother as all

Figure 8.1
Despair and Rage Themes

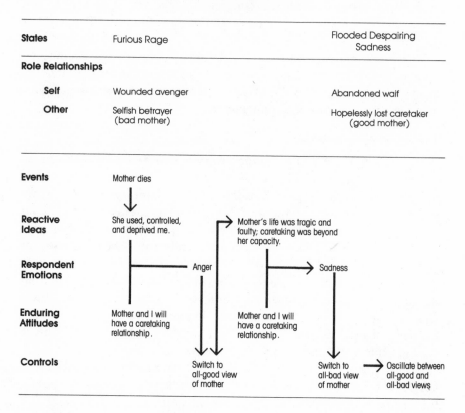

States	Furious Rage		Flooded Despairing Sadness
Role Relationships			
Self	Wounded avenger		Abandoned waif
Other	Selfish betrayer (bad mother)		Hopelessly lost caretaker (good mother)

good. She eased the threat of each affective state by an emotional reversal, accomplished by shifts in role relationship models.

Ellen's dilemma was that if she contemplated loving feelings toward her mother, she couldn't tolerate the disappointment of losing the untempered fantasy of a wholly restorative relationship with her. If Ellen experienced her unmoderated hatred toward her mother, she cast away potentially sustaining positive memories of the relationship. The prototypical borderline control of splitting was evident in these segregated views (a longed-for but never realized all-good mother of a loved and loving daughter, a dreaded all-bad mother of a hated and hate-filled daughter) and contributed to a profound impasse in the mourning process.

Ellen had contrasting beliefs about why her mother had neglected her. In one view, she had the idea that she was disregarded because she was a defective, unworthy, and unlovable daughter, a thought that engendered feelings of shame. When she attributed blame to her mother, perceiving her as selfish or defective, she experienced rage at her unjust treatment. This rage triggered further latent ideas that she hated her mother so much that she often wished the mother were dead, and was now pleased that she had finally died. These death wishes were at variance with her ideal for herself as a loving daughter, and Ellen felt both guilty and ashamed that others might view her as a diabolical, hate-filled person. She also feared loss of control of her rage, a fear that was not mere fantasy but was grounded in actual experiences of lapses in control.

A variation on the theme of rage over neglect was the hostility that Ellen felt toward her mother, not only for neglecting her but for manipulating Ellen through guilt to extract caretaking for herself. There was parallel resentment toward Ellen's roommate, her brother, and her previous therapist for "forcing her" to accommodate to their needs rather than supporting Ellen in her hour of grief. These disappointments all carried the meaning that others were not able to care for her, and instead that she was blackmailed into caring for them. This sense of obligatory self-sacrifice ran counter to Ellen's aims for autonomy and pursuit of her own needs, and triggered intense anger. Her feeling of rage again stimulated fears of loss of control, and activated a chain of images and thoughts that included a fear of personal fragmentation, guilt for being a horrible person harboring destructive fantasies, and fear that expression of this rage could be injurious to and, in the extreme, lethal for others. These dangers motivated controls, primarily splitting, which was accomplished by a dissociative, segregated appraisal of who was actually responsible. The alternative perspective was that Ellen's mother, her roommate, her brother, and her former psychologist were all justified in their neediness, and that she should accommodate to them (be their caretaker) without reciprocal expectations. In this view, she was forced to subjugate her needs to others in an act of emotional martyrdom, but was less threatened or overwhelmed with feelings of rage, shame, and fear, as shown in figure 8.2

These disparate representations of victims and victimizers differ from the switching of controls that accomplish role reversals in persons with neurotic-level obsessional characters. In the latter case, the contradictory views of self and others can be more readily contemplated simultaneously. In borderline patients, the views are segregated so that while one is active, there is no access to the alternative viewpoint. For example, the view that the mother calculatedly and sadistically extracted caretaking from Ellen could not be reconciled with the view that the mother was emotionally disturbed, frequently driven by a desperate sense of needi-

Figure 8.2
The Defensive Maneuver of Switching from the Attitude of Needing Care to the Attitude of Compulsively Providing Care

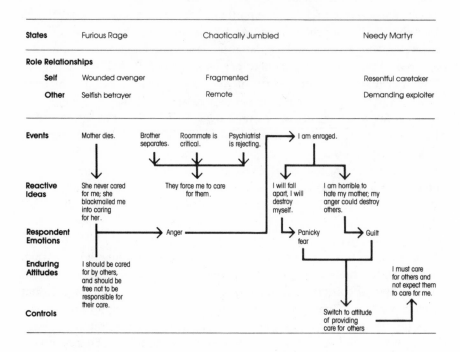

States	Furious Rage		Chaotically Jumbled		Needy Martyr
Role Relationships					
Self	Wounded avenger		Fragmented		Resentful caretaker
Other	Selfish betrayer		Remote		Demanding exploiter

ness, but when stabilized, was more giving to Ellen—who was then either too angry or too frightened to accept the overtures of caring.

Other fragmented meanings of the death included the view that the death was a gift and that Ellen could now cut the ties that bound her to her mother and be a free, independent woman. At times she felt that she was no longer in danger of being trapped, engulfed, and controlled by her mother, and may have been able, for the first time in her life, to integrate her tender, yearning feelings for others. One aspect of entry into a therapeutic relationship might be a trial of Ellen's more hopeful expectation regarding a new woman therapist who would not be as dangerous or unstable as her mother. It was difficult, however, to maintain this optimistic view (of her future in general, and her treatment in particular) since Ellen lacked the real competence to sustain herself as an independent person and vacillated between denying and seeking gratification of her dependency needs.

The Theme of Career Block. At the time of the pre-therapy evaluation, the patient presented herself as profoundly blocked with regard to the advancement of her career. She had become chronically entrenched in preparations for her dissertation. In the past, she had contemplated several other careers. The stagnation and confusion regarding the establishment of a clear career identity was symptomatic of a broader lack of cohesiveness in Ellen's own self-definition. In modeling the difficulties inherent in her choosing a career, each option was attached to a variety of negative images of herself that interfered with progress toward that career goal.

The Theme of Sexual Identity Diffusion. An important configuration of conflicted and unresolved ideas centered around the theme of bisexual attractions. At the time when Ellen entered treatment, she had failed to maintain a sustained attachment. While her pre-therapy description of her difficulties in sexual relations with men was somewhat sketchy, it subsequently emerged during the treatment and the follow-up evaluation that Ellen tended to experience panicky excitement and disorganizing fear of loss of control during sex. These feelings were related to the fear of being physically injured or merging with the other in sexual relations. The fearful arousal experienced during sex led to the *chaotically jumbled* state, in which Ellen experienced a sense of self-fragmentation. Intrusive images of physical mutilation threatened the coherence of her body image.

The Theme of Power. Ellen tended to react to important events in her life by attributing meanings that triggered images of herself as either very powerful or powerless in relation to these events. Powerful and pleasurable constellations would include the idea that she would eventually write the definitive thesis.

More often, however, she experienced her power as potentially dangerous. When her mother was still alive, Ellen believed that completing her thesis or being happily married would lead her away from her mother and would carry the potential of destroying her. On the surface, Ellen believed that she should assert her power to be a separate, independent person and to be aggressive, assertive, and sexual. However, each autonomous act of this nature carried with it an imagined devastating potential for others.

287

GENERAL STYLE AND CONTROL CAPACITIES AND THEIR IMPLICATIONS FOR
TREATMENT

Ellen's incapacity to tolerate simultaneous but contradictory views was
evident in her segregation of ambivalent feelings and attitudes into exclusively good and bad dichotomies. When in a positive emotional state, she
overgeneralized the view of her own idealized capacities and expressed
unwarranted overoptimism. When she was in a negative state, there was
a cascading progression of troubled emotions, self-hatred, and persecu-
tory images of others. Further, Ellen could not tolerate examination of
these disparate viewpoints, nor could she securely repress the frightening
bad representations. Instead, they remained dissociated from her conscious experience, only to flood into awareness when an idealized image
of herself or the other person was fractured by a disillusioning experience. She used intellectualization, isolation, repression, and suppression
to avoid emotional excitation and these threats of disillusionment.

Ellen's therapist was, for these reasons, confronted with a dilemma.
When Ellen was being clear and organized, she was distanced from the
ambivalent thoughts and emotions that were salient to her current dilemma. When Ellen offered insights into her problems, it was difficult to
determine which of these carefully articulated ideas and formulations
were new and relevant to her current distress. Some of the ideas that she
brought forward in a defensive intellectual manner stemmed from her
general knowledge and her particular experiences in past therapy. At the
same time, if the therapist directed Ellen's attention toward relevant but
dissociated topics, she temporarily lost her capacity for clear processing
of information.

The Process of Therapy

ESTABLISHING A THERAPEUTIC ALLIANCE AND MODULATED STATES

Many brief therapies show progression from an initial social alliance
through relatively rapid establishment of a therapeutic alliance to working through of conflictual themes. In contrast, this treatment was noteworthy for the difficulty in moving beyond the initial social alliance. The
risk of the positive and negative transferences, as summarized in table
8.5, seemed high throughout the therapy. At the same time, there was no
sense that once aroused, these transferences might provide the matrix for
useful insights. The working alliance, to the extent that it was estab-

lished, was tenuous. Ellen was fearful of being overwhelmed by her emotions, and maintained a rigidly overcontrolled and intellectualizing posture to defend against feeling.

Ellen's efforts to lessen her controls, involve herself effectively in the relationship with the therapist, and confront conflictual themes frequently precipitated actual or feared disorganizing emotions. There was no readily attainable intermediate zone of modulated emotional expression. The state transitions were from overcontrolled states, such as *controlled communicating* and *artificial and engaging,* directly to the undermodulated *chaotically jumbled, furious rage,* and *flooded despairing sadness* states, and then back to the zone of overcontrol. When Ellen was in an overcontrolled state, she was too remote from her feelings to work effectively on the implications of her loss. In the undermodulated states, she tended to view the therapist in terms of the negative transference views listed in table 8.5 (see p. 282). The most intensely negative transference reaction was one in which she was chaotically emotional and "too much" for the therapist. The therapist was either depleted and overwhelmed or surprised and repelled in this role relationship model. To counteract the threat of this negative transference, Ellen made very strong efforts to develop and maintain a social alliance.

For Ellen the social alliance took two forms. The first was to experience herself and her therapist as colleagues, consulting together in a detached, clinical manner (the *controlled communicating* state). A variant occurred in Ellen's friendly conversational style, characteristic of her *artificial and engaging* state. Whereas such social alliances allowed emotional distancing from the conflictual material and provided Ellen with safety in indicating problem areas to the therapist, these social alliances also served as a major resistance to the formation of a therapeutic alliance.

In spite of the medley of potential negative transference reactions shimmering beneath the surface, and the strong defensive efforts at maintaining a social alliance, a very tentative and fragile working alliance was gradually established during the therapy. The principal ingredients responsible for the establishment of this alliance were the therapist's tact, empathy, and avoidance of any recapitulation of traumatic aspects of earlier relationship experiences. Even so, Ellen remained worried that her seemingly supportive and caring therapist could be deceitful or dangerously intrusive like her mother. Ellen felt she might be tricked into a hopeful attachment only to be criticized, controlled through guilt and neediness, and alternatively smothered or neglected. These transference-based fears were unusually intense and varied (again, as summarized in table 8.5), leading to a level of mistrust that ran deeper than that usually observed in neurotic patients. Ellen's fears motivated her to repeatedly test the safety of the therapeutic relationship. With gradually building increments of trust, she was able to relate as a vulnerable person to a helping professional rather than as if she were a colleague or a personal friend of the therapist. The process of building the therapeutic relationship was very time-consuming, and the relationship was stabilized only toward the end of the brief therapy. As a result, time available for working through the mourning-related themes was limited. The eventual outcome was entry into long-term therapy.

THE EARLY PHASE OF TREATMENT: EFFORTS TO ESTABLISH A THERAPEUTIC ALLIANCE

In the first therapy session, Ellen indicated her potential for under-modulated emotional states and her method of keeping herself sealed off from this threat by strict controls.

Ellen: I am very deeply involved in the stuff that I am . . . going through, my relationship with my mother and her death.

Therapist: So there's no way to put it away?

Ellen: No. (*laughing*) No.

Therapist: It's part of what you're dealing with.

Ellen: That's what I'm really saying, is that this is clearly necessary now to go through. It's not like I can deal with the grief six months from now. I really don't have an escape.

Therapist: Mmmhmm. Are you in any sense feeling overwhelmed by it—in terms of the intensity of what you're experiencing?

Ellen: I was. I just went away for a week, and that's . . . changed it. Really beginning with the interview here, in which in the course of it, some of it . . . some of it was . . . frequently when I am talking I will have . . . (*trails off*)

Therapist: Mmmhmm.

Ellen: You know, insight in the process, and that partially happened, putting some things together.

Therapist: Mmmhmm.

Ellen: And . . . letting myself feel vulnerable. I mean, I had *just not allowed* anything to touch me for three to four weeks.

Therapist: Mmmhmm.

Ellen: At that point, and was just sealed.

Therapist: Mmmhmm.

Ellen: You know, just incredibly defended.

This sequence occurred during the first part of the first treatment session. At this early juncture, the therapist was alert to possible deficiencies in Ellen's capacity to tolerate affects. "There's no way to put it away?" She inquired about whether Ellen was overwhelmed by her emergent feelings of grief, which had in part been triggered by the pre-therapy evaluation. Later in the same hour, after Ellen described frightening, flooded states of sadness that occurred outside of the therapy, the therapist suggested that Ellen had "opened the door a little too far on her feelings." The therapist was telling Ellen that she, the therapist, did not expect Ellen to either totally seal herself off against her feelings, or strip away all her defenses. The message was that she could discuss her loss in tolerable, self-selected doses. This was reassuring, but Ellen could not entirely believe it.

Ellen then tested the therapist's capacity to tolerate emotional expression. She told the therapist in an intellectual manner about her fear of overwhelming the therapist were she to be less guarded.

> Ellen: I just didn't believe anybody would really . . . It's like I
> didn't believe anybody . . . underneath this feeling of . . .
> that I can't let down, is that I don't really believe that any-
> one has the strength to handle me if I let go.
>
> Therapist: Mmhmm.
>
> Ellen: And that's . . . specifically my mother.
>
> Therapist: Mmhmm.
>
> Ellen: And. . . .
>
> Therapist: That you'd . . . cause other people to fall apart, too?
>
> Ellen: Mmm, well, yes, that I will destroy other people if I let go.

While in the grip of this transference-based fear, Ellen experienced herself as needy and devouring and the other as frightened by—and in the extreme, destroyed by—the toxic quality of the overwhelming quantity of her need. In the next sequence, Ellen describes a discussion with a girlfriend who was able to tolerate her emotional displays:

> Ellen: And I was very surprised when she not only heard me and
> started responding . . . in ways that she used to, which was
> . . . helping me to interpret what was going on, but also
> said, "Why don't you come down . . . "
>
> Therapist: Mmmhmm.
>
> Ellen: " . . . and spend some time with me?" And I . . . I totally
> didn't expect that.

Therapist: Mmmhmm. How did you feel when she said it?
Ellen: Oh, I cried.
Therapist: Mmmhmm.
Ellen: And it . . . it was interesting. She misinterpreted the crying. Uhm, she thought it had to do with my not being able to do something that . . . and it had to do with just being . . . so relieved that my fears were not founded.
Therapist: Mmmhmm.
Ellen: And that I uhm, I would get . . . a particular kind of help that I wanted.
Therapist: So that was very meaningful to you.
Ellen: It was *very* meaningful, yeah.

This story about Ellen's girlfriend indicated a hoped-for ideal of how she could work with her therapist, who would also hear her, be responsive, help her "to interpret what was going on," and allow her to "come down and spend some time." The therapist empathically reflected that the availability of Ellen's friend was "very meaningful." Ellen and the therapist then discussed their work together, and how it could be very meaningful.

Toward the end of the first session, Ellen contrasted her reactions to her current therapist with her overly protective stance toward her previous therapist. She felt that the latter had been upset by her raw expressions of hopelessness and self-depreciation, attributing this feeling to her subjective belief that the therapist, like her mother, was vulnerable to his own deflations of self-esteem.

Ellen: Uh, and I feel, I guess, a little protective of my last therapist.
Therapist: Mmmhmm.
Ellen: I think there is something . . . and I am just thinking of this now, I mean, it's just a feeling I'm having, and . . . visualizing it . . . I think there is something in me that protected him from seeing all of me in some way, too.
Therapist: Mmmhmm.
Ellen: I guess because there is a . . . way in which he is self-deprecating; doesn't think of himself in real high terms.
Therapist: Mmmhmm.
Ellen: And . . . I think maybe it's male protective? . . . partly? You know, to protect the man, 'cause I am . . . (*pause*) terrific at protecting my father; and uhm . . . partly . . . you know, even . . . protecting a friend, you know. . . .

Therapist: Mmmhmm.

Ellen: . . . in a way, and I don't have those feelings around you. (*pause*) Partly because you're a woman, and partly because you're new.

Ellen indicated hope ("I don't have those feelings around you") but also pessimism ("It's only because you're new").

Early in the second session, Ellen reported that she was consciously letting her guard down (she labeled this "undefending") in order to confront her feelings about her mother's death. In the following segment of the transcript, the therapist and patient both address this shift in a way that is cautiously supportive of it. The therapist meanwhile is mindful of Ellen's difficulties in putting the lid back on her emotions so that she can continue to function.

Therapist: Sounds like you've set yourself as a task to relax and to dream, and it's almost like you're setting up a working process for yourself in terms of trying to deal with the feelings.

Ellen: Yeah, I had . . . I went to the symphony Friday night, and it started on the way over to the symphony . . . that I was . . . remembering some things uhm . . . about . . . mother. I had gone to the symphony . . . and you're right. I was doing a kind of *deliberate* (*intake of breath*) . . . trying to let down. I mean it's . . . I really call it a process of undefending, and uhm. . . .

Therapist: Mmmhmm.

Ellen: I'm really comfortable doing it *if I can manage it.*

Therapist: Mmmhmm.

Ellen: But if I *need* my defenses, then it's awful.

Therapist: Mmmhmm.

On the surface, this dialogue would seem to reflect an increasing engagement in the work of therapy. The unthawing of blocked feelings of grief would be a good prognostic sign in stable, overcontrolled, neurotic-level patients. In this instance, however, several factors mitigated against a view of therapeutic optimism. First, Ellen was reporting a deepening of her feelings of grief outside of the therapy, while maintaining an over-controlled stance during the session. The incident regarding the symphony was related in the *controlled communicating* state, with defensive distancing from the feelings described. Additionally, it appeared that the episode was an intrusive breakthrough of feelings rather than a gradual disinhibition (with feelings kept at tolerable intensity) that could promote working through and mastery. Ellen had already had the experience of therapy, and might have presented this episode as a gift to her therapist in an effort to please her, rather than as a working commitment to further explore her feelings of grief. Such an effort by a patient is analogous to the presentation of certain dreams early in the course of psychotherapy, which frequently are introduced to please the therapist.

In the next quote, which also came from the second session and immediately followed the one above, Ellen described the frightening shifts she experienced from tolerable to disorganizing grief.

> Ellen: It would just come pouring up in me and then I would (*anxious laugh*) you know, try to . . . hold it down a little bit so I didn't get hysterical in the middle of the, you know, of the symphony. And then . . . but I was real shaken and I was real depressed, and I was actually aware that I was feeling real depressed, and I thought well, that's good, you know, that you finally get to the point where you can sort of feel some of the sadness and some of the just, you know, whatever is coming up.
>
> Therapist: Mmmhmm.
>
> Ellen: And I was actually very comfortable with it, but I suppose I didn't realize that depression is something you . . . sort of need to take a little carefully.
>
> Therapist: Mmmhmm.
>
> Ellen: Anyway, I got home and . . . I guess that's when I had a little wine and turned on some music that normally would comfort me, and instead it uhm . . . I don't know what happened. I remember I . . . was writing some stuff, and it was getting . . . giving me a bunch of (*sniffling*) ideas and insights and stuff, and then all of a sudden there was this feeling of ter— (*voice breaking*) *being terrifically overwhelmed.*
>
> Therapist: So it sounds like you opened the door, but you opened it a little too wide.
>
> Ellen: Exactly.

The therapist's last remark was mentioned earlier. She later indicated that Ellen was afraid to allow strong feelings to be experienced during the sessions, and "opened the door" only when alone, and not when in active communication with others. This interpretation led to further work on potential negative transferences, but it did not alter Ellen's behavior to any major degree during the brief therapy.

Establishing a Focus. Ellen was from the outset intellectually committed to exploring the implications of her mother's death. Specifically, Ellen wished to work on conflictual aspects of her relationship with her mother, as they related to bad feelings she had about herself. Also, she consciously related long-standing problems in social, sexual, and academic functioning to disturbances in her relationship with her mother, and correctly appreciated that problems in these spheres had intensified since her mother's death.

Unlike certain patients in brief therapy who, for neurotic or manipulative reasons, present an initial focus that camouflages their real concerns, Ellen did not appear to have a hidden agenda when making her initial requests for help. The therapist sought to understand the complex linkages between the event of her mother's death and its historical antecedent—that is, the developmental unfolding of the mother-child relationship and of its then-current intrapsychic and interpersonal consequences. The connections that were identified were synthesized into the focus in a series of exchanges between Ellen and the therapist. This gradual clarification of the focus had its beginning in the first minute of the first treatment session.

Therapist: So maybe we could start off by your describing what it is that you're looking for in therapy, and what are. . . .

Ellen: Mmmmm.

Therapist: . . . the particular things that you found that have been problematic for you since your mother's death.

Ellen: Okay, uhm (*sighs*) . . . I'm specifically looking for, and it's sort of hard to get to it 'cause it's really . . . uh . . . uh . . . it's a deep level, uhm, and that's something, you know, that I suspect we'll discuss as I try to get to it. And whether that's really appropriate. . . .

Therapist: Mmmm.

Ellen: . . . to do here, and so on.

Therapist: Yeah.

Ellen: Uhm . . . I had been . . . the . . . the last therapy I had, which was a little more than two years. . . .

Therapist: Mmmhmm.

Ellen: . . . ended . . . about a year and a half ago . . . and it was through him that I was referred here.

Therapist: Mmmm.

Ellen: But uhm, I realized after my mother's death that there is . . . that there are some levels of dealing with what happened when I was ten or eleven.

Therapist: Mmmm.

Ellen: . . . the time of my parents' divorce and the time of my very complicated relationship with my mother; uhm, that I hadn't experienced, that I hadn't experienced is really the best way of putting it.

Ellen went on to relate that although she had had glimmerings of these complexities in her prior long-term therapy, she had been too fearful to pursue them.

Ellen: I had never realized it before, because I had some . . . neat images that summarize it. I just assumed that I remembered it.

Therapist: Mmmm.

Ellen: And I suddenly realized that I didn't, and that I began to have . . . stuff come up after my mother's death that I realize has been blocked. And the reason that it's so important is . . . uh . . . I've done a lot of thinking about it in the time since my therapy ended.

Therapist: Mmmm.

Ellen: And it's . . . it's . . . it, uh, is played out right now very heavily in a way that I hadn't fully faced, I guess.

Therapist: Mmmm.

Ellen: And that's what my dissertation is on—how adolescents leave caretakers.

Therapist: It was not an accidental choice.

Ellen had introduced a key word, "caretakers." The theme of caretaking in its many ramifications occupied a central place in this brief therapy and served as a conceptual bridge between past and current concerns. Ellen recognized that her block with respect to working on her thesis was somehow enmeshed with her confused feelings about caretakers in her own life. She went on to express the hope that therapy would free her from the work block on her dissertation.

Ellen next portrayed her present conflict with her roommate as a replay of the struggles with her mother. She indicated that the relationship with the roommate had reached a disturbing impasse. Ellen felt she could not afford to defer working on her grief since, in her view, resolution of the problems with her roommate was contingent on coming to terms with the parallel caretaking issues that had arisen in her relationship with her mother.

Ellen next described how depleted she had felt by the burden of caretaking that she had experienced in the weeks prior to her mother's death.

Ellen: I had gone to San Diego in early March, when she was in a leukemic crisis and expected to die immediately. . . .

Therapist: Mmmm.

Ellen: . . . and she didn't. She pulled through. My brother was too involved in his own problems to help out, and all this stuff went on, and I was involved in *terrific* amounts of caretaking.

Therapist: Mmmm.

Ellen: And it was very clear that it was what it was, and I had prepared . . . real well . . . because I was in real good shape before I left for it.

Therapist: Mmmm.

Ellen: Uhm, dealing with it, compartmentalizing, and being cautious of what I was doing and how I was defending, and it worked really well, for two weeks.

Therapist: Mmmm.

Ellen: And then all of a sudden I would start . . . I just fragmented . . . the last week . . . I was taking care of my two nieces and my brother who was . . . really falling apart. . . .

Therapist: Mmmm.

Ellen: . . . and my mother who was, you know, deeply ill. And then I came back here for a little over a month, and then my mother died. And then I went back again. . . .

Therapist: Mmmm.

Ellen: . . . for three weeks, with my brother collapsed and the kids hysterical and. . . .

Therapist: Mmmm.

Ellen: . . . with my brother trying to set up his office and feeling that he couldn't manage . . . you know . . . with so many responsibilities.

Therapist: So in a way, the crisis for you has really been being surrounded by all these needy people.

Ellen: Yeah; really deeply needy. And it is typical of me to . . . feel that it is a black-and-white situation; that if . . . other people are needy, I cannot get my needs met.

297

Therapist: Mmmm.

Ellen: I just can't afford. . . .

Therapist: . . . not even to have them?

Ellen: . . . not even have them, right. And I behave as though I don't.

The therapist called attention to Ellen's reflexive style of deferring to others by assuming responsibility in times of mutual neediness. Without concretely saying so, the therapist implied an agreed-upon focus: She and Ellen would explore this self-defeating pattern with the goal of permitting Ellen to set realistic limits on caring for others, and to feel safer in demanding some reciprocal caretaking.

The focus on caretaking was further elaborated later in the first session, when Ellen pointed out a relationship between the abuse she was tolerating from her roommate and her need to punish herself for past actions.

Therapist: What are you getting punished for?

Ellen: Uhm . . . everything. You know? (*anxious laugh*) I mean, everything from not being perfect . . . to . . . uh. . . .

Therapist: Mmmm.

Ellen: . . . to not being a perfect caretaker, to not having succeeded in saving my mother's life, to having . . . at the time I was eleven . . . having asked for my own needs.

Therapist: Mmmmm.

Ellen: And having in response being told that was a *terribly* threatening awful thing to do.

Therapist: Mmmmm.

Ellen: And I had no right to do it. And . . . then having said okay, then uhm . . . to hell with you, Mother, basically.

Therapist: Mmmm.

Ellen: Not that I could leave. . . .

Therapist: Mmmm.

Ellen: But I . . . then I won't give you anything.

Therapist: Mmmm.

Ellen: I will be a cost commodity from you . . . for you from now on. And in some sense that was true.

Therapist: Mmmm.

Ellen: I did . . . do that . . . uhm, in relation to my mother.

Therapist: So that choice had both the quality of anger, but also of insulation.

Ellen: Yes, insulation was *very* important.

Insulating herself from her mother's extreme demandingness had a quality of "cutting off her nose to spite her face" by intensifying her sense of lonely abandonment. At the same time, Ellen viewed insulation as a reprehensible act of aggression against her mother. She would sometimes resentfully undo such an act by assuming the parental role and treating her mother as a needy, helpless child. This would then create a vicious cycle by fueling further resentment over having to take responsibility for her mother at the sacrifice of having her own needs met.

WORKING THROUGH

Overview of the Phases of the Brief Therapy and General Characteristics of the Work of Therapy.   The demarcations between phases in this treatment were less sharply defined than in the average brief therapy. As already discussed, the social alliance persisted, the therapeutic alliance was tenuous, and working states were difficult to stabilize. Nevertheless, it is possible to trace some more gradual shifts in phases and relate these to relevant actions by therapist and patient. During the early phase, occurring predominantly in hours one and two, the social alliance was formed and was organized around two role relationships. In the first, the patient related to the therapist in a collegial manner, discussing her own psychopathology in the intellectualized, clinical terms characteristic of the *controlled communicating* state. In the second version of the social alliance, Ellen related to the therapist in the conversational style of the *artificial and engaging* state, chatting about her problems while remaining distant from her true feelings. In this initial phase, Ellen related the events leading up to and following the death of her mother, and then described troubled aspects of her relationship with her mother during childhood and adolescence. The therapist was supportive, empathically facilitating the presentation of current and historical material, and was largely unchallenging of Ellen's overcontrolled states.

During these early sessions, in the course of reviewing the events surrounding her mother's death, Ellen transiently entered more deeply into feeling states of sadness, anger, and vulnerability. She tested the therapeutic waters by risking some affective involvement. The therapist was not frightened by the expression of these feelings, did not condemn Ellen for being crazily out of control, was neither too intrusive and seductive nor too passively unavailable, and in general weathered the storm of Ellen's transference-based expectations. Many of the relevant therapist actions in the first few sessions were nonverbal. Ellen was sensitively attuned to the therapist's facial expressions, posture, mannerisms, and quality of voice as she monitored the therapist's reactions to her own emerging positive and negative feelings toward her mother. She was reassured by the therapist's empathic, noncritical clarifications, and was able to permit a modest relaxation of her controls. There was a gradual, incremental building of trust against the stubbornly persistent background of mistrust.

In the second phase of treatment, approximately between sessions three and six, there was some movement beyond an exclusive social alliance into a working alliance. Ellen entered the *struggle with vulnerability* state, which was pivotal for entry into the *irritable anger, needy martyr,* and *open crying* states. Ellen was struggling with intense and ambivalent feelings, primarily toward her mother but also toward her roommate and brother. Her style was to avoid the expression of feelings, particularly anger, that frightened her with the sense of loss of control.

To accomplish this avoidance, Ellen would segregate the conflictual implications of these close relationships into dichotomous all-good or all-bad meanings. Contemplation of exclusively bad images would trigger the emergent feeling of rage and bring on a collapse of perspective in which memories of sustaining qualities of the relationship were annihilated. Ellen would then attempt to retreat to an exclusively positive view of the relationship.

Beginning in sessions three through six, the therapist encouraged the patient to focus on positive views of herself and others. She permitted Ellen to deflect from the anger, sadness, and fear attached to negative images. The pattern of splitting was rarely interpreted, and relatively little processing was accomplished in working through negative images. Therapeutic effort was not directed toward making it more tolerable for Ellen to experience anger. Rather, the therapist was empathically tuned in to themes of sadness related to Ellen's mourning of the loss of idealized caretaking figures; the therapist steered clear of the hostility that Ellen felt for being cheated, tricked, used, seduced, and deprived. The combined effect was to encourage the *needy martyr* state, in which Ellen experienced herself as sad and needy but as forgiving of her mother, who was seen as justifiably needier and in many ways had actually deprived her daughter.

In the third phase of the treatment, primarily hours seven through ten, this trend toward work on lost positive aspects of the mother intensified and shifted in character. Ellen came to regard her mother as well-meaning, offering love and protection. She shifted to blaming herself for the breakdown in their relationship. She felt that she had sealed herself off emotionally in order to deny her dependency on her mother, to take flight from her sexual attraction to her mother, and to punish her mother by not reciprocating the latter's overtures of affection. In essence, such perceptions led Ellen to a view of herself as bad and her mother as good, a view that intensified states of sadness and guilt, and countered states of anger.

The therapist's effort to help the patient focus on good images of the mother extended also to working with the positive side of Ellen's ambivalence concerning her current struggles with her roommate and her brother, and with the therapist herself. Themes of anger toward these individuals were allowed to pass by relatively unchallenged, whereas empathic holding responses were utilized to encourage the further expression of sadness.

A similar tactic was employed to counter Ellen's deprecating views of herself. Just as Ellen was prone to intense and disorganizing hatred of others, she had difficulty with unmodulated all-bad images of herself. Experience of this personal sense of badness could trigger entry into the *furious rage, flooded despairing sadness,* and *chaotically jumbled* states by a mechanism similar to that described earlier in the discussion of Ellen's reaction to hateful feelings toward others. As a consequence of this state instability, and in an effort to protect the alliance against the risk of flight from intolerable feelings of worthlessness, the therapist made many remarks that tended to bolster Ellen's more positive self-images (before attempting to confront the opposite side of the split). The bolstering statements made by the therapist tended to occur at those moments when Ellen was hovering on the brink of threatening, overwhelmed states and was struggling to maintain an overcontrolled posture to protect herself from this threat.

WORKING THROUGH SPECIFIC THEMES

Despair over Loss of Closeness Theme: Mourning the Loss of the "All-Good" Mother. At the beginning of treatment, Ellen experienced intrusive pangs of sadness and yearned for the sought-after but largely unrequited closeness with her mother. The finality of her mother's death simultaneously intensified both the wish for a good mother and the reality that she had been deprived of such a mother. Thoughts about these subjects triggered sadness, fear of intolerable states of despair, and defensive avoidance of awareness of her loss. During the treatment, many clarifications were offered by both the patient and the therapist with regard to this theme, and some work on mourning the loss of an idealized good mother was accomplished. The therapist hoped to fortify Ellen's positive identification with the lost good mother, but this was difficult because Ellen also viewed the mother as a noxious self-object. The major effect of the therapist's interventions was to sidestep Ellen's sense of disillusionment by bolstering an idealized image of her as self-sufficient and self-nurturing.

Ellen would segregate themes of sadness at the loss of the good mother from themes of anger at the bad mother. For the most part, her alternating dissociations—which led to undermodulated extremes of both sadness and hostile reactions—were not challenged. When the therapist actively countered this pattern by simultaneously considering more tempered, ambivalent images, Ellen seemed incapable of processing, or even repeating, the information as arranged by the therapist. This difficulty in processing information makes it hard to deal with ambivalence in brief therapy with borderline-style patients.

Ellen's complexly overdetermined conflicts in her feelings of love for her mother did not progress to a resolvable form during the brief treatment. Ellen's defensive effort to deny her neediness and her feelings of love for her mother by insulating herself were interpreted to her. But linkages to fears of opening up and subsequently facing disappointment, manipulation, seduction, and abandonment were incompletely explored. Transference manifestations of these issues could only be dealt with in a circumscribed way. More direct interpretation of the transferences carried the threat of disrupting the unstable therapeutic alliance.

Additionally, the confusing crosscurrents of the patient's ambivalent feelings toward her mother and her murky communicative style combined to make it difficult to formulate which of these multifaceted transference issues was paramount at a given moment. In a complex, shifting field of transference reactions, Ellen's wishes for closeness, nurturance, and merger ebbed and flowed with fears of seduction, painful abandonment, loss of identity, manipulation, and persecution.

Rage at the Loss of the Abandoning Mother: Mourning the Loss of the "All-Bad" Mother. Limited progress was accomplished in working through the rage and abandonment theme, with modest shifts occurring in insight and attitude. Some anger at the mother was helpful to Ellen in that this affect helped her to establish a sense of her own separateness and to feel strong. However, contemplation of bad images of the mother threatened Ellen with entry into disorganizing rages; she responded with defensive avoidances that were largely unchallenged by the therapist. Unresolved was the specific issue of the patient's rage at her mother's suicidal threats, which had blackmailed Ellen into a position of forced responsibility for her mother and had resulted in the sacrifice of Ellen's own autonomous development. While this particular theme of omnipotent responsibility was only one strand in the broader cloth of Ellen's rage at her unavailable, unempathic, and seductively intrusive mother, it typified the limitation in working through of hostility in the brief treatment. The progress that was made in working on rage at bad mothering served as a useful prelude to Ellen's subsequent long-term therapy.

There was a repeated effort to locate a middle ground in which caretakers would be defined on a more realistic and less all-or-nothing basis. The therapist challenged the attitude that a person had to be all-supplying to be called a capable caretaker, and offered in place of it the idea that others could be limited caretakers without being deceitful, defective, or ambiguous. Part of the interpretive process involved clarifying Ellen's conflict over this theme and the degree to which it permeated her various life decisions and choices.

The expressive work, encouraged by the therapist's empathic elaboration, did allow Ellen to say somewhat more about ways in which her mother had been bad. She was able to do this while preserving a sense of control, both in the *controlled communicating* state and tentatively in the more affectively engaged working states. At times she talked angrily, as if at her mother, before the audience of the therapist (and the imagined audiences of the cameras) in a more controlled way than she probably could have done in the presence of her mother. Her degree of control helped to clarify the reality of some of her criticisms of her mother, and to differentiate real criticisms from fantasied ones. While this work was carried out in an *"as if" angry* state, it may still have been progressive for Ellen.

As part of the process of examining her resentment toward her mother, and due in part to the efforts at clarification by the therapist, Ellen was able to understand that in her current involvement with her roommate, she was acting out some angry feelings that stemmed from the relationship with her mother. These feelings of displaced anger were contrasted with Ellen's more realistic responses to her roommate's collusions and provocations. In short, these constellations of ideas about rage, abandonment, and fear of loss of control over anger became clear in terms of intellectual insight. Ellen was able to think about these ideas more and to separate, to some extent, themes of rage from themes of sadness. As a result, she was able to experience some grief. The therapeutic work mainly involved labeling of ideas and logical analysis of themes. In this manner Ellen gained some awareness and therefore some control over her anger, although there was far more left to do. The therapy might simply have been too brief for more to have taken place with a person who displayed such strong defensive stances and needs.

The limited accomplishments of the brief therapy can be contrasted with a hypothesized ideal for working through the loss of Ellen's mother: The patient would test the therapist along the previously modeled relationship dimensions to determine the therapist's reliability. The therapist could become the desired good mother substitute, and Ellen—with a secure and stabilized attachment to this substitute—could risk experiencing rage at her real mother. The therapist would facilitate this expression of rage by helping Ellen to examine her dissociative compartmentalization of feelings, to reassess the fantasized exaggeration of the dangers concerning her feelings, and to cease overgeneralization of segregated meanings. In addition, the therapist could help Ellen to discover that a modulated expression of ideas was not as dangerous as she feared. Realistic disappointments in Ellen's idealized longing for the all-good mother-therapist would be tolerable and would permit a gradually increasing capacity to form integrated good and bad images of others. Positive and negative transference distortions that arose would be interpreted as part of an evolving capacity to distinguish fantasy from reality. Taken in concert, these shifts could have led to progression along the lines of: "My mother was not all I wanted; I am marred by the relationship with her, but she is all I had. She satisfied some of my needs some of the time. I mourn that the past cannot be undone and accept my disappointments. I want more of the therapist, but I cannot have more of the therapist than I have. It is enough, so my plan is to go ahead anyway."

This route would have been more possible in a long-term time-unlimited therapy than in a brief time-limited therapy. From the outset, Ellen's progress in therapy was predicated on the safety of an enduring attachment to the therapist. Such an attachment permitted further risk-taking and gradual modification of her capacity to mourn.

The Theme of Ellen's Career Blocks

Work on Ellen's failure to consolidate a career identity was not a major focus of this brief therapy. The initial pre-therapy formulation of the impediments was confirmed by the patient's further in-treatment elaborations on this theme. In particular, the failure to consolidate a career was not seen as exclusively or even predominantly related to conflicts in a single developmental sphere, as would be more typical of a neurotic-level patient. Instead, there were multiple roadblocks to the resolution of Ellen's career identity. Interactive contributions came from all levels of development (especially separation-individuation), from pathology of the self-concept with unstable idealizations and devaluations, from struggles for control, and from conflicts concerning sexuality and competition.

For Ellen, successful self-definition within a career entailed multiple dangers that were associated with unacceptable, negative self-images. Establishing a career represented independence from, and therefore symbolic abandonment of, her mother. This perception led to guilt over separation and pleasure in surpassing her mother, themes that resonated with now-conscious death wishes toward the mother. Such wishes contributed to Ellen's sense of herself as a selfish destroyer. Choosing a career that would fulfill her creative impulses rather than conform to parental expectations involved risk taking and a clear sense of purpose. When Ellen contemplated such a course of action, she had a now-internalized tendency to condemn herself as a failure, a naive fool who ignored practicalities to pursue whimsical goals. Her past history of heterosexual and homosexual seductive involvements with art teachers colored the choice of pursuing an artistic career, arousing disturbing images of herself as a sexual wrongdoer. Completion of Ellen's dissertation on cross-cultural variations in child rearing was impeded by her unsuccessful efforts to resolve personal conflicts about caretaking through academic rather than therapeutic efforts. Her progress was also slowed by rage, depression, and confusion regarding her unresolved grief, which interfered with concentration and clear synthetic thinking. Narcissistic distortions in self-concept were apparent from Ellen's swings between grandiose projections of a timeless future in which to resolve these difficulties, and a self-devaluation tied to feelings that no resolution would ever be possible. Such distortions impeded realistic appraisal of her actual talents and shortcomings in working toward career goals.

The many negative self-images involved in Ellen's career block were largely unaddressed in the brief therapy. The therapist's tactic of bolstering Ellen's self-images extended to this theme as well; efforts were made to counter her self-doubts and to stabilize her self-image as a person who was sufficiently competent to complete the dissertation. At the same time, both the therapist and Ellen understood that such complex difficulties could not be resolved in a brief therapy, and that further treatment was indicated if Ellen wished to deal with them.

The Theme of Sexual Identity Diffusion

During the course of treatment, Ellen was able to reveal in elaborate detail the multiple factors that contributed to her difficulties regarding sexuality. Ellen's openness in this respect was a measure of her trust in the therapist. However, as with the other themes of grief and career identity, in a brief therapy it was impossible to work through the complex array of frightening states, perceived dangers to the self, and cognitive confusion that were characteristic of Ellen's experiences of sexual intimacy.

The Theme of Power

The patient introduced the theme of power and emphasized it particularly during the termination phase of the brief psychotherapy. She was both attracted to a sense of power and fearful of it. The attraction was linked to her realistic aims for mastery and her grandiose wishes to magically triumph over all the difficulties in her life. At the same time, grandiose destructive fantasies interfered with adaptive self-expression. Ellen feared that expression of her power would mean that she was burdened by omnipotent responsibility toward others, and that disturbing feelings, such as death wishes toward others, could materialize. On the flip side, she was very prone to experiencing herself as powerless and victimized by others, as in the idea of being emptied out by them. She saw herself as unable to transform her mother into someone who would love her or approve of her separate autonomous pursuits. Further, she regarded herself as unable to prevent the recurrence of her mother's leukemic illness, to organize her dissertation, to set appropriate limits with her roommate, and so on.

These issues of exaggerated power and powerlessness again reflected dissociated (split-off) all-good/powerful and all-bad/weak images. The intensification of this theme under the tensions of termination was not surprising given Ellen's fear of being powerless in the face of a traumatic abandonment and her defensive need to feel powerful to counter this threat. The therapist's bolstering statements at termination once again had the short-term advantage of shoring up Ellen's sense of power, while having the long-term disadvantage of sidestepping in the revision of both her powerful/grandiose and her powerless/deflated images.

THE MEANING OF BEING "ON CAMERA"

The television camera, as a symbol for an imagined wider audience, played a significant role during the therapy. At times when Ellen felt it was too dangerous to make the therapist the object of intense feelings, especially anger, she was able to try out these feelings "on camera" to a more abstract, impersonal audience who would eventually view the videotapes. Sometimes when Ellen feared alienating her therapist, she preserved the concept that a "good therapist" was behind the camera. She was able to counter feelings of defectiveness by imagining that the tapes would become useful teaching vehicles, and she fantasized conducting a research project with the tapes herself. In that way, she could experience herself as a consultant, more in control than would be a troubled person seeking help. Finally, the tapes represented a tangible material record of the treatment, something fixed that she could go back to in an effort to preserve the treatment process and the relationship with the therapist. (In general, Ellen lacked a sense of permanency of experience and could not remember the past with clarity.) The existence of the tapes also countered the sense of injury about termination that Ellen anticipated from the outset, feeling that the end of the therapy would be premature and traumatic for her. In all of these variations, Ellen developed a personal relationship to the research clinicians or students projected to be behind the television camera. Preserving the camera as a "good object" was useful in facilitating a therapeutic alliance and practicing the working through of intense feelings that Ellen felt to be too threatening to inflict on her all-too-real flesh and blood therapist.

Outcome

The first follow-up evaluation was four months after termination, or approximately seven months after the death of Ellen's mother. Between the last therapy interview and the first follow-up interview, Ellen experienced the emergence of a state of near-suicidal despair and called urgently for a reopening of a therapeutic contract. This was accomplished before the first follow-up, and the course leading to Ellen's turbulent state will be described in what follows.

At the first post-therapy evaluation session, Ellen's status as assessed through use of the Patterns of Individual Change Scale, and her pattern (see figure 8.3) was compared to those in the earlier figures in this book. One notes much less improvement between pre-therapy and follow-up levels. Symptomatology related to grief was not much changed and was at problematic levels. Ellen's symptoms were related, as will be seen, to her personal efforts to do the grief work of the therapy after the relationship with the therapist had ended. Because of Ellen's entry into time-unlimited therapy by the first follow-up, the ratings for the use of a support system were "improved." There was also improvement on the assertiveness dimension and in Ellen's ability to relate well to men and family. Intimacy, self-esteem, work identity, and relationship with the surviving parent showed little change.

STATES AND ROLE RELATIONSHIPS

Subsequent to the end of therapy and prior to the follow-up interview, Ellen went through a turbulent period of emotional upheaval. This period

Figure 8.3
The Pattern of Change: The Case of Ellen

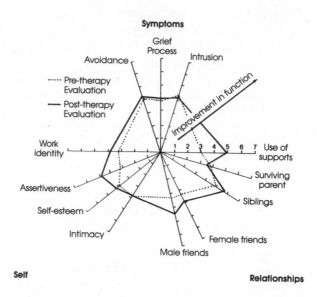

was preceded by two changes in her life. First, she moved out of the previous household that she had shared with her roommate, and purchased her own home using the inheritance from her mother. This life change increased her sense of having a secure place in the world that was all her own, and from which she could not be evicted. She did not actually resolve her differences with her roommate by asserting her right to remain in the shared household more on her own terms, but rather withdrew from the dangers of this confrontation by moving out. As was described earlier, conflicts with the roommate over the expression of power, self-assertion, guilty feelings of responsibility, and ambivalent sexual feelings paralleled Ellen's past unresolved reactions to her mother. Her failure to work through these issues and resolve them by taking flight from the relationship reflected ongoing difficulties in these domains, not just in her present troubles with her roommate but more fundamentally in relation to her mother.

Ellen also found a part-time job, which introduced structure into her daily routine, contributed to a sense of esteem and self-sufficiency, and kept her mind occupied with more practical and concrete matters, in contrast with her disquieting struggle to organize her dissertation. The effects of these two life changes were additive: Ellen's move to her own home diminished the aggravations with her roommate, and the new job contributed to a sense of confidence.

Ellen consciously decided that now she could better afford to risk experiencing her feelings of grief for her mother. She deliberately made a pilgrimage to the foothills of a mountainous region near her home. Ellen recalled how she had often walked with her mother through grassy meadows in a hilly region near her childhood home, and how her mother had taught her about wildflowers. Returning to a similar environment triggered feelings of sadness associated with a sense of her mother's presence. Initially, Ellen felt in control of this state, experiencing it as cathartic and bittersweet. However, after several weeks of grieving she felt unable to contain her sense of loss, and entered the *flooded despairing sadness* state for intervals that were too frequent and intense. The character of her grief shifted as well, from predominantly fond memories to guilty self-condemnations. The following excerpt from the first follow-up interview illustrates this sequence of events:

> Ellen: After a very short time, I uhm, was aware that the mountains was my mother's favorite place and a soothing place to be. I never had any . . . particular feelings about the mountains, and it was almost as though by being there, uhm, I felt . . . her presence and would . . . hear her talking about the brooks. . . .
>
> Evaluator: Mmmhmm.
>
> Ellen: . . . and trying to make us feel about it the way she felt about it. And then I could see her, you know, picking wildflowers and explaining things to us from the time I was little, and . . . we didn't go to. . . .
>
> Evaluator: Those are warm, sharing memories.
>
> Ellen: Right . . . so the first things were the warm, sharing memories, and the things that she loved. Uhm . . . (*tearfully*) this is going to cost a lot of emotion immediately, uhm, so that immediately . . . totally turned everything around, and then began to be able to feel the loss, which I hadn't even had a glimmer of. Uhm, not only from the time of her death, but at any time earlier.

The intensity of the sadness brought on by this self-imposed grieving stands in contrast to Ellen's predominantly overcontrolled stance during the brief therapy.

In the course of this follow-up interview, Ellen related how her experience in therapy had taught her to modify her need to rigidly intellectualize and begin "to feel," so that the work in treatment in part set the stage for the post-therapy grieving process:

> Ellen: And . . . so that came very powerfully, at first, there was the loss, and there would be these sudden moments which . . . I would feel . . . it was little . . . it was sort of like what I would . . . what I learned in the brief therapy about being able to feel . . . uhm . . . not just think. And, what I would have would be . . . stark, visual images of . . . feeling, not necessarily of anything happening, but a feeling, and, then associated things to it. And it would be like just . . . plunging into this well of feeling that at some point . . . and I would try, and then it's and . . . but it was very cathartic; and at some point I would feel, all right, that's enough, and come back out of it.
>
> Evaluator: So you were able to come out of it when you wanted to.
>
> Ellen: Yes, I was always able to come out of it. Right. Well, at least for a while. And then about three weeks ago I had two deep episodes in one day. They weren't . . . sometimes I would deliberately set the scene a lot. I mean I was doing it . . . I had everything organized. I would not see people very often, 'cause I wanted to have the emotional space, and because I was also very unpredictable in how much I was tolerant of people.

In Ellen's description of "plunging into this well of feeling," experiencing a catharsis, and then consciously putting the lid back on these emotions ("At some point I would feel, all right, that's enough, and come back out of it"), Ellen was wishfully thinking that she had developed a flexible way of moving through the intrusive and avoidant phases that occurred in connection with the stressful life event. Unfortunately, as is illustrated in the following excerpt, the intensity and conflictual quality of the intrusive pangs of sadness and guilt overwhelmed Ellen, and she entered disorganizing states of grief. The avoidances characteristic of much of the brief therapy period were replaced by disruptively intense states at follow-up:

> Evaluator: So you were kind of setting aside time for grieving.
>
> Ellen: Right.
>
> Evaluator: Mmmhmm.
>
> Ellen: Right. 'Cause I, you know, had so carefully . . . not allowed

it for such a long time . . . and . . . uhm . . . after the three weeks anyway, I had . . . I remember one evening that was especially painful, because . . . a lot of guilt started coming in, and it was really awful. I really felt that I was a terrible person (*starting to cry*) and . . . this is still hard, uhm, because of my inability to really give my mother any love in the two years that she was dying. Uhm, I was a good nurse. I was a good caretaker. I was a good organizer. I, you know, was efficient, and this stuff, but . . . but my emotions were kept distinctly out of it. And that felt very cold and very ugly, and I felt, you know, I was very unable to be independent of her. She certainly was the same way, but the pain was that . . . that I couldn't act . . . on my own feelings. I couldn't even, you know, acknowledge my own feelings. So I felt very kind of emotionally barren, and it was very painful to see that.

Thus, Ellen experienced herself as "very cold," unable to acknowledge or act on her own feelings, "emotionally barren," and unable to be independent of her mother. She kept a daily journal of her experiences in the mountains and even felt frightened reading it because, she wrote, "Whatever was coming out—they'll be very into fantasy."

Ellen was particularly alarmed when she had two of the deep, "plunging" episodes in one day. These episodes were characterized by intense emotions, fragmentary thoughts, and hallucinations involving a distorted body image. It is inferred that these were experiences of *flooded despairing sadness* punctuated by moments of jumbled confusion, guilt, and rage, with momentary loss of cohesion of an organized sense of self. It had been predicted earlier that Ellen was at risk for suicidal extremes of despair, and this was described in the next moments of the follow-up evaluation.

Ellen: I was standing at the easel painting a sunset scene over a lovely meadow I had recently visited, and uhm . . . all of a sudden I had . . . uhm, a suicide image . . . and it's . . . they're not specific . . . it was just a feeling of . . . I think I was having trouble with some detail of . . . of the perspective . . . and I just suddenly had this feeling of futility which was just, you know, it's . . . very weird. I . . . uhm . . . it was like . . . trying to paint something and getting . . . angry for a moment at my inability to get it right, or whatever.

311

Evaluator: Mmmhmm.

Ellen: And then having a feeling of futility . . . oh, what's the use, I'm really not an artist anyway, and having suddenly . . . jumping to what is the use.

Evaluator: Mmmhmm.

Ellen: Within, you know, a microsecond kind of time. And then flash images of . . . uhm . . . I don't think there was any particular suicide . . . act in my mind, but just . . . the feeling of kind of . . . not believing in the future, I guess.

Ellen took this suicidal impulse seriously, and coped with it by retreating into bed, reading herself to sleep, and calling the first thing in the morning to request further treatment. She told her therapist, "I have just had suicidal ideation and I think I need things—done in my life. One, I need some structure. I've tried three weeks with no structure, and doing a lot of grieving, and it . . . it was fine, but it has got to stop, right now." Her complaints at this time also included episodes of dazed distraction: in one instance she began to sew a button on a dress, forgot what she was doing, started to wash the dishes, left the water running, and went into another room to write a letter that she never finished. Such short-term memory lapses were particularly distressing because Ellen relied heavily on efficient intellectualizing processes as coping mechanisms to maintain her self-cohesion.

STATES AND ROLE RELATIONSHIPS BASED ON DIRECT OBSERVATIONS OF ELLEN IN THE FIRST FOLLOW-UP INTERVIEW

Ellen began the first follow-up interview in the *controlled communicating* state, with periodic overlays of the *artificial and engaging* state. There was an increased use of psychological jargon into the *controlled communicating* state. Ellen used intellectualization as a defense against feeling, or as a smokescreen to distract herself and the interviewer from closer scrutiny of what was being described. Ellen was able to sustain these overcontrolled states during the interview, up to the point where she began to describe the *flooded despairing sadness* and *chaotically jumbled* states that were experienced outside of therapy during the recent period of grieving. A review of Ellen's self-imposed grieving episodes precipitated entry into the *struggle with vulnerability* state, with frequent breakthroughs of the *struggle with crying* and *chaotically jumbled* states. Evoking these frightening memories of episodes of loss of control during the last month—that is, in Ellen's own words, "being adrift, pitched up and down like the high seas"—led to an actual loss of control during the interview, characterized by an immediate sense of confusion and despair. While Ellen attempted to stabilize the *controlled communicating* and *artificial and engaging* mix, she was unable to do so.

The *open crying* state, usually entered following a struggle with crying in the *needy martyr* state, was observed in the first follow-up interview. Exit from this state was provided by retreat to the overcontrolled states. Momentary experiences of *open crying* occurred when Ellen reviewed her frustrated efforts to establish a good feeling toward her father. Also, in acknowledging some positive memories of her mother—beginning with her brief therapy and extending into the self-imposed grieving—Ellen "totally turned everything around," so that she began to feel sadness, which she previously "had not even had a glimmer of." Ellen was aware that even recalling this period would "cost a lot of emotion immediately," and, in sharing these feelings during the follow-up interview, she shifted between the *struggle with vulnerability* and *open crying* states.

A triadic situation involving the patient, the evaluator, and the absent therapist (camera) was very apparent in all three follow-up interviews, but most noticeably in the first. This was a reversal of the in-treatment situation, in which Ellen had been "on camera" with the absent evaluator. During the first follow-up interview, in particular, Ellen "played" to the camera, projecting (predominantly in nonverbal ways) a message of despair to her former therapist, as if to say, "Aren't I needy?", "See how upset I am!", and "This is for you. Are you listening?" There was evidence of splitting of roles, with a denigration of the bad evaluator and implied praise of the now-idealized absent therapist. It was as if Ellen was saying to her therapist beyond the camera, "She [the evaluator] doesn't know what to talk about, but you and I do."

STATUS OF THE SPECIFIC THEMES

Despair and Rage: Mourning the Loss of the "Good" and "Bad" Mother. Ellen reported a marked intensification of feelings of sadness about the lost opportunity for closeness with her mother. These feelings ranged from a warm, cathartic nostalgia, with a comforting sense of the mother's presence, to painful self-condemnations for having isolated herself from her mother's loving overtures. Ellen was unable to sustain the fantasied loved-child/loving-mother relationship, which was evoked by memories of lyrical walks in the mountains in which she and her mother would share in a sense of the mystery of nature. This image of loving mutality, initially helpful in repairing Ellen's feelings of empty loneliness, paradox-

313

ically triggered intrusions of painful self-recrimination. If her mother was more caring than Ellen was previously willing to acknowledge, then it was Ellen's own fault that things had deteriorated between them.

This sequence can be summarized as follows: Before the brief therapy, Ellen predominantly felt herself to be the innocent victim of her mother's evil ministrations, and struggled with furious rage at this perceived betrayer. In the course of the brief therapy, an effort was made to bolster a positive image of Ellen as able to sustain herself, and at the same time to bolster a more balanced image of her mother as a person who was at times well-intentioned. This was in part accomplished by the therapist's efforts to interpret Ellen's bad image of her mother as a defense against her frightened longings for a good mother.

The attempt to restore the good-daughter/loving-mother model was continued by the patient in her post-therapy pilgrimages to the mountains, in which she experienced a state of *warm, mutual engagement.* This configuration was unstable, however, and Ellen shifted to a view of herself as a bad daughter who, in an exaggerated need for autonomy and for revenge, had cruelly insulated herself from a good mother who extended love to Ellen that was unrequited. This viewpoint led to flooded despair, hopelessness, and furious rage directed at herself, culminating in the suicidal wishes that had motivated Ellen's reentry into therapy. The shifts in her perceptions were noteworthy for the split-apart, shifting all-good or all-bad self and object images, as opposed to more realistic integrated, ambivalent images.

The Theme of Consolidating an Identity: Caretaking, Work, Sexuality, and Power.   Ellen's identity diffusions stemmed in part from her wish to care for herself and her fear that she had to stifle her own freedom out of an exaggerated sense of responsibility for others; from her wish to assert her sexuality, intellect, and anger; and from her fear that she would continually have to submit to the wills of others. At times she viewed herself as a resentful, powerless victim who had to submit to the needs of others; alternatively, there was an equally unacceptable view of herself as a dangerously destructive victimizer when she asserted her own needs. There was no middle ground of seeing herself and others as mutually sharing power. This theme was explored during the first follow-up interview.

Ellen reported having the strength to assert her needs with her roommate, but there was a vague, hollow ring to such claims. She was able to express some anger toward her roommate, but this emotion had the character of intrusive breakthroughs following strained suppression, and did not lead to problem-solving. Midway through the interview, Ellen discussed her problem with handling anger and related her difficulties in part to an identification with her father:

> Ellen: I mean I used to break things and . . . uhm . . . you know, have a lot of intense anger in inappropriate ways, and I'm still not . . . uhm . . . very good at learning how to express it in tactful or clear, easy-to-hear ways.
>
> Evaluator: Mmmhmm.
>
> Ellen: Part of the . . . I mean, my father is a violently, sarcastically angry person, always has been, and uhm, uhm, it's because of his constant, right-out-there anger that I probably don't have fear of anger, that some people grow up with, 'cause my father didn't repress it very much. . . .
>
> Evaluator: Mmmhmm.
>
> Ellen: But I've always used anger to hurt. I mean, I've expressed anger . . . it's very mixed in with hurt, because my father's anger was always very hurtful.
>
> Evaluator: Do you still have that on your mind?
>
> Ellen: Well, as I said it, I suddenly . . . I just suddenly realized that I was talking about . . . yes, I do. But, I can . . . I mean, that's, you know, one of the issues of the power thing was to try to separate power from . . . dangerous, threatening, hurtful behavior.
>
> Evaluator: Mmmhmm.
>
> Ellen: And I think I've separated that a little . . . you know, taking some real starts with that. The anger . . . uhm . . . I think that's still a problem. I think to feel . . . that . . . that it's all right for me to be angry, but that I need . . . angry . . . but that I need to . . . express it, and that I can express it in ways that are not hurtful.

The outcome of Ellen's blustering confrontation with her roommate was that Ellen deferred and moved out rather than claiming what was rightfully her own. She felt this was a triumph, and believed she had "retreated with flying colors." Her attitude reflected a sense that she had sufficient capacity for appropriate assertiveness, and also indicated a defensive idealization of the brief therapy.

In the sphere of sexuality, Ellen again exaggerated the accomplishments of the brief therapy and minimized her problems, in an ongoing struggle to support a positive image of herself. There was an unrealistic quality to Ellen's optimistic view of her progress since brief treatment. Among other problems, she had been unable to establish a satisfactory relationship.

The first follow-up also revealed Ellen's difficulties in resolving her career dilemmas. There was a seeming clarity in Ellen's insight concerning the contradictory pulls within her to organize or not organize her dissertation. Such intellectualizations, however, did not free her from her paralyzing ambivalence:

> Evaluator: What's going on with your doctorate? Are you . . .
>
> Ellen: Well, the (*half laughing*) . . . yes. That, uh . . . now that's an interesting . . . sometimes the question . . . how I react to the question is the best indication. (*laughs*) If . . . if I don't hit you, it's positive. (*laughs*)
>
> Evaluator: (*Laughs*)
>
> Ellen: One of the chores for this free period . . . and it has . . . I mean, I wanted to kick people who wanted to sit down . . . I mean, literally one day, my friend and another woman, both of whom have their Ph.D.'s, were sitting debating why I should finish the degree. And I got so angry because . . . one of the reasons for wanting this free time and the time alone was because I am . . . have been . . . always with my mother's . . . existence and so easily influenced . . . by what I thought she wanted or what I thought it . . . I should . . . you know. Finishing the dissertation would help take the stigma away from feeling like an emotionally unstable person, or . . .
>
> Evaluator: Mmmhmm.
>
> Ellen: All of the whole list of things that weren't . . . weren't perfect about me, and I also . . . I rebel, so I won't do the dissertation, and so it was like being caught. I couldn't go either way. I felt very strongly that I wanted . . . that I really didn't really care about the degree, on the one hand, and on the other hand . . . uhm . . . the only way to become an adult was to do the degree. So I'm trapped, and the only thing to do is to do nothing.
>
> Evaluator: Mmmhmm.
>
> Ellen: To not formally quit and to not do anything successfully. I mean, I could write reams as long as they don't really add up to the product.

In Ellen's characterization of her own efforts as "I could write reams as long as they don't really add up to the product," it can be seen that her energies at work, as in love, were dissipated in an unfortunate process of spinning her wheels while being disengaged from real accomplishment. She was caught between a rebellious wish to assert her autonomy by not completing her dissertation, and a need to define herself as an adult by feeling authentic in following through with her accomplishments.

Ellen continued to struggle to define herself as a separate person who could care for herself and not fall victim to the ties of exaggerated responsibility that bound her to others. The brief therapy threw this theme into bold relief and armed Ellen with an intellectual scaffolding on which to struggle toward less guilt and more autonomy. However, she still found herself "getting sucked in" by the problems of people whom she valued. Infatuations, particularly with others who were seen as similar to her in physical attributes or creative ideals, intensified the pull to fall into someone else's orb, stifling her autonomy in the process:

> Ellen: I felt this week suddenly aware that I was sucked in again . . . in this particular relationship so I am wary, and interested now about what that means and how to deal with it. I think I always had problems with ego boundaries with my husband. I always identified with him and . . . felt that we were . . . I used to . . . when we were first . . . knowing each other, and felt very close in some way that involved our both being . . . when we were both aspiring to being artists . . . I used to feel that we were somehow . . . the other half of each other in some ways.
>
> Evaluator: Mmmhmm.
>
> Ellen: Uhm . . . there was a bond. Well . . . with my present friend it's not like that, but I suddenly discovered that I let go of certain kinds of self-determination.
>
> Evaluator: Mmmhmm.
>
> Ellen: And in some sense it's . . . it's like what happens in an infatuation, which this has got some pieces of, though, it's because of his mind, and it's because of . . . the positive parts, and probably to some extent because of the negative parts . . . 'cause he . . . I think I identify with him.

Ellen's identification with her friend, which was based on both realistic attributes and those occurring in a process of projective identification, created a sense of entanglement with loss of clear boundaries of separation of self and other. This identification further contributed to Ellen's problem of responsibility toward others.

Brief therapy, with a time limit, was less helpful for Ellen than for the other patients described in earlier chapters. The treatment did, however, provide her with an experience of therapeutic relatedness. Her motivation for entering a time-unlimited treatment was not only a desire to stop the painful, flooding emotions but her belief that she would get positive benefits from the experience. She did engage in and make notable progress during longer-term therapy, as reported to the evaluating clinician a year later.

9

CHANGE IN BRIEF PSYCHOTHERAPY

O UR APPROACH to brief therapy, described in chapter 2, is problem-focused. Personality style is seen as an important factor in understanding symptom formation, therapeutic technique, and syndrome resolution. Our dynamic approach may also facilitate modification of some personality features. However, there are other approaches to brief therapy that aim more centrally at major personality change by focusing on character analysis. These approaches were described in chapter 1. In this final chapter we wish to address the question of the degree to which, in addition to symptomatic change, character change may occur.

Since the primary aim of our brief therapy approach is to improve immediate adaptation, and to analyze character only as it involves an impediment to this goal, our experience is in no way a test of what might be accomplished with a different technique. Nonetheless, our experiences in carefully reviewing cases are fairly unique, and it is not inappropriate to offer our opinions on change, based as they are on the information we had available. These opinions are based on our reviews of our larger archive as well as the representative cases presented here. Since our configurational analysis method provides some useful ways of thinking about change, we shall take up that topic according to the points of view, now familiar to the reader, that were used to formulate pre- and post-therapy status as well as the therapeutic process in the various case presentations. Thus, we shall consider changes in states of mind, and then issues such as changes in self-organization and core attitudes. In each category we shall contrast issues of problem-focused change with issues of organizational change in personality structure. We shall call the latter "character change," as is conventional in the literature of psychoanalytic psychotherapy.

Changes in States of Mind

In terms of problem-focused change versus character change, one can describe two types of alterations in states of mind. We have observed both types of change after brief therapies, but the former is the more common one.

PROBLEM-FOCUSED CHANGE

One important aspect of therapy is a communicative review of sequences of events that trigger entry into uncontrolled states of mind. As a result of such increased awareness, some people learn how to avoid triggers or learn ways of attenuating such states. Instead of explosive rage, the patient feels angry; instead of desperate panic, a pang of anxiety or period of tense dread may be experienced; instead of anguished and self-tormenting despair, there may be sadness and a sense of poignant loss. For example, Ann, by the end of her brief therapy (chapter 6), was able to feel tolerable sadness when faced with reminders of her father, rather than needing to ward off intense feelings of rage or grief.

CHARACTER CHANGE

A change in personality is manifested when, for the first time, a person is able to experience a new state. If never previously able to mourn a loss, he or she now can grieve. In addition, individuals may learn to enter states of mutuality and intimacy in a way that was previously not experienced. These changes in state patterns are best considered in terms of determinants such as self-concepts, role relationship models, and habitual patterns of information processing.

Changes in Self-Concepts and Role Relationship Models

As we discussed each case, a shift in a state of mind was explained, in part, as a shift in the relative predominance of particular self-concepts and role relationship models in organizing thought and action. In many cases, establishment of a therapeutic alliance helped patients to shift from a less competent to a more competent self-concept, which, in turn, led to more adaptive behavior patterns.

A shift from a damaged or bad self-concept to one that is competent may encourage adaptation by enabling the patient to process the meanings of a stressful life event. Such shifts may also serve a defensive aim, as when presentation of a pseudo-competent self-concept allows the patient to appear recovered and so not "have to" confront problems and turbulent feelings. Such defensive shifts to pseudo-competent self-concepts, occurring early in therapy, were especially noted in Ann (chapter 6), Harold (chapter 7), and Ellen (chapter 8).

PROBLEM-FOCUSED CHANGE

A person may enter therapy with a pattern of habitually activating a self-concept that is inappropriate to certain specific situations. A problem-focused change is one in which there is a conceptual plan to specifically avoid entry into states governed by certain self-concepts and role relationship models that occurred repetitively and maladaptively in the past. For example, instead of a timid, vulnerable self-view in a threatening situation, the person deliberately strives to maintain an assertive posture. This was the case for Marilyn (chapter 5), who, in working out the relationship with her lover, became better able to negotiate disagreements instead of seeing herself as overwhelmingly needy.

CHARACTER CHANGE

In character change, the individual develops a new basic view of self and other. This may be a more mature conceptualization of an existing self-image or role relationship model. Continuities between previously dissociated self and object concepts may be established, or the person may practice a new mode of relating to others, which in turn leads to new self-concepts.

Some of the patients whom we studied developed a greater ability to contain varied self-concepts within a complex, supraordinate view of the self (Horowitz and Zilberg 1983). That is, they came to realize that they had several self-concepts and views of the relationship with the deceased parent. By contemplating several views at once, they were better able to handle ambivalence. Anger associated with love does not occasion as much anxiety and guilt as when hostility is dissociated from affiliative feelings.

This type of change—that is, increased continuity between varied self-concepts and role relationship models—was facilitated by communication with the therapist (De Wald 1978). When the patients entered treatment they typically attempted to ward off feelings. They were unable to completely inhibit schematizations involving hostility or helplessness, and they had intrusive ideas and feelings. Their therapists encouraged a gradual but full expression of emotionally loaded ideas in a dose-by-dose manner. The patients carefully observed the therapists to see whether acceptance was genuine or was some kind of enticement that would lead to shameful exposure.

When various schematizations of self were communicated without occurrence of the feared punishment, revulsion, abandonment, or criticism, then the patient could identify with the therapist's accepting attitude. Self-concepts and role relationship models that were usually dissociated could then be contained within an overarching view. Such conscious recognitions of connections improved the adaptive functioning of the patients by reducing the likelihood of distortion in current interpersonal relationships. Acceptance by the therapist also led, in some patients, to what could be called a role change experience.

Discussion of Role Change Experience. Patients often began therapy in an overcontrolled state where they warded off expression of certain ideas and feelings in order to avoid the threat of certain role relationships. The most common role expectation of the therapy situation was that the therapist would criticize them or withdraw interest if he knew of the warded-off ideas and impulses. The therapists, in almost all instances, did not fulfill the patient's fearful expectation, behaving instead in an accepting and empathic manner.

Because the patients made repeated challenges to the therapist's stance of apparent acceptance of whatever they chose to express, it was often difficult to maintain empathy. The therapists were, however, aware of this problem. If they deflected momentarily from an accepting attitude, because of their own emotional response to a provocation, they would learn from their countertransference feelings, correct the countertransference problem, and return to an accepting stance. As a result, patients learned a new relationship, one of mutual give-and-take.

How does this role change experience compare with the corrective emotional experience described by Alexander and French (1946; Alexander 1950)? The concept of corrective emotional experience is based on providing something desirable in place of the errors or deficiencies in a patient's developmental history. The concept of the role change experience is based on the idea of helping a person to learn a new role relationship model in order to free him or her from repetition of a limited repertoire of behaviors. In this view, the preexisting schematizations of self and other are not erased. They do remain as potential ways of organizing experiences, and are likely to be reactivated during a regressive response to stress. The new patterns are practiced when in less vulnerable states of mind, and the patient then becomes more resilient in responding to stress without regression.

These two views—that of the corrective emotional experience and that of the role change experience—have different technical implications. In conceptualizing a corrective emotional experience, the therapist formulates a model of how the parent acted badly and then counteracts this model. The role change experience requires that the therapist maintain his part of the therapeutic alliance, valuing expression of warded-off ideas and feelings without being judgmental or authoritarian.

A role change experience in brief therapy may set in motion new learning that can continue to take place after termination. Indeed, the potential for character change may be found primarily in the internalization of actual transitions that began during the therapy, ones that take time to evolve into stable patterns. The brief therapy may not continue long enough for a sufficiently extensive series of trial behaviors with the therapist to take place. However, a brief therapy may instigate a start down a pathway, a start that may encourage the patient to set aside avoidant behaviors and try new life experiences in other relationships. These life experiences may then take place after therapy, leading to gradually evolving changes in self-concepts and role relationship models.

We have suggested that the permanence of a new relationship schematization depends on repetitions in actions, ones that may take place after therapy. The therapeutic context is limited by the adherence of the therapist to a relatively well-defined professional role. Praise, blame, and a lifelong, caring commitment are not part of the agreed-upon goals of the therapy. However, the therapist will have clarified and supported the patient's expressed wish for closeness, affection, sex, praise, and support in the context of current and future relationships. Hopefully, the patient will then go out and obtain such sustenance from outside relationships (Frank 1974).

These routes to change take time. If a patient has been impaired by a particular neurotic pattern of construing self and transacting with others, a newly developed pattern is only an ambition until it is channeled and solidified. An intimate relationship provides a good example. It takes time to find and know another person. If the relationship goes well, there may be a first phase of idealization followed by realization that the other person has both desirable and undesirable characteristics. In a patient unfamiliar with intimacy and acceptance, courting may be clumsy. Selection of a suitable partner may be clouded by repetition of neurotic criteria, even if these criteria have already been insightfully recognized. The patient may begin a new relationship while in brief therapy, have it terminate perhaps a few months after therapy has ended, and then go on to try another and another. If the patient is continuing along a new line of development, he or she may achieve a satisfactory end point a year (or much longer) after the end of therapy.

Sometimes the patient cannot tolerate alone the states of mind that occur when such trials of new relationship patterns are disrupted. Therapy may have to be resumed without a time limit, with the therapist acting as a sustaining figure while the patient continues his or her attempts. Also, in cases where a patient has very entangled and conflicted schematizations, many repetitions of regressive self-concepts and role relationship models—as well as many trials of new and alternative modes—may be necessary with a therapist before the patient extends new behaviors to outside relationships. Such repetitiveness is an indication that long-term treatment should be considered.

A special situation arises when the patient's conflicted relationship pattern is derived from interactions with a parental figure which in some real way parallels the experience with the therapist. In such instances, in order to develop a new role model, the therapist has to be especially active in interpreting and clarifying the difference between the therapist's role, within a therapeutic alliance, and the role attributed to him or her by the patient. For example, if the therapist is empathically listening and waiting for the patient to bring forth each new communication, the patient may experience the therapist as being exactly like a parent who was unduly passive and did not provide needed direction. This does not mean that the therapist should shift to a directive stance, as might be the case if one were providing a corrective emotional experience as suggested by Alexander and French. It does mean that it would be valuable to the patient for the therapist to clarify that his listening is for the purpose of actively understanding the patient rather than arising from a passive sense of helplessness or futility about how to provide direction. Information will be forthcoming when it will be useful to the patient.

On the other hand, if the therapist is active in establishing and maintaining a focus, the patient may have a sense of again being subjugated to the wishes of a domineering parent. In such instances, the therapist does not have to back off from the useful technique of focusing a time-limited therapy. Nor does he have to become passive and especially gentle. Instead, the therapist may continue the tactic of establishing a focus, but should also communicate that the aim is to facilitate the patient's own movement, not to dominate him.

In short, establishing the difference between one role relationship model, characteristic more of transference reactions, and another, characteristic more of a therapeutic alliance, does not necessarily mean providing a real relationship experience opposite from that of the transference. The therapist may provide clarification of the differences in situations where there is similarity but not exact congruence.

The new relationship experience will usually involve a modification of the therapeutic alliance over the course of even a brief therapy. The early therapeutic alliance is based on preexisting role relationship models, with elements that could be considered maternal and paternal transference or sibling rivalry (Stone 1961). In the course of the treatment, some new possibilities for the relationship with the therapist are discovered. The therapeutic alliance itself is modified in an evolutionary manner. For example, in the case of Connie (chapter 4), the first establishment of the therapeutic alliance was one in which the therapist, as an expert professional, was regarded as being like the idealized father. The transference element was to regard him as a supportive caretaker. When the therapist gave interpretations in later sessions, the supportive therapeutic alliance was modified in the direction of a more confrontative one. However, the new model of relationship in the therapeutic alliance contained the concept of being confrontative to be supportive, not scornful, an experience she had not gained with her father.

In patients who use overcontrol as a substantial defensive effort, there may be establishment of what might be called a pseudo-therapeutic alliance. These patients maintain *artificial and engaging* states, as described for Ann in chapter 6 and Ellen in chapter 8. Their behavior has been called a transference resistance in the course of psychoanalytic treatment. With such patients, the therapist needs to clarify that there is an opportunity to establish more intimate communication without danger. This means analyzing the differences between the therapeutic alliance and the social alliance (with the latter characterized by the artificiality of engagement) as well as analyzing the warded-off but potential and threatening transferences (Rowland 1967; Freud 1912; Sterba 1940; Gill 1982).

Change in Information Processing

Most patients come to therapy to relieve symptoms. However, they also frequently seek help because they recognize that some current life plan is being thwarted by their own conflicts, limitations, avoidances, indecisiveness, or irrational attitudes. Prototypically, the patient with a hysterical personality style enters treatment not only because of anxiety but also because of a recognition of excessive dependency masqueraded by a driven fraudulent activity that has begun to feel unrealistic. The person with a compulsive personality style may come partly because of depression but also because he or she is aware of procrastination that is associated with useless ruminations and false starts in divergent directions. The narcissistically vulnerable person may come because of a sense of inert, frozen apathy. The borderline patient often enters because of a sense of chaotic, depersonalized emptiness that prevents any effective course of action.

With people who have these personality styles, change can be considered in terms of movements toward relative completion of an actively conflicted and stymied train of thoughts and feelings. This change may take place both in terms of modification of enduring irrational attitudes, and in terms of modification of the ways in which information processing is regulated.

PROBLEM-FOCUSED CHANGE

In the patients presented in this book, a problem-focused change was exemplified by a working through of a mourning process and a consequent reduction in the grief-induced symptoms of intrusion and numbing. Such a change can be accomplished by dealing with particular styles of defensiveness without necessarily modifying them. For example, Connie (chapter 4), Marilyn (chapter 5), and Ann (chapter 6) came in with prominent symptoms and had virtually none at follow-up, despite the fact that their defensive styles remained virtually the same.

Symptom reduction seemed to be accomplished through relative completion of a previously, compulsively repeated, but blocked train of important thought. In the cases in this book, the death of a parent had instigated trains of thought that were stymied within the mourning process. These were referred to as the salient themes for working through in each case. When focused contemplation in therapy can be given to such themes, the formerly blocked and conflicted aims can be resolved, leading toward the completion of a mourning process. Because each step of such trains of thought is usually associated with strong negative feelings, the progression of thoughts is modulated by controlling operations. Sometimes the same associative elements and sequences occur repetitiously in the thought cycle, without progression toward completion. That is, the ideas repeat intrusively but unproductively. Moreover, a patient's avoidance of ideas or of generalized zones of thought also impedes progression. In such instances, psychotherapy may involve examination of the warded-off implications of a stressful event.

The relative completion of a train of thought about a theme, or a decision on how to resolve a conflict, can often be accomplished in brief therapy. The mechanism of change is alteration of a patient's defenses, which is brought about both by pressure from the therapist and by the sense of safety that is provided. To exert pressure, the therapist persistently focuses attention on topics that will move the patient further along the route of the blocked train of thought; to provide safety, the therapist works to build a therapeutic alliance in which emotions can be expressed and then helps the patient to make conceptual gains as fantasy is differentiated from reality.

This working through of an incipient, incomplete, but important train of thought seems to be most readily accomplished when the patient has been using inhibition of thought as a coping or defensive style, as is the case with the hysterical personality style. The compulsive personality style is more complex, containing both inhibitory and switching defenses. The overcontrolled states of mind in the compulsive personality are harder to set aside during the therapy, and the first maneuvers through the train of thought may take the still defensive form of intellectualizations and generalizations. With the narcissistic patient, the distorted meanings pertaining to the train of thought need to be dealt with tactfully in order to avoid a confrontation that is perceived as too critical. With all types of patients, a continuously deepening development of the theme while still in the therapeutic context is necessary in order to reach a point where the patient acknowledges as his own the previously warded-off train of thought.

CHARACTER CHANGE

As the patient reappraises the meanings of the stressful life event, previous attitudes that are no longer in accord with real life circumstances are revised. The revision may be either current or far-ranging. To the degree that it is far-ranging, the change process involves important modifications in basic assumptions about the world.

Because of the interactive quality of mental processes, no single enduring attitude can be altered without entanglement with a network of other beliefs (ones fundamental to the epistemology of the person as described by Bateson in 1972). The changes made are not ones of "exterminating" the irrational enduring attitude; they are ones of developing more rational predominant counterattitudes.

Patients often have a tendency to mentally speak to themselves in specifically irrational terms, yet can learn to speak to themselves in terms of more rational ones. This concept, from our psychodynamic point of view, is in agreement with the observations made by cognitive-behavior therapists such as Beck (1976; Beck and Emery 1984) or by rational-emotive therapists such as Ellis (1962): patients may learn to modify their states of mind through an inner dialogue, learned and rehearsed in the therapy sessions, in which they counteract some repetitive, irrational assumption of inferiority or blame.

Changes in Styles of Defense. Some hysterical patients have commented during post-therapy evaluations that they have learned how to slow down their impulsive pace of action and instead to devote time and effort to thoughtful planning. The clarity of ideas achieved during psychotherapy has provided such patients with a new experience in awareness—one that they can sometimes repeat with volitional effort. This shift in thematic contemplative ability is the only change in information-processing style noted in the cases we studied. It should also be noted that patients with a hysterical style of information processing may develop clearer ideas about important, conflictual themes during psychotherapy, and then repress these ideas so that they are no longer retained as insights by the time of follow-up evaluations, even though a symptom remission may be maintained.

While we have not been impressed with any pronounced modifications of defensive styles as a result of these brief therapies, the consequences of a persisting style may be modified in several important ways. If the patient can adapt to life in a way that reduces stress, then he or she will less frequently be in states where extreme defensive operations are necessary.

Another type of change may occur as the person gains an awareness of his or her personal defensive style: volitional efforts may be made to counteract the repetitive defensive modes that involve preconscious processing. For example, patients with compulsive personalities may gain awareness that they process ideas and emotions in a parallel fashion, with one level involving communicative contact with a companion and another level involving private, even secretive contemplations of opposite meanings associated with the ideas. The latter mode would be expressed, if at all, only as leakage through nonverbal communications.

Patients may also learn to recognize that their simultaneous, parallel modes of processing information are used to erase the meaning of each of them. This awareness does not seem to stop defensive maneuvers, such as intellectualization or undoing, but at times the patient may be able to notice and consciously reflect on them. He or she may then become more openly communicative about the previously private mode of thinking. At the very least, the patient will usually be better able to monitor and contemplate ideas and feelings that are dissociated. Once the threat of out-of-control states is examined reflectively, the threat of being flooded with emotion seems less likely, and the person can discuss themes more openly. Part of the patient's motivation is a decision that "now is the time to do it, " a decision fostered by the time limit in brief therapy.

Conclusion

The principal aim of these brief therapies—to work through stress-related and personality-related problems of a focal nature—often could be accomplished within the specified time limit. Major revision of character style seemed to be a goal seldom accomplished during the brief therapies that were conducted along the lines we described in this book. Some types of personality change were noted in patients who gained from new experiences with the therapist and then continued developmental progress after completing the brief therapy.

Even when the main aim of a brief therapy is to work through stress induced by recent life changes, the personality of the patient can be very important. The more flexible the personality, the more the therapy process can focus on working through trains of thoughts to reduce strain. The more restrained, rigidly stereotyped, and limited the person's personality style, the more this style itself impedes the working-through process. In this book we have examined some of the traits presented in the more stereotyped styles. In doing so, we have sought to understand how personality affects both symptom formation and healing.

REFERENCES

Abraham, K. 1921. Contribution to a discussion on tic. In *Selected Papers on Psychoanalysis*. New York: Basic Books, 1966.

———. 1924. A short study of the development of the libido, viewed in the light of mental disorders. In *Selected Papers on Psychoanalysis*. New York: Basic Books, 1960.

Adler, A. 1958. *What Life Should Mean to You*, ed. A. Porter. New York: Capricorn.

Adler, G. 1977. Hospital management of borderline patients and its relation to psychotherapy. In *Borderline Personality Disorders*, ed. P. Hartocollis. New York: International Universities Press.

Adler, G., and Buie, D. H. 1976. The process of psychotherapy in the treatment of borderline patients. Presented at the 11th Annual Tufts Symposium on Psychotherapy, Boston, Mass.

Alexander, F. 1950. Analysis of the therapeutic factors in psychoanalytic treatment. *Psychoanalytic Quarterly* 19:482–500.

Alexander, F., and French, T., 1946. *Psychoanalytic Therapy: Principles and Applications*. New York: Ronald Press.

Ayllon, T., and Michael, J. 1959. The psychiatric nurse as a behavioral engineer. *Journal of the Experimental Analysis of Behavior* 2:323–34.

Balint, M.; Ornstein, P. H.; and Balint, E. 1972. *Focal Psychotherapy*. Philadelphia: J. B. Lippincott.

Basch, M. F. 1980. *Doing Psychotherapy*. New York: Basic Books.

Bateson, G. 1972. *Steps Toward an Ecology of Mind*. San Francisco, Calif.: Chandler Publishing.

Beck, A. T. 1976. *Cognitive Therapy and the Emotional Disorders*. New York: International Universities Press.

Beck, A. T., and Emery, G. In press. *Cognitive Therapy of Anxiety*. New York: Basic Books.

Beck, A. T.; Rush, A. J.; Shaw, B.; and Emery, G. 1979. *Cognitive Therapy of Depression*. New York: Guilford Press.

Blacker, K., and Tupin, J. 1977. Hysteria and hysterical structures: Developmental and social theories. In *Hysterical Personality*, ed. M. Horowitz. New York: Jason Aronson.

Bordin, E. S. 1974. *Research Strategies in Psychotherapy*. New York: Wiley.

Budman, S. 1981. *Forms of Brief Therapy*. New York: Guilford Press.

Burke, J. D.; White, H. S.; and Havens, L. L. 1979. Which short-term psychotherapy? *Archives of General Psychiatry* 36:177–86.

Butcher, N. J., and Kolotkin, R. L. 1979. Evaluation of outcome in brief psychotherapy. *Psychiatric Clinics of North America* 2:157–69.

Dahl, H. 1980. A structural theory of the emotions, ed. J. DeRivera. *Psychological Issues* 10:4, Mono. 40.

Davanloo, H. 1979. Technique of short-term psychotherapy. *Psychiatric Clinics of North America* 2:11–22.

———, ed. 1980. *Short-Term Dynamic Therapy*, Vol. 1. New York: Jason Aronson.

DeWald, P. A. 1978. The process of change in psychoanalytic psychotherapy. *Archives of General Psychiatry* 35:535–42.

Diagnostic and Statistical Manual of Mental Disorders (3rd ed.). 1980. American Psychiatric Association.

Easser, B. R., and Lesser, S. R. 1965. Hysterical personality: A reevaluation. *Psychoanalytic Quarterly* 34:390–405.

Ellis, A. 1962. *Reason and Emotion in Psychotherapy*. New York: Lyle Stuart Press.

———, 1973. *Humanistic Psychotherapy: The Rational-Emotive Approach*. New York: McGraw-Hill.

Ferenczi, S. (1920). The further development of an active therapy in psychoanalysis. In *Further Contributions to the Theory and Techniques of Psychoanalysis*, ed. J. Rickman. London: Hogarth Press, 1950.

Ferenczi, S., and Rank, O. 1925. *The Development of Psychoanalysis*, trans. C. Newton. New York: Nervous and Mental Disease Publication Company.

Fishman, S., and Lubeticin, B. (1980). Personal communication as cited in G. T. Wilson, Behavior therapy as a short-term therapeutic approach. In *Forms of Brief Therapy*, ed. S. Budman. 1981. New York: Guilford Press.

Frank, J. D. 1974. Therapeutic components of psychotherapy. *Journal of Nervous and Mental Diseases* 159:325–42.

———. 1978. *Effective Ingredients of Successful Psychotherapy*. New York: Brunner/Mazel.

French, T. M. 1958. *The Integrations of Behavior*, Vol. 3. Chicago: University of Chicago Press.

———. 1970. The cognitive structure of behavior. In *Psychoanalytic Interpretations: The Selected Papers of Thomas M. French*. Chicago: Quadrangle Press.

Freud, A.; Nagera, H.; and Freud, W. E. 1965. Metapsychological assessment of the adult person: The adult profile. In *Psychoanalytic Study of the Child*, ed. R. S. Eisler, A. Freud, H. Hartmann, and M. Kris. New York: International Universities Press.

Freud, S. (1900). The interpretation of dreams. In *Complete Works of Sigmund Freud* (standard ed.), ed. and trans. J. Strachey. London: Hogarth Press and the Institute of Psychoanalysis, 1953.

———. (1912). Dynamics of the transference. In *Complete Works of Sigmund Freud* (standard ed.), ed. and trans. J. Strachey, 12:97–109. London: Hogarth Press, 1958.

————. (1919). Lines of advance in psychoanalytic therapy. In *Complete Psychological Works* (standard ed.), Vol. 17, ed. J. Strachey. London: Hogarth Press, 1962.

Frosch, J. 1983. *The Psychotic Process.* New York: International Universities Press.

Gaarder, K. 1971. Control of states of consciousness: I. Attainment through control of psychophysiological variables. *Archives of General Psychiatry* 25:429–35.

Garfield, S. L., and Bergin, A. E. 1978. *Handbook of Psychiatry and Behavioral Change* (2nd ed). New York: Wiley.

Gedo, J., and Goldberg, A. 1973. *Models of the Mind.* Chicago: University of Chicago Press.

Gill, M. M. 1954. Psychoanalysis and exploratory psychotherapy. *Journal of the American Psychoanalytic Association* 2:771–97.

Gill, M. M. 1982. *Analysis of Transference.* Vol. 1: *Theory and Technique.* Psychological Issues Monograph No. 53. New York: International Universities Press.

Glover, E. (ed.) 1955. *The Technique of Psychoanalysis.* New York: International Universities Press.

Goldberg, A. 1973. Psychotherapy of narcissistic injuries. *Archives of General Psychiatry* 28:722–27.

Gomes-Schwartz, B. 1978. Effective ingredients in psychotherapy: Predictors of outcome from process variables. *Journal of Consulting and Clinical Psychology* 46:1023–35.

Green, A. 1977. The borderline concept. In *Borderline Personality Disorders*, ed. P. Hartocollis. New York: International Universities Press.

Greenspan, S. I., and Cullander, C. 1973. A systematic metapsychological assessment of the personality. *Journal of the American Psychoanalytic Association* 21:303–27.

Grinker, R. R.; Werble, B.; and Drye, R. C. 1968. *The Borderline Syndrome.* New York: Basic Books.

Grotstein, J. S. 1981. *Splitting and Projective Identification.* New York: Jason Aronson.

Gunderson, J. G., and Singer, M. T. 1975. Defining borderline patients: An overview. *American Journal of Psychiatry* 132:1–10.

Hartocollis, P. 1977. *Borderline Personality Disorders.* New York: International Universities Press.

Holt, R. R. 1968. Comments made during the panel "Psychoanalytic Theory of Instinctual Drives in Relation to Recent Developments." Reported to H. Dahl. *Journal of the American Psychoanalytic Association* 16:613.

Horowitz, M. J. 1973. Phase oriented treatment of stress response syndromes. *American Journal of Psychotherapy* 27:606–15.

————. 1974. Stress response syndromes: Character style and brief psychotherapy. *Archives of General Psychiatry* 31:768–81.

————. 1975. Sliding meanings: A defense against threat in narcissistic personalities. *International Journal of Psychoanalytic Psychotherapy* 4:167–80.

————. 1976. *Stress Response Syndromes.* New York: Jason Aronson.

————. 1977a. Cognitive and interactive aspects of splitting. *American Journal of Psychiatry* 135:549–53.

———— (ed.). 1977b. *Hysterical Personality.* New York: Jason Aronson.

————. 1977c. Hysterical personality: Cognitive structure and the processes of change. *International Review of Psychoanalysis* 4:23–49.

————. 1979. *States of Mind.* New York. Plenum.

————. 1981. Self-righteous rage and the attribution of blame. *Archives of General Psychiatry* 38:1233–38.

————. 1982. Strategic dilemmas and the socialization of psychotherapy researchers. Presidential address, Society for Psychotherapy Research. *British Journal of Clinical Psychology* 21:119–127.

Horowitz, M. J., and Becker, S. S. 1972. Cognitive response to stress: Experimental studies of a "compulsion to repeat trauma." In *Psychoanalysis and Contemporary Science*, Vol. 1, ed. R. Holt and E. Peterfreund. New York: Macmillan.

Horowitz, M. J., and Kaltreider, N. 1980. Brief psychotherapy of stress response syndromes. In *Specialized Techniques in Individual Psychotherapy*, eds. T. Karasu and L. Bellak. New York: Brunner/Mazel.

Horowitz, M. J.; Krupnick, J.; Kaltreider, N.; Wilner, N.; Leong, A.; and Marmar, C. 1981a. Initial psychological response to parental death. *Archives of General Psychiatry* 38:316–23.

Horowitz, M. J.; Marmar, C.; Weiss, D. S.; DeWitt, K.; and Rosenbaum, R. Research on brief psychotherapy: The relationship of process to outcome. *Archives of General Psychiatry.* In press.

Horowitz, M. J.; Marmar, C.; and Wilner, N. 1979. Analysis of patient states and state transitions. *Journal of Nervous and Mental Diseases* 167:91–99.

Horowitz, M. J.; Wilner, N.; Alvarez, W. 1979. Impact of Event Scale: A Measure of Subjective Stress. *Psychosomatic Medicine* 41:209–18.

Horowitz, M. J.; Wilner, N.; Kaltreider, N.; and Alvarez, W. 1980a. Signs and symptoms of post-traumatic stress disorder. *Archives of General Psychiatry* 37:85–92.

Horowitz, M. J.; Wilner, N.; Marmar, C.; and Krupnick, J. 1980b. Pathological grief and the activation of latent self-images. *American Journal of Psychiatry* 137:1157–62.

Horowitz, M. J., and Zilberg, N. 1983. Regressive alterations of the self-concept. *American Journal of Psychiatry* 140:284–89.

Jacobson, E. 1964. *The Self and the Object World.* New York: International Universities Press.

Jones, E. 1929. Fear, guilt, and hate. *International Journal of Psychoanalysis* 10:383.

Jones E. 1955. *The Life and Work of Sigmund Freud*, Vol. 2. New York: Basic Books.

Kaltreider, N.; Becker, T.; and Horowitz, M. J. 1984. Relationship testing after parental bereavement. *American Journal of Psychiatry* 141:243–46.

Kaltreider, N.; DeWitt, K.; Lieberman, R.; and Horowitz, M. J. 1981a. Individualized approaches to outcome assessment: A strategy for psychotherapy research. *Journal of Psychiatric Treatment and Evaluation* 3:105–11.

Kaltreider, N.; DeWitt, K.; Weiss, D. S.; and Horowitz, M. J. 1981b. Patterns of Individual Change Scales. *Archives of General Psychiatry* 38:1263–69.

Kaplan, J.; Freedman, A.; and Sadock, B. 1980. *Comprehensive Textbook of Psychiatry*, 3rd ed. Baltimore: Williams and Wilkins.

Kazdin, A. E., and Wilson, G. T. 1978. *Evaluation of Behavior Therapy: Issues, Evidence, and Research Strategies.* Cambridge, Mass.: Ballinger.

Kelly, G. 1955. *The Psychology of Personal Constructs*, Vols. 1 and 2. New York: Norton.

Kernberg, O. 1967. Borderline personality organization. *Journal of the American Psychoanalytic Association* 15:641–85.

———. 1975. *Borderline Conditions and Pathological Narcissism*. New York: Jason Aronson.

———. 1976. *Object Relations Theory and Clinical Psychoanalysis*. New York: Jason Aronson.

Klein, G. S. 1976. *Psychoanalytic Theory*. New York: International Universities Press.

Klein, M. 1952. Notes on some schizoid mechanisms. In *Developments in Psychoanalysis*, eds. M. Klein, P. Heimann, and J. Riviere. London: Hogarth Press.

Knapp, P. H. 1974. Segmentation and structure in psychoanalysis. *Journal of the American Psychoanalytic Association* 22:14–36.

Knight, R. P. 1953. Borderline states. *Bulletin of the Menninger Clinic* 17:1–12.

Kohut, H. 1971. *The Analysis of the Self*. New York: International Universities Press.

———. 1977. *The Restoration of the Self*. New York: International Universities Press.

Krupnick, J., and Horowitz, M. J. 1981. Stress response syndromes: Recurrent themes. *Archives of General Psychiatry* 38:428–35.

Lazare, A. 1971. The hysterical character in psychoanalytic theory: Evolution and confusion. *Archives of General Psychiatry* 25:131–37.

Lazarus, A. 1980. *The Practice of Multi-Modal Therapy*. New York: McGraw-Hill.

Luborsky, L. 1976. Helping alliance in psychotherapy. In *Successful Psychotherapy*, ed. J. L. Cleghorn. New York: Brunner/Mazel.

———. 1977. Measuring pervasive structure in psychotherapy: The core conflictual relationship. In *Communicative Structures and Psychic Structures*, ed. N. Friedman and S. Grand. New York: Plenum.

Luborsky, L.; Singer, B.; and Luborsky, L. 1975. Comparative studies of psychotherapies. *Archives of General Psychiatry* 32:995–1008.

Mack, J. E. (ed.). 1975. *Borderline States in Psychiatry*. New York: Grune and Stratton.

Mahoney, M. J. 1974. *Cognition and Behavior Modification*. Cambridge, Mass.: Ballinger.

Malan, D. H. 1963. *A Study of Brief Psychotherapy*. New York: Plenum.

———. 1976. *Frontiers of Brief Psychotherapy*. New York: Plenum.

———. 1979. *Individual Psychotherapy and the Science of Psychodynamics*. London: Butterworth.

Mandel, H. P. 1981. *Short-term Psychotherapy and Brief Treatment Techniques: An Annotated Bibliography, 1920–1980*. New York: Plenum.

Mann, J. 1973. *Time-Limited Psychotherapy*. Cambridge, Mass.: Harvard University Press.

———. 1980. Time-limited psychotherapy (Course No. 65). American Psychiatric Association, 133rd Annual Meeting, San Francisco, Calif., May 3–9, 1980.

Mann, J., and Goldman, R. 1982. *A Casebook in Time-Limited Psychotherapy*. New York: McGraw-Hill.

Marks, I. 1978. Behavioral psychotherapy of adult neurosis. In *Handbook of Psy-*

chotherapy and Behavior Change (2nd ed.), ed. S. Garfield and A. Bergin. New York: Wiley.

Marmar, C.; Marziali, E.; Horowitz, M. J.; and Weiss, D. S. The development of the therapeutic alliance rating system. In *The Psychotherapeutic Process: A Research Handbook,* ed. L. Greenberg and W. Pinsof. New York: Guilford Press. In press.

Marmar, C.; Wilner, N.; and Horowitz, M. J. Recurrent patient states in psychotherapy: Segmentation and quantification. In *Process Measures in Psychotherapy Research,* ed. L. Rice and L. Greenberg. New York: Guilford Press. In press.

Marmor, J. 1953. Orality in the hysterical personality. *Journal of the American Psychoanalytic Association* 1:656–75.

———. 1979. Historical aspects of short-term dynamic psychotherapy. *Psychiatric Clinics of North America* 2:3–9.

Marmor, J., and Woods, S. (eds.) 1980. The *Interface Between the Psychodynamic and Behavioral Therapies.* New York: Plenum.

Marziali, E.; Marmar, C.; and Krupnick, J. 1981. Therapeutic alliance scales: Development and relationship to therapeutic outcome. *American Journal of Psychiatry* 138:361–64.

Masterson, J. F. 1981. *The Narcissistic and Borderline Disorders.* New York: Brunner/Mazel.

Meehl, P. E. 1973. Why I do not attend case conferences. In *Psychodiagnostics: Selected Papers.* Minneapolis: University of Minnesota Press.

Meichenbaum, D. 1977. *Cognitive-Behavior Modification: An Integrative Approach.* New York: Plenum.

———. 1980. *Cognitive Behavior Modification.* New York: Plenum.

Menninger, K. 1958. *Theory of Psychoanalytic Technique.* New York: Basic Books.

Moras, K., and Strupp, H. H. 1982. Pretherapy interpersonal relations, patients' alliance, and outcome in brief therapy. *Archives of General Psychiatry* 39:405–9.

Murray, H. 1938. *Explorations in Personality.* New York: Oxford University Press.

Nagera, H. 1976. *Obsessional Neuroses: Developmental Psychopathology.* New York: Jason Aronson.

Neu, C.; Prusoff, B.; and Klerman, G. 1978. Measuring the interventions used in short-term interpersonal psychotherapy of depression. *American Journal of Orthopsychiatry* 48:629–36.

Ornstein, P. 1978. *The Search for the Self: Selected Writings of Heinz Kohut,* Vols. 1 and 2. New York: International Universities Press.

Parloff, M. 1982. Psychotherapy research evidence and reimbursement decisions: Bambi meets Godzilla. *American Journal of Psychiatry* 139:718–27.

Peterfreund, E. 1971. Information systems and psychoanalysis: An evolutionary biological approach to psychoanalytic theory. *Psychological Issues* 7, Monograph 25/26.

Piaget, J. 1937. *The Construction of Reality in the Child.* New York: Basic Books.

———. 1950. *Psychology of Intelligence.* trans. by M. Piercy and D. E. Berlyne. New York: Harcourt, Brace, and Company. Originally published, 1947.

———. 1970. *Structuralism.* New York: Basic Books.

Rank, O. (1924). *The Trauma of Birth.* New York: Robert Brunner, 1952.

———. 1947. *Will Therapy.* New York: Knopf.

Reich, W. 1949. *Character Analysis*. New York: Farrar, Straus, and Giroux.

Rowland, A. 1967. The reality of the psychoanalytic relationship and situations in the handling of transference-resistance. *International Journal of Psychoanalysis* 48:504–10.

Rush, A. J.; Beck, A. T.; Kovacs, M.; and Hollon, S. D. 1977. Comparative efficacy of cognitive therapy and pharmacotherapy in the treatment of depressed outpatients. *Cognitive Therapy and Research* 1:17–37.

Salzman, L. 1968. *Obsessive Personality: Origins, Dynamics, and Therapy*. New York: Science House.

———. 1980. *Treatment of the Obsessive Personality*. New York: Jason Aronson.

Sandler, J., and Joffee, W. 1969. Towards a basic psychoanalytic model. *International Journal of Psychoanalysis* 50:79–90.

Schafer, R. 1976. *A New Language for Psychoanalysis*. New Haven, Conn.: Yale University Press.

Shapiro, D. 1965. *Neurotic Styles*. New York: Basic Books.

———. 1981. *Autonomy and Rigid Character*. New York: Basic Books.

Shapiro, E. R. 1978. Research on family dynamics: Clinical implications for the family of the borderline adolescent. In *Adolescent Psychiatry*, Vol. 6, ed. S. C. Fernsterheim and P. L. Giovacchini. New York: Basic Books.

Sifneos, P. E. 1966. Psychoanalytically oriented short-term dynamic or anxiety-producing psychotherapy for mild obsessional neuroses. *Psychiatric Quarterly* 40:270–82.

———. 1972. *Short-Term Psychotherapy and Emotional Crisis*. Cambridge, Mass.: Harvard University Press.

———. 1979. *Short-Term Psychotherapy: Evaluation and Technique*. New York: Plenum.

Singer, M. T. 1977. The borderline diagnosis and psychological tests: Review and research. In *Borderline Personality Disorders*, ed. P. Hartocollis. New York: International Universities Press.

Smith, M. L.; Glass, G. V.; and Miller, T. I. 1980. *The Benefits of Psychotherapy*. Baltimore, Md.: Johns Hopkins Press.

Sterba, R. 1940. The dynamics of the dissolution of the transference resistance. *Psychoanalytic Quarterly* 9:363–79.

Stone, L. 1961. *The Psychoanalytic Situation*. New York: International Universities Press.

Stone, M. J. 1981. Borderline syndromes: A consideration of subtypes and an overview, directions for research. *Psychiatric Clinics of North America* 4:3–24.

Strupp, H. H.; Hadley, S. W.; and Gomes-Schwartz, B. 1977. Psychotherapy for better or worse: The problem of negative effects. New York: Jason Aronson.

Ullman, L., and Krasner, L. 1969. *A Psychological Approach to Abnormal Behavior*. Englewood Cliffs, N.J.: Prentice-Hall.

Volkan, V. D. 1976. *Primitive Internalized Object Relations*. New York: International Universities Press.

Wallerstein, R. S. 1976. Psychoanalysis as science: Its present status and its future tasks. *Psychological Issues* 9:198–228, Monograph No. 36.

Wallerstein, R. S., and Sampson, H. 1971. Issues in research in the psychoanalytic process. *International Journal of Psychoanalysis* 52:11–50.

Waskow, I. E. 1981. The psychotherapy of depression collaborative research program: The first year experience. Workshop at the 12th Annual Meeting of the Society for Psychotherapy Research, Aspen, Colo.

Weiss, J. 1967. The integration of defenses. *International Journal of Psychoanalysis* 48:520.

Weiss, J.; Sampson, H.; Gasner, S.; and Caston, J. 1981. Further research on the psychoanalytic process. *Mount Zion Psychotherapy Research Group Bulletin* No. 4.

Weissman, M., and Klerman, G. 1973. Psychotherapy with depressed women: An empirical study of content themes and reflection. *British Journal of Psychiatry* 123:55–61.

Weissman, M.; Klerman, G.; Prusoff, B.; Sholomskas, D.; and Padian, N. 1981. Depressed outpatients: Results one year after treatment with drugs and/or interpersonal psychotherapy. *Archives of General Psychiatry* 38:51–55.

Wilson, G. T. 1981. Behavior therapy as a short-term therapeutic approach. In *Forms of Brief Therapy*, ed. S. Budman. New York: Guilford Press.

Wilson, G. T., and Evans, I. M. 1976. Adult behavior therapy and the therapist-client relationship. In the *Annual Review of Behavior Therapy: Theory and Practice*, Vol. 4. New York: Brunner/Mazel.

Zetzel, E. 1968. The so-called good hysteric. *International Journal of Psychoanalysis* 49:256–60.

INDEX

Outcome of therapy: *(continued)*
patient, 200–204; with hysterical patient, 105–9; with more disturbed hysterical patient, 150–57; with narcissistic patient, 253–58

Panic attacks, 112, 262
Panicky emptiness state, 214, 218; role relationship models and, 223; themes related to, 225, 228
Pan-neurotic symptoms, 262
Parloff, M., 7, 24
Pathological grief, predisposition to, 39, 57; in compulsive personality, 178; in hysterical personality, 88–89; in more disturbed hysterical personality, 125; in narcissistic personality, 225
Pathological styles, 69
Patterns of Individual Change Scale, *xiii*, 105, 150, 204, 256, 307
Perceptual manner: of hysterical personality, 71; *see also* Information processing
Personality disorders: exacerbation of, 35; in *DSM–III*, 68–69; *see also* Borderline personality; Compulsive personality; Hysterical personality; More disturbed hysterical personality; Narcissistic personality
Peterfreund, E., 52
Phobic reactions, 3, 165
Piaget, J., 27
Polarizations, 173–74
Positive transference: of borderline patient, 288; of compulsive patient, 186–88; of hysterical patient, 87, 93; of more disturbed hysterical patient, 134–35; of narcissistic patient, 224–25, 249
Post-Traumatic stress disorders, 32, 35, 39; *DSM-III* category of, 68
Power, theme of, 287, 314–17; working through, 306
Presenting complaints: of borderline

patient, 266–67; of compulsive patient, 164–68; of hysterical patient, 75–76; of more disturbed hysterical patient, 114–15; of narcissistic patient, 212
Problem-focused change: in information processing, 326–27; in role relationship models, 321; in self-concepts, 321; in states of mind, 320
Procrastination theme, 228–29, 236, 241; outcome and, 254–56; working through, 244–49
Pre-oedipal character structure, 110
Pre-oedipal factors, 4
Projection, 261
Projective identification, 261
Prusoff, B., 23, 24
Psychiatric history, 7
Psychoanalysis: theory of defense in, *xii*; time-limited, 3–6
Psychodynamic history, 7
Psychophysiological disorders, 112

Rage, 57; *see also Distraught rage* state; *Explosive rage* state
Rage at loss of abandoning mother theme, 283–87, 313–14; working through, 302–4
Rank, O., 4, 5
Rational-emotive therapy, 328
Rationalization, 181
Reality testing: borderline personality and, 265; in corrective emotional experience, 5; with narcissistic patient, 46
Reflective, active, earnest state, 86; working through in, 99, 103, 105
Regression: in corrective emotional experience, 5; in long-term therapy, 6
Reich, W., 73, 110
Rejection, vulnerability to, 121
Relationships: in configurational analysis, 54–56; *see also* Role relationship models
Remorseful self-disgust state, 214, 215,

217, 218; role relationship models and, 221; themes related to, 227–28; working through and, 244
Repression, *xii*, 71, 288
Resistance, *xii*, in behavior therapy, 25; of borderline patients, 266, 289; of compulsive patients, 163, 164, 183–85; of hysterical patients, 81, 94–96; interpretations of, 11; of narcissistic patients, 211; transference, 325
Restorative care, 4
Restorative fantasy, 210
Reversal of affects, *xii*
Role change experience, 322–25
Role–playing technique, 238–39, 249
Role relationship models, 54; of borderline personality, 274–83, 307–13; of compulsive personality, 172–77, 190–91; changes in, 107–9, 153, 156, 201–2, 321–25; defensive organization of, 85, 175–76, 218–19, 276–77; desired, 63; development of repertoire of, 221–22; dreaded, 64; dreaded compromise, 65; of hysterical personality, 73, 82–87; implications for therapy of, 85–87, 122–25, 176–78, 222–25, 281–83; of more disturbed hysterical personality, 121–25; multiplicity of, 277–81; of narcissistic personality, 218–25; repetition of, 42; resistance and, 185; splitting and, 261; therapeutic alliance and, 93
Role representations, 5, 6
Role reversal, 181, 228
Rowland, A., 325
Rush, A. J., 32

Sad crying state, 81, 87; working through and, 99, 102, 105
Sad-needy state, 117, 118, 143; modification of, 151, 154
Sadness and comfort theme, 225
Sadness state, 223
Sadness theme, 88
Sadock, B., 5

Salzman, L., 163
Sampson, H., 52
Sandler, J., 52
Schafer, R., 52
Searing guilt state, 168, 170; resistance and, 184
"Seeding" technique, 6
Selection of patients, 7–8, 10, 14–16, 18–19
Self-concepts, 54; of borderline personality, 274–81; capacity for maintaining, 69; changes in, 107–9, 153, 156, 201–22, 321–25; of compulsive personality, 172–75; development of repertoire of, 221–22; of hysterical personality, 71, 82–85; of more disturbed hysterical personality, 111, 121–22; multiplicity of, 277–81; of narcissistic personality, 218–22; positive, therapist's support of, 138; roles and aims used in organization of, 62; therapeutic alliance and, 92
Self–formulation, organizational level of, 69
Self–objects: and borderline personality, 301; and more disturbed hysterical personality, 111, 121–22; and narcissistic personality, 218; and pathological grief, 125
Self-righteous rage state, 214–17; role relationship models and, 221; themes related to, 228; working through and, 247
Separation, 4
Separation–individuation, 276
Severely distraught state, 117, 118, 120, 141, 142, 147, 154, 157; defensive style in, 127; and pathological grief, 125; therapeutic alliance and, 129, 130
Sexual identity diffusion theme, 287, 314–17; working through, 305
Sexuality: of borderline personality, 269, 280; of compulsive personality, 162, 175, 201; of hysterical personality, 85; of more disturbed hysterical personality, 112
Shapiro, D., 161, 162